The Memoirs of
Admiral H. Kent Hewitt

1887–1972

NAVAL WAR COLLEGE *HISTORICAL MONOGRAPH SERIES NO. 15*

The historical monographs in this series are book-length studies of the history of naval warfare, edited historical documents, conference proceedings, and bibliographies that are based wholly or in part on source materials in the Historical Collection of the Naval War College.

The editors of the Naval War College Press express their special gratitude to all the members of the Naval War College Foundation, whose generous financial support for research projects, conferences, and printing has made possible the publication of this historical monograph.

The Memoirs of Admiral H. Kent Hewitt

Edited by Evelyn M. Cherpak

NAVAL WAR COLLEGE PRESS
NEWPORT, RHODE ISLAND
2004

Library of Congress Cataloging-in-Publication Data

Hewitt, H. Kent (Henry Kent), 1887-1972.
 The memoirs of Admiral H. Kent Hewitt / edited by Evelyn M. Cherpak.
     p. cm.
Includes index.
 ISBN 1-884733-20-4 (pbk. : alk. paper)
 1. Hewitt, H. Kent (Henry Kent), 1887-1972. 2. Admirals—United States—Biography. 3. United States. Navy—Officers—Biography. I. Cherpak, Evelyn M. (Evelyn May), 1941- II. Title.
 V63.H48 A3 2004
 359'.0092—dc21

2002004601

TABLE OF CONTENTS

Acknowledgments	ix
Introduction	xi
I. Early Years, 1887–1906	1
II. Duty in USS *Missouri*, 1906–1907	13
III. The Round-the-World Cruise, 1907–1909	19
IV. Duty in USS *Connecticut*, 1910	33
V. Pre–World War I Assignments, 1911–1916	37
VI. USS *Eagle*, 1916–1917	47
VII. World War I to 1922	63
VIII. Fleet Assignments and the NWC, 1923–1935	75
IX. Cruise in USS *Indianapolis*, 1936	85
X. Pre–World War II Assignments, 1937–1940	101
XI. Convoy Duty, 1941	115
XII. Preparing for Operation Torch, 1942	125
XIII. The Voyage to North Africa, 1942	149
XIV. Operation Torch, 1942	159
XV. Sicily and Anzio Invasions, 1943	177
XVI. Operation Anvil-Dragoon and Aftermath, 1944	199
XVII. War's End and Twelfth Fleet, 1945	213
XVIII. Twelfth Fleet, 1946	233
XIX. Twelfth Fleet and Return to USA, 1946–1947	249
XX. The United Nations, 1947	267
XXI. The United Nations and Retirement, 1948–1949	277
Index	282
Titles in the Series	291

ACKNOWLEDGMENTS

I owe a debt of gratitude to the following individuals at the Naval War College who supported the publication of this work: Dr. Robert Wood, former Dean of the Center for Naval Warfare Studies, Dr. Thomas Grassey, former Editor of the Naval War College Press, and Dr. John B. Hattendorf, Ernest J. King Professor of Maritime History and Director of the Advanced Research Department. Professor John Clagett of Middlebury, Vermont, also encouraged the publication of this memoir.

The Admiral's daughters, Mrs. Leroy Taylor of Middletown, Rhode Island, and Mrs. Gerald Norton of Annapolis, Maryland, cooperated fully with this endeavor and graciously provided me with biographical information on their ancestors.

Barbara Prisk did a superb job of typing the manuscript, and the editing skills of Patricia Goodrich of the Naval War College Press improved the manuscript. A grant from the Naval War College Foundation made possible the publication of this work.

EVELYN M. CHERPAK
Portsmouth, Rhode Island

Editor's Note: While care has been taken to present Admiral Hewitt's memoirs as written, in some places the wording has been revised for clarity. Similarly, punctuation has been adjusted, and capitalization has been brought into conformance with present-day standards. The original manuscript is available for scholars in the Naval War College Naval Historical Collection.

INTRODUCTION

Memoirs as sources fill an important gap in the historical record. They tell us how an individual lived, what he did, and what he thought about how he lived and what he did. Such are the memoirs of H. K. Hewitt, admiral in the United States Navy, whose active duty career spanned the first fifty years of the twentieth century, including World War I and World War II, when he played a leadership role in the Allied invasions of North Africa and Southern Europe.[1]

The Hewitt memoirs are part of the Admiral's personal papers that are located in the Naval Historical Collection at the Naval War College.[2] A portion of the collection was presented to the Naval War College Foundation by Admiral Hewitt's wife, Floride Hunt Hewitt, in 1973 and a second portion by his daughter, Mrs. Floride Hewitt Taylor, in 1976. The papers consist of letters, memoranda, and telegrams that treat the amphibious operations in North Africa and Southern Europe; an extensive collection of career photographs, including shots of the landings in Morocco in 1942, wartime leaders and dignitaries he met as Commander of the Twelfth Fleet; and certificates, commissions, citations, and honorary degrees. The Naval War College archives contain lectures, correspondence, and papers written by Hewitt that supplement his collection.

Admiral Hewitt had a long and close association with the Naval War College throughout his naval career. He lectured at the College in 1924 and 1925 on naval gunnery, and in 1943 on Operation TORCH. He graduated from the College in 1929 as a member of the senior class and remained on the staff in the Department of Operations, Strategy, and Tactics for the next two years. In 1947, College president and classmate Admiral Raymond A. Spruance asked him to spend several months at the College, where he lectured on his wartime experiences. He returned again in 1952 to speak to students on the employment of allied forces in the Mediterranean during the war. In 1976, Hewitt Hall, which houses the College library, student study carrels and classrooms, was named in his honor. Given his distinguished naval career and connection with the Naval War College, it is appropriate that his memoirs are now published in the Naval War College Historical Monograph series.

Admiral Hewitt's memoirs cover his ancestry, boyhood, early education, U.S. Naval Academy experience, and his entire naval career until his retirement in 1949. There is no mention of his activities in retirement. In 1949, he settled in Orwell, Vermont, in a farmhouse named "Foretop," where he spent the remaining years quietly, writing his memoirs as well as articles and book reviews for the U.S. Naval Institute *Proceedings* and traveling to Newport, Rhode Island, and Annapolis, Maryland, until his death in 1972. As in most personal accounts, some events and career experiences are given more weight than others. The round-the-world cruise in USS *Missouri* from 1907–1909; convoy duty in World War I; the 1936 cruise in the *Indianapolis*, transporting President Franklin D. Roosevelt to the Pan American Conference in Buenos Aires, Argentina; the planning and execution of Operation TORCH; his command of the Twelfth Fleet in 1946; and membership on the United Nations Military Staff Committee, his final active duty assignment, are covered in great detail. Less detail is accorded his role in the investigation of the debacle at Pearl Harbor on December 7, 1941; Operation HUSKY, the invasion of Sicily in 1943; Operation AVALANCHE, the invasion of Salerno; and Operation ANVIL-DRAGOON, the invasion of Southern France in 1944. The latter operations, he felt, were fully covered in other sources, including Samuel Eliot Morison's *History of United States Naval Operations in World War II*.[3]

The Hewitt memoirs also bring to life the peacetime and wartime political, military, and diplomatic leaders of the first half of the twentieth century as well as the crowned heads of Europe. Throughout his naval career, especially when he reached flag rank, Hewitt had to plan and execute combined operations with Army Generals George Patton, Dwight D. Eisenhower, Mark Clark, Marine Corps General Holland Smith, U.S. Admiral Richard Conolly, and Royal Navy Admirals John and Andrew Cunningham. In the course of his career, he met Lord Louis Mountbatten when he went to England to investigate British amphibious planning prior to Operation TORCH; he reported to President Franklin D. Roosevelt and Chief of Naval Operations Fleet Admiral Ernest J. King throughout the war; and when he commanded the Twelfth Fleet, he made visits to Norway, Sweden, Holland, Denmark, and Greece, where he called on their monarchs, and to Portugal and Turkey, where he met heads of state. Even as a young officer, he was in the company of President Theodore Roosevelt, and later Rear Admiral William S. Sims, head of U.S. naval operations in European waters during World War I. His naval career afforded him the opportunity to travel, to meet world leaders, and to have a breadth and depth of experience unavailable to his civilian counterparts.

The memoirs reveal the character of the man as well. Admiral Hewitt was a quiet and unassuming wartime officer, an expert in amphibious operations that he mastered, literally, on the job, who did not receive the public recognition that other more flamboyant military leaders did. He was intelligent, dignified, honorable, and a man of high principles, whose leadership qualities and competence were recognized by his military confreres and superiors. This was evidenced by the many decorations he received for military service from both the United States and foreign countries and by his promotion to four-star rank in 1945.[4]

On September 15, 1972, Admiral Hewitt died in Middlebury, Vermont. He was buried in the U.S. Naval Academy Cemetery in Annapolis, Maryland.

NOTES

1 For biographical sketches of Admiral Hewitt, see John H. Clagett, "Skipper of the *Eagle*: Rehearsal for Greatness," U.S. Naval Institute *Proceedings*, Vol. 878 (April 1976), pp. 58–65; John H. Clagett, "Admiral H. K. Hewitt, U.S. Navy: Part I—Preparing for High Command," *Naval War College Review* (Summer 1975), pp. 72–86, and John H. Clagett, "Admiral H. K. Hewitt, U.S. Navy: Part II—High Command," *Naval War College Review* (Fall 1975), pp. 60–86; Stephen Howarth (ed.), *Men of War: Great Naval Leaders of World War II* (New York: St. Martin's Press, 1993), pp. 313–330; Roger Spiller (ed.), *Dictionary of American Military Biography* (Westport, Conn.: Greenwood Press, 1984), pp. 466–469; Clark G. Reynolds, *Famous American Admirals* (New York: Van Nostrand Reinhold Co., 1978), pp. 119–150.

2 For a complete description of the papers, see H. K. Hewitt Papers, Manuscript Register Series No. 11, Naval Historical Collection, Naval War College, Newport, R.I., 1985. The Naval Historical Center, Washington Navy Yard, Washington, D.C., has a small collection of Hewitt manuscripts with a checklist prepared by Martha Crawley in 1979. The Columbia University Oral History Research Office interviewed Admiral Hewitt for their oral history program. The oral history is available on microfiche at the Naval War College Naval Historical Collection.

3 Samuel E. Morison, *History of United States Naval Operations in World War II*, Vol. IX: *Sicily-Salerno-Anzio, January 1943–June 1944* (Boston: Little, Brown and Company, 1954), pp. 3–314; Vol. XI: *The Invasion of France and Germany* (Boston: Little, Brown and Company, 1957), pp. 221–292.

4 Admiral Hewitt received the Navy Cross, Knight Commander of the Bath, Croix de Guerre with Palm (France), the Russian Order of Kutuzov, Legion of Honor, the Distinguished Service Medal (both Army and Navy), the Order of the Southern Cross (Brazil), the Order of Abdon Calderon (Ecuador), the Order of King George (Greece), the Order of Nichan Iftikar (Tunisia), the Order of Sts. Maurizio and Lazare (Italy), the Order of Orange-Nassau (Netherlands), and the Order of Leopold and Croix de Guerre (Belgium); his campaign medals include the Naval Expeditionary Medal, the Dominican Medal, the Victory Medal, the American Defense Medal, the American Area Campaign Medal, the World War II Victory Medal, and the European-African-Middle Eastern Campaign Medal.

*Hackensack High School
(New Jersey Historical Society)*

I Early Years, 1887–1906

The following notes on my life history, interspersed with more complete narratives on interesting occurrences or more important events, are jotted down for the benefit of my family and, I may say, at their insistence.

I was born on February 11, 1887, in my maternal grandfather's house on what was then known as the Kent Place on Polifly Road (or Terrace Avenue), about a tenth of a mile south of Essex Street in the southern outskirts of Hackensack, New Jersey. My father, Robert Anderson Hewitt,[1] godson and namesake of the Robert Anderson[2] of Fort Sumter fame, was the son of Charles Hewitt[3] of Trenton, New Jersey, and his wife was Anna Conrad.[4] My grandfather Hewitt was president of the Trenton Iron Company for years and, as such, was instrumental in turning out some of the first steel rifle barrels to be manufactured in this country for the Union Army in the Civil War. Be it noted that, as were many of his family, he was an inventor, but one who failed to capitalize on his inventions and merely used them to improve the process in his plant. My father, denied college on account of a boyhood eye injury, nevertheless became a mechanical engineer. Notes on the genealogy of the Hewitt family will be found elsewhere in my papers and in the book *Those Were the Days*, written by my father's first cousin, Edward Ringwood Hewitt.

My maternal grandfather, Henry Frederick Kent,[5] for whom I am named, was born in New York City, as was my grandmother, Charlotte Mumford.[6] He was a New York businessman. My mother, Molly (or Mary) Kent,[7] was the eldest of four sisters and three brothers, all of whom, in my youngest days, were living in "The Big House on the Hill." It is surprising, since my father and mother each were members of such large families, that I should be an only child. But such is the case.

Being the only child among so many adults, it was natural that I should receive considerable attention. If it had not been for strict parental discipline (for which I am duly thankful), I would probably have been badly spoiled. I never knew my grandfather Hewitt, but I was a favorite of my grandfather Kent, who died when I was about six. I can remember him well.

It was a bit lonely being the only one of my age in that big place. I had no one to play with prior to my school days, except on one of those rare occasions when some child was brought by carriage to spend the day. Thus, I was much left to my own devices. This had one advantage in that I learned thoroughly how to amuse myself, a knowledge which, at times, has stood me in good stead. I had plenty of adult male companionship on Saturday afternoons and Sundays, but during the rest of the week my father and uncles all commuted to business in New York City.

Things were better after I started going to school, and especially after I got my first bicycle and was able to get around on my own. But it was not until after I got into high school that I really began to be one of the gang, to pal around with boys of my own age whom I liked. In grammar school, most of my friends, boys and girls, went to "Uptown School" (State Street), whereas I had to go to the "Downtown School" (Union Street). It wasn't a question of being snobbish or not liking some of the boys there, but most of them had a different background and different ideas about what they wanted to do.

After my freshman year in the high school, the old family place was broken up, and my parents and I moved to a residence uptown where I was nearer most of my intimate friends. There, I became more involved in athletics than I had been, due primarily to my lonely start, but I never became very good at them. Tennis was my best game, but never more than mediocre. My highest attainment was to become a substitute halfback on the high school football team, but I was pretty light for that. But we boys used to cover most of northern New Jersey on our bicycles on Saturdays and take very long walks on Sunday afternoons; most of my friends were not permitted to ride bicycles on Sunday.

In school, I was usually interested in learning. I liked mathematical subjects and they came more or less easily to me. But I do not think that I was in any sense a grind.

The high school was a good one, presided over by a splendid teacher, Dr. Nelson B. Haas. I took the scientific or classical course, which included algebra, geometry, general history, Latin, German, and rhetoric. Also, as I remember, some physics. All went along smoothly, and if I looked ahead at all, it was with the hopeful idea of going to Stevens Institute of Technology in Hoboken to become an engineer.

As to church affiliations, we belonged to Christ Church (Protestant Episcopal), where I was baptized and later confirmed. My father was superintendent of the Sunday School, so I was regular in my attendance there. I was a choir boy from a fairly early age, until my voice changed. Then I became a crucifer and acolyte. The latter was a necessity in our church, because our dear old rector, Dr. William Welles Holley, was a cripple and had to be helped up and down the altar steps. Not only did he have a wooden leg, but he became quite rheumatic in his old age. Also, I was a member of the Bell Ringers Guild in which we boys took turns on Sundays at playing hymns on the chimes, which had to be done by pulling the right rope at the right time. My prize accomplishment there was to play "Softly Now the Light of Day" in two-bell chords.

One Monday evening in May 1903, toward the end of my high school junior year, the local evening paper came out with a notice that Congressman Hughes of the 6th New Jersey District would hold a competitive examination in Paterson the following Saturday for an appointment to the Naval Academy. It gave the requirements as to age, subjects, etc. Somehow, I got the idea that it might be fun to try it. I hadn't the slightest notion of being able to win it—in fact, any idea of ever going to West Point or Annapolis was beyond my fondest expectations— none of my family knew anyone in politics. When I broached the subject to my father, he gave his consent to my trying, but said that if I did, I had better take it seriously. So, after supper, he took me right up to call on Dr. Haas, the principal, at his house.

Dr. Haas was a rather stern man who was held somewhat in awe by most of the students. The student body was small enough, however, so that he knew most of them personally, at least those of the upper classes. He told me that he did not know what chance I would have, that there was another boy in the school who had been preparing for this exam for some time (he had had advance information), but said that if I were to take it seriously, I had better work. He suggested that I should not come to school for the rest of the week, but to study each day just what he specified, and to come to school at 3:00 p.m., when he would quiz me and give me my work for the following day. He advised me not to worry about the mathematics subjects, in which he knew I had good marks, but to concentrate on the subjects which I had not studied since grammar school days, such as United States history and geography. I was fortunate in having such a mentor.

I doubt if ever in my career I put in more concentrated hard work than I did in those four days, Tuesday to Friday inclusive. Up early, a bit of exercise, and then uninterrupted study until time to meet my tutor. Then a little relaxation, a bit more study, and early to bed.

To reach Paterson on time Saturday morning, it was necessary to take an early morning train. They ran with some frequency in those days. The exam was administered by a committee of school teachers and took place in one of the public schools. As I remember, about thirty or so boys reported. We wrote out our names and addresses and placed them in a sealed envelope with a number. Only our assigned number was placed on any of our papers, so that there was no chance for favoritism. We worked from about nine a.m. through until about four p.m., with an hour out for lunch to which we were treated by Congressman Hughes at a nearby restaurant.

I knew some of the questions which were asked, but was not at all sure about others. I returned home and rather dismissed the whole thing as an interesting experience. During my usual Saturday evening job at the Hackensack Public Library as a librarian's assistant, I told friends who inquired that I did not think I had done very well. And on Monday, I resumed my regular schoolwork.

At school, the following Wednesday or Thursday, during a Latin class, someone walked into the room and handed our professor a message. He read it, stopped the class, and announced that I had won the appointment. I was so utterly surprised that I almost went through the floor and was barely able to get on my feet and say a few words, as I was asked to do.

There being a sharp rivalry between Bergen County schools, my unexpected success was deemed a real victory for Hackensack. As a result, I was treated that night to a sort of school rally and carried around as if I were a real football hero, something I had never experienced before nor have ever since.

This brought my regular schoolwork to a close. It was then necessary to buckle down to prepare myself for the Naval Academy entrance examination, which I did, again under the voluntary guidance of Dr. Haas.

Having been directed to report to the Academy on June 15, my father took me down to Annapolis, where, through friends, we found a place to board at the Misses Buchanan's (daughters of Admiral Franklin Buchanan,[8] one of the early superintendents) just outside the main gate, 2 Maryland Avenue. It was all very strange and very exciting to me.

The examination was held in the newly completed armory, some 100 or more of us working under very warm conditions in the Naval Academy's wide-arm recitation chairs. It took us from Monday through Friday to cover all the subjects, and it was a pretty grueling test. After this, there was nothing to do but wait, making frequent trips to the main gate to examine the lists of candidates posted there, as the marking was completed. Finally, I saw my own name posted, accepted, with a passing grade in all subjects except United States history, which was only a 2.3. The trouble there was that I was asked too many questions involving dates, which I always seemed to have difficulty in remembering. But my good marks in the mathematical subjects carried me through.

Midshipman H. K. Hewitt at the U.S. Naval Academy, Annapolis, MD, 1903

The next thing was the physical examination, held in the old sick quarters (between the present Officers' Club and the Modern Language building). Everything here went all right until they stood me up, *sans* clothing, face to the wall. Then there was a great consultation by the medical examiners, who finally turned me down, alleging that I had curvature of the spine, something which was news to me. My bitter disappointment may be imagined.

My father, however, a determined man if ever there was one, immediately whisked me off to Washington. He was sure that there was nothing wrong with me. It so happened that the then Chief of Bureau of Medicine and Surgery, Doctor Rixey, was an old friend of the Trenton, New Jersey, Hewitt family, so we were granted an audience and listened to sympathetically. Dr. Rixey appointed a special board in the Bureau, which went all over me again. The result: a finding that I had no curvature of the spine, but a left tibia half an inch shorter than the right, which, when I stood with my heels flat on the floor, brought my left hip lower than my right and gave my spine a slight apparent curve. That minor defect, which had never bothered me before, nor has since, was promptly waived, and, to my overwhelming joy, I was cleared for entrance.

Thus it happened that on a warm 29th of June 1903, I was sworn in as a midshipman by the Superintendent, Rear Admiral Willard H. Brownson,[9] and entered into the summer training of a plebe. We were all quartered in what was then known as Main Quarters, an old building that was situated between the present locations of Sampson Hall and the Officers' Club, with an entrance fronting on a walk about where the road north of the museum is now. There being about 300 of us, we formed a battalion facing south along the walk between Maryland Avenue and the main entrance of Main Quarters. I was assigned to a room on the third floor with Francis P. McCarthy, a youth from Troy whom I had never met before. In fact, I knew none of my classmates prior to my arrival in Annapolis for the examination.

Plebe summer was taken up with elementary instruction in infantry and artillery drill, in seamanship, in gymnastics, and in swimming. Our awkward squad drill master was the famous Swordmaster Corbesier,[10] a very military Frenchman rumored among us as having been cashiered from the French Army as a result of a duel in which he was victorious. In learning the proper position of attention, none of us will ever forget his injunctions to "Oop de haid, out of the chaist, in da belly."

In seamanship, we had many an afternoon of boats under oars and sail, mostly in the heavy double-banked twelve-oared cutters of those days. The oars seemed like trees, and many a wrist ached after an afternoon's session of boat maneuvers with Lieutenant "Bull" Evans in charge.[11] We learned our knots and splices, and our signal flags in the sail loft of the new Seamanship Building, and, on the ground floor, we sat around the waterline-up model of the full-rigged ship *Antietam*[12] to learn the nomenclature of sails, spars, and rigging. Our time was fully taken up, and there was no need to rock anyone to sleep when taps was sounded at 10:00 p.m.

All went serenely until the first of September when the practice cruise ended—the upper classmen going on their September leave and the "unsats" remaining with us to make up the subjects in which they were down. These few taught us the "rates" and served to make us understand that plebes were but a low form of life.

October saw the commencement of the academic year and the formation of the brigade into two battalions of four companies each, in which the Class of 1907, being the first one appointed on a two per congressman and senator basis, outnumbered the other three classes. Meal formations were along Maryland Avenue, one battalion behind the other, facing west toward Main Quarters. The four classes were quartered in the Main Quarters and in three wooden annexes, A and B behind Main, and C east of Maryland Avenue near the present tennis courts. I was quartered in Annex A with a new roommate, R. T. Hanson, and assigned to the Seventh Company, captained by the present Rear Admiral H. S. Howard (Ret.).[13]

The academic work was interesting to me, and I got along rather well, finding myself in the first math section after the marks of the first month were posted. Our routine was two recitation and study hours in the morning and one of each in the afternoon, followed by a drill, except on Wednesday p.m. when the extra time was devoted to athletics. On Saturday, there was one recitation and study period and one drill period in the morning, with the afternoon free. Sunday routine was as it is now, except that plebes never got out except on special request to dine with their parents. For exercise, outside of drills, I played tennis and walked. I went out for no athletic teams. In the first place, I was no good at them, and, in the second, I was too light for most of them. Knowing no one in Annapolis, my Saturday afternoon liberties, when my conduct grade permitted them, consisted mostly in wandering around Annapolis and environs and indulging in waffles and maple syrup at Wiegard's on State Circle (now Tilghman's) or having ice cream sodas at Gilbert's drugstore (now the Central). The exciting event of the plebe year, of course, was the trip to Philadelphia for the Army-Navy game, which, sadly enough, we lost 40–5, in spite of our captain, Bill Halsey.[14] There was no Christmas leave. We even had study hour Christmas night. Afternoon drills, however, were omitted. Some midshipmen were lucky to have their parents, sisters, or sweethearts come to Annapolis to be with them in their free hours.

At the end of the first term, I was forced to change roommates. Hanson and I both stood well, but two classmates in our company, also roommates, were in danger of bilging.[15] So we swapped, each taking on one of the unsats. I think that was fortunate for me, because in helping my roommate, I probably gave more time to each subject and became more thoroughly grounded than I otherwise would have. I was interested in most of my subjects, but I also liked doing things other than study.

June Week of 1904 was, of course, an exciting occasion for the Class of 1907, for we had become "youngsters" at last. There were drills and exercises for the Academic Board, the June Ball, with parents and friends from home attending, and last, but not least, the embarkation for our first practice cruise. I was assigned to the old battleship *Massachusetts*,[16] veteran of '98, on which I spent the first half of the cruise. The second half I was in the steam frigate *Hartford*,[17] veteran of an older war; she had been Farragut's flagship at Mobile Bay. The immortal words "Damn the torpedoes, go ahead" were emblazoned on her gun deck. On both ships, we were busy learning the rudiments of our profession and doing the more menial tasks assigned midshipmen, such as manning the boat falls, the ash whip, etc. But what sticks out most in my recollection were the thrills of the aloft work on the *Hartford*. This was not entirely new, for we had had alongside-the-dock sail drills in the full-rigged training ship *Chesapeake*,[18] and we had all—to be called seagoing by our fellows—climbed to her main truck and spiked our white hats on her lightening rod. But sitting on the fore-topgallant crosstrees of a heavily rolling ship at sea, at times seeing nothing under you but water, was another matter. There were a few who couldn't take it, but most of us survived. Fortunately for me, I was never seriously troubled by seasickness.

Our itinerary that summer did not take us beyond the New England coast. Our stops were mostly at such places as New London, Connecticut, and Rockland, Maine, where we had famous times. We soon found that we were not unwelcome at summer resorts, where there were often more young ladies than there were young gentlemen to dance with them. On Sunday mornings, we were not granted liberty, but, on special request, we were permitted ashore to attend church. This was undoubtedly not only good for our souls but excellent strategy on coming into a new port. After service, we were usually greeted by many friendly parishioners and introduced into the most desirable circles.

August 31 found us off Annapolis, excitedly preparing for our first leave, on which we departed early the following day. And what a time that was!—back home with old friends and, as I look back at it, perhaps a bit the center of attention at parties in my midshipman's uniform. And, just before we were to return to Annapolis on September 30, there was for us a lucky break; there came an entirely unexpected extension of our leave because of a typhoid epidemic among the new plebe class. Many, from points further away, were caught already en route. Thus it was that I was able to gather in three of my good friends for an additional wonderful ten days.

Midshipman H. K. Hewitt on the parade grounds of the U.S. Naval Academy, Annapolis, MD, 1903.

The beginning of our youngster academic year found the Second Battalion, of which I was a member, quartered in the just completed Boat House Wing, as it was then called, of Bancroft Hall. The First Battalion remained in the old Main Quarters and Annexes A and B. Annex C was made into a recitation building. The other wing of Bancroft Hall, then called the Armory Wing, was not yet ready for occupancy. The office of the officer in charge, as we called him, remained in Main Quarters, Bancroft Hall being more the responsibility of the Second Battalion midshipman officer of the day. This had its advantages, for no sooner did the officer in charge leave Main Quarters headed for Bancroft Hall on an inspection than the First Battalion officer of the day passed the word down by telephone. Nevertheless, fairly good order and discipline was maintained, and we got on with our work.

Third Class year passed on uneventfully, pretty much as the previous year, except for more advanced studies and drills and the privilege of being a youngster rather than a lowly plebe. And then there were the hops which now could be attended and the consequent initiation of friendships with the young ladies of Annapolis and their families. The Class of 1905, as had 1904, graduated in February and was given its Farewell Ball by 1906, which succeeded to officer of the brigade. On March 4th the brigade participated in inauguration ceremonies and the parade. June Week rolled around almost before one knew it, and immediately after the June Ball we were once more embarking for a cruise.

This time, I spent the first half of the cruise on the monitor *Florida*,[19] later renamed *Tallahassee* when the battleship *Florida* was built. She was quite a craft, quite a roller, in fact, but we learned a lot in her when we got our sea legs. One personal experience in her is probably worth recounting. While no one was allowed to smoke, except First Classmen at stated times, it had long been a Third Class rate to have a class pipe with a bowl with silver inlaid class numerals, etc., of which one was very proud, even if he did not smoke it. While on watch in the *Florida* engine room, understudying the throttleman, with hot oil and steam everywhere and a heavy roll on, I made the mistake of showing off my pipe, intending to try it out with a little of the Bull Durham cigarette tobacco I had. "Oh, no!" said the throttleman, "let me give you some real tobacco." With that he pulled out a bar of the old navy cut plug, and with his knife, shaved me off a pipeful. My pride, of course, would not let me refuse, so I lighted up. I fear that I turned green before finishing, but I got away with it.

Our itinerary that summer was much the same as before, except that the *Florida* reached as far north as Eastport, Maine. On the second half of the cruise, again on the *Hartford*, we had added responsibilities, and I became a foretopman and the captain of the foretop. One of the duties of the foretopmen on the *Hartford*, on getting underway, was to tend to the anchor chain, which on that ship was something of a job. First, a bit of chain had to be roused up from the chain locker and brought to the capstan by a number of hearties using long chain hooks. Then, as the anchor was hove in, the chain had to be "lighted" aft with the same chain hooks from the capstan to the chain pipe leading to the chain locker. Usually, it was difficult for the captain to find enough hands for this arduous task, but in Annapolis Roads on the morning of September 1, all hands were only too anxious to assist, and the ship got underway in jig time.

Second Class leave was as happy as the previous one. By then, my parents had moved into their own house on Maple Avenue in Hackensack, and here again I had some of my classmates as guests, although this time there was no extended leave.

The beginning of the 1905–1906 academic year found the whole brigade quartered in Bancroft Hall, the First Battalion in the Armory Wing. Now, for the first time, brigade formations were held on Bancroft Hall Terrace—during the previous year, they had been held along the walk between Maryland Avenue and Bancroft Hall, just north of the "lovers lane" area. And the new Bancroft Hall Mess Hall was now put in commission. But chapel was still held in the old armory building between the present officers' tennis courts and the engineering building, the new chapel still being under construction.

In February, 1907 gave 1906 its Farewell Ball. At this ball, "Anchors Aweigh" by Bandmaster Zimmerman, 1907's own class march, was played publicly for the first time, and after the graduation exercises we became the senior class supplying officers of the brigade. Officially, however, we were still the Second Class. In order that we might be more strict with our subordinates and not tend to any favoritism, all of 1907 in the First Battalion were transferred to the Second, and vice versa. Thus I found myself to be the second petty officer (insignia and star) and left guide of the Sixth Company. By then we had six companies to a battalion. My roommate of the previous two years, A. G. Dibrell, succumbed to his academic difficulties, and I had a new roommate, a grand fellow, Riley F. McConnell,[20] who years later was the best man at my wedding.

By the second term of Second Class year, we were getting more and more professional subjects, a great deal of navigation, and much gunnery, engineering, and seamanship. But we were continuing our language courses. In those days, but two languages were offered, French and Spanish. We majored in one of the two but were given one term of the other in order to get a foundation. I had chosen Spanish for two reasons: first, because it was reputed to be the easier (as it is), and second, because I thought it would be the more useful in my profession, the

Midshipman H. K. Hewitt in his whites at the U.S. Naval Academy, 1906.
(Naval Historical Collection)

Navy then having so much to do in the Spanish-speaking areas of the Caribbean, Central America, and South America.

Before the end of the term, we learned that 1907 was to be split into three sections, the first to graduate in September 1906; the second in February 1907; and the third in June 1907. This was done because of the need for junior officers in the fleet, which was being augmented by the many new battleships built as a result of Teddy Roosevelt's efforts. The mark for assignment to the First Section was, as I remember it, an average of 3.12. Eighty-seven of us made it, and so, instead of going on to the First Class practice cruise, we remained at the Academy for what we termed a forced draft First Class course.

The three-month period available for this course was divided into two terms of six weeks each, with a Semi-An and a Final. The eighty-seven were formed into three divisions of twenty-nine each, which rotated for a week afloat down the bay on the monitor *Nevada*,[21] and two weeks of academic work ashore. It was a summer of hard work and a productive one, but not without its pleasant side. For one thing, we were ordered to wear our officer's whites—of course without the shoulder marks but much superior to the midshipman's whites of those days; and second, we were allowed out in town daily after our work was over. We felt, indeed, like officers already. Our association with the new plebes (Class of 1910) was minor; we scarcely deigned to notice them.

I had one personal experience that summer which might have been serious and unquestionably cost me some numbers. Sunday afternoon, the day prior to the start of our mid-summer Semi-An, while on liberty out in town, I was suddenly taken with a feeling of nausea. I went right back to quarters and took to my bunk. I forced myself to go to supper formation, but on arriving in the mess hall, the smell of food made me almost actively ill. The officer of the day excused me on the condition that I report to evening sick call, which I certainly had every intention of doing. Throwing pajamas and toilet articles into a laundry bag, I managed to drag myself over to the old Sick Quarters, there to await my turn with the young doctor on duty. After listening to my tale of woe, he only gave me a prescription. I said, "Doctor, aren't you going to put me on the list?" "No," said he, "there's nothing much the matter with you. You are just trying to get out of that exam." That made me mad. I said, "Doctor, I am in the First Section. I don't have to dodge exams. In fact, I'd rather take this one on time. But the way I feel now, I doubt if I could even get to it." After a lot of argument, he finally consented to put me on the list and to turn me in at Sick Quarters. "But," said he, "I'll probably get in trouble for it." I spent that whole night up, and for days, I ate nothing but the white of egg on cracked ice. In justice to the doctor, who was new and had undoubtedly been thoroughly indoctrinated on the habits of some midshipmen, he came to me the next day and apologized, acknowledging that I really was sick.

I missed the whole exam week and on return to duty, still weak, I had to take a makeup exam on one of the hottest days we had, way up under the roof of the old physics lecture room. Naturally, I did not do as well as I otherwise might have. And *then* I had to make up for all the lost recitations.

In spite of all that, I survived, and on September 12 graduated number thirty in the class. That was a great day with parents and friends present and our new passed midshipman's shoulder marks on our shoulders.

Graduation leave for some of us was very short, for President Roosevelt was coming to witness target practice in the fleet. So it was that on September 26, just two weeks after graduation, I reported on board the USS *Missouri*[22] at Provincetown, Massachusetts. And the following day we received the president on board and fired a battle practice for him. Naturally, I was little more than a spectator, but it was an experience.

NOTES

1 Robert Anderson Hewitt (1861–1929). Father.

2 Robert Anderson (1805–1871). U.S. Army officer who, in command of troops in Charleston harbor, defended Fort Sumter when it was bombarded on April 12–13, 1861, by the Confederates.

3 Charles Hewitt (1824–1870). Paternal grandfather.

4 Anna Conrad Hewitt (1823–1898). Paternal grandmother.

5 Henry Frederick Kent (1827–1893). Maternal grandfather.

6 Charlotte Mumford Kent (?-1914). Maternal grandmother.

7 Mary Kent (1862–1945). Mother.

8 Franklin Buchanan (1800–1874). First superintendent of the U.S. Naval Academy, 1845–1847.

9 Willard H. Brownson (1845–1935). Rear Admiral. U.S. Naval Academy, Class of 1865; superintendent, U.S. Naval Academy, 1902–1905.

10 Antoine J. Corbesier was appointed swordmaster at the U.S. Naval Academy in 1865.

11 Robley D. Evans (1846–1912). Rear Admiral. U.S. Naval Academy, Class of 1865. He was nicknamed "Fighting Bob" because of wounds received during the assault on Fort Fisher, North Carolina, in 1865. He commanded the Great White Fleet in 1907 but was forced to resign in 1908 because of ill health.

12 USS *Antietam* (Screw sloop). Wooden ship launched in 1875 and redesigned as a stores ship. She served in this capacity in Philadelphia from 1876 to 1887.

13 Herbert S. Howard (1884–1977). Rear Admiral. U.S. Naval Academy, Class of 1904.

14 William F. Halsey (1882–1959). Fleet Admiral. U.S. Naval Academy, Class of 1904; Commander, U.S. Naval Forces, South Pacific, 1942–1944; Commander, Third Fleet, 1944–1945; Fleet Admiral, 1945.

15 Bilging: Flunking.

16 USS *Massachusetts* (BB-2). Commissioned in 1896. During the summer of 1904, she served as a training ship for U.S. Naval Academy midshipmen.

17 USS *Hartford* (Screw sloop). Commanded by David Farragut at the Battle of New Orleans, 1862 and the Battle of Mobile Bay, 1864.

18 USS *Chesapeake* (AM). Renamed *Severn* in 1905.

19 USS *Florida* (Monitor No. 9). Renamed *Tallahassee* in 1908.

20 Riley F. McConnell (1884–1940). Captain. U.S. Naval Academy, Class of 1907.

21 USS *Nevada* (Double-turreted monitor). Renamed *Tonopah* in 1909.

22 USS *Missouri* (BB-11). She sailed with the Great White Fleet around the world, 1907–1909.

USS Missouri *(BB-11)*
(Naval Historical Collection)

II *Duty in USS* Missouri, *1906–1907*

When I reported on board the *Missouri* (one of five classmates so assigned), I was detailed as junior officer of the Third Division under Lieutenant F. D. Berrien,[1] who had the after 6-inch guns of the secondary battery on the main deck. One of my first duties was to assist in rendering honors to President Theodore Roosevelt, who came aboard the following morning accompanied by then Lieutenant Commander William S. Sims[2] and by the president's great friend, marine artist Henry Reuterdahl.[3] Sims, it may be remembered, was the one who, having gotten Roosevelt's ear, was primarily responsible for a real advancement in our Navy's methods of gunnery training. The *Missouri* stood well in the fleet in target practice scores, and the purpose of the presidential visit was to witness her so-called battle practice.

Thinking of that practice, as compared to present-day methods and equipment, brings to mind the truly remarkable changes that have taken place in these fifty-odd years, not only in the range and effectiveness of naval gunfire, but in the development of such things as guided missiles. Practice was held at an anchored target with the ship at about ten knots on a straight course, with ranges between 6,000 and 8,000 yards. The guns and the turrets were directed by individual pointers and trainers using telescopic sights (at that time a great advance), who struggled to have their horizontal wire or vertical wire on the target at the instant of hearing the salvo signal. With any movement of ship at all, this required long training and great skill. Fire control, which, when I first came aboard, I thought had to do with a conflagration, was in a very elementary stage. Ranges and deflection settings were passed to individual sight-setters at the guns by jury-rigged or improvised voice tubes from the tops, as were the spotter's corrections, "up 200," "right 2," etc. The usual result was that no two sights were set quite the same at the end of the firing. The firing signals were by buzzer, also jury-rigged, rung from the top, two shorts for "stand-by" and a long one for "fire."

Being new on board, I was assigned no station except to observe, which I did, from the topside. I must say, having never experienced anything like it, that I was quite lifted off my feet by the first salvo of four 12-inch guns and eight 6-inch.

President Roosevelt was indeed his own energetic self, up into the tops, down into the engine and firerooms, messing with the crew, congratulating the gunpointers, and being photographed with them. Reuterdahl made many sketches of these activities.

I soon settled down to the life of a junior officer aboard ship. We had a fairly congenial mess in the steerage, and veterans of the Class of 1906 were quick to show the new men of 1907 the ropes. Besides our regular work in our division and in our part of the ship, that of assisting the division officer, those of us who were on deck stood regular watch as junior officer of the deck. When we got to the Boston Navy Yard for overhaul, as we did in October, this became an actual port watch as officer of the deck, with the regular wardroom watch officer taking a supervisory day's duty.

On my first watch of this sort, I almost got into trouble. It was the mid-watch and I had been carefully instructed that it was part of my duty at night to make occasional inspections below to see that all was well. I was determined to carry out this duty conscientiously, but being new, I did not yet know my way around very well. Consequently, when the Marine corporal of the guard came to make one of his routine reports, I directed him to accompany me, carefully informing the seaman anchor watch that I was inspecting the ship. What I did not know was that the latter was more green than I. It so happened that the speaking tube and bell from the bridge to the quarterdeck was just inside the deckhouse, under the stateroom of the navigator, who was a rather nervous and excitable person. It was customary for the signalman on watch to call the quarterdeck to report liberty party men coming down the dock. Repeated unanswered calls roused the navigator, who, being the acting commanding officer, got up to see what it was all about. Not finding the officer of the deck but only a rather sleepy anchor watch, the only information he got was that "The officer of the deck went up the dock with the corporal of the guard." That was too much for the navigator. When I duly returned from my below decks inspection, I found quite a veritable reception committee—the navigator and most of my messmates who were on board, one having already been designated as my relief to take the watch and the remainder getting ready to deploy through the yard on a search expedition. In the end, I was exonerated, but it was a long time before I was allowed to live it down in the mess.

After New Year's 1907, we left the Navy Yard, joining the other battleships of the Atlantic Fleet for the move to the West Indies, and particularly Guantánamo Bay, for winter training. At that time it was the unusual practice, rather than the usual, for ships to steam in formations, so junior officers of the deck were kept with their eyes glued to the stadimeter to read the distance from the next ahead, and officers of the deck were constantly ringing up "three turns faster" or "two slower" in an effort to keep the ship within 50 yards of prescribed position. Failure to do so was quite likely to result in penalty to the officer of the deck concerned and to the captain as well.

The month of January in Guantánamo was spent primarily in landing force training, with the ship's battalion (four bluejacket companies and a Marine company) and the regiment to which it belonged camped ashore on Deer Point, near the big rifle range. I well remember several very hot days ashore in charge of a working party clearing our prospective camp site of cactus and other brush. Our time in camp was mainly taken up on the rifle range, qualifying as many marksmen as possible (a good rifle shot was supposed to make an excellent gunpointer), but there was also a good bit of infantry and artillery training. They were long days of hard work, relieved by a refreshing swim at the end. Most of us were ready to turn in when darkness fell.

February brought with it my first and perhaps most important experience with disaster relief. In February, Kingston, Jamaica, suffered a most devastating earthquake. Communications being what they were in those days, it was not until the following day that we heard of it in nearby Guantánamo, and not until the day after that were the *Indiana*[4] and *Missouri*, under Rear Admiral C. H. Davis,[5] able to reach the stricken city with extra medical personnel and supplies drawn from the remainder of the fleet. As we entered the harbor in the early morning, we were astonished to see that the point at Port Royal had apparently sunk, as evidenced by partly submerged palm trees. And worse was yet to come.

Conditions on shore in the city were chaotic. Local officials appeared to be in a daze, and there was no effective organization to alleviate the situation. Buildings had been wrecked and streets were filled with debris together with the bodies of people who had been felled and buried by falling walls. Many injured were completely unattended. In the large penitentiary, convicts, released from their cells during the tremor, were refusing to return and were threatening to break out. The United States Navy, which was welcomed with open arms by city authorities, promptly went into action. A field hospital was set up on shore, manned by all available medical personnel. Working parties were landed to clear up debris, pull down dangerous walls, dispose of bodies, and to furnish whatever assistance was required. Food and fresh water were made available. And upon request of the warden of the prison, an armed company of bluejackets was landed from the *Indiana* to restore order there. The Marines happened to be ashore in Guantánamo undergoing field training.

The dead had lain for two days, first under a tropical downpour and then under a tropical sun. The resulting stench was nauseating, even reaching the ships via the gentle trade wind and thence down below through the ventilating systems. To prevent epidemics, something had to be done promptly.

My first duty was to visit ashore, with our chaplain, a number of American tourists marooned on one of the piers but hoping to board an early arriving ship. They had been without food or water since the earthquake, and some were slightly injured. We ministered to them as best we might and, as I remember, most were taken aboard one or the other of our ships. One woman exclaimed to me with tears in her eyes that the American flag as we came in that morning was the most beautiful sight she had ever seen.

My next job was in charge of one of the many busy working parties. An old photograph in one of my albums pictures me directing the pulling down of an unsteady wall. Another shows the gruesome sign of cremating corpses found in the street. Loaded carts were carrying others away. There was no attempt or possibility of identification. One man implored me to help dig into what was left of his house to see if the remains of his wife were there. They were. It was a day one would like to forget, but which one cannot. I have never been back to Kingston. I should like to see it under happier circumstances.

The Governor-General of Jamaica was somewhere in the interior of the island, out of communication, and he did not come to Kingston until a day or two after our arrival. Unfortunately, he was an "Americanophobe." He was infuriated that we, rather than the British navy, were in the stricken city. He was incensed that we had landed forces under arms without his authority, although these had been requested by those on the spot, in an emergency. He demanded that our field hospital be withdrawn. This, reluctantly on our part, had to be done, in spite of the pleas of the patients that they not be left. Leading civilians apologized to many of us publicly at the conduct of their governor. But the situation had became such that Admiral Davis felt we could be of no further use. Accordingly, he withdrew his ships to Guantánamo and turned about a navy supply ship which was en route, for Governor Swettenham[6] insisted that the provisions and other supplies it carried were not needed. We knew they were. This unfortunate incident resulted in a diplomatic apology to the United States from Britain and the prompt recall of Governor Swettenham.

The fleet came north again in time for those of the first section of the Class of 1907 who could be spared to return to Annapolis to attend the 1907 Class german and the Farewell Ball with the Third Section of the class, who were then graduating. Naturally, a wonderful time was had by all, with old friends in the Academy and in town.

Most of that summer was spent in the Hampton Roads area, in connection with the Jamestown Exposition. At the opening, there was a large naval review at which ships of many nations were present, including one even from as far away as Japan. Each United States ship had an opposite number to entertain, that of the *Missouri* being the British cruiser *Roxburgh*.[7] There was much visiting and entertaining back and forth between the officers' messes, and many friendships were made. The events were marred by one tragedy. A launch from the *Minnesota*,[8] carrying officers back from a ball at the exposition after midnight, in low visibility, was caught under a towline between a tug and a car barge and sunk with the loss of all on board. When it failed to turn up, a search was started. It was found the following day by dragging. Several of my classmates were lost with it.

The late fall found most of the ships in their assigned navy yards preparing for the coming cruise around South America to the West Coast. The *Missouri* left Boston in early December for the fleet rendezvous in Hampton Roads, with full bunkers and a deck-load of coal, most of which was washed overboard in a gale we experienced en route.

NOTES

1 Frank D. Berrien (1877–1951). Rear Admiral. U.S. Naval Academy, Class of 1900.

2 William S. Sims (1858–1936). Admiral. U.S. Naval Academy, Class of 1880. Naval aide to President Theodore Roosevelt, 1908–1909; Commander, U.S. Naval Forces operating in Europe, 1917–1919; president, Naval War College, 1917 and 1919–1922.

3 Henry Reuterdahl (1871–1925). American naval painter and journalist.

4 USS *Indiana* (BB-1). Commissioned in 1895, she took part in the Spanish American War, then served as a training ship for Naval Academy midshipmen and naval guns crews through World War I.

5 Charles H. Davis (1845–1921). Rear Admiral. U.S. Naval Academy, Class of 1865. Division Commander, Battleship Squadron, North Atlantic Fleet, 1904–1907. He aided victims of the 1907 earthquake in Jamaica.

6 Sir Alexander Swettenham (1845–1933) was educated at Cambridge University. He served in diplomatic posts in Ceylon, Singapore, and British Guiana before his appointment as captain-general and governor-in-chief, Jamaica, 1904–1907.

7 HMS *Roxburgh*. Armoured cruiser, 10,850 tons; 450' x 68.5'; built by London & Glasgow Company in 1904.

8 USS *Minnesota* (BB-22). Commissioned in 1907, she was one of sixteen battleships of the Great White Fleet that sailed around the world, 1907–1909.

Ships of the Great White Fleet visited Auckland, New Zealand, from August 9–15, 1908, where the officers and crew were warmly received and feted. (Naval Historical Collection)

III   *The Round-the-World Cruise, 1907–1909*

Fifty years ago, the backbone of the United States Navy—in fact, the major part of it—was en route around the world. It was a historic event and an invaluable and unforgettable experience for those fortunate enough to be aboard one of those white and spar-colored ships. No one now in active service is old enough to have made that cruise, but we old-timers of the classes of 1907 and before remember it well. Even 1908, which joined in San Francisco after graduation, got in on half of the cruise.

It was passed midshipmen of the classes of 1906 and 1907 (and later, 1908) who manned the junior officers' messes, the steerages, stood the junior officers' watches, took boat officer duty, and the many other odd jobs which fell to the lowly. The lordly ensigns, commissioned only after two years at sea, were in the wardroom and standing top watch.

How did the remarkable voyage come about? It did not start as a world cruise. As we got underway, all we knew was that the Atlantic Fleet, our sixteen battleships plus a few small destroyers and one or two auxiliaries (about all we had then), was to proceed to the Pacific via the Straits of Magellan. (The Panama Canal was not yet in being.) For some time, even then, the situation in the Far East had been growing more and more threatening. Finally, President Theodore Roosevelt made the decision to concentrate our major naval strength in the Pacific in preparation for any eventuality, but with the hope that this gesture would thoroughly discourage any oriental belligerent intent.

So it was that in early December 1907 the fleet assembled at Hampton Roads. There, on December 16, immaculate and freshly painted, it put to sea, passing in review before President Roosevelt, who was flying his flag on the presidential yacht *Mayflower*. Rails were manned and officers were decked in special full dress: cocked hats; epaulets; high-collared, double-breasted, white satin-lined swallow tail coats; and gold-striped trousers. The midshipmen, of course, merely had their usual caps, frock coats with gold shoulder knots, and narrow-striped trousers. It was an overcast, raw, blowy day as I recall, and all hands on deck, especially those on the forecastles and the open bridges, were happy when pipe down finally sounded.

Our commander in chief, the famous Admiral Robley D. (Fighting Bob) Evans, one of the heroes of Santiago, had advised the President that his command was "ready for a fight or a frolic." Ready we undoubtedly were by the standards of those days, but, as we can better realize today, there were serious deficiencies. Twenty-two individual guns, using pointer fire with improvised fire control, could, in smooth weather, make rapid-fire hits in short bursts on canvas screens 1,600 yards away. Larger latticework targets, slowly towed on fairly well-known courses, could be hit with a few salvos at around 8,000 yards. But fire control and loading arrangements were crude, and effective fire could not be long sustained.

The fleet was far from being what later became termed well-balanced. The flotilla of six small destroyers assigned was very short-legged and could not be fuelled at sea. Consequently, it had to follow an entirely different itinerary and was rarely present with the larger ships. Also, since there were no cruisers whatever, the fleet had no eyes.

The battleships, however, were highly proficient in maneuvering and station-keeping and in visual signaling. Naturally, they became more proficient as the cruise progressed. Where initially the junior officer of the watch was required to keep his eye glued to the stadimeter, and frequent changes in revolutions were rung up to maintain the required distance, toward the end, the officer of the deck was satisfied to cock a seaman's eye forward to note the position of the top of his jack staff with reference to the waterline of his next-ahead. It was a matter of pride to keep position with a minimum of revolution changes.

Radio (wireless telegraphy) was in its infancy and its range very short. The vacuum tube had not yet been introduced. Experimental radio telephones, intended for very short-range inter-ship communication, were hastily installed in each battleship pilot house before sailing. But no one ever seemed to get them to work satisfactorily, or at all.

Coal, of course, was the fuel. And that meant a day or more of hard, dirty work during each stay in port, and several days thereafter to clean up ship and personnel. No one was spared. One night might find one black as the ace of spades with one's division among the coal bags in the hold of a collier, and the next, in evening dress, at the governor general's ball. The few colliers the Navy possessed were entirely inadequate for the task of supplying the required fuel, which was, throughout the cruise, furnished for the most part by means of British tramp steamers. This was a lesson, for under war conditions with a neutral Britain, our fleet would have been practically immobile.

Of recreation on board ship there was little. There were no movies, no radio, no television. Occasionally, in good weather, there might be a "smoker" on the forecastle—boxing and wrestling—or a minstrel show. Each ship had its band, which made a great contribution. But there were so many drills and so many watches to stand (better than a watch in four or five was a rarity) that one had little time for anything else.

As to food, ships had iceboxes that were iced from ashore, and ice machines of capacity barely enough to supply the daily needs of the messes. After about a week at sea there would be no more fresh provisions, and the messes would be reduced to potatoes and what we called sea stores—smoked and canned meats and fish, canned fruit and vegetables.

After passing the Capes of the Chesapeake, the battleship fleet headed south toward its first port of call, Port of Spain, Trinidad. It was organized in four divisions of four ships each, each two divisions forming a squadron. Except in narrow waters, it normally cruised in line of squadrons (the two squadrons abreast, each in column), but sometimes it formed line of divisions. The cruising speed, the economical speed of most of the ships, was ten knots.

My own ship was the *Missouri*. It was my good fortune to have been detailed as assistant navigator and to continue as such until our arrival in California. Not only did this give me fine experience piloting and sights of all sorts in both north and south latitudes, it permitted me to be on the bridge entering and leaving port and whenever anything of interest was going on.

The trip to Trinidad was uneventful. It was pleasant to get south of Hatteras and into a more balmy atmosphere. The *Missouri*, I remember, made a detour into San Juan to land a sick man. No one got ashore, but we did see the harbor and the Morro. The fleet anchored off Port of Spain on December 23 and remained until the 29th, a Christmas week primarily occupied with coaling ship and holding field day. At best, Christmas in a strange land is a sad occasion. But there were, however, parcels to open, and some diversions ashore. The principal of these were the Christmas races in the Queen's Park Savannah, where many a young officer lost some of the five-pound gold pieces in which we were paid, and the visits to the Queen's Park Hotel to sample its good food and its famous concoctions—its green swizzles and planter's punches. (Twenty-nine years later, on the occasion of Franklin D. Roosevelt's presidential visit to South America, I and one of my classmates revisited the Queen's Park and found that the punch had lost none of its savor.)

From Trinidad to Rio de Janeiro was one of our longest legs, and I can remember that the "coal eater" *Maine* had a close call making it. Ships' ventilating systems not being what they are today, it got pretty hot, and many slept on deck. The big event, of course, was crossing the line and the initiation of thousands of "pollywogs." King Neptune, who probably had never before flown his flag simultaneously on so many ships, and all his court had a mighty busy day. One of those pollywogs little thought

Battleship Organization–Atlantic Fleet
Upon Departure Hampton Roads,
December 16, 1907
Rear Admiral Robley D. Evans, Commander in Chief

First Division	Third Division
Connecticut (F)	*Minnesota* (F)
Kansas	*Ohio*
Vermont	*Missouri*
Louisiana	*Maine*

Second Division	Fourth Division
Georgia (F)	*Alabama* (F)
New Jersey	*Illinois*
Rhode Island	*Kearsarge*
Virginia	*Kentucky*

that years later, as senior "shellback," he would be directing the president of the United States, the senior pollywog, to set the lookout watch for "Davey Jones."

Not to be forgotten also was the celebration of New Year's Day. It would be fun to read an anthology of those mid-watch logs, written in verse, as they always used to be on the first watch of the year.

Rio at its best, with the entire Brazilian navy assembled, received the fleet with open arms on January 12. There were innumerable parties, but the high spot, in my recollection, was the luncheon given the officers of the fleet atop the Corcovado,[1] with a magnificent view of the city and world famous harbor spread out below.

One of my recollections is that of going ashore one hot morning with the chief quartermaster and a hack chronometer, journeying by trolley car and afoot to the astronomical observatory on a hill within the city limits in order to observe the transit of the sun across the local meridian. By such means only was it possible to determine accurately chronometer error. The days of easy radio "ticks" were yet to come.

Departing from Rio on January 21, the fleet once more turned south. No stop was scheduled for Montevideo or Buenos Aires, probably because it would have been undiplomatic to visit the one without the other, and the long trip up the Rio de la Plata with its shallow channel of varying and unpredictable depths was considered impracticable for such a force. We did, however, have a visit off the La Plata from a very smart unit of the Argentine navy.

It was not until January 31 that we entered the Straits of Magellan, anchoring overnight in Possession Bay. The following day we proceeded in daylight to Punta Arenas,[2] then the most southern city in the world, to meet our waiting colliers and to be greeted by the Chilean cruiser *Chacabuco*.[3]

Punta Arenas was a bleak, frontier-like sort of place, with little to offer in the way of recreation, except the many bars. One of our first sights was an enormous sign along the waterfront, "Special Prices for the American Fleet," a statement we soon found to be true but in an opposite sense than the one intended to be conveyed! There was, however, little to purchase other than a few souvenirs made of guanaco feathers. My principal recollections of the visit are of a rather tough tour of duty as a junior officer of the shore patrol and of a day in the plaza taking observations with a vibrating magnetic needle to determine the local strength of the earth's magnetic field.

Mentioning of the last brings to my mind the tremendous task set by the Hydrographic Office for the fleet's navigators, to say nothing of the assistant navigators. Our time being prior to the days of the gyrocompass, each battleship had about six magnetic compasses—the standard compass abaft the bridge, and steering compasses on the bridge, in the pilot house, conning tower, central station, and steering engine room. Orders were directed that each ship "swing ship" near the latitude of Hatteras, again near the magnetic equator, and, finally, near the latitude of the

Straits, to determine the errors of each compass uncompensated. Then, of course, the compasses had to be re-compensated and the ship swung for residual errors. In addition, the magnetic directive force (very little in the conning tower and below decks) at each of the compass stations had to be determined by vibrating needle. With all of this, a great mass of compass data was to be computed and submitted to the Hydrographic Office. It required many midshipman-hours. Whatever use was made of all this information, I never knew. Probably it still reposes deep in the Hydrographic Office archives.

Well before daylight on February 7, in time to round Cape Froward at first light, the fleet got under way in single columns, led by the *Chacabuco*. And then began an unforgettable twenty-four hours on the bridge for at least one assistant navigator. I realize now, much better than I did then, the heavy responsibility that rested on the shoulders of Admiral Evans in getting all those ships safely through that tortuous passage under the conditions to be encountered.

The weather in the Straits of Magellan is always capricious. Sudden blows, or "williwaws," may occur, and fogs suddenly shut down. The water is deep, the shores steep-to, and currents swift and unpredictable. There is no anchoring ground, and, once in, large ships must keep going. In spite of the magnificent scenery, towering cliffs, distant glaciers, and cascades dropping in silver threads to the shore, many officers heaved a sigh of relief when late that night, in a thick fog, the fleet reached the open Pacific.

The next port of call for the battleships was Callao,[4] but en route, the fleet steamed into and out of the semicircular open roadstead of Valparaiso,[5] there to be reviewed by the president of Chile from aboard the anchored cruiser *General Baquedano*.[6] It was a beautiful, clear, balmy day, and the long white and spar-colored column presented a thrilling sight. As the flagship passed the headlands, a flag signal fluttered down, a puff of white smoke appeared from each starboard side, and, from each fore and main, the Stars and Stripes and the Chilean ensign. Thus was inaugurated the fleet's salute to a friendly nation.

To our starboard, Chile reciprocated with the huge, living welcome sign, made by bluejackets, in white against the green terrace of the entrance fortification. The harbor was crowded with gaily decorated small craft and shipping, and at the farther end was the *Baquedano*, full-dressed with our ensign at the main, and yards manned. Each ship, as it passed, rendered presidential honors, rails manned, guard at "present," band sounding four ruffles and playing the Chilean national anthem, and, when clear of the reviewing ship, firing another twenty-one-gun salute. I am sure that it was as memorable an occasion for our Chilean friends as it was for us.

Because of the nature of the harbor, arrival at Callao on February 20 was not as spectacular, but the usual honors were exchanged and our welcome was none-the-less warm. The Peruvians outdid themselves in hospitality, and there were many parties for officers and men, not only in Callao, but in the beautiful and interesting nearby capital, Lima. All saw the bones of Pizarro[7] reposing in the cathedral there, and many officers and men were able to make trips up into the Andes on the breathtaking Arroyo railroad.

The fleet had with it for training five or six Peruvian midshipmen who wore our uniform and performed the same duties as their United States colleagues. Naturally they were happy to be home for a while and to see their families and friends. One of those midshipmen, a messmate of mine, subsequently had a distinguished career in his own navy, becoming *contra-almirante* and, later, Minister of Marine.

All hands were sorry to say *adios* to Peru on February 29. The next stopping place, this for work and not for frolic, was Magdalena Bay on the West Coast of Baja California. Here we stayed for a month, March 12 to April 11, holding target practice, admiral's inspections, and various other exercises, including athletic competitions, plus fishing which afforded about the only diversion. Other than a few fishermen in the tiny settlement of Magdalena, there were no inhabitants.

It was well that there was this interlude, because the arrival of the fleet on our own West Coast was the signal for a series of festive visits, parties, and parades which lasted from the time we arrived off San Diego on April 14 until we finally departed San Francisco, westbound, on July 7. By that time, most of the junior officers, to say nothing of others, had lost much sleep, if not weight.

Since San Diego harbor could not accommodate such a fleet, we anchored in the open off Coronado and North Island. Liberty parties were sent in to San Diego in long lines of sailing launches (no motor launches then) towed by the ships' steamers. Most of the officer activities centered around the old Coronado Hotel—the ships' boats landing at the hotel pier.

After four active days there, the fleet went on to the Los Angeles area, one division anchoring off Long Beach, one off San Pedro, one off Santa Monica, and one off Redondo. The present Long Beach harbor was nonexistent, and the only shelter was the original short San Pedro breakwater.

After eight days filled with sightseeing and social activities in Los Angeles and its beaches, the fleet, on April 25, moved up to Santa Barbara. Here again it was the recipient of an uproarious welcome and overwhelming hospitality. Next came equally busy two or three-day visits at Monterey and at Santa Cruz. Finally, on May 6, 1908, the Atlantic Fleet, augmented by several units of the Pacific Fleet, made a majestic entrance into the Golden Gate—a spectacle watched by most of the population of San Francisco, we thought, as we saw the dense masses of people on every hill and vantage point.

We thought we had been welcomed there, but the reception given us by the city of San Francisco surpassed everything we had theretofore experienced. After a big shore parade, there was a succession of banquets and fleet balls and many other pleasant social activities in the city of San Francisco itself and the surrounding bay area.

Shortly after our arrival, Rear Admiral Evans, who had not been too well, was relieved, and a few days later, Rear Admiral G. S. Sperry[8] became commander in chief. Some changes were made in the composition of the battleship fleet also. The *Maine*[9] and the *Alabama*,[10] neither of which had been noted for their fuel economy, were replaced by the *Nebraska*[11] and the *Wisconsin*.[12] The *Nebraska* joined the Second Division, the *Virginia*[13] transferring to the Third to replace *Maine*. The *Wisconsin* took the place of its sister ship in the Fourth Division, becoming its flagship.

Since the Puget Sound area refused to be slighted, the reconstituted fleet, on May 18, sailed for Seattle and other Puget Sound ports. After a round of visits there, the fleet returned to San Francisco on May 31. By this time, it appears that the tension in the Pacific had become somewhat relaxed. Whether this was due to the westward movement of the fleet or to other causes was a matter of conjecture. Personally, I believe that T. R.'s "big stick" had much to do with it. Whichever was true, it soon became known that we were not to remain on the West Coast but to proceed to the Far East and then back to the East Coast via Suez and the Mediterranean. That prospect, for most of us, was not hard to take.

At Magdalena, I had been assigned to the engineer division for the tour of duty which every passed midshipman was required to have. But before we left San Francisco, our ensign signal officer was detached. To my delight it was decided that I, having spent much time around the bridge, was to be the best qualified relief. So I soon found myself boss of the signal bridge with its detail of one chief quartermaster and sixteen "signal boys."

After many fond farewells (and minus some class rings), the fleet passed through the Golden Gate on July 7 in its long column and headed for Hawaii. It was a pleasant voyage with many drills as a shakedown after our months in port. Our first stop was Lahaina Roads, Maui, where we coaled and cleaned up prior to our ceremonial arrival off Honolulu on July 16. En route to that port, the fleet detoured slightly to pass within sight of the leper colony on Molokai for the benefit of those poor people. This was a result of a request to the president by the famous Father Joseph,[14] who was devoting his life to them.

No one who has ever been to Hawaii could doubt the character of the "aloha" accorded the fleet here. Except for the flagship, all had to anchor offshore. But the weather was good and we had no trouble in making the beach.

The memory of that visit consists mostly of leis, of energetic sightseeing, of surf-riding, of luaus, of hula dancing, and of beautiful concerts in the moonlight under the palm trees at the old Moana Hotel. Ever since, I have had a love of real Hawaiian music. One of the main events was a daylong trip to the sight of the proposed Pearl Harbor Naval Base, then nothing but a harbor surrounded by cane fields. We traveled on the Hawaiian Railroad with native entertainers in each car, and upon arrival took a boat trip out to the harbor entrance. Little did we dream of what would happen there thirty-three years later!!

The Hawaiian stay was all too short, and July 22 found us at sea again, this time on the longest leg of the cruise, the seventeen-day haul to Auckland, New Zealand. By calendar, it was eighteen days, because we skipped a day crossing the 180th meridian, a new experience for most of us. As we passed Samoa, the station ship *Annapolis*[15] came out to have a look at us, rendering honors with her picturesque Fita Fita's guard. By the time we reached Auckland on Sunday morning, August 9, we were thoroughly fed up with sea stores and ready for a bang-up dinner at the best hotel. Unfortunately, we reckoned not with the Sunday habits of the good New Zealanders, for, after a good afternoon walk viewing the city, we found nothing available at the best hotel but what was called a high tea, and that not until 9:00 p.m.

The high spot of the New Zealand visit was a wonderful trip to the world-famous hot springs region of Rotorua. There we shivered a bit in the cold mountain air, but were entertained royally. Particularly to be remembered there were the native Maori dances, and the Maori war yell, which some of us were able to give months afterward. Other events in Auckland, besides official parties, were the races and the inevitable parade in which I always seemed to participate as regimental adjutant. (The *Missouri*'s captain, being the junior, was the Third Division regimental commander.)

It was but a short haul, August 15 to 20, from New Zealand to Sydney, Australia. In Rio, we thought we had seen the most beautiful harbor in the world, but here was one to compete, a matter of universal local pride. "How do you like our harbor?" were almost the first words of our new Sydney acquaintances.

There is no question but that Australia gave the fleet its warmest welcome outside of our own country. And we were made to feel at home, for the people were so like our own. The Sydney visit was full of the usual functions and entertainments. And here again were races and a big parade. The fleet was not able to provide four regimental bands for its landing force, and one was lent to our regiment by an Australian-Scottish regiment. It was an unusual sight to see American Marines and bluejackets led by kilted pipers and drummers.

It was evident that the Australians were also feeling the menace from the north, and they attributed our cruise to it, because there were many street banners with such signs as "Down with the Yellow Peril" and "Blood is Thicker than Water." No doubt this contributed to the cordiality of our reception.

Our busy eight days in Sydney were followed by another week (August 29–September 5) in Melbourne where all the functions, parades, festivities and general hospitality of the previous port were repeated. It would have been impossible to say in which of the two we had a better time.

Continuing around Australia, the fleet arrived in Albany, West Australia, on September 11, remaining until the 18th, a week spent primarily in renewing fuel supplies. Albany then was a small and new town, and while the reception again was hospitable, there was little to do on shore.

Since September 12 was the second anniversary of the graduation of the first section of the Class of 1907, its members were due for their full stripe, subject to passing their final examinations. These were given to those of us in the fleet during the Albany visit, and in spite of the fact that there had been little or no time to "bone," practically all, as we later learned, managed to pass.

The voyage from Albany to Manila, which was reached on October 2, was a peaceful one through tropical seas with the occasional sighting of palm-covered islands. It was, of course, a thrill to pass in by Corregidor as Admiral Dewey[16] had done a little over ten years before with a much smaller force, to see Cavite in the distance, and to anchor off Manila itself. Unfortunately, however, Manila was in the throes of a cholera epidemic and liberty was either not to be had or severely restricted. My recollection consists of only one daytime visit to the old Army-Navy Club in Intramuros and an evening dance at the Army post of Fort McKinley.

During our trans-Pacific voyage, Japan had been extending most insistent invitations for the fleet to visit that country. These having been accepted, the fleet left Manila Bay on October 9 en route to Yokohama. Before arriving there on October 18, however, it ran into a true old-fashioned typhoon, the first and the worst storm of that type I personally have ever experienced. I remember our being in line of squadrons at double distance, barely making steerageway. I recall pitching and shipping heavy seas, our rolling to dangerous angles and having lifeboats at quarterdeck davits smashed to smithereens. I recall being shot from one wing of the signal bridge to the other, only saved from going over the side by the weather cloth. And I wondered how the firemen and coal passers ever kept their feet on the fireroom floor plates.

A miraculous rescue took place during that storm—a combination of courage and splendid seamanship. In the murk, to our starboard, the "man overboard" signal was noted on a ship of the First Squadron. Since the lowering of a boat in that weather would have been out of the question, we naturally gave the poor fellow up for lost. But, not so. To our amazement, we intercepted a signal some minutes later from the second astern of the original ship reporting that she had the man safely aboard. It developed that the sailor, being a good swimmer, had kept his head and had reached the copper ring life buoy dropped to him. The rescuing ship had smartly hove to windward, and, drifting down toward him, recovered him by heaving a line.

Somewhat battered and weary, we arrived in Yokohama on October 18, there to be greeted by the assembled Japanese fleet and to receive the official welcome of the Japanese government. We were treated with the greatest hospitality, but it was an organized hospitality rather than the spontaneous sort to which we had grown accustomed. We officers were given embroidered silk passes on the government railroad. Pretty high school girls were at the Yokohama and Tokyo railroad stations to serve us tea, and often school children waving Japanese and American flags were lined up to see us pass on official occasions. Each ship had a Japanese host ship which strove to see that we were well cared for, and there were garden parties and entertainments galore in Tokyo. All enjoyed seeing the sights and the manners of a land so utterly strange to us. It may be that the contacts then made served to delay what happened later.

Upon leaving Yokohama on October 25, the fleet divided, the First Squadron proceeding directly to Manila Bay for target practice, arriving October 31. The Second Squadron, to which my ship was attached, went to Amoy for a visit of courtesy to the Empire of China. There we had an interesting time, but we saw nothing of the native city of Amoy, for there, also, a cholera epidemic was raging. We were allowed to visit only the foreign settlement on the island of Kulangau, where we were given the privileges of the big British club. Along the shore near the city, however, the Chinese government had built quite a large compound especially for the entertainment of the American fleet. There were shops, theaters, and many places of entertainment for us, all done in regal, old-time Chinese style. We were fascinated by our Mandarin hosts with glass balls atop their hats, colored as per their rank. One night I attended a large official Chinese dinner—birds' nest soup, sharks' fins, chopsticks, and all. The following night, I was present at another sumptuous dinner, this time, European style. The week passed all too rapidly, and on November 7 the Second Squadron rejoined the fleet in Manila Bay.

The month of November was spent by the fleet in target practice and other exercises, and this time, the cholera having died down, we got a real chance to see Manila and the surrounding country. Also, I remember a short visit to Subic Bay by my ship during that period. But by December 1 we were on our way again, this time with thoughts of home, not by Christmas, of course, but not too long after. And the idea of mail meeting us, rather than chasing after us, was pleasant.

It would have been interesting to have had a look at Singapore, but that was not to be. We passed it by for a week's stay, December 13 to 20, at Colombo, Ceylon. My memory of that consists primarily of a highly interesting trip to Kandy, one of the reputed sites of the Garden of Eden, with elephant rides, many pleasant activities at the Galle-Pace Hotel on the shore near Colombo, and the ever-present jewel peddlers, who would not even let one enjoy a cup of coffee in peace at a sidewalk cafe or a hotel porch. Undoubtedly, there were bargains to be had if one knew one's stones; otherwise one was apt to be fleeced. But many officers came home with some beautiful opals.

Christmas and New Year's Day were spent at sea, en route to Suez. Forlorn they might have been had it not been for the receipt of a big Christmas mail at Colombo and the knowledge that at last we were really homeward bound. I am sure that all the poetic mid-watch logs of January 1 were in cheerful vein.

The period from January 3 to January 10 for some ships was spent at Suez in transiting the Canal and at Port Said, many of the officers and enlisted men making the trip to Cairo. There they missed none of the sights, the mosques, the Coptic churches, the Nile, and, of course, camel rides to the sphinx and the pyramids. I was hauled from one wide pyramid step to the next by Egyptian guides until the top was reached, and I will remember the eerie effect of the sphinx by moonlight.

From Port Said, detachments of the fleet spread out all over the Mediterranean, visiting such ports as Naples, Villefranche, Marseille, Tripoli, Malta, Algiers, and Tangier. Several ships, including the flagship *Connecticut*,[17] proceeded to the aid of the stricken inhabitants of Messina, recently devastated by a severe earthquake.

The *Missouri* and the *Ohio*[18] were lucky to be assigned to the Piraeus, the seaport of Athens where we were moored, each between a Greek and a Russian man-of-war, anchored by the bow with stern to the breakwater. The presence of the Russian squadron was supposed to be due to the fact that Queen Olga[19] of Greece, the wife of King George I,[20] was a Russian princess. The carrying out of international naval custom at colors, the proximity of the ships (50–100 yards apart), and the fact that each had bands resulted in a musical pandemonium each morning of the visit. Each ship played its own national anthem, then the Greeks switched to ours, and the Russians and ourselves to the Greek. The concert ended with all officers and men still at attention, with the Greeks and ourselves playing the Russian anthem, and the Russians playing the "Star Spangled Banner."

The week at the Piraeus was fully taken up seeing the interesting sights of Athens and enjoying Greek hospitality. I still remember delightful meals at the Hotel Grande Bretagne, with delicious after-dinner Turkish coffee. (Thirty-eight years later, revisiting Athens with my flag flying on another and much larger *Missouri*, in the course of a few remarks at an official dinner at the same Grande Bretagne, I was to recall the coincidence of my previous visit as a midshipman, and a ship with the same name.)

King George I, a Danish prince who had been trained as a naval officer in the British navy, honored the *Missouri* with an official visit. Queen Olga accompanied him, and the two of them went over the spotless ship from stem to stern, evincing great interest in everything. The King, when I had brought my division to salute, stopped to say a few pleasant words to me. Much to my subsequent embarrassment, I responded with "Yes, Sir" instead of "Yes, Your Majesty," as I realized I should have done. It was my first contact with royalty.

After leaving Athens, the *Missouri* and *Ohio* spent a couple of days at Salonika, followed by three in Smyrna (now Izmir). Salonika at that time was under Turkish sovereignty, and we were greeted there by some of the Turkish fleet. Several Turkish officers were assigned to each of the two ships as guests for our trip home, and we found them to be most interested in their profession and personally likeable. They regaled their hosts with large quantities of Turkish cigarettes and the famous Turkish paste, locum.

By February 1, all the fleet had reassembled at Gibraltar, preparatory to its transatlantic passage. We were received by the Governor General, with the Royal Navy present, and the garrison, with the greatest of friendly cordiality. We spent five days in seeing the sights of the Rock, in shopping, and, of course, coaling. The mail that greeted us at Gibraltar brought with it the long-delayed ensign's commissions for the First Section of 1907. I guess most of us picked up some good British gold lace. My chief signal quartermaster, en route home, sewed on my first half stripe.

With loud cheers and with long homeward-bound pennants streaming astern, the fleet got underway for the last leg of the journey on February 6. All was excitement, with the prospect of being greeted by wives, sweethearts, parents, or friends upon arrival. The trip was uneventful except for a little bad weather, a night false alarm "man overboard," and being met by units of what we probably called the Home Fleet, among which were the new small battleships *Idaho*[21] and *Mississippi*[22] (destined to be sold to Greece in 1914). Since we could have entered Hampton Roads on February 21, there was considerable growling at having to delay for the ceremonial entry the following morning. But that was soon forgotten.

Early on the morning of Washington's Birthday, 1909, the fleet completed its circumnavigation of the globe by passing once more in review off the "Tail of the Horseshoe" before President Roosevelt in the *Mayflower* and the secretary of the Navy in the *Dolphin*[23]—this time, in-bound.

Thus was written finis to what was indeed a memorable voyage.

After the presidential review of the fleet upon its arrival in Hampton Roads, the various ships dispersed to their respective navy yards, which for the *Missouri* was again Boston, for overhaul and for the granting of leave to officers and crews. My turn for thirty days leave, which I spent at my home, did not come until March 5. During that period I was made a Mason by my own father, who was then master of the lodge in Hackensack.

Upon my return from leave, having duly received my commission as ensign, I left the steerage (junior officers' mess) and became a regular watch and division officer, being given charge of the ship's second division, which manned the forward 6-inch guns. Upon completion of our overhaul, we soon embarked on the usual routine of gunnery and tactical exercises.

NOTES
1. Corcovado. Famous Hunchback mountain in Rio de Janeiro's harbor, 2,310 feet high.
2. Punta Arenas, Chile. A small naval base is located there.
3. *Chacabuco*. Chilean protected cruiser. 4,300 tons; length 360'; beam 46 1/2'.
4. Callao, Peru. Port city.
5. Valparaiso, Chile. Port city and naval base.
6. *General Baquedano*. Training ship of the Chilean navy, launched in 1898. 2,500 tons; 240' x 45 3/4' x 18'. She was named after General Manuel Baquedano, who led the Chilean army to victory in the War of the Pacific, 1879–1882.
7. Francisco Pizarro (ca. 1475–1541) was a soldier, explorer, and conqueror of the Inca empire in Peru in 1532. He was killed by the followers of Diego de Almagro, his partner in the conquest, with whom he had quarreled and whose execution he had ordered three years earlier.
8. Charles S. Sperry (1847–1911). Rear Admiral. U.S. Naval Academy, Class of 1866. Sperry commanded the Fourth Division, Second Squadron of the Great White Fleet in the *Alabama*. When Evans became ill in May 1909, he assumed command of the Great White Fleet.
9. USS *Maine* (BB-10). Ship of the Great White Fleet. She returned to New York in October 1908 with the *Alabama*.
10. USS *Alabama* (BB-8). Ship of the Great White Fleet. She completed the circumnavigation of the globe ahead of the other ships, arriving in New York in October 1908.
11. USS *Nebraska* (BB-14). She joined the Great White Fleet in San Francisco in 1908 for the world cruise.
12. USS *Wisconsin* (BB-9). Ship of the Great White Fleet.
13. USS *Virginia* (BB-13). Ship of the Great White Fleet.
14. Father Joseph Damien de Veuster (1840–1889). Belgian Roman Catholic priest and minister to the leper colony in Molokai Island, Hawaiian Islands. He improved living conditions for the lepers and died of the disease himself.
15. USS *Annapolis* (PG-10). She served as station ship at Tutuila, Samoa, 1907–1911.
16. George Dewey (1837–1917). Admiral. U.S. Naval Academy, Class of 1858. Famous for his destruction of the Spanish fleet at the Battle of Manila Bay in 1898, he was promoted to the rank of Admiral of the Navy in 1903.
17. USS *Connecticut* (BB-18). Ship of the Great White Fleet, 1907–1909. She served as flagship during the round-the-world cruise.
18. USS *Ohio* (BB-12). Ship of the Great White Fleet.
19. Olga of Greece (1851–1926). Queen of Greece. She married King George I in 1867.
20. George I of Greece (1845–1913). King of Greece from 1863 to 1913.
21. USS *Idaho* (BB-24). She took part in the naval review in 1909 at Hampton Roads, Virginia, for the returning Great White Fleet.
22. USS *Mississippi* (BB-23). Stationed in the Caribbean, the ship joined the Great White Fleet for the naval review at Hampton Roads on February 22, 1909.
23. USS *Dolphin* (PG-24). She participated in departure ceremonies for the Great White Fleet in 1907, and welcoming ceremonies upon its return in 1909.

USS Connecticut *(BB-18) was the flagship of the Atlantic Fleet from 1907–1912. (Naval War College Museum)*

IV *Duty in USS* Connecticut, *1910*

In May of the following year, 1910, the *Missouri*, being then one of the oldest battleships in commission, was ordered in reserve with a reduced complement. Her captain, the famous Captain Bill Rush,[1] who had taken over the command the previous fall, was transferred to the *Connecticut*, the fleet flagship. I was complimented by being asked to go along. Accordingly, on May 14, I reported to the big flagship and was assigned to her second division, which manned the forward pair of 8-inch turrets. This was the beginning of an interesting year, which included, at the end of 1910, an unforgettable visit to Britain and France. Under the Commander in Chief, Rear Admiral Seaton Schroeder,[2] two divisions of battleships, including the new dreadnoughts *Delaware*[3] and *North Dakota*,[4] paid courtesy calls at Portsmouth, England, and Cherbourg, France, one unit going to each and then exchanging places. The flagship *Connecticut*, with its division, went first to England, where we arrived about November 15. Officers and men were given opportunity for visits to London. Thus it was that five of us from the *Connecticut*'s wardroom spent the last week in November taking in all the sights we could of that historic and interesting city.

December 2 found me back in London, this time on duty to attend the luncheon in the Guild Hall given by the Lord Mayor for the officers of the fleet. We wore our frock coats, and it was a most interesting and enjoyable occasion. Instead of returning immediately to Portsmouth, I was ordered to wait over until the following day to take charge of the *Connecticut* detail attending the Lord Mayor's luncheon for enlisted men, since my classmate bringing them up was, instead, to take part in a football game at the Crystal Palace. The officer's uniform, I was informed, was to be service dress (the old braided blouse with closed high collar). Arriving so attired at the railroad station, I discovered, to my horror, that the officer I was relieving, and all the others, were dressed in frock coats. Unfortunately, my shipmate was a much bigger man than I, with very long arms. But there was nothing to do but to dive into a compartment and exchange coats as best we could. It was not so bad for him, although he had difficulty in buttoning my blouse, for he was soon to change into "cits" at the club. But for me, it was a different matter. I had to parade through the streets of London leading my platoon in a coat reaching below my knees, with sleeves almost to my fingertips, and a collar two sizes too big, then attend the official luncheon, and after that, a reception at the American embassy given by our ambassador, Mr. Whitelaw Reid.[5] My discomfort may well be imagined.

My sense of unease was no-wise lessened when I found myself sitting at the head table directly opposite the Lord Mayor himself and Commander Sims, newly appointed captain of the *Minnesota,* who, as senior officer with the party, was representing the commander in chief. I spent most of my time during the luncheon pulling up my coat sleeves, so that a little of my shirt cuffs would show, and trying with one hand to gather my coat in the back so that it would not look quite so full in the front. It was in this situation that I listened with awe to Sims's famous "blood is thicker than water" Guild Hall speech. I fully agreed with all that he said, but, even as an ensign, I could not help thinking that there were bound to be diplomatic repercussions. And there were. Not so many months later, another fleet detachment was sent on a visit to Kiel in an effort to soothe ruffled German feelings. But Sims's prediction came true when the British Empire was in difficulties, not only once, but twice.

By December 10, Battleship Division One had taken the place of the Second Division in Cherbourg, and I had my first glimpse of France. It was fun to walk about the Norman countryside, to watch the cider-making then in progress, and to enjoy the product. December 16 found a party of three of us, with like tastes, in Paris for a stay until nearly Christmastime, during which we made the very best of our opportunities from early morning until late at night. We developed a simple system, which I think had much to recommend. We each contributed a like number of *Louis d'or,* in which we were paid, to a fund handled by one of our number, the paymaster, who then paid for everything—thus obviating a lot of figuring as to who owed for this and who for that. When the balance ran low, it was sweetened by each again chipping in. Another of the party, who was probably the most well read historically, told us all about the sites and other things we saw. The third, who was I, was appointed the navigator, whose duty it was to decide where we were going and to make the necessary arrangements. It worked like a charm, and we needed no guide.

We returned to the ship in Cherbourg all too soon—in fact, just in time to participate in coaling ship on the 23rd, an operation which we would have been delighted to miss. While still covered with coal dust, I was greeted with the news that I was to chaperon the *Connecticut*'s contingent to a Christmas dinner being given that night for our enlisted men by the mayor and city of Cherbourg. And not only that. I was informed that *Monsieur le Maire* was to present a cup to our commander in chief, which I, as his representative, would receive—making suitable acknowledgement in French. Since, as will be remembered, my French training at the Naval Academy was a bit sketchy, I begged a messmate, who was a better French scholar, to write a speech for me, which I proceeded to memorize.

The dinner came off well and was enjoyed by all. The mayor made a very cordial speech, most of which I was able to understand. Before commencing my reply, I told our bluejackets the gist of what he had said and warned them that I was going to try to express our thanks and would call on them at the end for three cheers for our hosts, the mayor, and the city. Then, with my best French pronunciation, which probably had a trace of Spanish, I launched into my prepared remarks, departing a little here and there as seemed necessary. How well they were understood I do not know, but I did note that the British consul at my side was at times doubled up with laughter. However, I finished off with *"Nous vous souhaitons une Joyeuse Noel."* That and the ensuing rousing cheers were understood and the occasion ended on a happy note.

NOTES

1 William R. Rush (1857–1940). Captain. U.S. Naval Academy, Class of 1877.

2 Seaton Schroeder (1849–1922). Rear Admiral. U.S. Naval Academy, Class of 1868.

3 USS *Delaware* (BB-28) was commissioned in 1910. She served in the Atlantic Fleet and in 1914–1915 she protected American interests on the east coast of Mexico. During World War I, she joined the Sixth Battle Squadron, British Grand Fleet, during exercises and protected American ships laying the North Sea mine barrage.

4 USS *North Dakota* (BB-29) was commissioned in Boston in 1910. She served with the Atlantic Fleet and as a training ship for midshipmen at the U.S. Naval Academy. She was an honor escort for HMS *Natal* that returned the body of Ambassador Whitelaw Reid to the United States.

5 Whitelaw Reid (1837–1912). Ambassador to the Court of St. James, 1905–1912; formerly editor-in-chief of the *Herald Tribune*, 1872–1889.

USS Flusser (DD-20)
(Naval Historical Collection)

V Pre–World War I Assignments, 1911–1916

In January 1911, eight battleships were en route from Cherbourg, France, to Guantánamo Bay, Cuba, the winter exercise base of the United States Atlantic Fleet. Shortly after their arrival, they were scheduled to have their annual admiral's inspection. Instructions had been issued that a man-overboard drill might be held during the passage, on signal from the flagship, at a time when ships were in such a formation that they could be maneuvered independently. Each ship was to have a dummy on the bridge ready to be tossed overboard to simulate an actual man.

In those days, the fleet flagship had an after bridge, called the flag bridge, from which the admiral made his signals. The forward bridge of the flagship was required to read, answer, and execute signals from the flag bridge, just as on any other ship.

I was an ensign, a watch and division officer on the flagship *Connecticut*. Through no fault of my own, and for reasons which make a separate story, I had, at the direction of the commander in chief, been placed under suspension for two days for alleged "negligence as officer of the deck."

My first watch upon release from suspension was an afternoon watch. As was customary, I took over the deck at 1230, as soon as I had finished my lunch in the wardroom. Naturally, I was resolved to be a very alert young officer of the deck and to let nothing escape me. The two divisions of ships were in an unusual formation, one division astern of the other, with each division in a forty-five degree line of bearing, with the right flank advanced. There was a moderate sea, with wind and sea on the port bow.

At two bells (1300), I happened to be looking aft just in time to see a signal hoisted on the after bridge. It was "UY," which, in the tactical signal book, meant "Exercise at Man-Overboard." It was one of the signals all watch officers knew by heart. But I was surprised at its being made in that weather; so I looked at my signal book to make sure. It was right. By the time I could look aft again the signal was down, "executed." Time was already being taken on me.

I didn't like the sea (for a drill), but it looked as if it could be done. The fleet was in a formation from which ships could maneuver independently to give lee to and pick up a starboard lifeboat. So, with my heart in my mouth, I ordered "Throw over the dummy. Man overboard. Full speed astern both engines. Man the starboard lifeboat. Fire the signal gun. Break the 'N' halfway."

Glancing aft, I noticed another signal flying from the flag bridge. It was "YE," meaning "Repeat signals," the signal usually used to inaugurate flag hoist signal drill, often held at 1300. With a sinking sensation I realized that the first signal had been a mistake. But as well try to stop an avalanche as halt that man overboard drill. Every ship in the formation had fired its gun, was flying the man overboard signal, had dropped life buoys, and was lowering a boat. Our own boat was practically in the water. One had to go ahead.

The captain came tearing up on the bridge, very red in the face from his rapid run up from his cabin way aft. I told him exactly what had happened. Soon the admiral's orderly appeared, presented the admiral's respects, and stated that the admiral would like to see the captain on the after bridge. When the captain returned, he was more red-faced than ever and said, "Hewitt, I will relieve you. You lay aft and see if you can explain to the admiral."

At the initial alarm, the admiral had come up onto the quarterdeck to see what was going on. He inquired of the executive officer, who had by then taken charge of things on the quarterdeck, if he could see the man. The exec said, "Sir, there isn't any man. I believe this is a drill." "Drill," said the admiral, "Who stopped my fleet for a drill?"

When I arrived in the august presence, I was kept standing at attention for some moments before the admiral looked at me with a cold glance and said, "Well, young man, what have you to say for yourself?" I said, "Sir, the after bridge hoisted 'UY.'" He said, "The after bridge hoisted no such signal, sir." All I could say was "aye, aye, sir." And with that, I was dismissed.

On my return to the ship's bridge, I could not find a man who could verify what I had seen, not even the signalman. The after bridge watch, to a man, flatly stated that no signal had been hoisted but "YE." I began to doubt my own sanity, and I felt sure that my naval career was ended. In the meanwhile, however, our own boat and those of the other ships had been safely recovered without casualty, and for that I gave devout thanks.

But the good flag lieutenant, who was friendly to me, finally thought of asking the next ship astern what signal had been hoisted at 1300. Back came the same answer, "UY." Result: apologies from the admiral to the ship, a very relieved ensign, and severe punishment dealt to the flag signal watch for lying.

It seems that as a joke, prior to signal drill, some of the signal boys had mixed up the flags in the flag rack, thinking to have some fun with their mates. The mistake was quickly seen and the hoist hauled down for correction, as they thought, before it would be seen and acted on. Then they were too scared to admit what had happened.

And, as a final happy ending, the eventual admiral's inspection report bore this notation: "No opportunity was had of holding man overboard drill in connection with the inspection, but on a recent occasion when the lifeboat was lowered unexpectedly, it was very creditably handled."

Upon the return north of the battleships from their usual winter exercises based on Guantánamo, and the arrival of the *Connecticut* at the New York Navy Yard for overhaul, I had completed almost four years on a battleship since my graduation. I had risen to a fairly senior watch officer in the fleet flagship. It was time, if I was to round out my experience, to go to a smaller ship with increased responsibilities. Consequently, I was happy to receive orders in June to report to the destroyer *Flusser*,[1] a 750-ton coal-burner. The first oil-burning destroyers of like tonnage were just then being introduced to the fleet. The *Flusser* had a complement of only three officers in addition to the skipper, who was a lieutenant commander. Although still only an ensign, I was senior to the other two officers. Consequently, I became the executive officer, the navigator, the torpedo officer, the commissary and, eventually, when the engineer was detached and the officer complement was reduced by one, I became the engineer officer as well. I felt like sort of a pooh-bah. But it was a wonderful experience, although plenty of work was involved. With the captain absent, on the sick list, or on leave, I had the pleasure of taking the ship to sea several times, once for night maneuvers and once for a full power run. And several times, I had to put her alongside a dock when making a good landing was a bit tricky. On the last of those, a pretty difficult one, my then skipper, Lieutenant Bill Halsey, calmly stayed in his cabin when I reported, "ready for getting under way," and said, "Put her in." My heart was in my mouth, but I got away with it.

Having completed my three years as an ensign (after two years as passed midshipman) and having successfully passed the examinations, mental and physical, for promotion, I was commissioned a lieutenant, junior grade, as of September 13, 1911.

By the fall of 1912, the Fleet Destroyer Flotilla had been augmented by many new oil-burners. Accordingly, the coal-burning destroyer division, including the *Reid*,[2] *Flusser, Lamson*,[3] and *Preston*,[4] was ordered in reserve at the Navy Yard, Charleston, and most of the officers were detached. Commander Sypher,[5] whose assistant navigator I had been in old *Missouri* days, having become executive officer of the comparatively new dreadnought battleship *Florida*,[6] invited me to her; and on October 26, upon reporting in accordance with my orders, I was assigned to the First Division with number 1 turret. This also made me officer of the forecastle on getting underway and coming to anchor.

Duty on the *Florida* was very pleasant and interesting, including the usual target practices and maneuvers, but nothing exceptional happened until the spring and summer of 1913. While still in Guantánamo on winter exercises, I had received orders detaching me to home and to await orders. Since I was a bachelor and liked my ship and my turret, I had no desire whatever to go ashore. Accordingly, when the *Florida* reached Hampton Roads, on the way north, I went to Washington on two days leave and managed to get my orders rescinded upon my agreement to stay with the ship for at least another year.

From Hampton Roads, the ships went to New York, and the *Florida* entered the Navy Yard in May for an extended overhaul; of course, that gave me the opportunity to see something of my home in Hackensack and also something of a young San Francisco lady then visiting an aunt in nearby Paterson, whom I had met in Monterey five years before during the World Cruise. At the end of two weeks, when she had to return to San Francisco, we were engaged and I was bitterly regretting my agreement to stay at sea for another year.

Shortly after reporting to the *Florida*, probably during the following month of November, that ship was sent out to meet and escort into New York HMS *Natal*,[7] bringing back the remains of our ambassador in London, Mr. Whitelaw Reid, to his own country—the same Mr. Reid whose reception I had attended two years previously in an oversized frock coat. On the way in, the *Natal* inquired of the *Florida*, "Which side are we to put to the jetty?" Somewhat to our embarrassment, we had to explain that there would be no jetty, that both ships would moor in the North River, slightly above 96th Street. No dock of any sort was made available to us.

That being the case, and without even a tug being assigned to help, the *Florida* had to make arrangements for the landing of the body with her own resources. She was equipped with a couple of fifty-foot steam launches, called picket boats, with a large cockpit in the stern for officers, a smaller one forward, and a housing over the machinery spaces. The coxswain steered from a wheel on deck slightly abaft the stack. To carry the heavy leaden casket, the after cockpit of one of these boats was decked over. Eight husky chief petty officers were detailed as body bearers, and I was placed, by my friend Commander Sypher, in charge of the operation.

The task might have been fairly simple were it not that at the time for the landing, a strong southerly wind was blowing up the river which, against an outgoing tide, made a rather bad chop. The personnel, necessarily standing on deck, and the heavy coffin would make the boat distinctly top-heavy. We shoved off with an admonition to lash the casket securely, and with the added comment from the executive officer to me that I might as well take a turn of the same lashing about myself. And well I knew that if I lost that valuable cargo, I might as well go along with it.

The *Natal* riding to the ebb tide with stern to wind, we went alongside bow to stern so that on shoving off we would be headed into the wind. Our destination was a landing float at 96th Street, somewhat further down river. The casket was slowly lowered over the side by the *Natal*, with all due honors, but was received and secured by us with considerable difficulty, for we were bobbing up and down violently with the chop. I got the distinct impression that the British on deck did not think too highly of the treatment we were according our late representative to their country.

When we finally cast off, I took the wheel from the coxswain myself and went ahead dead slow. There was a coal pier extending well into the river just south of the float which offered some chance of a lee. Accordingly, I edged slowly over toward it with the chop slightly on our starboard bow. When at last we reached that cover, I heaved a big sigh of relief, put the wheel over, and headed into the dock.

Thereafter, getting the heavy casket with some difficulty up the narrow ramp from the heavy float and placing it in the hearse, we accompanied it to the Cathedral of St. John the Divine and participated in the very impressive service there.

However, all's well that ends well. The *Florida* was not due to leave the yard until late in September. Accordingly, I was able to secure thirty days leave from August 15. The train trip to San Francisco seemed endless. But on August 23, Floride Hunt[8] and I were married in her home by Bishop Nichols of California; I was attended by my erstwhile Academy roommate, Riley McConnell, as best man, and two other classmates. We spent the first days of our honeymoon at the old Del Monte Hotel in Monterey, where we had first met.

Returning to Hackensack a few days before my leave was up, I received a telegram from my friend, Commander Sypher of *Missouri* and earlier *Florida* days, who was then in the Navy Department, advising me to put in a request at once if I wanted to go to the Naval Academy. Since nothing would have suited me better, I started to draft a telegram to the Bureau of Navigation, which years later became the Bureau of Personnel. But that did not seem enough to my forehanded bride. She insisted that I should plead my case in person. So the two of us, that night, boarded a train to Washington, and I was at the Navy Department bright and early, while my wife waited in Lafayette Park and fed the pigeons. The Department was then in the old State-War and Navy Building. As luck would have it, and my luck seems to have been consistently wonderful, I encountered my captain in the detail office. He agreed to my detachment, provided it was delayed until after the *Florida*'s short-range battle practice in late October. This was agreed by the detail officer and my orders were promised me. Nothing was said about my previous agreement to stay at sea, a subject which I was careful not to bring up.

I greeted my bride in the square with the good news, and we decided that we would go promptly to Annapolis to seek a place to live. I had already begun to learn that I was married to a most efficient as well as charming young woman. Arriving by the first available train (there *were* trains then), we soon found accommodations in Carvel Hall,[9] and we set out to the town in one of Chaney's best victorias,[10] looking at everything there was to rent. Almost anything seemed good to me, who had never had a home of his own. But nothing quite came up to the style to which one from the Bay City was accustomed, until we were told of some new houses being built just outside the Upshur Row Gate, which were to be completed by the end of October. When we looked at them there was nothing up but the studding, and I had little idea of what they would look like. But my better half declared that she liked the arrangement very much. The next thing I knew, we were calling on the owner, another Navy wife, and Floride was selecting the wall paper and the hangings.

This settled, I visited the superintendent's office to see what assignment was in store for me. I had requested a professional department—navigation, seamanship, or ordnance and gunnery, or else mathematics. But the aide told me that, there being no vacancy in any of those departments, I would be detailed to the department of English and history. I was disappointed, not that I disliked those subjects, but I felt that I was better qualified to instruct in one of the others. I was happy to have anything.

With target practice over, I was detached from the *Florida* in Hampton Roads, journeyed to Baltimore via night boat, met my wife at the Pennsylvania Railroad Station, and arrived at Carvel Hall on October 22. On my way to the Superintendent's office to report, I encountered a classmate on Maryland Avenue who informed me that, finding that he had been assigned to the department of mathematics and I to English, he had engineered an exchange. He hoped that I did not mind. Indeed, I did not. So began a three-year assignment to that department, which I know was of much professional benefit to me. I found that I liked to teach, and I derived great satisfaction when I felt that I was able to make a midshipman understand what seemed to him a knotty problem.

In early 1914, I was examined at the Washington Navy Yard for promotion to lieutenant, and in May received my commission, dated January 11, 1914. I had already received orders to the USS *Idaho* for the coming practice cruise, and I accompanied the head of the department of navigation, Captain J. F. Hines,[11] to Philadelphia to act as a navigator in bringing that ship to Annapolis. At the end of June week, on the embarkation of the midshipmen, I reported on board as a watch officer and as an instructor in navigation. My wife went to San Francisco to be with her ill mother.

The practice cruise went to the Mediterranean, with Naples as the first port of call. Many of the officers and the midshipmen made trips to Rome, but I, for financial reasons and because I thought I should have many other opportunities, contented myself with seeing Pompeii, Herculaneum, and Amalfi. I certainly did not then realize that when I next saw those shores, twenty years later, I would be in command of an invasion fleet. And little did I realize, while still in Naples on June 28, what the event in Sarajevo on that day was going to mean to Western Europe, and to all of us. Assassinations of royalty in Europe seemed more or less commonplace and of no concern to us younger officers. We joined the Italian man-of-war and the Austrian cruiser in the harbor in half-masting our colors and thought no more of it. But things began to happen.

A little later we learned that our ship was to be sold to Greece and the USS *Maine*, which had also been in reserve, would join us in Villefranche to bring the *Idaho* personnel and midshipmen home. In that port on July 30, with European war clouds gathering, we turned the ship over to a Greek crew which had arrived by merchant ship. The USS *Idaho* went out of commission when our colors were hauled down at sundown. I spent the night on board in charge of a caretaking American detachment. Likewise, a lieutenant was in charge of the skeleton Greek crew. The Greek officer could speak no English and I no Greek, but we managed to get along in broken French. The Greeks took over the auxiliary fireroom watch at midnight, and at 0800 hoisted the Greek national ensign and commissioned the ship as His Hellenic Majesty's Ship *Lemnos*. Then, with my detachment, I departed to the *Maine*.

Our midshipmen, having worked hard to clean up the *Idaho* for its turnover, had now to work equally hard cleaning up the *Maine*, which had come over very short-handed. They got plenty of training with deck hose, holy-stone, and squilgee. But they were able to enjoy, as we all did, the sights of Villefranche and Nice, and even of not-far-distant Monte Carlo. The plot was now rapidly thickening. On the afternoon of August 1, I was officer of the deck of the *Maine*, at anchor in the harbor of Villefranche. The new *Lemnos* had already departed for Greece. Suddenly I heard a report of a cannon from the fort at the harbor entrance and simultaneously a string of signal flags going up at the signal station. From the shore there were sounds of cheering. Turning to the French bumboat woman, who had been a daily visitor selling us souvenirs and

Lieutenant H. K. Hewitt on the bridge of USS Eagle *(PY), 1916. (Naval Historical Collection)*

whatnot, I asked her if she knew what all that meant. Her only reply was to wring her hands and exclaim, "*C'est la guerre! C'est la guerre!*" As so it was, for it was the declaration of the French mobilization.

We remained at Villefranche a few more days, but they were days of extreme interest. Watching the mobilization, we marveled at the way the reserves rolled in, reported to the *caserne*,[12] donned their uniforms and equipment with practiced ease, and marched off. We noted how promptly the tunnels, bridges, and other strategic points were placed under guard, and could not help but think what would happen in our own country in a similar emergency, with our very small regular army and no military reserves other than the militia of the several states. But some of the French reserves had to go to war dressed in the old blue coats and bright red trousers of by-gone days.

After helping out stranded American tourists by depositing a good sum in gold on their behalf with the American consul at Nice, we departed for Gibraltar and home. We travelled at night with all lights on, and a searchlight trained on our colors hoisted at the gaff. Even then we were closely scrutinized by several fully darkened French men-of-war, which passed close aboard.

The search was on for the German *Goeben*[13] and *Breslau*,[14] which were loose somewhere in the Mediterranean. When we reached Gibraltar, we found it in a state of war, unwilling to take us into the inner harbor or to give us any coal. In consequence, we crossed over to Tangier where we got enough coal to take us back to Annapolis, which we reached in time to send the midshipmen on their regular leave.

I, too, was granted thirty days leave, part of which was spent with Floride in Atlantic City and part in Hackensack, listening to the news from Europe, which was far from good. Returning at the beginning of the academic year, I resumed my regular duties in the department of mathematics.

This year passed rapidly, as did the summer of 1915, which I spent at the Academy with temporary duty in the executive department and in the department of navigation. During this summer, on August 27, our first child, Floride Hewitt,[15] was born. We were by then occupying quarters at 31 Upshur Road. At the end of the succeeding academic year, I was due for sea duty once again.

I was ordered to command the USS *Eagle*[16] (my first command), a 434-ton converted yacht, which had been taken over as a gunboat in 1898 and had subsequently been converted to a survey ship for work in the West Indies and Caribbean. She was armed with two ancient 6-pounders in the stern, but was well-equipped with motor boats and had an exceptionally large crew for her size. I took her over on June 30, 1916, in the North River in New York, relieving Lieutenant Commander Aubrey K. Shoup.[17] She had just come up from her winter survey season and was on her way to the Navy Yard in Portsmouth, New Hampshire, for her annual summer overhaul and leave period for officers and men.

NOTES
1. USS *Flusser* (DD-20). Commissioned October 28, 1909. A ship of the Atlantic Torpedo Fleet, she cruised in the Caribbean and in New England waters until 1916.
2. USS *Reid* (DD-21). Commissioned December 3, 1909. A ship of the Atlantic Torpedo Fleet.
3. USS *Lamson* (DD-18). Commissioned February 10, 1910. A ship of the Atlantic Squadron, she cruised in Caribbean and New England waters.
4. USS *Preston* (DD-19). Commissioned December 21, 1909. A ship of Destroyer Force, Atlantic Fleet.
5. Jay A. Sypher (1871–1928). Commander. U.S. Naval Academy, Class of 1891.
6. USS *Florida* (BB-30). Commissioned September 15, 1911. Flagship of Division One of the Atlantic Fleet. She participated in exercises in the Caribbean and off the East Coast.
7. HMS *Natal*, cruiser, *Warrior* Class. Laid down in 1904 and completed in 1908. 480'L.
8. Floride Hunt (1888–1973). Native of San Francisco, Calif. She married H. Kent Hewitt in 1912. Her grandfather, William Hunt, was secretary of the Navy, 1881–1883, and U.S. ambassador to Russia. She was buried at the U.S. Naval Academy, Annapolis, Md.
9. Carvel Hall Hotel was the home of William Paca, colonial governor of Maryland. In 1900 it served as a popular hotel for Naval Academy dates and a rendezvous for officers as well as midshipmen.
10. Victoria. A four wheeled carriage with a calash top and raised seat for the driver.
11. John F. Hines (1870–1941). Captain. U.S. Naval Academy, Class of 1892.
12. Caserne. A military barracks.
13. *Goeben*. Battle Cruiser. 22,640 tons; Length 610 1/9'; Beam 96 3/4'.
14. *Breslau*. Small Cruiser. 4,550 tons; Length, 446'; Beam 43'.
15. Floride Hewitt (1915–). Admiral Hewitt's daughter is married to Captain Leroy Taylor, U.S. Navy (Ret.) and lives in Middletown, Rhode Island.
16. USS *Eagle* (Patrol Vessel-Converted Yacht). Purchased by the U.S. Navy in 1898. She saw service in the Caribbean where she protected U.S. interests.
17. Aubrey K. Shoup (1880–1931). Captain. U.S. Naval Academy, Class of 1904.

USS Eagle (PY) conducted surveys off the coast of Haiti and protected American lives and property during unrest in Cuba in 1917. (Naval Historical Collection).

VI   USS Eagle, 1916–1917

As mentioned previously, the *Eagle* was a converted yacht, later fitted out for survey work. For this purpose, it carried an unusually large crew for its size—eighty-six men. In addition to the captain, it had three line officers and a two-stripe paymaster. The captain was a lieutenant, the executive officer a lieutenant (j.g.), and the other two were ensigns.

The motive power was a single reciprocating engine driven by steam from a single coal-burning Scotch boiler, which was also the only source of steam for the auxiliary machinery. The *Eagle*'s best speed was about nine and a half knots, which I soon found could be realized only in a calm sea with no head wind.

For boats, there was a motor sailing launch, a motor whale boat, a motor dory, and a pulling whale boat. Since most of these boats were stowed high over the after-deck house, the ship was inclined to be a bit top-heavy.

The forward deckhouse, with a beautiful interior paneling of mahogany, housed the wardroom or officers' mess, abaft of which was the tiny captain's cabin. The other officers had staterooms below, of fairly good size, with ports just above the waterline (always dogged tight at sea). The after deck house, abaft the machinery spaces, housed the crew's sanitary facilities. The crew was quartered below decks, both forward and aft.

After a slow and foggy passage around the Battery, up the East River, and through Long Island Sound and Vineyard Sound, the *Eagle* reached Portsmouth, New Hampshire, and the Navy Yard to begin its long overhaul and leave period. It was a pleasant summer, part of which was spent by me at the Hydrographic Office and Naval Observatory in Washington, receiving special instruction to fit me for the survey work ahead.

At long last the ship departed from Portsmouth on November 2, with Charleston, South Carolina, as the first port of call, a necessary stop to replenish our very limited coal supply in order to reach Guantánamo. This part of the trip was not bad, albeit a bit hard on new officers and members of the crew who had not yet acquired their sea legs. The *Eagle* had a motion all her own.

Leaving Charleston on November 6 or 7 (Election Day) in the teeth of a bad easterly blow was another matter. It was impossible to take the direct course for the Crooked Island Passage, because doing so would put the ship in the trough of the sea where she would roll dangerously. It was necessary to tack down, first taking the wind and sea on the port bow and then changing course to put it on the port quarter. In the latter situation, she had a tendency to roll well over to starboard and hang there. Often I had to use left rudder to bring her up. There was not much sleep, and little rest for anyone. Also, very little to eat, because it was practically impossible to keep anything on the galley stove. We subsisted primarily on hot soup and coffee, which our valiant steward and cooks managed somehow to supply. My cabin, opening on the main deck, was untenable. What relaxation I got was on a cot lashed to the rail behind a bridge weather screen, fully clothed, even in my oilskins. It was a great relief, after six days of wallowing around, to sight finally Watling Island Light and to get into the lee of Crooked and Acklins Islands.

The extra steaming we had done, coupled with a casualty to our feedwater heater, caused us to burn an excess of coal, so much so that I began to fear our ability to reach Guantánamo, particularly if the bad weather should continue. The nearest port of any size was in Nipe Bay, Cuba, and we might even have trouble making that. Searching our sailing directions, I found that small quantities of coal were sometimes available at Matthew Town, on the lee side of Great Inagua, which was practically on our route. So, in there we put, to be received in most friendly fashion by the only two white men on the island, the British Commissioner and the owner of the only store. They constituted the entire government, including the police and the judiciary. Fortunately, there was a little coal on hand, which was made available to us. It came out to us from the beach in small oar-propelled boats and was loaded aboard entirely by female labor, women in the boats filling small baskets and passing them up to other women on staging hung over the side. Never had we seen such a coaling. While all this was going on, our new white friends took us ashore to see the island. After our ordeal, it was a strange sensation to be standing on terra firma. In fact, at first the ground seemed to be going up and down under us. We found that the sole industry of Great Inagua was salt, obtained by natural evaporation of sea water in great salt flats, and that this business was at a standstill because of the scarcity of shipping in wartime. Most of the male population eked out a bare living by stevedoring in the West Indies, shipping on vessels which called for them on the way south and which returned them on the return voyage. After a night at anchor, during which all hands enjoyed their first real sleep in a long time, we continued our voyage and reached Guantánamo without further event.

Orders left much to my own initiative. The *Eagle*, independent of the Atlantic Fleet, operated directly under the United States Naval Hydrographic Office. I was given specification for the surveys to be accomplished, but which was to be first and which was to be last was left to me. In addition, I was authorized to proceed to ports at my discretion at due intervals for liberty and recreation.

After fueling and victualing at Guantánamo, we proceeded to Port de Paix, a small port on the north coast of Haiti, to chart its harbor and approaches, working from a previously established observation point. We found that locating one of these was almost as exciting as finding a buried treasure. Our directions would give us distances and bearings from certain easily found marks. There we would dig, possibly under a cairn of rocks, to find a copper tack with a cross mark inscribed on its head, imbedded in a small block of concrete. The village and its surroundings showed interesting evidences of the French colonial era, particularly in the old stone fort, which was largely intact.

Completing the Port de Paix survey in a few days, and returning to Guantánamo, we received orders to pick up a naval civil engineer, Commander Leonard M. Cox, and make a reconnaissance of Samana Bay on the northeast coast of Santo Domingo with a view to determining its practicability as a fleet base. After a preliminary look at the bay, we took time out to spend Thanksgiving Day at nearby San Juan, Puerto Rico. During the following week, while we were again in Samana Bay, our Marines having occupied Santo Domingo as a result of a revolution, the United States proclaimed a temporary military government for that republic. We already had Marines in neighboring Haiti. Having located a possible site for a small repair base on the north side of Samana Bay, and having given a detachment of Marines some assistance at Sanchez, we returned Commander Cox to Guantánamo and then entered upon our next survey project, which was to connect by triangulation an established observation point at Mole St. Nicholas with another on the south side of Haiti's northwest peninsula, east of Baie de Henne. After getting that work started, we returned to Guantánamo just in time to celebrate Christmas with our friends at the naval station. New Year's we spent at Santiago, to give our crew a good liberty and to see the site of the 1898 battle. I should have liked to have gone to Kingston, Jamaica, to revisit the scene of the earthquake ten years earlier and also to survey its facilities and the language, but Britain was at war and I had been advised to avoid the ports of a combatant. However, we found pleasure in joining with the Cubans in their celebration of the holiday.

At Santiago we encountered Doctor McDonald and Civil Engineer Gayler, who had arrived with their families by train from Havana. They were under orders as, respectively, public health officer and public works officer for the government of Haiti and were seeking means of getting to Port au Prince. I volunteered to carry them as far as Guantánamo, which was only a short daylight run. Arriving there, they found no prospective transportation to Haiti, other than by *Eagle*. But a special dispatch to Washington brought an authorization for the *Eagle* to detour via Port au Prince en route to its survey area. So we departed eastbound, carrying as passengers two extra officers, two women, and three children, whose overnight accommodation presented a real problem. It was solved by stretching a canvas curtain down the middle of the passageway in the officers' country, with women and children on one side and men on the other. Most of the ship's officers, when not on watch, bunked in the wardroom. I spent the night on the bridge helping the ship buck a heavy trade-wind sea. Under these conditions, the *Eagle* had an annoying habit of diving down into the trough of a sea and then trying to play submarine, refusing to rise to the next unless we stopped the engine momentarily. This did not contribute to the comfort of most of the passengers. Dr. McDonald, however, like an old sea dog, frequently joined me in a pipe on the bridge. After a tempestuous night we finally gained the lee of Haiti and landed our passengers, most of them looking a bit peaked. It was a voyage they will probably remember.

January and most of February were fully occupied with our work between Mole and Henne Bay. It was highly interesting work, which kept all hands actively engaged, some in triangulating, some in building signals, some in boats running lines of soundings in shallow water, and the ship itself running soundings further to seaward. One of the most interesting things to me was seeing the evidence everywhere of the original French colonial civilization in that area. In the little town of Mole Saint Nicholas itself, there was the ancient church, ministered by an old French priest and two or three French nuns, who, with the Frenchman in charge of the cable station and the ex-Marine sergeant captain of *gendarmerie*, were the only whites in the whole area. The natives were friendly enough, always greeting me with a "*Bon jour, mon general*" when, on my reconnaissance expeditions riding the priest's horse, I met them along the trails. These trails were of interest for, although overgrown with cactus and passable only on foot or on a horse or a burro, they were based on old French military roads, evidently constructed with great engineering skill. These led to the old stone forts guarding the harbor entrance, abandoned a century or so ago but still practically intact, even with some of the old muzzle-loading cannon and stores of cannon balls. It was fun to explore them. Another interesting relic was the ruins of what had apparently been a sizeable barracks on the military road close to the town, with slits so cut in the thick walls as to permit a musket to be brought to bear over a wide angle.

With the *Eagle*'s limited coal and supply-carrying capacity, it was necessary to return to our base at intervals of not over ten days or two weeks. Thus it happened that we were in Guantánamo on Washington's birthday to follow the motions of the Commander in Chief, and most of the Atlantic Fleet, south for the winter training, in dressing ship—which brings to mind a laughable incident that occurred on our arrival. Since poultry and eggs were exceedingly cheap in Haiti, we were in the habit of bringing in supplies of them for our friends at the naval station. This time was no exception. Our crew, considering the rough work in which they were engaged, was normally allowed to wear almost anything. But this time we were to meet the fleet, so all hands were gotten into immaculate whites. Passing close aboard the flagship, with the crew at quarters and apparently everything looking fine, I was horrified on glancing aft, just as the flagship sounded attention for us, to see a flock of chickens parading up and down our midship awning. They had broken out of the crates stowed on the after deck house at just the wrong moment. The CINC saw them, I am sure, for he was on the quarterdeck with several of his staff, watching us through binoculars. We heard nothing about it, but it was embarrassing when we were trying to make a good impression.

Our survey in the Cap Foux area was almost, but not quite, completed. We did not know that we were not to return to it. But so it was. Early in February, a revolution had broken out in Cuba, headed by José Miguel Gómez,[1] leader of the Liberales, who claimed that the recent re-election of the Conservative Menocal[2] as president had been obtained by unfair means. The island was in a condition of unrest, from east to west. On February 25, I received orders to report for duty to the Commander in Chief of the Atlantic Fleet, and, by him, I was ordered to proceed to the north coast of Cuba to protect American life and property, first investigating the situation at Nuevitas.

As I have said, the *Eagle* had a complement of five officers and eighty-six men, and its armament consisted of two antiquated 6-pounders with open sights that dropped down every time the gun was fired. In addition, it had two equally antiquated machine guns that usually jammed after firing a few rounds. For small arms, we had six .45-caliber automatic pistols and a box of twelve Springfield rifles. By dint of special pleas around the fleet and at the naval station, we managed to acquire six more pistols and twenty-four more rifles, giving us enough to equip a landing force of thirty-six men, with a few pistols for those left on board.

We arrived at Nuevitas on February 27 and, immediately upon anchoring, were visited by the Spanish and Danish consuls. There was no American consul. These gentlemen informed me that the alcalde (mayor), the local police, and the officials of the custom house had disappeared and, thus, that there was no government. In addition to that, a band of revolutionists had raided the town and set fire to the railroad station and a sugar warehouse. I decided to return with them and investigate the situation for myself, in the meanwhile directing that our landing force be made ready.

There appeared to be no particular American interests in Nuevitas, but in view of the Monroe Doctrine, the purpose of which is to prevent interference by outside powers in the affairs of the nations of the Americas, I concluded that it was my duty to extend U.S. protection to the life and property of European nationals as well as of our own.

The consuls conducted me on a tour in an old Model T Ford, and I found that they had not exaggerated conditions ashore. The town was on a neck of land with only one road leading into it. With the idea of determining how best to defend the town against future raids, I had them drive me out this road to look over the terrain. Coming up a slight rise, we were astonished to meet, coming up the other side, a band of fifteen or more armed horsemen, the like of which I had never seen before outside of the movies. They were dressed in a variety of costumes, mostly dungaree trousers with any kind of a shirt, and wore big straw hats. They were draped with many *bandoliers* of ammunition, had rifles slung across their backs and, in addition, were armed with long machetes. Had I not realized how dangerously real it was, I should have thought it was a comic opera.

We stopped, and the horsemen stopped. The officer who accompanied me and I were in white uniform and carried our automatic pistols. The leader of the band dismounted and came toward us. We got out of the car with the Spanish consul who was interpreting for us. The *insurrecto* presented me with a paper on which it stated in pencil that he, Citizen González, was appointed "a Captain in the *Ejército Constitucional*" (Constitutional Army), signed by General Caballero. I acknowledged these credentials politely and stated that the United States was taking no sides whatsoever in the unfortunate state of affairs in Cuba, the people of whom we regarded as our friends, and that my only orders were to protect the life and property of U.S. citizens and those of other friendly nations. This apparently satisfied the *capitán*, who now asked me if he might have my permission to enter the town, stating that his men had been in the field for a long time and were anxious to visit their families.

The reply to this query required some thought. While I strongly doubted the reason given for the visit, I could see no legal justification for denying the entry of Cuban citizens into a Cuban town so long as no interference with my mission was involved. Accordingly, I answered that I could see no objection to this so long as order was maintained. I might add that two lone naval officers would have had difficulty enforcing a contrary decision.

El capitán next informed me that he had orders from his general to obtain certain supplies of saddlery and blankets from the custom house. Would that be all right? I thought to myself "What business have I interfering with a Cuban custom house?" Yet, American property might be involved. My consul friends whispered that they believed this matériel mentioned was consigned to an American sugar mill up the railroad, but that if we could obtain keys to the custom house, we might check the manifests. So I answered that I would ascertain the ownership and advise him and would oppose no objection to his commandeering anything that was strictly Cuban.

Then came another poser. He had orders to get certain additional supplies from the stores. Might he do that? "No objection," said I, "provided that they are paid for." The captain, however, had no money but would give *vales* (IOUs) given by the Constitutional Army. I solved that one by saying that I would not object, provided the merchants agreed to accept the *vales*.

So into town went the cavalcade, we following in our jitney, headed for the custom house, whence from which I sent my junior officer off to the ship with orders to the executive officer to get the landing force ashore "*lo mas pronto posible*" (as soon as possible).

The custom office was in a state of complete confusion. But we managed to find the manifests for which we were looking and verified the fact that they represented the property of U.S. citizens. There was nothing to do but to tell *el capitán* that the saddlery he was after must not be touched. Setting off with my consul interpreters to find him, we sighted, down the main street, a ring of mounted men outside the entrance of one of the principal stores. Inside were the captain and the storekeeper with a large pile of articles on the counter. This looked more like a raid than a peaceable acquisition of supplies and certainly gave no appearance of family reunions.

As I entered to speak to the rebel leader, he drew his gun. My own hand went back toward my pistol, but I must admit that I had little thought of winning any gun duel at that point. But, to my utter amazement, he proceeded to unload his revolver and restore it to its holster. I learned later that it was reported that I had told him that I would not talk to him unless he disarmed himself. My interpreter may have said it, but I do not think so. Anyway, I gained quite an undeserved reputation in Nuevitas.

Questioning the merchant as to whether he was willing to accept the rebel *vales*, he hesitated, looked at the lone American naval officer and then at the ring of men surrounding his door, and then declared that he was. So the purchases were duly wrapped and carried off. Sensing the situation, however, I told Captain González that in order to avoid any possible misunderstandings, I would accompany him to any other stores he intended to visit. This did not appear to please him in the least. He mounted his horse, gave an order to his men, and off they galloped. And, just as they disappeared down one end of the main street, there appeared at the other end a column of advancing American bluejackets—a most welcome sight.

Since there was no way to insure that the frustrated rebels would not return in force, it was necessary for the *Eagle*'s little force to take some measures for defense. Headquarters was established at the custom house, and breastworks were set up utilizing bags of sugar, which were readily available. On the ship we got a kedge anchor and warped around so that our stern 6-pounders would bear on the access road. And out that road we established agents provided with a Very pistol and colored signals stars to advise us of the coming of any armed party. Unquestionably, word of our preparations got out and probably served to discourage an attack. Nothing happened to disturb the peace, except that one of our patrols on shore that night had to quiet down a couple of American citizens who had been celebrating our arrival somewhat too freely.

When night came, I reported the situation and my action to the commander in chief by radio. We had but one operator, and it was only at night that our radio transmitter could reach Guantánamo, just across the island, something that seems hard now to believe.

After a couple of uneventful days, a company of well-disciplined and very trim-looking regular Cuban troops rolled in on a special railroad train. They were under command of an apparently efficient young officer whose name I remember because it was the same as that of a famous bullfighter I had seen in Algeciras three years before—Belmonte. I was most happy to turn Nuevitas over to him and to withdraw our landing force.

I relate this incident at some length because it illustrates how important it was that a young officer, even a lieutenant, should have a fair grasp of the fundamentals of international law. It was most gratifying later on to receive a copy of the following letter from the Commander in Chief to the Chief of Naval Operations:

1. The USS *Eagle* arrived Nuevitas, Cuba, on 27 February at 8:40 a.m. Conditions at Nuevitas were found to be serious. No force in city to preserve order. About noon a small party of revolutionists entered the town with apparent intention to loot the custom house and stores.
2. The commanding officer of the *Eagle*, Lieutenant H. K. Hewitt, U.S.N., immediately landed a force to protect the custom house and nearby warehouses.
3. The Commander-in-Chief considers that the commanding officer of the U.S.S. *Eagle* acted with commendable promptness and good judgement, and that an appreciation of his initiative, decision, and good judgement should be entered upon his record.

(Signed) H. T. Mayo[3]

I might add one thing more. The law says somewhere that in the absence of a U.S. consul, the senior naval officer in a foreign port is empowered to act in his behalf. In this connection, while in the harbor of Nuevitas, I was called upon to settle a dispute between the master of an American merchant ship and a member of his crew. This I did, after much thumbing of the copy of the Revised Statutes I found in my ship's library. Never again in my career did I have to act as a consul.

With the Nuevitas situation satisfactorily resolved for the time being, we received orders to proceed east to Nipe Bay, another large harbor on the north coast, to investigate and report the situation there. We arrived on March 3 to find comparative quiet, but much revolutionary activity in the hinterland. Like most bays on Cuba's north coast, Nuevitas included, Nipe had a narrow entrance which opened westward into a larger body of water. At the west head of the bay was the fairly large town of Antilla, with railroad connections and an American consul, but few American business interests. But at Preston, on the south shore of the bay, near the entrance, was a large sugar mill, together with its attendant sugar plantations, belonging to the United Fruit Company. And, up in the mountains, just south of Preston and connected to it by private railroad, were open iron ore mines of the

Spanish-American Iron Company at Felton. Another beautiful but smaller bay, just to the west, Banes, was the shipping port of the United Fruit Company's large Banes sugar mill. (Batista[4] was born in Banes.) Mayarí, a Cuban town a few miles inland from the south shore of Nipe Bay, was the reputed headquarters of rebel forces in the vicinity. (Castro[5] came from Mayarí.) There had been threats of raids on the various American activities and some burning of cane fields.

After estimating the situation and conferring with the managers of the American activities concerned, I dispatched my executive officer, Lieutenant (j.g.) Jerome K. Lee,[6] with about eighteen men, by sugar railroad from Antilla to Banes and took the *Eagle* alongside the dock at Preston. From there, I sent my engineer officer, Ensign H. E. Paddock,[7] with six men, up to Felton and proceeded to guard the mill at Preston with the ship and remaining personnel. By this time I had been officially informed of the great importance of safeguarding the sugar supply, in view of the threatening war situation. And I was beginning to realize that the Cuban *insurrectos* had great respect for the U.S. flag and the U.S. uniform—so much so that a few men wearing that uniform could accomplish much.

Feeling that the establishment of friendly relations with the revolutionary commander in the vicinity might be of help, I arranged a conference with him at Mayarí. Proceeding there on horseback, accompanied by one officer and an interpreter, and guided by a company guard from the Preston mill, I was received with due honor by a mounted guard in the same sort of nondescript attire I had previously encountered in Nuevitas. The general, who was quite dark in color, politely led me into his headquarters, a one-room shack furnished with a broken-down chair and two old iron beds without mattresses. I sat on one of these beds, on the bare springs, and the general sat on the other. In the doorway, with a rifle across his knee, sat who I assumed to be the corporal of the guard, for he wore corporal's chevrons pinned to his ragged civilian shirtsleeves with huge safety pins. During the discussion, if the corporal disagreed with the general or had other ideas to advance, he apparently felt free to say so and did.

I carefully explained to the general that the United States felt nothing but the most friendly feelings for the Cuban people, that we considered that the establishment of a government satisfactory to them was entirely their own affair, and that my only purpose was to safeguard the lives and legitimate interests of U.S. citizens. The general replied that friendship between our peoples had been firmly cemented in 1898 by the blood shed by them then in a common cause and that the only thing the *Liberales* wished from our government was that we take steps to insure a free and fair Cuban presidential election. He solemnly promised to respect American property. With this conclusion, we shook hands and I departed.

Things in the Nipe area being apparently under control, I decided to take the *Eagle* into nearby Banes Bay, visit our detachment there, and see that situation firsthand. The trip in was interesting, not only because we entered through a narrow, tortuous channel between high bluffs, like a canyon, but because we had various landing forces on shore, and therefore, the ship, when underway, was very short-handed. We even had mess attendants in the chains taking soundings. But almost anyone on the *Eagle* could do whatever might be required. Some of our engineers were very good helmsmen.

The town of Banes and the sugar mill were some distance from the dock, which was reached by a private sugar railroad. With the ship safely alongside the dock, I went up to a town on a railroad automobile, where we were warmly greeted by the local manager, Mr. Harold Harty, and the other leading United Fruit Company officials of the plant. I had taken with me our civilian hydrographer, Mr. Leo M. Samuels, who was as handy as any officer on the ship and made an excellent aide.

One might say that the town of Banes was divided into two parts, one being the Cuban town, and the other being that which housed the sugar mill and the American employees of the United Fruit Company. There had been no trouble, but there were revolutionary forces under another general in the Cuban part of the town. After an apparently satisfactory conference with him and a very pleasant dinner with Mr. and Mrs. Harty and others of his staff, Mr. Samuels and I, armed only with our trusty automatics, started back for the dock via the railroad auto. A little way outside the town we saw in the headlights a body of horsemen ride across the track, signaling us to stop. On requesting the reason, we were told that they had orders to permit no one to leave the town. They were still firm when I told them in no uncertain terms just who I was and that they had no right to stop an officer of the U.S. Navy on official business. There was nothing to do but retrace our steps.

Not understanding just what was going on and being acutely aware of the numerical inferiority of our forces, I decided that the only thing to do was to put on a bold front. Contacting our bluejacket sentry on my way down the main street toward the general's headquarters, I ordered him to alert Lieutenant Lee. I then strode into a rebel conclave, demanding to know by what authority they dared to interfere with me in the execution of my duty. Further, I demanded an apology and an assurance that there would be no further interference. These I received, the general insisting that it was all a mistake and offering me an escort on my way. On the way back to the company railroad terminal, I was met by a line of bluejackets, advancing with fixed bayonets to the rescue of their skipper. We reached the ship without further event, and the next morning returned with it to Nipe Bay and Pristine.

By the middle of March, the Nipe-Banes area situation apparently being satisfactory, we had withdrawn our landing forces and returned to Nuevitas. Everything there still being under control of the government forces, we were directed to proceed to Manatí to investigate and report. This, after some search on my charts, I found to be a small port some thirty miles east of Nuevitas. The bay had the same characteristics as those already mentioned for other north Cuban harbors. The detailed chart of it which we had was, according to the captain, based on an old Spanish survey dated some time in the 1830s. The soundings of the narrow entrance and the wide bay to the westward of it indicated plenty of water for *Eagle*'s draft of twelve feet and showed marker buoys at the point of turn. There was little or nothing to determine the exact position of the town or the mill which we presumed to be there. However, as we steamed along the coast, we sighted a tall stack and plotted it as being near the western head of the bay. About the same time, we received a message broadcast from some merchant ship to the effect that rebels were attacking the Manatí sugar mill and that immediate assistance was required. Preparations were made immediately to dispatch our landing force, under Lieutenant Lee, in our motor launch.

We entered the narrow channel cautiously, utilizing every navigational aid in our possession, Mr. Samuels assisting the officer of the deck, and me on the bridge. On the way in, we passed a dock with freight cars on it and a steamer alongside, obviously the shipping terminal for the mill. However, it seemed evident that with an attack on the mill in progress, there was little chance of rail transportation to town and it behooved us to get as near the head of the bay as we could to land our men there. So we continued on to find none of the chart buoys and only fisherman's stakes at the turn. With some four fathoms under us and in a position determined as best we could with tangential bearings of the chartered shoreline, we started our turn into the wide bay with right standard rudder, proceeding very slowly. At first the ship seemed to answer all right, but finally I had to give her full rudder to bring her around. Shortly thereafter, the leadsman sang out, "By the mark two," and I promptly rang up an emergency "Back Full." We came to a sudden stop and no amount of backing produced any result. We were aground, hard and fast. This was my first command. What was going to happen to my naval career?

The ship, however, was in no immediate danger. Our first thought had to be for the emergency at the mill, so away went our motor launch up the bay with the landing force. Then, observing the tide to be ebbing, we dropped a bower anchor and ran a kedge anchor out from the stern to prevent the ship from being swung around and "broaching to" on the shoal. We found that we were in mud, and a hasty inspection below showed no sign of any structural damage. The little ship was heavily framed and stoutly built of Norway iron.

Very soon a launch appeared, coming from the direction of the shipping dock. It bore a pleasant young American-educated Cuban, the assistant manager of the mill, wondering what in the world we were doing where we were. We told him, and why. He said that the company stores had been raided and that there had been threats of cane burning, but no attack whatever was in progress. (It later developed that the message we received had been originated by an excitable Cuban doctor.) He volunteered all possible assistance. As it happened, however, we needed none.

Fortunately, when we grounded, it had been half tide. At low tide we listed somewhat, but as the tide rose again to near high, we were able to pull off, turn around, and get alongside the shipping dock. In accordance with Navy regulations, I made a full report of the grounding, fully expecting a Court of Inquiry and probably a General Court. My relief may well be imagined when a month or so later, I received a communication from the Chief of Naval Operations acknowledging the receipt of my report and informing me that it had been placed on file.

To return to the affairs of the *alzamiento*, which was what the Cubans called their current revolution—it was near nightfall on March 17 when the *Eagle* landing force made a landing in the northwest corner of Manatí Bay, and after dark by the time they had covered the three miles to the sugar mill and its surrounding company town. They were received with open arms. Comfortable barracks for the men were established in the railroad station, and Lieutenant Lee was put up in the company guest house adjacent to the residence of the manager, with whom he was invited to mess. It was there, later, that I joined Lieutenant Lee, who was staying, with intervals for necessary trips to Guantánamo, during most of our five-week occupation of the Manatí mill.

Although the Manatí Sugar Company was, and is, an American company, its resident manager was a Spanish nobleman, the Marques San Miguel de Aguayo, a colorful character, if there ever was one. Although he knew a little English, he insisted on speaking Spanish, which was fine practice for me. And when he took us out on the locomotive to look over the sugar plantations, he took the throttle himself and drove the little engine at hair-raising speeds.

The country around Manatí was in a state of unrest, and there were many rebel bands gradually being pushed in towards us by the government forces who became more and more truculent and demanding. Consequently, we were forced to take all possible precautions. A cavalry squad was formed with eight bluejackets mounted on company horses, led by one of our coxswains, who had served an enlistment in the U.S. cavalry. He intrigued the Cubans by trick feats of horsemanship, such as picking up his sailor hat from the ground at full gallop. For artillery, we mounted one of our machine guns in a Model T Ford, and the other in a railroad automobile. The remainder of our detachment formed the infantry.

The cavalry was used to establish mounted patrols and as a support for the artillery, which several times dashed out into the cane fields to support workers fighting cane fires that had been set. In fact, so prompt was the response on several such occasions, this type of sabotage was eventually abandoned. Somewhat later, when one particularly belligerent rebel leader threatened an attack if his demands for supplies were not honored by the company, we removed our 6-pounders from the ship, mounted them on the *mirador* (lookout tower of the mill), and placed several shots through a target near a crossroads outside the town. The target being carefully left in place for passers-by to see, we heard no further threats.

It was at Manatí on April 6 that we received notice of our declaration of war against Germany. We promptly restored our armament to the ship and painted war color over our white and spar-color, with a gray paint obtained from the mill.

Two weeks later, we became part of the newly established Caribbean Patrol Detachment under Rear Admiral E. A. G. Anderson.[8] On one of our trips to Guantánamo and return, we had landed a Marine detachment at Preston to guard the iron mines at Felton. We now established a small Marine detachment at Manatí and radio personnel to man the company's new radio facilities offered to the Navy, and departed with the good ship for our new duty.

Cuba had joined the United States in declaring war on Germany, and the revolution appeared to be on the wane. The U.S. Caribbean Patrol Detachment cooperated with the small Cuban navy in an endeavor to ensure that Cuban waters and the nearby Bahamas should not be clandestinely used as bases of supply for the enemy submarines. In the course of this work, the *Eagle* visited most of the ports on the north coast of Cuba, many of which were isolated and had little rapid communication with the outside. Reliable American citizens and allied nationals were enlisted as information agents and were given codes by which to communicate. Many friendly Cuban fishermen were interviewed and promised their help.

By May, the *Eagle* was seriously in need of an overhaul. Her lone Scotch boiler had been under steam constantly since the preceding fall, and her bottom had become foul, reducing her already low speed. Permission was finally obtained for us to proceed to Key West for four or five days for docking and minor emergency repairs. Taking advantage of this, I got word to my wife (who, with our little daughter, had been sojourning with my parents in Hackensack) to join me there. She came down by the Florida East Coast Railroad, which still ran to Key West, arriving a few hours after the ship did. Meeting her at the station in the early morning, before I had had a chance to report to the commandant, I found the commandant's car also awaiting her, the chauffeur having orders to bring her right to the commandant's quarters. The commandant, Commander Warren J. Terhume[9], and his wife, both natives of Hackensack and old friends, had been alerted by my mother. They insisted that we stay with them and gave us a little private suite in the same house, which, many years later, was occupied by President Truman as a vacation White House. They were truly good samaritans. What an experience it was to supervise the work on my ship, hauled out on an adjacent marine railway, from a comfortably shaded upstairs porch! But the respite was all too brief. Soon we were back on our regular patrol, during the course of which we were able to revisit the scenes of most of our previous activities. Well do I remember a pleasant Fourth of July dance at Banes, where it was so hot that my white uniform blouse was stained by the cigars carried in my breast pocket.

By mid-July came orders to report to the Military Governor of Santo Domingo, Admiral H. S. Knapp,[10] for such duty as he might desire. Arriving at Santo Domingo

City, we moored in the Ozama River across from the city, anchored by the bow upstream and with our stern secured to the same tree reputed to have been used by Columbus to moor his *Santa Maria*. We found the city highly interesting with its ancient fortifications and other relics of original Spanish colonization, not the least of which were the reputed remains of Columbus himself in the Cathedral.

During our service with the military governor, we made a thorough patrol of the Dominican coast, from Puerto Plata on the north to Barahona on the south. There being no coal available in Santo Domingo, we had to get it by mining the bunkers of the old armored cruiser *Memphis*,[11] which had been wrecked by a tidal wave the previous year just outside the river mouth. In this, we were fortunately assisted by prison labor from the local jails. It was rather spooky down below, because, as the old ship rocked back and forth on the rocks with the swells, it gave forth loud sepulchral groans. Once on the deck, the coal had to be loaded into a small barge bobbing up and down between the hull and the inshore cliff and then towed by the governor's barge around to us in the river.

I received my appointment as a lieutenant commander (temporary), dated August 31. In mid-September, we were detached from our Dominican duty and ordered by Admiral Anderson to Havana for duty in connection with training the Cuban navy, which consisted mainly of the small cruiser *Cuba* and several lightly armed converted yachts. I found the Cuban officers and men friendly and eager to learn. Due mainly to scarcity of ammunition, they had had little or no gunnery training. It was indeed an experience to be giving talks on gunnery in Spanish and to be conducting shipboard drills in that language.

Finding that my stay in Havana was likely to last for two or three months, I called my little family to join me there, which they did via railroad again to Key West and ferry to Havana. I found a comfortable place for them in an American boarding house in Vedado, a residential suburb of Havana. Thus we were able to take in the sights of that old city together. And we were pleasantly entertained by the Cuban friends I had made during my previous activities.

Throughout the season of likely hurricanes, having no mind to be caught in one at sea in my little cockleshell, the *Eagle*, I had kept a watchful eye on the barometer, on wind direction, on weather reports, and the location of the nearest safe port. I finally did experience a severe hurricane, but inside Havana harbor, well secured to a mooring buoy over the site of the wreck of the *Maine*. It proved to be a rather harrowing twenty-four-hour affair. Although moored to the buoy by both chain and Manila hawser,[12] in fact everything we had, we still had to keep going ahead on the engine to ease the strain, and using our rudder in a more or less fruitless effort to check our wild yaws. Even at that, we nearly sideswiped a large adjacent car ferry when we occasionally yawed toward each other. When things quieted down and I got ashore, I found that my wife, too, had had a harrowing time, huddling behind the heavy shutters of her boarding house and worrying about me.

About November 10, we set out for Cienfuegos, westbound around Cape San Antonio, with the intention of checking on Cuban naval activities on the south coast and eventually returning to Havana. Off the Cape, we received radio orders from Admiral Anderson to proceed to Galveston, Texas, to exchange officers and crew there with the USS *Dorothea*.[13] The *Dorothea* was a considerably larger and more heavily armed converted yacht which had been used on the Great Lakes for the training of naval militia. It had been commanded by a rather aged Coast Guard officer but otherwise manned by naval militia officers and crew. Admiral Anderson wanted his regulars on the larger vessel and had received departmental authority for the exchange. So far as I know, it is the only case on record of such a ship-to-ship transfer.

Among the exhibits in my personal file is an order signed by me and directed to myself, dated November 15, 1917, ordering one Lieutenant Commander Hewitt, upon relief, detached from command of the USS *Eagle*, to report immediately to the USS *Dorothea* for duty in command of that vessel, with suitable endorsements duly supporting detachment, and assuming command—all signed by the same person. I might add that it took the Bureau of Personnel months to straighten out the records of personnel involved—if it ever did.

NOTES

1 José Miguel Gómez (1858–1921). Liberal party candidate. President of Cuba, 1909–1913.

2 Mario García Menocal (1866–1941). A member of the Conservative party, he was president of Cuba, 1913–1920.

3 Henry T. Mayo (1856–1937). Admiral. U.S. Naval Academy, Class of 1876.

4 Fulgencio Batista (1901–1973). Commander in chief of Cuban army and virtual dictator of Cuba from 1933–1959. His regime was corrupt and practiced terror against political opponents. On January 1, 1959, he fled Cuba after Fidel Castro's successful guerrilla campaign against him.

5 Fidel Castro (1927–). Political leader and revolutionary who transformed Cuba into the first Communist state in the Western Hemisphere.

6 Jerome A. Lee (1890–1967). Commander. U.S. Naval Academy, Class of 1913.

7 Hubert E. Paddock (1892–1980). Captain. U.S. Naval Academy, Class of 1915.

8 Edwin A. G. Anderson (1860–1933). Rear Admiral. U.S. Naval Academy, Class of 1882. He served as Commander, Squadron 1, Patrol Force, Atlantic Fleet, 1917.

9 Warren J. Terhume (1869–1920). Commander. U.S. Naval Academy, Class of 1889.

10 Harry S. Knapp (1856–1923). Rear Admiral. U.S. Naval Academy, Class of 1878. He was military governor of Santo Domingo and representative in Haiti, 1917–1919.

11 USS *Memphis* (Armored Cruiser 10). Commissioned in 1906 as USS *Tennessee*, she was renamed in May 1916. The *Memphis* was on a peacekeeping mission to the strife-ridden Dominican Republic when a tidal wave in the Santo Domingo harbor wrecked the ship, leaving 40 men dead and 204 injured.

12 Manila hawser is a strong rope used to secure a ship.

13 USS *Dorothea* (Gunboat). Built in 1897 and acquired by the U.S. Navy in 1898, she served in Mexican waters and along the southern United States during 1917 and 1918.

Franklin D. Roosevelt, Assistant Secretary of the Navy, Josephus Daniels, Secretary of the Navy, Edward, Prince of Wales, and Rear Admiral Archibald H. Scales, Superintendent of the Naval Academy, in Annapolis, MD, November 14, 1919 (Naval Historical Collection)

VII World War I to 1922

1917–1922

The *Dorothea* may have been well fitted out for lake cruising, but it was far from adapted to deep sea work. In addition, its engineering plant had not been well maintained, its water tube boilers were in poor shape, and its electric generator was of a high-speed hotel design, the gyroscopic effect of which put too much pressure on the bearings with a rolling ship, resulting in overheating. We had so much trouble right at the outset on leaving port that, instead of heading directly across the gulf toward Key West, where we were to join Admiral Anderson, I decided to proceed along the coast for a while toward the mouth of the Mississippi. It was well that I did; we rolled around for several hours in a norther, while the engineers struggled to patch up the lone feed pump. And there were other breakdowns. I limped into the Mississippi and up to the New Orleans Navy Yard, where I anchored early one morning just as the feed pump finally gave up the ghost. We had to have a tug put us alongside, an indignity to which I had never before submitted.

Consultation with and inspection by the Navy Yard authorities revealed that we must have work done which would require over a month to complete. This was authorized. So there was I in New Orleans, with my family in Havana. Fortunately, they were able to secure an early passage to New Orleans on a United Fruiter. We passed a pleasant Christmas and New Year's Day in a delightful boarding house where we had real old Southern cooking. During this time, my fine executive officer, Lieutenant Lee, was taken from me and ordered to Queenstown, Ireland, for destroyer duty.

We finally got away from New Orleans in early January, and after a short stay in Key West, where we were inspected by Admiral Anderson, we resumed our humdrum patrol duty. The only events worth noting were our experiences with the new battleship *Mississippi*, which had been sent during this time down to Guantánamo for shakedown and training. For the lack of anything else available, the *Dorothea* was assigned to her as a sort of tender. When she was maneuvering off Guantánamo, we were supposed to act as a sort of anti-submarine screen, something it was rather difficult to do in a ten-knot ship with no listening gear. At the end of one particularly wearing day, I saw our call pennant go up on the *Mississippi*, which we immediately answered. My good signal quartermaster had to ask for a repeat on the ensuing semaphore message. Again he had to ask for a repeat. This time I put my own glass on it. The trouble was that the signalman sending was not careful at holding his arms horizontal or at forty-five degrees, so that, for instance, one could not tell whether he meant an "A" or a "B." The moment I got the first few words, I guessed the rest and proceeded with my ship accordingly. After receiving our eventual acknowledgment, the *Mississippi* made me a flag signal "*Dorothea* pay more attention to signals." That was just too much, under the circumstances, for me. I sent back "Your signal was promptly answered. It was very poorly transmitted." Later, when both ships returned to port, a *Mississippi* launch came alongside, with an officer bearing an official letter addressed to me quoting the above signal, stating that it was considered highly insubordinate and directing me to make immediate written explanation.

I sat down and carefully wrote a report describing all the circumstances. The more I thought about it, the more I thought that I had better deliver my letter in person. So off in my gig I went to face the music. When I was finally admitted to Captain Philip Andrews'[1] cabin, I was told in no uncertain terms what he thought of my giving the *Mississippi* a "badly done." I told him that I had had no thought whatever of being insubordinate, that I had been trying to anticipate his wishes throughout the day, that my ship had answered his call immediately, and that I myself, an ex-signal officer, had difficulty in reading the signal because of the indistinct way the signalman made his letters. He finally seemed to understand my position and the interview terminated on a much more cordial note than it had begun.

The *Mississippi* duty finally ended with a more or less comic-opera anti-minesweep of the entrance to Guacanayabo Bay by the *Dorothea* on one end of an improvised sweep and the Cuban *Veinte Cinco de Mayo* (25th of May) on the other. Captain Andrews' subsequent letter to Admiral Anderson thanked him for the services rendered by the vessels of his patrol and "especially those of the *Dorothea*, which was particularly attentive."

Since the dispatch of our destroyers overseas, I had felt that my place as an officer with destroyer experience was with them. It annoyed me to learn of others without such experience, many my juniors, being ordered to destroyer command. I had repeatedly made official requests for such duty, only to be informed that I was needed where I was and that there was no relief available for me. No directories were being issued, and I had no means of knowing what friends, if any, I had in the department. But, finally, I received an official letter from the Bureau of Personnel on some other matter, signed by a classmate of mine. I wrote a personal letter to him at once, setting forth my tale of woe. Result—within two weeks orders came detaching me from the *Dorothea* and ordering me to the Receiving Ship *New York* to await further orders. On May 27, at Key West, I was relieved by Lieutenant Commander Cecil M. Gabbett, U.S. Coast Guard.[2]

On the way north, via railroad, I stopped in Washington to see what my prospects for future war duty really were. The detail officer in the Bureau of Personnel informed me that I would probably be ordered as executive officer of a transport. I pleaded hard for destroyer duty, citing my previous experience, but got nowhere. However, after waiting over a month in New York, during which I was actively employed by the commanding officer of the Receiving Ship to investigate certain serious irregularities which had turned up in the handling of drafts of enlisted men for sea duty, I finally received the orders I wanted to Queenstown for duty in connection with the prospective command of a destroyer. With a detail of five or six other officers, I sailed from New York about July 12 on the White Star liner *Baltic*, which was carrying a large number of U.S. troops and a U.S. military hospital unit.

The voyage across was uneventful, except that we naval officers stood daytime anti-submarine lookout duty and were put in charge of the lifeboats to which our hospital nurses were assigned. We arrived in Liverpool on July 26—where I was met with a change of orders to proceed to Brest, France, instead of Queenstown.

From Liverpool, with several officers junior to me, I went by train to London, a strange, quiet, blacked-out London. The party of which I was in charge was put up overnight in a YMCA hut in one of the London parks, which one I do not remember. It might have been Grosvenor Square. Next day we entrained at Southampton, where, after waiting until dark, we boarded a cross-channel steamer for a night crossing to Le Havre. Arriving in Le Havre in the early morning and breakfasting there, we finally got a slow train for Paris which landed us in a pitch black *gare*, well after dark. Fortunately, we were met by a representative of the U.S. Navy with transportation and arrangements for our accommodations in some little hotel. Due to wartime conditions in both France and England, we had to manhandle our own considerable baggage which included all our clothing and other equipment for duty on board ship.

Since there was no train for Brest the day after our arrival, we spent two nights in Paris. This gave us an opportunity to have a look around this war-torn city, so different from what I had seen previously, and to attend an evening performance at the Folies Bergère with hundreds of other servicemen on leave in the city. It was really spooky walking back to our hotel through the dark streets.

On July 31, we had a long train ride to Brest, where we reported to Rear Admiral H. B. Wilson,[3] our naval commander there. The next day, I reported to Captain A. G. Howe[4] on the USS *Conner*,[5] for my make-you-learn cruise, during which I also acted as his executive and navigator.

The U.S. destroyers based in Brest were engaged in escorting convoys to and away from ports on the French coast, such as Brest and St. Nazaire, through a zone five or six hundred miles off the coast, which in those days was considered to be the limiting operating range of the enemy submarines. They would take out a westbound convoy right to this limit, then pick up an inbound troop or cargo convoy and escort it to its destination. Often, due to bad weather and resultant navigation difficulties both for the escort and the convoy, it was necessary to spread out on a wide scouting line to avoid missing the all-important contact. Outside of the anti-submarine escort zone, these convoys were safeguarded back and forth on the Atlantic by an old battleship or cruiser called the ocean escort, to protect them from surface raiders. So many were the convoys, and, consequently, so busy were the destroyers, that they rarely had more than a day or so for refueling and provisioning in port after a week or more at sea.

On my first trip out with the *Conner*, we had a little excitement in that we picked up many of the survivors of the French cruiser *Dupetit Thouars*,[6] for which we received the official thanks of the French Navy upon our return to port. On the second trip with an outbound convoy, the American transport *Mount Vernon*[7] was torpedoed. Fortunately, no other ship in the convoy was hit, and the *Mount Vernon* was gotten safely back into Brest, where she was repaired sufficiently to be sent home.

By September 18 I was ordered to the destroyer *Cummings*[8] preparatory to relieving Commander Owen Bartlett[9] of the class ahead of mine, who was being sent home for rest and to commission a new destroyer. About the same time, I received an appointment as a commander (temporary). After another trip on the *Conner* to take the place of Captain Howe, absent on temporary duty, I assumed command of the *Cummings* on October 1. Other than for a false alarm or two, and some perhaps which were not, there was nothing particularly eventful in our trips during September and October.

During one of our two-day respites in port at the end of October, I received orders to report to a naval examining board on shore for examination for promotion to the permanent grade of lieutenant commander. The orders were addressed to Lieutenant Hewitt. The senior medical examiner, an old navy doctor I had never seen before, read my orders, looked at me, then again at the orders, and then again at the three full stripes on my sleeve, and finally said, "What the h—— are you, anyway?" Considering the exigencies of war service, my professional examination was made brief and entirely oral, only one question being asked in each required subject. The board must have checked my record, because my seamanship question was, "You are in command of a small vessel in the Caribbean in the month of September and the barometer does thus and so, and the wind does thus and so, what do you do?" With that satisfactorily answered, I was congratulated and returned to my ship. Would that some of my other examinations had been as simple.

On November 11 I was at sea with the *Cummings*, senior officer of the escort of a loaded eastbound troop convoy. When the good news of the Armistice was received by radio, there was much rejoicing and blowing of whistles and hoisting of brooms to the yardarms. The crew of the *Cummings* executed a snake dance all around the deck. Hardly had this celebration subsided and everyone begun to relax, when one of the transports made the submarine alarm signal. The war was supposed to be over, but maybe some submarine had not gotten the word. There was nothing to do but to go to general quarters and come around at full speed to the attack. Nothing developed. Probably it was a false alarm.

One of the strangest sensations after the armistice was to be running at night with all lights on. We had become so used to completely darkened ships that it had become even easier to judge one's distance from ships next ahead without lights. Nothing much happened during the rest of November, except that the *Cummings*, as one of the longer-legged destroyers, was detailed to the detachment that was (proceeding, via fueling at the Azores) to meet and escort the *George Washington*,[10] in carrying President Wilson[11] to the peace conference.

That assignment led to another experience which shows the importance of a navigator using every tool at his command and also having good luck. The *Cummings*, since the very beginning of our overseas destroyer participation in the war, had been operating out of Queenstown and Brest, with little opportunity for overhaul. Consequently, its engineering plant was not in the best of shape. In addition, it had but one condenser and, thus, unlike other destroyers with two, it could not run on one engine while making repairs. A leaky condenser meant rapid salting of the boiler water with consequent damage to boiler tubes and priming, the carrying over of considerable water with the steam to the turbines.

About two days out on our run to the Azores, tests of our feed water began to show serious salting. It was necessary either to stop dead in the seaway, open up the condenser, locate the leaky tube and plug it, or return to port. The escort commander ordered me to do the latter, so I turned about and headed on a northeasterly course for Brest. The weather was such that we had been unable to get a sight since our departure, and continued that way during our return. Our position could only be estimated by dead reckoning. South of Brest there was a shoal called the Chausse du Seine, which stuck out like a finger for some miles from the coast. About six miles in from its tip, there was a lighthouse, but under the weather conditions at that time of year, one could rarely see six miles. Also, there was usually an easterly inshore set on that part of the Brittany coast. I figured what I thought was a reasonable allowance for that set. Doubling it, I laid a course that I felt sure would lead me well clear of the dangerous shoal.

At that time, present day sonic depth finders had not been invented. The only way one could take soundings was by the hand lead for lesser depths and the deep-sea lead for greater depths. The latter required practically stopping the ship. By our reckoning, we were due to be off the tip of the shoal by about eight p.m. By seven, I began checking my figures. Surely, I had made an ample allowance. But suppose I had not! I was anxious to get in and did not want to stop. But stop I did for a deep-sea sounding at 7:30. "No bottom at 100"—all was well. But, still, I was uneasy. At 7:45, I took another sounding. Fifteen fathoms, quickly confirmed by the hand lead as twelve. Nowhere, except directly south of the shoal, could one get such a sounding! I turned west at slow speed, feeling with the lead for the 100-fathom curve. I had run west for about ten miles before I was able to feel my way around the shoal. My ship and I had been saved by a premonition, or rather by Divine Providence, and the caution which every navigator should exercise.

The remainder of the night was spent in moving cautiously toward the approaches to the Goulet, the steep-to and narrow entrance to Brest harbor, using our lead and bearings from the newly installed and untried radio direction finder on shore. Finally, we anchored in a thick fog in a position we thought to be just to the north of the entrance channel, the deepest part of the approaches, to wait for daylight. Underway at dawn, we proceeded slowly on a course slightly diagonal to the channel, endeavoring to find it with the lead. Suddenly the bow lookout let out a yell, and I backed emergency on both engines. As I moved the telegraphs astern, a line of white appeared under the bow and then, gradually, out of the mist, there appeared a rocky height—the high land at the entrance and the breakers under it. I thought that ship would never stop moving ahead, although we had been going at bare steerageway. But finally she did. As I stopped, preparing to straighten out, I looked astern and recognized a beacon on a rock in the middle of the Goulet, apparently passing us. We had been caught in a strong flood tide and were being carried through broadside to or nearly so. By the time I could get headed again on our course, the fog had lifted and we found ourselves inside the harbor. We heaved a sigh of relief and went alongside our tender for repairs. My chief engineer told me later that when they first opened the throttle on the backing turbines, nothing seemed to be going through but water—the result of our badly salted condition.

When the *George Washington* finally arrived with President Wilson, all the Brest and Queenstown destroyers were there to meet her. It was the usual low visibility, but a chain of destroyers stationed at visibility distance with searchlights on were used to mark navigation dangers, and other destroyers with veteran pilots led the big ship in. As she entered the Goulet, she had an escort of destroyers on each side, all in best uniforms with crews manning the rail. It was indeed an occasion.

The *Cummings* had been one of those longest overseas. So on December 16, we found ourselves one of a detachment of about five, flying long homeward-bound pennants, en route to Philadelphia via the Azores and Bermuda as fueling stops. Christmas was spent in the mid-Atlantic in somewhat rough weather, but all was cheery, except for one thing; one of our men had become sick with what my chief pharmacist's mate thought to be scarlet fever. We immediately isolated him as best we could, and because I had been through a scarlet fever quarantine on the old *Missouri*, I knew what precautions to take, such as breaking out and scrubbing all the men's clothing and holding daily neck and throat inspections. There was a doctor in the detachment, but it was too rough to transfer him. Contacted by our newly installed radio telephone, he confirmed the diagnosis, the treatment, and the preventive measures.

All went well until we arrived at Bermuda. Apparently there had never been a case of scarlet fever on the island, and they did not want any. No vessels were ever allowed to enter the narrow entrance channel without a pilot, yet they would not allow a pilot to board. But we had to have fuel, and our fuel supply was in the inner harbor off Hamilton. The problem was finally solved by putting a pilot in a steam launch, which was to follow closely. Safely anchored, the *Cummings* got its only view of Bermuda through a porthole, while our comrades enjoyed warm hospitality ashore. Our sick man was received at the hospital at the Naval Base. When it came our turn to go alongside the fuel barge, its crew abandoned ship and we had to attend our own moorings and fuel connections.

Although no more cases of the fever developed on board, our quarantine troubles were not yet over. Several days later, New Year's, which was celebrated at sea, we arrived at the League Island Navy Yard (Philadelphia) to learn that we were not to berth with our fellow destroyers, that we were to be segregated in the back channel, and that I was to allow no one ashore until further orders. Considering the long overseas wartime service of my officers and crew, and the fact that my wife was awaiting me in a Philadelphia hotel, this was a little hard to take. The young naval doctor who visited us informed me that the quarantine would last until we were inspected by the senior medical officer. Questioned as to when that might be expected, I was told "probably sometime the next day." With that, I blew up and directed him to present my compliments to the commandant (having no idea who he was) and say, most respectfully, that I demanded an immediate inspection. In less than half an hour, an official car came tearing down the dock bearing the senior medico. He proved to be very nice and, when the situation was fully explained to him, said that it was all a mistake and released us forthwith. When the glad news reached the crew, you could have heard the cheer in Independence Square. Off went the first leave and liberty party in jig time. When I finally reported to the commandant, I found him to be none other than the famous Admiral Charles F. Hughes,[12] with whom I was to serve in the future in several capacities. He stood for no delay in our inspection.

After the *Cummings*' long overseas service, one would have thought that the ship would be allowed adequate time for urgent repairs, and officers and crew opportunity for a decent leave; but not so. Transports bringing home troops had priority on yard work, and we got little attention. About two weeks after arrival at the yard, despite my repeated protests, we were forced to sail to join the fleet in Guantánamo for maneuvers. Nothing more foolish nor more damaging to the spirit and morale of the crew can be imagined. And it did not help matters to be officially censured later for breakdowns and poor matériel performance.

Upon the return north, I was detached from the *Cummings* in New York and took over command of the *Ludlow*,[13] a newer World War I destroyer, on April 22. In mid-May we formed part of the destroyer detachment deployed across the Atlantic to guard the first trans-Atlantic NC-4 flight. After the planes passed safely overhead, we returned to the coast. In New York again, on June 27, I was detached in accordance with my welcome orders to the Naval Academy, where I reported three days later after a trip down in my first automobile.

How pleasant it was, after three years of eventful but sometimes difficult sea service, to be at peace, to be reunited with one's family, and to be back at the dear old Naval Academy and once more on Upshur Row. This time I was assigned to the department of electrical engineering and physics under Captain Burrell C. Allen.[14] I found the work there most rewarding. Not only did I enjoy instructing once more, but it gave me a splendid opportunity to further my knowledge of chemistry and electricity, in which my own course as a midshipman had been rather short. My previous mathematics training stood me in good stead.

In addition to my academic work, I was fortunate enough to be elected as secretary-treasurer of the U.S. Naval Institute before my first year was up. This brought additional duty but also extra compensation. I have always been happy to have had this all-too-brief association with the Institute—it taught me much.

As a commander, I had hoped that this tour at the Academy might be for three years, as the previous one had been, but it was not to be, perhaps fortunately so, because it put me in a better sea-shore cycle for what happened later. With the arrival of the new superintendent, Admiral H. B. Wilson, in the summer of 1921, I was detached. Having been away from big ships by then for eight years, I expected and wanted duty as head of department of a battleship. And, considering my previous experience, the logical assignment would have been as navigator. Instead, with the logic often exercised by the Bureau of Personnel, I was ordered as gunnery officer of the *Pennsylvania*,[15] then the flagship of the Atlantic Fleet. Probably the Navy Department wanted to give me all-around experience.

When on August 13 I reported on board to Captain Althouse,[16] the *Pennsylvania* was completing an overhaul in the New York Navy Yard, preparatory to being transferred to the Pacific Fleet. I found plenty to do, learning the ins and outs of my gunnery department, particularly the director system, an innovation since I had departed from the *Florida* years before.

About the time we departed for Panama, in September, some trouble arose between Costa Rica and Nicaragua, which caused a battalion of Marines to put aboard for transport to the Canal Zone. Having arrived in Balboa on the Pacific side, we were held for some time with the Marines still aboard, pending developments.

When the flare-up subsided, we landed the Marines for return to Quantico, and we continued on to San Pedro. When we arrived, we reported to our division commander, the energetic Admiral Hughes, whose flag was on our sister ship *Arizona*,[17] and were immediately plunged into a very tough schedule of inspections and gunnery exercises in which we did not do very well. In fact, we got a most unsatisfactory report, which I fear had a serious effect on poor Captain Althouse's record. He was detached soon afterward and relieved by Captain John F. Hines, an excellent officer with whom I had been previously associated.

The *Pennsylvania* really was in poor shape. She was not clean as current naval standards went, and not only did she have a green gunnery officer, but there had not been a proper recent opportunity for gunnery training. As Fleet Flag in the Atlantic, she had been somewhat sacrosanct and had been spared many routine inspections. Her poor reputation had preceded her to the Pacific, which largely explains the "initial course of sprouts" we were put through. This was a good lesson and began the gradual improvement which culminated in her winning the battle efficiency pennant the following year as well as coming within an ace of the gunnery trophy the same year (losing it only due to an unfortunate casualty to a little lost-motion spring in the director train system).

The two-year tour as gunnery officer of the *Pennsylvania* was strenuous, but most pleasant and interesting and also very valuable. In the spring of 1922, the fleet had its annual maneuvers in the Hawaii area and the following year off Panama. During the Panama fleet concentration, several advanced practices were fired by battleships at our first radio-controlled target, the old battleship *Iowa*, veteran of Santiago. How strange it was to see a ship of that size stopping, going ahead, and turning this way and that without a soul on board. Due to our gunnery standing, the *Pennsylvania* was chosen to fire one of these special practices. We opened fire with our forward turrets to starboard, then turned toward the target, maintaining our fire as we came around, and finishing with the target to port. To complicate matters still further, we had to fire from a new installation—a gyro-stabilized director below decks in the plotting room. We did fairly well, and got a commendation for it. Unfortunately, in the last scheduled exercise, the *Mississippi* was directed to use armor-piercing shells instead of the special thin-walled projectiles previously used, and the poor old target was sunk. It had been hoped to preserve it for future use, but probably the fear of Army Air Force propaganda was too great. Billy Mitchell et al.[18] would have filled the press with accounts of how the big battleships had fired for days at an old hulk without sinking it, whereas it could have been dispatched with one aircraft bomb.

NOTES
1. Philip Andrews (1866–1935). Rear Admiral. U.S. Naval Academy, Class of 1886.
2. Cecil M. Gabbett (1882–1940). Captain. U.S. Coast Guard.
3. Henry B. Wilson (1861–1954). Admiral. U.S. Naval Academy, Class of 1881.
4. Alfred G. Howe (1878–1970). Rear Admiral. U.S. Naval Academy, Class of 1901.
5. USS *Conner* (DD-72). Commissioned in January 1918, she served with U.S. Naval Forces, Europe, escorting convoys to French and British ports. Damaged by *U-82* in September 1918, she returned to Brest for repairs, having lost thirty-six sailors. She was one of the ships that escorted President Woodrow Wilson to the Paris Peace Conference, 1918.
6. *Dupetit Thouars* was built in 1901. She was torpedoed on 7 August 1918 in the North Atlantic by a German submarine.
7. *Mount Vernon*, formerly the *Crown Princess Cecilia*, was built in Stettin, Germany, in 1906. The ship was interned in Bar Harbor, Maine, when World War I was declared and then was transferred to the U.S. Navy. She was used as a troop transport during the war.
8. USS *Cummings* (DD-44). Commissioned in September 1913, she served with U.S. Naval Forces, Europe, as an escort ship and on anti-submarine patrols.
9. Owen Bartlett (1884–1950). Commander. U.S. Naval Academy, Class of 1906.
10. USS *George Washington* (AP). Commissioned in September 1917, she served as a troop transport in World War I and carried President Wilson and U.S. representatives to the Paris Peace Conference in 1918.
11. Woodrow Wilson (1856–1924). President of the United States, 1913–1921.
12. Charles F. Hughes (1866–1934). Admiral. U.S. Naval Academy, Class of 1888.
13. USS *Ludlow* (DD-112). Commissioned in 1918, she joined Mine Squadron 2, Fleet Base Force, in 1921, in Hawaii, where she remained for eight years.
14. Burrell G. Allen (1881–1967). Rear Admiral. U.S. Naval Academy, Class of 1901.
15. USS *Pennsylvania* (BB-38). Commissioned in June 1916, she joined the Pacific Fleet in 1922, operating in the Caribbean and Pacific Ocean.
16. Albert Althouse (1870–1954). Captain. U.S. Naval Academy, Class of 1891.
17. USS *Arizona* (BB-39). Commissioned in October 1916, she joined the Atlantic Fleet in 1921. From 1921 to 1929 she was based at San Pedro, serving as flagship for Battleship Divisions 2, 3, and 4 in the Pacific Ocean and Caribbean waters.
18. William Mitchell (1879–1936). Aviator and Army officer. He served in World War I and headed the aviation branch of the Army. In 1920, he was appointed brigadier general. A champion of air power in the 1920s, the independence of the air arm, and the effectiveness of the airplane vis-à-vis the battleship, he was demoted for his views. In 1926 he resigned from the Army.

Vice Admiral Louis R. de Steiguer with Commander H. Kent Hewitt in 1926. (Naval Historical Collection)

VIII *Fleet Assignments and the NWC, 1923–1935*

The summer of 1923 found me due once more for duty on shore. By then I had received two commissions as a permanent commander, the latter dating back to my birthday, February 11, 1922. Our second daughter, Mary Kent,[1] was born in the Seaside Hospital, Long Beach, California, on July 5, 1923, and a few days thereafter I was en route, alone, by train to Washington, D.C. At the request of Captain Chauncey Shackford,[2] the director, I had been ordered to the Naval Operations Division of Fleet Training as head of the gunnery section. This was a most complimentary detail, since it gave me cognizance not only of battleship target practice but of other types as well.

I arrived in Washington just in time to be assigned the job of Adjutant of the Naval-Marine Brigade, participating in the funeral ceremonies for President Harding.[3] Never have I had such a hot day. Before it was over, I had gone through two complete suits of white uniform. The poor Marines, up from Quantico in their dress blues, were dropping out like flies.

Three years spent in fleet training were full of hard work but also of interest. Professionally, it was most rewarding, and I found my mathematical training of great value in analyzing the results of target practice to establish where fault lay or where improvement in operational methods or matériel installations were indicated. The work of getting out the annual Orders for Gunnery Exercises and Report of Gunnery Exercises itself was tremendous. The annual visits to the fleet to witness special practices were also most interesting.

After my second year in Washington, I had wanted to go to the Naval War College, but Admiral Hughes, who had relieved Captain Shackford after my first year, refused to let me go. It was July 17, 1926, when I finally left the Navy Department, pursuant to my next orders to sea.

Having had two years of duty as the head of a department of a battleship, I thought of going back to my old love, command of a destroyer. In fact, I did succeed in obtaining such orders. But prior to proceeding in accordance with them, I received an invitation which I could scarcely turn down to serve on the staff of Vice Admiral Louis R. de Steiguer,[4] newly appointed Commander, Battleship Divisions, Pacific Fleet, as aide and gunnery officer. This was to be my first experience with staff duty of any sort. It proved to be interesting and professionally valuable.

After a short leave with my parents in Hackensack and a delightful week in Yellowstone Park with my family, I reported, on September 4, on board the flagship *West Virginia*[5] at San Pedro and was soon deeply immersed in my new duties, particularly with respect to the routine fall target practices. In addition to being the gunnery officer, I found myself to be the staff tactical officer, which meant that, with the assistance of the flag lieutenant as plotter and under the supervision of the admiral, I practically ran the tactical handling of the division of which the admiral was in immediate command and the battleships as a whole during maneuvers. My earlier training as a signal officer certainly stood me in good stead.

I had been somewhat reluctant to accept service with Admiral de Steiguer, because he had the service reputation of being what might be mildly described as difficult. I soon found him to be a very able officer with the perhaps unfortunate trait of flying off the handle if he thought things were not going right or someone was not on the job. He wanted no "yes" men around him but people who knew what they were doing, and he did not hesitate to tell them so.

Once one gained his confidence, all was usually well. But that did not prevent occasional battles royal. Some years later I ran into a younger officer who had been serving on the *West Virginia* at the time, who said to me, "Sir, you are the first officer I ever heard damn an admiral." "What," said I, "I, damn an admiral?" "Yes, sir," said he, "You were arguing on the bridge over what signal to make for some maneuver, and Admiral de Steiguer said 'D—— it, Hewitt, you are wrong.' And you came right back at him with 'D—— it, Admiral, I am right.'" He might have added that the admiral finished off with "All right! Go ahead and make a d—— fool of yourself."

The joint Atlantic-Pacific Fleet maneuvers in the spring of 1927 were held in the Panama area, after which the entire U.S. fleet transited the Canal and paid a visit to New York. That was fine for me, because amidst the various official festivities, I was able to see something of my parents and old friends of my native town. However, the Pacific Fleet was soon on its way back to the West Coast.

The summer of 1927 was spent in the Puget Sound area, as was then customary. During this period, Admiral de Steiguer succeeded to the four-star command of the Pacific Fleet, and I followed him to the flagship *California*[6] as fleet gunnery officer. That brought me in contact with the gunnery of all fleet types, cruisers, destroyers, submarines, and air, as well as the battleships. Our chief of staff was Rear Admiral Harris Laning,[7] with whom I was to be later associated at the Naval War College. On this staff, also, I had much to do with fleet tactics and with war planning. It was another interesting year, culminating with fleet maneuvers in the spring of 1928 in the Hawaii area.

With the relief of Admiral de Steiguer as CINC Pacific Fleet in June 1928, I also was detached, with the orders that I had long sought, to the Naval War College at Newport, Rhode Island.[8] It was my opinion then, and one which was thoroughly confirmed by my subsequent experience, that at least a year at that college should be an absolute requisite to advancement to higher command in the Navy.

I enjoyed my year greatly, a year with no command responsibility, during which I had ample opportunity for study and reflection, for learning the art of estimating situations, making decisions, and writing orders or plans to place them in effect, and I practiced what I had learned by the solution of strategical and tactical problems and playing them out on the game board. The student commander of a major force, or one of its subdivisions, was faced with making the same sort of decisions which might fall to his lot in actual war.

When it came time for graduation, I felt that I was just beginning to scratch the surface of the things I wanted to know. I was delighted as well as honored when I was asked to remain at the college and join the staff.

My War College year was marred by a personal sorrow. On my father's 72nd birthday, on May 7, 1929, I called him by telephone to wish him well. He was apparently feeling fine and in good spirits. The following morning he had a stroke. Before I could reach Hackensack from Newport, he was gone. It was as he would have wished. I could not imagine him as a hopeless invalid. He was a fine man as well as a wonderful father, and I felt his loss deeply. I owe much to him.

The president of the War College during my first year there was Rear Admiral J. R. P. Pringle,[9] a splendid officer with whom I had been associated in one way or another since my midshipman days, when he was one of our instructors. He and his family had been next door neighbors on Upshur Row when I was first married. He was succeeded by Admiral Laning as president.

In my first year on the War College staff, I was assigned to the operations department, which had to do with planning the tactical and strategic problems, studying the solutions submitted by the students, and managing the playing out of the war games. I assisted the planning officer, Captain George B. Wright,[10] a brilliant officer who would have gone to the top had not a heart condition brought his early retirement and his subsequent demise. It was a great compliment to be given his planning section when he went to sea.

As the spring of 1931 approached, I had to think of my own next sea duty, particularly as during that period I would probably be coming up for selection for captain. It was almost a *sine qua non* in those days that one had to have had a successful tour of duty as executive officer of a battleship to have much chance for further promotion. Having had duty as head of department of a battleship, what I really wanted was the command of a division of destroyers, which I felt actually to be better training for higher command. But, in accordance with Admiral Laning's urgent advice, I duly put in a strong request for the executive officer billet, citing my reasons. The Bureau of Personnel replied that it regretted there was no vacancy available and that I would have to take a destroyer division instead. Too bad! But my effort to get the other duty was on record.

My new command was Destroyer Division Twelve of the Pacific Fleet, consisting of the *Southard*,[11] *Hovey*,[12] *Chandler*,[13] and *Long*.[14] These were World War I destroyers, but still going strong. I broke my division commander's broad pennant temporarily in the *Hovey* on June 10, 1931, transferring later to the regular flagboat, *Southard,* when it became available after Navy Yard overhaul. After a summer in the Puget Sound area, we went south for the customary fall target practices and tactical exercises in the San Pedro–San Diego area. It was a delight to handle a fine division of fast craft.

In connection with this duty, I should record an incident which illustrates graphically the slender thread by which a naval officer's career sometimes hangs (the margin between successes and disaster), even though its explanation requires a rather long story.

Some years previously, destroyer tactics had visualized an attack on a battle line by coming in from a position well ahead, firing the torpedoes of one broadside, then reversing course and firing the other. The torpedo practice laid out for destroyers had reflected this. When I was in fleet training, we found that many destroyers, in order to insure the best possible score, were taking entirely too much time to make a cautious approach for the firing of the second broadside, an entirely unrealistic procedure, for they would theoretically be under serious gunfire. Accordingly, it was decided to introduce a time factor, based on a comparison between what we considered to be a reasonable elapsed time between broadsides and the actual time by which torpedo hits would be multiplied to produce a final score.

During the first year that this time factor rule was in effect, one brilliant destroyer captain conceived the bright idea of training his torpedo tubes thirty degrees on each bow and setting the torpedo gyros thirty degrees left or right respectively so that the torpedoes, when launched, would parallel the course of the ship. Thus, he could steady his ship on the course he wanted the torpedoes to take, fire both broadsides simultaneously, slow his ship long enough for the torpedoes to get ahead, and then turn away. With an interval of zero between launchings, his time factor would be infinity, and all he needed for an infinite score was one torpedo hit, which he got. This presented fleet training with a problem in determining destroyer gunnery standings, but it did serve the purpose of introducing a very valuable improvement in torpedo tactics.

To use this method of torpedo fire with an attacking division of destroyers, a system of quick deployment was devised by which the column leader turned ninety degrees right and then immediately back to the original course; number 2, forty-five degrees right then back to course; number 3 kept straight ahead; and number 4 put on flank speed and sheered slightly left to bring him up on the line. This formed the division very promptly in line on the original course, in position to launch torpedoes ahead.

On the occasion which I am about to relate, Destroyer Squadron Four, operating out of San Diego, was to make a simulated daylight attack on a division of battleships steaming south from San Pedro. Navy planes were to "box in" the battleships with a smoke screen, and the destroyers were to attack as the ships emerged from the smoke. One division of the squadron was to operate in a southeasterly sector, one from the southwestward and the third, my own, from the southward, in the center. There was a little natural haze in the air, and there was a slight breeze from the northward.

Destroyers had no ship-to-ship radio phones at that time, but they did have whistle signals for making simultaneous turns in low visibility, with which, fortunately, I had thoroughly drilled my division. As I approached the smoke screen on a northerly course, I decided to make a quick deployment with the purpose of getting my boats on a line about right angle to the expected target bearing, then to move back and forth on an easterly or westerly course awaiting the enemy's appearance. What I failed to note was the rapidity with which the smoke screen was moving toward me with the wind. Hardly had the quick deployment been initiated when we found ourselves in a smoke so thick that one could not see the jack staff as we moved at some twenty knots toward a formation of battleships somewhere ahead. It was an awful moment, requiring that something be done, and, that, quickly. Reaching for the whistle cord, I blew one long blast (turn right), followed by four toots (4 x 15 = 60 degrees). Thankfully, I heard #2 repeat, then #3, and then #4. Thereupon, I blew one short blast (execute), and we put the rudder right. About halfway through the turn we came out in the clear to see our battleships about 1,500 yards away, steaming right toward us. A flag signal to fire port torpedoes hastily executed, and another sixty-degree right turn, and out we went through the smoke again. There probably never was such a torpedo attack, and the battleships would hardly have had time to fire more than two or three shots at us. But I think that it gave me some of my first gray hairs. And I certainly offered a devout prayer of thanks at the safe outcome. But risks sometimes have to be taken, even in peace-time training for war.

In the spring of 1932, the Pacific Fleet held joint exercises with the Army in the Hawaii area. The first of these, designed to test the Hawaiian defense plans, represented an attack on the islands by a naval force coming from overseas. Destroyer Division Twelve was assigned as plane guards for Carrier Division One, the *Saratoga*[15] and *Lexington*,[16] under Admiral Harry Yarnell.[17] From a position well to the northward of Oahu at nightfall, this force made a fast run-in during the night, made a pre-dawn Sunday morning launch of planes in rough weather, and recovered them successfully after a simulated surprise attack on Pearl Harbor and Army air fields and defense installations. Little did we realize that we were rehearsing what would actually happen in less than ten years, with such disastrous results.

Having been fortunate enough to be selected for promotion to captain by the selection board meeting the previous December (in spite of my failure to have battleship executive officer duty), I took my examinations for promotion in May, after the Pacific Fleet returned to West Coast bases. I had looked forward to another year with my destroyers, but it was not to be. Without being consulted in the matter, I was ordered to the staff of Admiral Luke McNamee,[18] the new Commander in Chief, Pacific Fleet, as operations officer, a title which more precisely described the duties of what previously had been called the assistant chief of staff. I was complimented and pleased with the prospect of interesting duty but, as always, hated to leave my command. However, I was able to put on my fourth stripe before leaving and to receive the kind congratulations of my captains and other officers. Before reporting to Admiral McNamee on August 11, I spent about six weeks in charge of the Destroyer Gunnery School.

A distressing event requiring an important decision by me occurred shortly after the change of commands in the fleet, which occurred during the customary summer visit to the Puget Sound area. The battleships were anchored in Port Angeles, just across the sound from Victoria, British Columbia, to which it was connected by ferry. Admiral McNamee and the chief of staff had gone to Victoria for the day. My old friend and mentor, Admiral Pringle, had been made vice admiral as Commander, Battleship Divisions, Pacific, and it was no secret that he was slated to become the next Chief of Naval Operations. Unfortunately, shortly after taking over his new command, he had to take to his bed. Hardly had Admiral McNamee left when Admiral Pringle's chief of staff and the *West Virginia*'s doctor came to the *California* with the news that it was urgent that the admiral be gotten to the naval hospital in San Diego as promptly as possible by the most comfortable means available. And, also, that Mrs. Pringle and their daughter were most anxious to accompany him, which was strongly recommended.

This was something that seemed to require immediate action, without awaiting the departmental authority that would ordinarily be required. It seemed to be a heavy responsibility for a newly made captain to take upon himself, but my training had always been, when faced with the necessity of making a decision for my immediate commander, to place myself in his shoes and take the action I thought he would want me to take. The flagship *West Virginia*, in any event, was due to go south two weeks later for an overhaul. So, in the name of the CINC, I directed the *West Virginia* to proceed at once to San Diego at best speed and authorized the embarkation of Mrs. Pringle and Miss Pringle. A priority despatch was transmitted to the Navy Department, informing them of this action and the reason therefore. By the time Admiral McNamee returned on the afternoon ferry, the *West Virginia* was well on the way, and I was awaiting him on the landing with the news. I was glad to learn that he approved of my action.

The Navy lost a wonderful officer a little over a month later when Admiral Pringle died in San Diego. It was some comfort to know that I had been of some assistance to him and to his family. Admiral Pringle's place in the fleet was taken by another fine officer, Admiral Sellers.[19]

The autumn of 1932 was taken up with the usual target practices and tactical exercises, during which the time of the operations officer was fully occupied in preparing schedules, working on war plans and, when underway, assisting in the tactical handling of the fleet. These were followed by the usual Christmas–New Year period of leave and relaxation, and, in the spring of 1933, by a fleet concentration and joint strategic and tactical exercises.

In March of 1933, while the fleet, fortunately, was at its home bases, California (and especially the Long Beach area) experienced a severe earthquake. This involved a personal experience which may be worth setting forth for the record.

At this time my family was living in an apartment on First Street on the eastern outskirts of Long Beach, one block inland from the beach, on fairly high ground. With my wife were her semi-invalid mother, our ten-year-old daughter, and an elderly maid who had followed us from Coronado. Our older daughter was in the east at Vassar. It was Friday and my wife and I were to have tea with one friend in Pasadena and to have dinner with another. Arriving at the tea, we found our hostess rather white faced and saying that she had just felt quite a heavy earthquake shock. In the car, we had felt nothing. Since there was no visible damage, we thought nothing of it. But later, during dinner, our first hostess rang up to inquire if we had been listening to the radio and to inform us that there were reports of serious damage in Long Beach. The first direct report we heard over that medium was that "Long Beach was on fire and under control of the Navy." Immediate attempts to reach the family were fruitless, all telephone lines to the area being cut. This did nothing to allay our natural anxiety.

The trip back to the coast was made as rapidly as possible, via several detours around damaged areas, arguments with state police as to why we should be allowed to enter the stricken area, and finally, permission to pass down a narrow side road, given by a friendly civilian wearing the arm band of volunteer police. We saw no signs of a conflagration, the absence of which was confirmed by the sight of an idle fire truck and its crew sitting on the ramp outside of its damaged station. When we arrived, we found our apartment completely dark and no one in it. Inspection revealed little interior damage other than furniture tossed around, a grandfather's clock thrown across the living room, and the contents of a medicine cabinet dumped into the washbasin below. Outside, great chunks of a concrete chimney littered the driveway. Electricity was on, but not gas.

To our relief, we eventually found the missing members of the family safely parked in a car across the street. My sister-in-law, temporarily in Long Beach, had come to the rescue. Our attempts to reoccupy our apartment were defeated by recurring heavy shocks, which finally forced a decision to spend the night in our cars in the open spaces of a nearby park. The Navy had taken over, and patrols from its fleet landing force were everywhere. There were reports of danger from an expected tidal wave, which I discounted. Anyway, we were on relatively high ground. At dawn, we returned to the apartment, where my family finally consented to my moving them to Pasadena, which we knew to be undamaged. I cooked breakfast boy scout style over a driveway fireplace made of concrete blocks with a top from our gas stove. We learned that many families had been taken out to the ships, but that was impracticable for my mother-in-law.

I drove to Pasadena in uniform to avoid being stopped anymore, and thus had no trouble. I finally returned aboard the *California* and to duty shortly after lunch. Never on a man-of-war had I ever seen the sight which greeted me—infants' apparel strung all along the wardroom passageways.

The damage to the city of Long Beach was very serious. All the public schools were flat. Had the quake occurred during school hours, thousands of children would have been lost, my own little girl among them. As it was, there were few casualties.

The culmination of the year of scheduled fleet activities soon rolled around, and with it, Admiral McNamee's relief, and on May 20 my own detachment to duty at the Naval Academy. The superintendent, Admiral Hart,[20] had approved my assignment there and, upon my reporting at the end of June, ordered me to relieve Captain Louis McBride[21] as head of the department of mathematics, my old

Captain H. Kent Hewitt, Head of the Mathematics Department at the U.S. Naval Academy, with faculty members, ca. 1934. (Naval Historical Collection)

department. Naturally I was delighted, for, under Admiral Hart and later under Admiral David W. Sellers, I was able to spend almost three happy years doing work in which, next to handling ships, I was truly interested and most enjoyed. And I enjoyed the associations with and friendship of my fellow heads of department on Porter Row.

NOTES

1 Mary Kent Hewitt (1923–) graduated from Connecticut College and attended graduate school at Middlebury College. She is the wife of Captain Gerald Norton, U.S. Navy (Ret.) and resides in Annapolis, Md.

2 Chauncey Shackford (1877–1964). Captain. U.S. Naval Academy, Class of 1899.

3 Warren G. Harding (1865–1923). President of the United States, 1921–1923. The Washington Conference on Naval Limitation took place during his administration in 1921–1922.

4 Louis R. de Steiguer (1869–1923). Rear Admiral. U.S. Naval Academy, Class of 1889.

5 USS *West Virginia* (BB-48) was commissioned in December 1923. In 1924 she was flagship for the Commander, Battleship Divisions, Battle Fleet.

6 USS *California* (BB-44) was commissioned in August 1921 and served as flagship of the Pacific Fleet for twenty years, 1921–1941.

7 Harris Laning (1873–1941). Rear Admiral. U.S. Naval Academy, Class of 1895. President of the Naval War College, 1930–1933.

8 Naval War College, Newport, R.I. was established in 1884 by Rear Admiral Stephen B. Luce. The Navy's senior educational institution prepares naval officers for positions of higher command.

9 Joel R. P. Pringle (1873–1932). Vice Admiral. U.S. Naval Academy, Class of 1892. President of the Naval War College, 1927–1930.

10 George B. Wright (1883–1942). Captain. U.S. Naval Academy, Class of 1901.

11 USS *Southard* (DD-207) was commissioned in 1919 and was named after Samuel L. Southard, secretary of the Navy.

12 USS *Hovey* (DD-208) was commissioned in 1919 and named after Ensign Charles E. Hovey, who was killed on the island of Basilan in the Philippine Insurrection.

13 USS *Chandler* (DD-206) was commissioned in 1919 and named after secretary of the Navy William E. Chandler.

14 USS *Long* (DD-209) was commissioned in 1919 and named after secretary of the Navy John D. Long.

15 USS *Saratoga* (CV-3) was commissioned in November 1927. She was the first of the Navy's fast carriers attached to the Pacific Fleet.

16 USS *Lexington* (CV-2) was commissioned in December 1927. She joined the Battle Fleet on the Pacific coast for battle problems and fleet training exercises.

17 Harry Yarnell (1875–1959). Admiral. U.S. Naval Academy, Class of 1897.

18 Luke McNamee (1871–1952). Admiral. U.S. Naval Academy, Class of 1892. President of the Naval War College, 1933–1934.

19 David Sellers (1874–1949). Admiral. U.S. Naval Academy, Class of 1894.

20 Thomas Hart (1877–1971). Admiral. U.S. Naval Academy, Class of 1897.

21 Lewis B. McBride (1880–1947). Captain. U.S. Naval Academy, Class of 1901.

Captain H. K. Hewitt reviews the crew of the USS Indianapolis, *1936 (Naval Historical Collection)*

IX *Cruise in USS* Indianapolis, *1936*

The time passed all too rapidly. In early 1936, I was once more due for duty at sea, this time for a large ship command. Command of the heavy cruiser *Indianapolis*[1] became vacant in January, and Admiral Sellers consented to my detachment to her, provided the department would agree to my delaying until the end of the first academic term. Fortunately, they did, and on February 29 (lucky leap year) I was on my way once more to the West Coast, leaving my family in Annapolis. After joint fleet exercises in the Panama area, my ship was due for a three-month overhaul at the New York Navy Yard. I assumed command of the Scouting Force flagship of Admiral Arthur Hepburn[2] on March 16, and shortly thereafter left with the fleet for Panama and the usual tactical exercises and joint problems with the Army.

Upon completion of the scheduled exercises, we transited the Canal and proceeded north, where, at the end of May, we hauled down Admiral Hepburn's flag. He had been detached to duty in Washington. Not due in New York until the end of June, and under orders to act independently, I seized the opportunity to proceed up Chesapeake Bay and anchor in Annapolis Roads for the Naval Academy June Week. This was much enjoyed by the officers and gave the men an opportunity to see the Academy and visit nearby Washington and Baltimore. And my daughter enjoyed having a tea given for her midshipman friends in the captain's cabin. Incidentally, I was distressed to discover a bad dent in the punch bowl that had been in its case in the admiral's cabin. To my relief, when the bowl was emptied of its fruit juice contents, an inscription was uncovered noting that the dent had been made by the fragment of a Spanish shell on July 4, 1898.

The summer passed quickly, with my family ensconced in a small apartment in the old but comfortable Hotel Margaret on Brooklyn Heights, an apartment with a delightful view of the East River, Governor's Island, the lower end of Manhattan, and the passing shipping. Much against my wife's will, she preceded me to the West Coast in order to settle the family in time for the opening of school. I was scheduled to rejoin the fleet in the Pacific upon completion of our overhaul in September.

En route south, after my departure in late September, the *Indianapolis* was ordered to put into Hampton Roads, and her captain was directed to report personally to the Chief of Naval Operations in Washington. Having done so, I was informed, very confidentially, that if President Roosevelt were re-elected, the *Indianapolis* would be assigned to carry him to the Pan-American Conference[3] to be held at Buenos Aires on December 1, and that, pending final decision, I was to operate in the Chesapeake Bay–Hampton Roads area carrying out such exercises as were practicable. I was enjoined until further directed not to divulge our ultimate planned destination to anyone, not even to my executive officer, Commander Badger,[4] my old flag skipper of Destroyer Division Twelve days.

So began a pleasant month of anti-aircraft practices, emergency drills, school of the ship for officers, etc., interspersed with weekends in port—Hampton Roads, Annapolis, Baltimore, etc.—for liberty and recreation. The fact that these visits happened to coincide with the Navy football schedule was duly noted and commented on by my erstwhile Academy friends. When, after orders to a North River pier in New York for Navy Day, I appeared at a game in Princeton, the remarks were loud and to the point. "What the heck *was* I supposed to be doing?" When my *Floride*, marooned in Long Beach, heard of all these doings in which she would like to have participated, she vowed never to travel ahead of me again.

After Navy Day (October 27), we were sent into the New York Yard to be fitted out for our prospective cruise. As soon as the election results were known, this became public. A special elevator and other fittings necessary to the accommodation of a crippled president were installed, and we received our official orders. In accordance therewith, we arrived alongside the dock at Charleston, South Carolina, on November 16, thereby to be joined by the cruiser *Chester*,[5] under my classmate, Harry J. Abbett,[6] which had come around from the West Coast to act as escort.

At 8:00 a.m., November 18, President Roosevelt arrived by train in Charleston, to be met by the governor, the mayor, and a cadet honor guard from the Citadel as well as others. On the *Indianapolis* and the *Chester*, all hands were in full dress and the rails were manned. "Attention" was sounded as he drove alongside. The full guard and band were paraded and eight side boys were at the gangway. As the president worked his way up the special narrow brow with a high rail on which he could support himself, there was no sound except the trill of the boatswain's pipe, gradually rising in note as he came up. Instead of sounding off as he came over the side, in accordance with usual procedure, I waited as I had been advised to do until he reached the top and then had time for his son James[7] to take his arm to enable him to remove his silk hat. Then the Marine guard presented arms and the band broke into the four ruffles and flourishes, followed by the "Star Spangled Banner." As that finished, I stepped forward to greet him. (Since we were alongside the dock in the city, we fired no salute, but the *Chester* in the stream did so as we broke the president's flag at the main.) As I shook his hand, I said, "Mr. President, the *Indianapolis* is most happy and honored to have you on board." He grasped my hand, looked at me with a smile, and said, "Well, Skipper, I am mighty happy to be here." That immediately put me at my ease with him then and throughout the ensuing cruise, during which he never called me anything but Skipper. After all, it was "something" to receive the head of the nation on board one's ship and to have the responsibility for his safety.

The president went up the elevator from the well deck to the upper deck and thence forward to the rail abaft number 2 turret where he could look over and wave to the crowds on the dock. We were scheduled to be under way at 9:00 a.m., but it required quite a little planning to ensure that all the presidential baggage and entourage with their effects, and the newspaper men as well, were safely aboard us or the *Chester*. It necessitated good work on the part of the executive officer and department heads, but all went well. Commander Badger reported the ship ready for getting under way and the lines singled up. Just as we let go, and the ship began to move ahead, two bells were struck. Later, as we left the harbor and steadied on our southerly course, the president commented to me, "Skipper, I noted that you were right on the bell." He knew nautical terminology and liked to be treated as a flag officer. Throughout the cruise, he had charts—with courses plotted—parallel rulers, and dividers in his admiral's cabin, and he was always furnished with the 8 a.m., noon, and 8 p.m. positions, which he plotted and checked.

Our schedule required comparatively high speed, around a twenty-five-knot average. Consequently, I usually started out at about twenty-seven knots in order to make allowance for the possibility of having to slow down later on due to bad weather or low visibility. In case of the latter, I usually put the *Chester* in the lead in order to avoid the possibility of the president being involved in a collision. Radar was not yet in existence.

After a pleasant, fast passage in reasonably good weather, we reached Trinidad early in the morning of November 21 and went alongside our waiting tanker, anchored in the northern part of the Gulf of Paria, a short distance south of the Dragon's Mouths. This was in no way an official stop, so the president and party spent the day fishing around the many islands at the entrance of the Gulf. But we did have a visit from the colonial secretary, representing the governor.

With our ships alongside the tanker and not scheduled to depart until about 4:00 p.m., Abbett and I decided to go ashore in Port of Spain for lunch. We wanted to stretch our legs a little bit and see how much we remembered of a port we had not visited since Christmas twenty-nine years earlier, when we were young passed-midshipmen on the battleship around-the-world cruise. We did pretty well, for we walked straight to the Queen's Park Savannah and the Queen's Park Hotel without asking directions. There we relaxed on the spacious veranda, enjoyed one of the famous planter's punches, and had a delicious lunch. Since we were getting under way at 4:00 p.m., we had decided to allow ourselves just one refreshing drink, and the final choice was the result of considerable debate—between the planter's punch and a green swizzle. We made no mistake.

Back on board, with the fishing party duly returned and secured, and with our tanks full of fuel, we were soon on our way, at speed, out another of the Dragon's Mouths, and headed easterly around the bulge of South America. These Dragon's Mouths, passages between islands into the Gulf of Paria, are quite picturesque, and the presidential party enjoyed them.

Two events which occurred during the passage to Rio de Janeiro were indicative of the current German interest in South American affairs. One was the early evening passage overhead of the *Graf Zeppelin*, en route home from Brazil. Messages were exchanged to and from the president. The other was a daylight meeting with a northbound German cruiser, which passed the *Indianapolis* with rail manned and guard paraded, and fired a twenty-one-gun salute with the stars and stripes at the fore. Usually a foreign salute is returned gun-for-gun, but in the case of a salute to a head of a nation, international custom requires that it be returned only when made by the head of another nation. Accordingly the salute was merely acknowledged with a polite message of thanks.

The crossing of the equator was observed on November 24 with the traditional ceremonies. On the previous day, it was my duty and pleasure, as the oldest and the senior "shellback," to order the senior "pollywog," the president of the United States, to set a lookout watch for King Neptune's emissary, Davey Jones. This he did, and his son James, his military aide, "Pa" Watson,[8] and others were duly posted, suitably attired in aviator's helmets and jackets, wearing boxing gloves, and using two inverted hose nozzles, lashed together, as binoculars. Shortly after sundown, "Davey's" hail was heard and answered, and the royal messenger boarded over the starboard chains. I was informed that the *Indianapolis* was entering his Majesty's realm, that we were to be ready to receive the King on the following morn with proper honors, and that all landlubbers, pollywogs, and similar low forms of life on board were to be prepared for arraignment before the Royal Tribunal. Davey then departed the way he had come.

King Neptune and his retinue, Queen Amphitrite, the Royal Judge and Prosecutor, the Royal Police, the Royal Barber, and the bulls and bears arrived as scheduled. With the ship "hove to," His Majesty was piped over the side with eight side boys and greeted by the captain, who turned the ship over to his command. When the Royal Flag was broken at the main truck, alongside that of the president, it was the first time, so far as I can determine, that those flags had ever been flown simultaneously from the same mast. The King and Queen mounted their thrones, the Judge took his seat on the bench, the Royal Police set about rounding up the pollywogs, and the bulls and the bears, and the Royal Barber prepared to carry out whatever sentences might be imposed.

On the previous day, while the Davey Jones lookout was being stood by the members of his party, the senior pollywog had been set to fishing from the boat deck into a bucket off the fo'c's'l deck. After much patience and several tugs on his line, he had succeeded in catching two fish, one labeled Maine and the other Vermont, the two states he had not succeeded in carrying earlier that month. Now, after viewing the preliminaries with much amusement, and at his own insistence, he was hailed before the Royal Judge. In spite of an eloquent defense, he was sentenced—sentenced to explain to the Royal Court just why he had failed to carry the above-mentioned states. This he did in an amusing speech that was carried over the ship's public announcement system. Then he resumed his chair on the boat deck to witness the proceedings.

It had been suggested to me privately that it might be well for me to use my good offices with the Royal Court to ensure that Mr. James Roosevelt be treated with similar dignity. But Mr. Roosevelt, when he learned of this, would have none of it. Consequently, when he was arraigned, he was sentenced to the Royal Works. This consisted of being properly shaved and lathered by the barber, being tripped into the pool, and there ducked by the bulls and bears, then seated in the stocks for a term, and finally being consigned to the brig on bread and water. A similar fate, although not always so hard, met most of the others.

Captain H. K. Hewitt's Crossing the Line certificate, November 24, 1936 (Naval Historical Collection)

Mr. Roosevelt, however, was released in time to join his father and others of his party with me for luncheon in the captain's cabin. As a memento, I have a page of my *Indianapolis* Guest Book, headed November 24, 1936, Latitude 0° 00′, Longitude 37° 00′ W, autographed by all present.

November 26 was Thanksgiving Day. The president kindly invited the executive officer, Commander Oscar Badger, and me to dine with him and the members of his party in the admiral's cabin. It was a most pleasant informal affair with the president at the head of the table, genially carving an enormous turkey.

Since we were due to enter the harbor of Rio de Janeiro early the next morning, I excused myself early in order to supervise the necessary preparations and to check the navigation carefully. The sea was a bit rough and the visibility not too good. We had left the Navy Yard all freshly painted and spic and span, but the paint must have been of poor quality, because a lot of it had washed off our bow, exposing large patches of the underlying red lead. This was no condition in which to make a state entrance to a foreign port. In an effort to remedy the situation, we had made enough speed to anchor for a few hours after daylight in the lee of an island in the approaches to Rio. Unfortunately, the lee was insufficient to prevent a considerable swell. The boats we put over the side would first be below the regular waterline, and, as they rode up, the painters would take a few ineffectual swipes with their brushes before the boats descended again. Staging over the side was of no use because of the flare of the bow.

So it was that we entered the beautiful harbor of Rio precisely on schedule at 8:00 a.m., with all hands at quarters and in full dress, but with the ship itself looking somewhat disreputable. As we passed in, leading the *Chester*, the Brazilian ensign was broken at the main simultaneously with the first gun of our twenty-one-gun national salutes. When these had been answered from the shore, every Brazilian man-of-war in the harbor opened up with a twenty-one-gun salute to our president, flying the Stars and Stripes at the fore, and bringing it down with the last gun.

As we proceeded slowly up the harbor toward the city, our ambassador, Mr. Hugh Gibson,[9] came off in a boat to meet us. We hove to and received him aboard with honors. I came off the bridge to greet him, and thereby hangs a slightly amusing tale, showing how the most carefully laid plans may sometimes "gang agley." We were to receive so many officials and with so many different types of honors that a detailed schedule of events was made out, mimeographed, and furnished to all concerned. The reception of the ambassador required eight side boys, the guard and band, and four ruffles and flourishes followed by the national anthem. The ruffles and flourishes went off all right, but then the band broke into something strange. Suddenly, I realized that what they were playing was the Brazilian anthem. I had to stop them and start them all over again on the "Star Spangled Banner." Mr. Gibson, who I discovered had a splendid sense of humor, wore a broad grin.

As the *Indianapolis* was warped alongside her dock, with the *Chester* astern of her, we were greeted by a massed band of Brazilian Marines, and another mass of enthusiastically cheering school children who sang the "Star Spangled Banner" for us in English, a courtesy which could hardly have been repaid in kind in our own country.

Our dock was in a park area immediately in front of the handsome building of the Touring Club do Brazil. As we ran out our special brow, the Brazilians decorated it on each side with potted palms, and at its end erected a graceful reception tent. Here President Vargas[10] received his honored guest with all due ceremony, both from the shore and from the ship.

The Brazilian navy kindly assigned me an English-speaking aide with whom, after the presidential party had been whisked off to a guest house and to an official luncheon, I went to pay my official respects to the commander in chief of the Brazilian navy and to the minister of marine. There was an atmosphere of great cordiality throughout.

Unfortunately, not many of our men could be given the opportunity to see much of the beautiful city of Rio. Many of them were engaged in a desperate effort to get the hull repainted so that it would give proper credit to our chief executive. But as many as possible were given short liberties. Some of the senior officers enjoyed a very pleasant luncheon given by the members of our naval mission.

In the afternoon, I had the privilege of hearing President Roosevelt address the Brazilian Congress, where he was tendered an enthusiastic ovation, receiving honors coming and going from an elite infantry regiment in colorful full dress uniforms.

In the evening, President Vargas gave a state dinner for our president at the beautiful Intermerarty Palace of the Brazilian foreign office. At the reception immediately preceding this affair, I received from the hands of President Vargas the award of the Order of the Southern Cross (*Cruzeiro do Sul*) with the rank of commander. Owing to our scheduled departure at 10:00 p.m., it was necessary to start the dinner at eight, an unheard of early hour for Rio. It was a magnificent affair, not only for the wines and the cuisine, but for the setting and the decorations. From where the presidents sat at the head table, one could look out onto a beautiful patio with swans gliding about a moonlit pool. On the tables were masses of orchids, and more orchids in sprays adorned the walls. In our full evening dress uniforms, Abbett and I sat almost directly opposite the two presidents and listened with interest to the toasts. President Roosevelt remained seated during the drinking of the toast to him. But in making his reply to President Vargas, he struggled to his feet. This involved latching his braces, pushing himself up onto them, hanging on to his high-backed chair while he worked himself around to its rear, and then having someone hand him his wine glass. This took an appreciable interval during which silence reigned. Knowing how sensitive he was about his affliction, one could appreciate what this cost him. But his remarks were splendid and much to the point.

After this, I was forced to make an unobtrusive departure as soon as possible in order to return to my ship, shift into full dress, and be prepared to receive the president and get under way promptly on his return. With a police escort, we drove through streets lined with troops holding back the large crowds waiting to say farewell.

For ordinary officials, honors are normally rendered by a man-of-war only between the hours of 8:00 a.m. and sundown. But the regulations do not make this distinction for a head of state. Therefore, when the president came aboard, the rail was manned, the guard and band paraded, and side tended. No salute was fired because we were alongside the dock. Tired though he must have been, the president went immediately to the boat deck to wave to the crowds on the dock and to witness the beautiful fireworks display from the old fort, for which we hove to in the middle of the harbor.

As the *Indianapolis* cleared the dock, Captain Bastedo,[11] the president's naval aide, reported to me in some consternation that the president's valet was missing. This was serious, because the president relied on him heavily. So the *Chester* was told to remain at the dock and take all necessary steps to find him. Everyone was much relieved, later, to receive a signal that the *Chester* had him on board and would transfer him to us at sea. It seems that this elderly and highly respectable colored gentleman, after seeing the president off to the state dinner, had walked out to see some of the sights before returning to the ship. Not being in uniform and knowing no Portuguese, he was unable to explain himself to the police and military cordon guarding the dock. It was there that emissaries of the U. S. naval mission, assisted by the Brazilian Secret Service, found him trying to battle his way in. When he reported to me on board the *Indianapolis*, he vowed he was never going ashore again.

The following day, November 28, a Saturday, was the day of the annual Army-Navy football game. Arrangements had been made to have a play-by-play account broadcast, and facilities were set up on the well deck, in the charge of an ex-Navy football star, to follow the situation. The weather was good, and all hands not on duty and the presidential party were in attendance. The Army team was a heavy favorite and was ahead in the score until the last few minutes of play when the Navy slipped over a touchdown and won the game. I have never seen anyone laugh so hard as the president as he ribbed "Pa" Watson, his military aide. Incidentally, that gentleman later had to go around the ship passing out bills to various naval officers (including the captain) whom he had inveighed into accepting bets through pride of service but with little hope of gain.

In the meantime, we had been exchanging messages with the commander of the Argentine *Escuadra de Mar,* to whom we gave our position, course, and speed. Early on the beautiful Sunday forenoon of the 29th, dead ahead, we sighted a cruiser flanked on each side by two destroyers at sufficient interval to form a scouting line. All hands were called to quarters, and the guard and band paraded in preparation to return expected honors.

Upon sighting us, the Argentine destroyers immediately closed in to form a column of two on each flank of the cruiser, which proved to be the new fine-looking *Almirante Brown*.[12] With her rail manned, her guard at present, and her band playing our national anthem, the *Brown* passed down our port side, and then, while firing a twenty-one-gun salute with our ensign at her fore, swung in smartly to take station astern of the *Chester*. Anyone familiar with the tactical handling of ships knows this to be a most difficult maneuver, particularly at high speed. It requires being at exactly the right distance abeam and putting the helm over at exactly the right moment. It was executed with precision, testifying to the smartness of the

Argentine navy—a smartness I had noted twenty-nine years earlier when an Argentine division had greeted the southbound battleship fleet of Admiral Evans. The destroyers, rendering similar honors, passed us on each side, then, turning outward, took stations on each bow as an escort.

Very shortly afterward, the main body of the *Escuadra de Mar* was sighted. This consisted of the battleships *Moreno*[13] and *Rivadavia*[14] (American built), another cruiser, and more destroyers. They passed us, rendering honors, but continued on a northerly course. Our escort, the *Almirante Brown* and destroyers remained with us.

The channel to Buenos Aires up the muddy Rio de la Plata being long, tortuous, and shallow, with depths subject to change not only with up-river rain or drought conditions but changes in wind direction, it had been originally contemplated that the *Indianapolis* would put into the port of Mar del Plata, the president completing his trip to the Argentine capital by rail. This plan met with objection from the Argentine government, which was extremely anxious to receive the president with ceremony, on his ship, directly at Buenos Aires. The problem was solved by having several of our destroyers, which were fitted to take the president, meet the *Indianapolis* off Montevideo and accompany her up river. Thus, if we grounded or sucked our condensers full of mud, the president would still be able to arrive on schedule. The *Chester* would be left at Montevideo.

In the middle of the night of November 29–30, we arrived off the lightship at the entrance to the narrow river channel, having previously detached the *Chester* and been joined by our two U.S. destroyers. Here we picked up our Argentine river pilot. The *Almirante Brown* and the Argentine destroyers took position ahead to lead us. I might mention that my Spanish stood me in good stead because most of the messages exchanged with the Argentine ship were in that language. But it was not so with our pilot, who insisted on using his extraordinary English for his directions to us. I feel sure that I could have more easily interpreted his orders to the helmsman had he used his native tongue.

It was all night on the bridge for the skipper, the navigator, and the pilot. Fortunately, conditions at the time were favorable, and although it looked at times as if we were ploughing through liquid mud, our condensers held up. In the forenoon we passed the Argentine River Squadron, anchored in a wider deep spot in the river. Being at anchor, they were full-dressed with signal flags from stem to stern. The usual honors were exchanged, after which we continued toward Buenos Aires.

Turning out of the main river channel into the still narrower channel to the harbor of Buenos Aires, we were taken in hand by two tugs, one ahead and one astern. This was necessitated by shallowness of the water and the scant maneuvering room. Also, we were met by a flotilla of innumerable gaily dressed pleasure craft, some under sail. Passing through the very narrow breakwater entrance, we were placed alongside a splendid dock profusely decorated with American and Argentine flags.

Here, a fine looking battalion of Argentine naval cadets with its band rendered honors, and President Justo[15] waited to welcome President Roosevelt.

After the usual ceremonies, the two presidents were driven off with a splendidly uniformed and mounted escort through the broad streets of the beautiful city lined with soldiery (in German-type uniforms) to hold back the tremendous crowds. It was another magnificent reception. From then on, the president's time was fully taken up with luncheons, dinners, and other festivities, as was, in a lesser manner, that of his entourage and the officers of the ships. Both nights that we were there, Buenos Aires never seemed to sleep, and there were crowds on the dock looking at the ship from dusk until dawn.

Many were the courtesies offered to me personally by the Argentine navy. With my Argentine aide, a very pleasant young *Capitán de Corbeta* (lieutenant commander), I, of course, made my formal calls on the minister of marine and the commander in chief of the Navy. Later, I was very pleasantly entertained at the Naval Club, where I met informally most of the senior naval officers in Buenos Aires. A most unusual courtesy was the offer of a telephone call to my wife in Long Beach, California. They called her the night before to ensure that she would be on hand to receive my call, then put the call through the following morning at a pre-arranged time. I talked to her from my desk in my cabin, and it was as clear as if she were in the next room. Though brief, it was the longest telephone call I have ever made, or probably ever shall.

December 1 was the opening day of the Pan-American Conference for which the president had come, and he made one of his usual excellent speeches, which I am sure did much to promote Pan-American solidarity and friendship for his own country. In the evening, there was a splendid state reception and dinner which I, again, had the privilege of attending. In addition to the two presidents and the highest Argentine officials of state and church, there were present the delegates to the conference and the entire diplomatic corps of Buenos Aires, many with their families.

The Latin Americans seem always to take it as a compliment when their English-speaking neighbors to the north attempt to speak their language, even though poorly. Knowing this, I interjected a remark in Spanish during a conversation with two Argentine ladies who spoke perfect English. Immediately their faces lighted up, and one exclaimed "Oh! *El Capitán habla Español.*" Then they launched into a torrent of Spanish in which I completely foundered.

I failed to mention that on the 30th, our first night in port, the officers of our navy were given a very hospitable reception at the American Club by the large American colony in Buenos Aires. This was followed by a late dinner given by members of our naval mission (all dinners in Buenos Aires are late). They were both most enjoyable, but I must say that, having had no sleep the previous night, I was very glad to climb into my bunk about 2:00 a.m. for a few hours rest.

We were scheduled to depart shortly for Montevideo, after noon on the 2nd, so that the worst part of the river channel could be navigated during daylight. In spite of a rather heavy rain, the president was still hailed enthusiastically by dense crowds upon the occasion of his return to the ship. And as we drew away from the dock and headed out of the harbor, we were again escorted by many pleasure craft.

An event had occurred the previous evening which had saddened the president. The well-known elderly secret service man, Gus Gennerich, who was an almost constant companion and who usually slept within call, succumbed to a heart attack. His remains were brought aboard in the morning, with instructions that they were to be treated with due respect, but that they were to be kept where they would not serve as an unnecessary reminder to the president. They were placed in an out-of-the-way spot in one of the aircraft hangars.

Shortly after midnight, after dropping our pilot, we anchored near the entrance lightship, in the broader reaches of the La Plata, in order to get a few hours of needed rest prior to getting underway for our ceremonial entrance to Montevideo, which was scheduled for 10:00 a.m. on December 3.

Captain H. K. Hewitt bidding farewell to President Franklin D. Roosevelt after his successful South American visit aboard USS Indianapolis (CA-35), December 1936. (Naval Historical Collection)

Montevideo extended to our president another tumultuous welcome. A large area adjacent to our dock was kept clear of the crowds by a cordon of police and troops, and at the foot of the quarterdeck brow was another reception pavilion decorated with Uruguayan and U.S. flags. Here President Roosevelt was greeted by President Terra[16] and driven off to the Presidential Palace, escorted by a squadron of lancers in dress uniforms mounted on beautiful black horses.

At the very pleasant state luncheon given by President and Señora Terra, the president made another of his well-received addresses. Before the luncheon, with my Uruguayan aide, I had an opportunity to see the principal sights of Montevideo and a nearby *playa*.

Later in the afternoon, after the president had returned to the ship for our departure, the crowd was allowed through the lines and down on the dock, which soon became black with humanity. The pressure from those in the rear, struggling to get a closer view, was so great that we were fearful that many of those in front would be pushed right over the edge of the dock. In fact, there really was great danger of it, but, fortunately, nothing happened. We left the dock amidst cheers and the playing of bands, and headed out right past the spot where only three years later the *Graf Spee*[17] was to meet her end.

During our few hours in Montevideo, we had taken on a full load of fuel and were now prepared for a fast run back to Trinidad. No oil was taken in Buenos Aires in order to keep our draft at a minimum for the trip down river. No stop was made on the way north, except for a few hours in the open sea off Cabo Frio in Brazil to permit a little fishing by our distinguished passenger.

Our visit to Trinidad this time was official, and all the usual formalities were observed. Due to the shallowness of the water, we could go alongside no dock. Instead, we anchored as close to Port of Spain as possible, and a small island steamer came alongside to transport the president to the landing for his official welcome and a luncheon at Government House by the governor general. Prior to that, we received a call from the commanding officer of the French cruiser *Jeanne d' Arc*,[18] which I was to see more of in later years. She was in port on a cruise with midshipmen from the French Naval Academy.

The date was December 11, 1936, only a day or two after we had received the news of the abdication of King Edward VIII. Therefore, when at the governor's luncheon the president rose to propose the toast to the king, we probably participated in the first official toast to King George VI by the head of another nation. This luncheon was a very pleasant affair. My partner to my left was the wife of the chief justice of the island, who told me how particularly interested she was to meet the president, since her father had known his father. I sensed that she referred to Theodore Roosevelt, which proved to be the case, so I had to straighten her out on the relationship—family and political.

At dusk we passed out the Dragon's Mouth once more, completely fuelled, and bound for home via the Mona Passage between the islands of Hispaniola and Puerto Rico. The president had expressed a desire, however, to go fishing at early dawn off Aves Island, a small uninhabited island some miles to the eastward of our direct route. This presented a bit of a problem, since the island was only about three-quarters of a mile long with a maximum elevation of some twelve feet, and it had to be reached at first light. To cover the distance in time required about twenty-five knots, and the strength of the crosscurrents to be encountered could not be accurately predicted. It would be easy to miss the island altogether or, more unfortunately, to ground on an outlying shoal.

I discussed the matter with my senior aviator, Lieutenant Commander Cleaves.[19] We could use only our starboard catapult, since the one on the portside was blocked by the presidential elevator. And we had never launched planes in complete darkness when the pilots had no horizon to guide them on takeoff. But Cleaves assured me that if we would give him a horizontal beam with our starboard signal searchlight, he would be all right. So at 4:00 a.m. we successfully launched Mr. Cleaves, who, proceeding ahead, found the island and led us to it. At first light, we hove to off the island and got out our motor whaleboat with the president in it. He had a most successful morning.

The remainder of the voyage was successfully completed without event, and the *Indianapolis* and *Chester* arrived at Charleston at dawn of the 15th of December as scheduled. The president and his party were disembarked with all honors at 8:00 a.m. He gave us a "Well Done" and wished us Merry Christmas. Then began furious preparations for our speedy return to our base in California, fuelling, provisioning, dismantling and landing the president's elevator and other special facilities, and, last, taking aboard the Christmas trees which had been ordered in advance of our arrival. Naval appropriations at that time being at low ebb, cruisers were under orders to restrict their speed in ordinary circumstances to fifteen knots in order to economize fuel. With no president aboard, this would apply, making it impossible to reach our home port by Christmas, from which we had been absent for nearly eight months. Someone must have whispered this to the president, because, without any mention of it by me, he had sent a dispatch to the Secretary of the Navy saying that he hoped that the *Indianapolis* and *Chester* would be authorized to make sufficient speed to reach their home ports by Christmas. Naturally, this was granted. The effect on the morale of officers and men may well be imagined.

All hands worked so fast that we were able to leave our dock at 10:00 a.m. after only two hours alongside. Out we went, at speed, into the teeth of a gale and into low visibility. But this time, the senior officer present in *Indianapolis* had to shoulder the responsibility of leading. As we went south, the weather improved, and we were able to make Colon in time for the first daylight transit of the Canal on December 18. Safely through, we headed along the coast and finally north to our

Letter of appreciation from President Franklin D. Roosevelt to Captain H. K. Hewitt on the conclusion of the cruise to South America in USS Indianapolis, 1936 (Naval Historical Collection)

destination. The only time we slowed down, and that temporarily, was when an unexpected Tehuantepecker sea came aboard our well deck, bashed in the starboard hangar curtain and damaged one of our planes. A Tehuantepecker is a sudden storm which sometimes arises off the Gulf of Tehuantepec as a result of a norther in the Gulf of Mexico across the isthmus.

We dropped anchor in the harbor of San Pedro before eight on the morning of December 24. As the anchor went down, up went our Christmas trees to the mastheads, following the motions of the others already in port. So ended a memorable cruise in which two ships had covered about 18,000 miles in thirty-six days, an average of 500 miles per day, including stops.

NOTES

1 USS *Indianapolis* (CA-35). Commissioned in 1932, she was used by President Franklin D. Roosevelt several times prior to the 1936 cruise to South America. The ship was sunk by Japanese torpedoes on May 30, 1945 on the way to Leyte, PI.

2 Arthur J. Hepburn (1877–1964). Admiral. U.S. Naval Academy, Class of 1897.

3 Pan-American Conference, Buenos Aires, Argentina, 1936. President Roosevelt's opening speech pledged solidarity and cooperation among Western hemisphere nations in the face of war.

4 Oscar C. Badger (1890–1958). Admiral. U.S. Naval Academy, Class of 1911.

5 USS *Chester* (CA-27). Commissioned in 1930, she escorted the *Indianapolis* with President Roosevelt aboard to the Pan-American Conference.

6 Harry J. Abbett (1884–1972). Captain. U.S. Naval Academy, Class of 1907.

7 James Roosevelt (1907–1991) went to the Pan-American Conference at Buenos Aires as his father's aide, holding the rank of lieutenant colonel, USMC. Public outcry caused him to resign his rank, but he continued as a member of the White House staff.

8 Edwin M. Watson (1883–1945). U.S. Military Academy, Class of 1908. Major General, U.S. Army; military aide to President Franklin D. Roosevelt, 1933–1941. In 1939, he was named appointments secretary to President Roosevelt.

9 Hugh Gibson (1883–1954). Foreign Service Officer and ambassador to Brazil, 1933–1937.

10 Getúlio Vargas (1882–1954). President of Brazil, 1930–1945, 1950–1954.

11 Paul H. Bastedo (1887–1951). Rear Admiral. U.S. Naval Academy, Class of 1908.

12 *Almirante Brown* (Cruiser) 1929. Displacement 6,800 tons; Length 533 1/4'; Beam 58'; Draught, 16 1/4'.

13 *Moreno* (Battleship) 1911. Displacement 27,940 tons; Length 577 1/2'; Beam 95'; Draught, 28'.

14 *Rivadavia* (Battleship) 1911. Displacement 27,940 tons; Length 577 1/2'; Beam 95'; Draught, 28'.

15 José A. P. Justo (1876–1943). General and president of Argentina, 1932–1938.

16 Gabriel Terra (1872–1942). President of Uruguay, 1931–1938.

17 *Graf Spee*. 10,000-ton German pocket battleship launched in 1936.

18 *Jeanne d' Arc.* (Training cruiser) 1930. 6,496 tons; Length 525'; Beam 57 1/2'; Draught 17 3/4'.

19 Willis E. Cleaves (1902–1964). Rear Admiral. U.S. Naval Academy, Class of 1924.

Rear Admiral H.K. Hewitt, Commander, Cruiser Division 8, in USS Philadelphia *(CL-41), October 1940.*
(Naval Historical Collection)

X *Pre–World War II Assignments, 1937–1940*

After the Christmas–New Year holiday season at our homeport, which all hands naturally enjoyed to the utmost after their long absence, the *Indianapolis* resumed the flag of the Commander, Scouting Force, by now Vice Admiral W. T. Tarrant.[1] We were soon again engaged in the normal fleet routine of target practices and maneuvers. This year joint exercises were held once more in the Hawaii area. I enjoyed them to the utmost, particularly as my time on the *Indianapolis* was, regrettably, approaching its end.

The number of captains to be given experience in command and the number of large combatant ships available to accommodate them was such that no one could hope to retain command for more than eighteen months. For me, this period would end in mid-September 1937. In the meanwhile, however, Vice Admiral J. K. Taussig,[2] the prospective Commander, Cruisers, Scouting Force, had done me the honor to ask me to be his chief of staff when he assumed his new command in June. This would curtail my *Indianapolis* cruise by three months, but would be the most interesting duty and, in addition, would give me at least another year at sea. I was happy to accept.

Nevertheless, it was with a feeling of great nostalgia that I put my ship alongside the tanker in San Pedro harbor for the last time and handed my binoculars over to the chief quartermaster. Not only was I leaving a wonderful ship and ship's company, but I realized full well that I would never be handling a ship again. Before another tour of sea duty became due, I would either be a passed-over captain slated for retirement or a flag officer.

The sadness I felt at turning over my ship to another, even a good friend and fine officer like Captain Thomas C. Kinkaid,[3] was nothing like my grief when eight years later I learned of her sinking by Japanese submarine torpedoes, with the loss of her many officers and crew. I felt exactly as if I had lost a dear relative or close friend. One of my treasures is a watercolor of the ship by the famous marine artist Arthur Beaumont, given to me by my ship's company on the occasion of my detachment.

On June 7, immediately on leaving the *Indianapolis,* I reported to Admiral Taussig on the *Chicago*[4] and assumed my new duties as his chief of staff. There could be no finer man to work with, and I shall always remember not only the fine experience that my service with him gave me but his many kindnesses and the things he did to further my career. The Cruisers, Scouting Force comprised all the heavy (8-inch) cruisers in the active fleet, and most of them at that time were commanded by classmates and good friends of mine, all of which made for pleasant relations. I know it was a happy command from the admiral down.

Tactically, the heavy cruisers were organized in four divisions of four cruisers each. While Admiral Taussig was the commander of all four divisions, he also personally commanded one division. When handling two or more divisions as a group, instead of trying to do two jobs at once, he always turned over the direction of his own division to me. This was splendid training for one who hoped that some day he might have a similar division of his own.

In the spring of 1938, fleet maneuvers were once more held in the Hawaii area. They included a series of tactical exercises in which senior flag officers rotated in command of opposing task forces. The task force that Admiral Taussig commanded won a rousing victory by taking prompt and decisive action at the very beginning of the problem, an action which a simple study showed was the only practical way of ensuring accomplishment of the assigned mission. The details were worked out by me with the assistance of the operations officer. But it was Admiral Taussig, of course, who approved the solution and made the decision to carry it out. However, as I learned some years later, when Admiral E. J. King[5] congratulated Admiral Taussig on the result, he took no credit for himself, but assigned it to me. It was like him. I have thought since that, possibly, this may have had some bearing on the confidence Admiral King as CINC, U.S. Fleet and Chief of Naval Operations later showed in me, with its consequent effect on my subsequent career. It is one of the many debts I owe to my old "Chief," who made such a wonderful reputation in World War I and who would have liked so much to have been young enough to serve afloat in World War II.

July 1938 and detachment to shore duty came along all too soon, though I was happy at the thought of having a period when I could see more of my family. The president of the War College, Admiral Charles Snyder,[6] had kindly invited me to serve on his staff, a duty I should have enjoyed very much had it involved assignment to government quarters. Unfortunately it did not. Government quarters in those days were a great financial advantage to captains, a matter of importance with children at college and boarding school. Consequently, I was happy to receive instead orders as Inspector of Ordnance in charge of the Naval Ammunition Depot, Puget Sound, which was situated on an arm of the Sound, about five miles from the Navy Yard at Bremerton. This depot, with that at Mare Island, was an ammunition-issuing and overhaul point for the Pacific Fleet and was the depository for at least half of its reserve ammunition. It was on a beautiful site and included some thousand acres of land, a large part of which was forested with a good growth of

Douglas fir. The inspector had a very comfortable house, with a beautiful lawn sloping toward the water, a large garden in the rear, both floral and vegetable, a fruit orchard, and an efficient gardener to care for them. From the personal point of view, it could not have been more delightful, and I found the duty, when I got into it, both important and highly interesting.

On the personal side, one of the first things we did after my arrival in Bremerton was to stage a beautiful outdoor wedding on my lawn for our daughter, Floride, to the then Lieutenant LeRoy Taylor.[7] Her sister, Mary Kent, soon to attend Annie Wright Seminary in Tacoma, was the maid of honor. They were married by the Navy Yard Episcopal chaplain at an altar backed by greens in a Gothic arch and a background of Douglas firs. It was a beautiful as well as a happy occasion.

On the official side, I was soon engrossed in acquainting myself with the operations of the depot and with all its facilities, including the amount and type of ammunition on hand and the means of handling it and delivering it to the fleet. In familiarizing myself with the lay of the land, I was greatly aided by finding that the Marine guard had four riding horses for the ostensible purpose of providing for a mounted patrol. On horseback, I was not only able to get healthful exercise but to visit almost every part of my extensive realm daily.

All transportation for ammunition in and out of this depot was via water—barges being brought in through a narrow but deep water passage from Puget Sound near the Navy Yard and placed alongside our lone dock. This dock was connected with the various magazines and shops by a local depot gauge railroad, the motive power for which was provided by a single storage battery locomotive which, at the end of an eight-hour work day, had to be recharged for some ten to twelve hours before again being available. The magazines themselves were located singly in forest clearings over a large area, a situation which lent itself very well to confining an accidental explosion to one magazine but made them excellent targets for attack from the air. There was no underground storage. In other words, nothing had been done to meet the conditions of a modern war, which even then threatened.

The depot personnel consisted of one lieutenant commander as executive officer, one chief gunner, a small Marine guard headed by a captain, a chief pharmacist's mate, and an efficient, loyal, and stable civilian work force, large enough to handle routine operations. This was augmented somewhat later after the outbreak of the war in Europe in September 1939.

Everything worked smoothly, according to routine, but a little too much so, I found. For instance, it was customary to hold the weekly fire drill on Fridays at 11:30 a.m. As a result, everyone began to knock off work and stand by just before that time. This being no measure of effectiveness in an emergency, I changed this procedure to having drills at unexpected times, both day and night, and got the Bremerton fire chief to give special instruction to our Marine guard, who were responsible for manning our pumper and were practically the only personnel available outside working hours. Often, instead of telephoning in an alarm, the drill was started by setting off a smoke pot in a safe place to see what would happen. Once the executive officer and I, at night in damp weather, set fire to an abandoned shack in a clearing. The response was most gratifying.

Once familiar with the workings of the depot, I began to interest myself in our war plans—the amount and kind of ammunition we were supposed to be able to deliver to ships on each day after mobilization had been declared. Analysis soon showed that we had neither the ammunition on hand nor the facilities for timely assembly and delivery to come anywhere near meeting our commitments. The situation was so very bad that I made an urgent top secret report to the Bureau of Ordnance. To this and our other demands for more rolling stock and other needed equipment, the only response, until the war in Europe broke out in 1939, was "disapproved due to lack of funds."

Next, I tried to find out what plans there were, if any, for the defense of the depot in the event of hostilities. Well, little did I know from our own fleet exercises how vulnerable we would be to a fast carrier raid. And I have already mentioned what perfect targets our magazines were from the air. Anti-aircraft defense was, of course, an Army function. The staff of the naval district knew nothing about it and referred me to the commander of the Coast Artillery District, who in turn sent me to Corps Area Headquarters at Fort Lewis. There, with the assistance of Lieutenant Colonel Mark Clark,[8] I finally dug up a plan by which a National Guard anti-aircraft battalion from somewhere in the Mid-West, arriving on or about M+20, was assigned to defend the Bremerton Navy Yard and supposedly the ammunition and torpedo depots as well. A lot of help that would have been if the Japs had, just a few years later, decided to come further east!

My association with Army authorities at Fort Lewis led to what was to me an interesting and instructive experience. I was invited to be present with the Regular Army Third Division during a two or three-day field maneuver. Accompanying the headquarters of the general who was commanding one of the sides, I was surprised to learn how similar in many ways was the broad conduct of naval operations and Army field operations. Many of the problems, the exercises of initiative by subordinates, the constant need for intelligence of the enemy, and communication difficulties were the same. The principal difference was that things happened much more rapidly at sea than on land.

An interesting sidelight is that my Fort Lewis acquaintance, Colonel Clark, was next encountered, unexpectedly, with General Eisenhower[9] at a combined operations exercise in Britain in June 1942, when I was visiting Vice Admiral Lord Louis Mountbatten.[10] He was then a brigadier general. In 1943, I was landing his Fifth Army at Salerno. And the Third Division, whose maneuvers I had witnessed, was to be landed by forces under my command four times during operations in the Mediterranean Theater.

Owing to the size of the ammunition depot, entry to which was prevented only by several miles of high, steel fence tipped with barbed wire, sentries at two gates, and a weak roving patrol, a destructive raid by a small band of organized saboteurs would have been relatively easy. In view of the threatening situation that existed, particularly after September 1939, I felt that this possibility should not be overlooked. Accordingly, we staged several very realistic exercises in which Marines from the Navy Yard were rushed by truck to the reinforcement of the small depot guard (the second in command of the Navy Yard guard happened to have been my Marine officer on the *Indianapolis*). The results of these exercises served to strengthen my plea for the strengthening of the depot guard, a plea which was, somewhat later, granted in part.

An event important to me occurred in December 1939. The annual board for the selection of flag officers met, and when the list was published, my name was among the fortunate ones. Two others, similarly affected, were then present in Bremerton in command of battleships. Both joined me at the depot in a mild celebration. They were I. C. Kidd[11] who, unfortunately, was to lose his life on the *Arizona* less than two years later, and my old friend and classmate, Raymond Spruance,[12] who was to win fame in the Pacific.

There was one more special event at the ammunition depot which I believe is worth recording for its historical interest. It will be remembered that under the Lend-Lease Act, the president had been authorized to transfer or sell to Great Britain and her allies surplus arms and munitions no longer required for our own defense. One Friday night in 1940, shortly after the debacle of Dunkirk, I received a high priority secret dispatch declaring certain categories of small arms ammunition in our stores to be obsolete and directing immediate shipment of several million rounds by fast freight to the Overseas Trading Corporation in New York, not later than the following Sunday afternoon. At the same time, the naval district informed me that barges with the necessary empty freight cars would be delivered to the depot dock the following morning.

Since the depot was on a five-day week, not working on Saturdays, I had to call in our civilian personnel on an emergency overtime basis. In they came and turned-to with a will. They knew perfectly well where it was going. By the dint of almost superhuman efforts, using commandeered trucks as well as our lone storage battery locomotive, we got it all loaded and away by midnight Saturday. It was almost our entire reserve supply of machine gun and small arms ammunition for the Pacific Fleet. Years later, I learned from the British army officer who, subsequent to Dunkirk, commanded an important defense sector on the south coast, that his forces were desperate for ammunition, being down to some seventy-five rounds per man.

My promotion to rear admiral was supposed to wait until a vacancy occurred on the regular Navy list. This was not expected until some time in 1941, at least. However, shortly after the aforementioned small arms ammunition shipment, I found myself under orders to report to the Canal Zone about August 1 as the relief of Rear Admiral J. W. Wilcox[13] in command of the Special Service Squadron and, upon assuming command, to hoist my flag as a temporary rear admiral. I was to be relieved as Inspector of Ordnance in charge of the Ammunition Depot by Captain J. W. Rankin.[14]

It was exciting, of course, to go to one's first flag command, but I left Bremerton with great regret, a regret which was heightened by the farewell garden party at the depot given me by the civilian employees, all of whom attended with their families. It was a spontaneous and heart-warming exhibition of real friendship that I shall never forget.

My widowed mother had come west in 1938 to be present at her elder granddaughter's wedding, but after a short visit had returned to her home in New Jersey. In order to see her again, it was natural that I should proceed to Panama via New York, which we did. But thereby arose another personal problem of the sort that is all too common incident to a naval career. Our younger daughter had just graduated from Annie Wright Seminary in Tacoma and was destined for college. Because I had thought it probable that my next sea duty would be with the Pacific Fleet, we had applied to Scripps College for her. She had been accepted and her matriculation fee had been paid. We contemplated no change, in spite of going to Panama, because her sister, then living in San Diego, could look out for her. While in Hackensack, just two weeks before sailing to Panama, we received a telegram that my son-in-law had just had orders which would take him to Brooklyn in the fall, thereby leaving Mary Kent on the West Coast with no close relative nearby. Fortunately, her papers had also been submitted to Connecticut College in New London. I immediately got in touch with their committee on admissions and explained the situation. Not only did they graciously accept my daughter, although their list had been made up, but Scripps, equally graciously, refunded the admission fee. Mary Kent arrived east to be with her grandmother just in time to see her parents off by United Fruit liner to Panama.

The irony of it was, as will be seen, that by December, my wife and I were back in California. However, everything worked out for the best in the long run.

With a month's leave, plus travel time from Bremerton to Panama available, we journeyed via San Francisco and Hackensack to see my mother and thence sailed from New York in late July on a United Fruit liner. Here my previous association with the United Fruit Company in Preston and Banes on the *Eagle* during the revolution of 1917 paid off. When some of my old friends, now in responsible positions at the United Fruit main office in Boston heard the news, they not only arranged to have me seen off by officials in New York, but to have me moved from the stateroom provided by the Navy to an upper-deck suite with a parlor, bedroom, and bath. So we had a pleasant and luxurious voyage to Cristobal, the first sea trip I had ever made with my wife, and the first one in which I did not have in some manner to work my way.

Met on landing by a naval representative, we were soon on our way across the Isthmus via Panama Railroad to the city of Panama. There we took up temporary quarters in the famous Tivoli Hotel, just inside the Canal Zone.

On the very next day, August 3, I had the pleasure of putting on rear admiral's shoulder marks for the first time, of breaking my flag on the USS *Erie*,[15] moored at Balboa, and of receiving my first salute, thirteen guns. My new command, the Special Service Squadron, was a small unit composed of the gunboats *Erie* and *Charleston*[16] (which was absent under overhaul) and a few old World War I four-stack destroyers. Its primary duty was that of showing the flag, cultivating friendly relations, and protecting American interests in the Caribbean and Central American area and on the West Coast of South America. We belonged to no fleet but operated directly under the Chief of Naval Operations. Since much of our work would be diplomatic, I had been advised to provide myself with a complete set of flag officer's full dress uniforms (at a cost equal, it must be said, to one year's difference in pay between captain and rear admiral).

My first few days were taken up with official calls, first on Rear Admiral Sadler,[17] Commandant of the Naval District, and then on Colonel Edgerton, Governor of the Canal Zone, Lieutenant General Daniel Van Voorhis,[18] Commanding General of the Canal Zone, and Major General Jarman[19] of the Coast Artillery, Commander of the Panama Canal Defenses. Those completed, I was taken under the wing of our minister to Panama, Mr. William Dawson,[20] and made calls on the president of Panama and most of the diplomatic corps, carefully omitting the German and Italian ministers. In the meantime, also, we were busy moving into the quarters on Quarry Heights, ANCON, vacated by my predecessor.

At that time, with the war going on in Europe and the threatening situation in the Pacific, the defense of the Canal was receiving considerable attention. A glance at a chart quickly reveals the strategic location of the Galápagos Islands in this connection as an outlying base for air, submarine, and surface patrol operations. (Equally true for radar, of which little was known at that time.) Accordingly, arrangements had been made with the friendly Ecuadorian government for a joint Ecuadorian-American reconnaissance of these highly interesting islands by the Commander Special Service Force and a party of senior Ecuadorian military and naval officers who were to take passage in my flagship. Thus, on August 9, I departed from Balboa for Guayaquil with the *Erie* and destroyer *Tattnall*,[21] arriving the 11th. Ecuador being well named, we barely crossed the line in doing so, but the pollywogs in the detachment were duly initiated.

The trip up the fairly deep river to Guayaquil was interesting, with the strong flowing current carrying down branches of trees and other objects apparently washed from the shores. Anchoring off the city close in to the shore was easy, as the ship never swung. At Guayaquil, we were met by those who where to accompany us to the Galápagos and shown the utmost courtesy. We saw all there was to see of that thriving city, the metropolis and principal port of Ecuador.

On our short run to the Galápagos, we had the chance to become thoroughly acquainted with our guests and to establish a most cordial relationship. The senior of these, the chief of staff of the Ecuadorian army, Colonel Urrutia, was a splendid officer of Indian extraction who had undergone training with the Italian cavalry. In addition to Spanish, he spoke Italian fluently, but little or no English. Here again my slight knowledge of Spanish came in handy, and we apparently got on famously.

So much has been written about these remarkable islands and their flora and fauna that it would be out of place for me to attempt to describe them. Suffice it to say that they fully lived up to expectations and that our visit there was one of the most interesting experiences I have had. The Spanish name for them is El Archipiélago de Colón (The Archipelago of Columbus), but they were named Galápagos by American whalers after the giant turtles of that name which they caught and loaded there to serve as fresh meat on their way to and from the Bering Sea. These same whalers, outgoing, left mail there in a barrel in what became known as Post Office Bay, to be picked up and ultimately delivered by homeward-bound vessels. We visited Post Office Bay and found a mail barrel still there, but no mail in it. Charles Darwin,[22] who visited these islands, made them famous in his writings, and one small islet is named for him.

Returning to Guayaquil, we received orders to attend the inauguration of a new president, Señor Arroyo de Rio,[23] at Quito, and to assist Mr. Dawson, our minister at Panama, who had been named as special ambassador to represent the United States. I shall never forget our trip up to that beautiful and interesting capital, high in the Andes, with a few of the senior officers and my band. It was made in a special self-propelled car and took all day, from early morning until after dark, and with a two-hour stop in Riobamba, half-way up, for a sumptuous repast (*almuerzo*) given by the military commander of that district. We had been warned by our medical officer that to avoid mountain sickness in the unaccustomed high altitude, we should be sparing of exercise, food, and drink. On this occasion, the last two were rather hard to observe, considering the bountiful delicious food, the many toasts requiring response, and the diplomatic necessity of showing appreciation for the hospitality. However, no ill effects were felt and all arrived in good form to be most comfortable in Quito's best hotel, the Metropolitano, right on the beautiful and picturesque central plaza. The views en route were simply indescribable, including a close look at snow-capped Chimborazo.

The ceremonies and festivities incident to the inauguration lasted about three days, and I believe I attended all of them. Besides the inaugural ceremony itself, there were many parades, balls, and receptions. At one of these I received the Order of Abdon Calderón at the hands of the minister of defense, Señor Galo Plaza.[24] I remember that during the inaugural parade for which I occupied an open car, I had to remain with my hand at salute the whole time, for we no sooner passed one band playing their national anthem than we came to another doing the same thing.

Between official functions, I found time to see something of the city and its environs and to do a little shopping. The Ecuadorian Indians are skillful silversmiths, and one of my purchases was a little hand-wrought group of a laden llama, followed by his master playing some sort of a musical instrument and by the wife bearing a water jar on her back and knitting as she walked along. I had seen the real thing repeatedly on the country roads outside the city during my two horseback rides with my friend Colonel Urrutia.

Returning to Guayaquil, we were soon back in Balboa with many pleasant memories. There was another incident connected with this trip, however, that is worth recording. It became necessary to refuel the destroyer *Tattnall* at a Peruvian port on the Gulf of Guayaquil. We duly radioed Lima and received the necessary permission. When I next saw the skipper of the *Tattnall*, he was openmouthed. He had had the "red carpet" rolled out for him. It seemed that my old Peruvian friend of the *Missouri* and Around-the-World Cruise days, Carlos Rotalde, now a vice admiral and Peruvian minister of marine, had thought that I was coming in. Thus, nothing was too good for the *Tattnall*. I had hoped to go to Callao later and renew our old acquaintance, but it was not to be.

In view of what happened at Pearl Harbor a little over a year later, I particularly want to give the account of a day I had spent with General Jarman, at his invitation, after my return to the Canal Zone. After inspecting the fixed defense of the fortified islands on the Pacific side, he took me into the jungle, where his troops had mounted anti-aircraft batteries on hilltop sites in clearings hacked out by themselves, with searchlights and all necessary communications. The crews were living in tents under mosquito net, maintaining a twenty-four-hour watch, and slowly building their own barracks with matériel prepared and trucked out from the main Army ports. All was ready for action at a moment's notice. How different over a year later at the much more exposed Hawaii, where anti-aircraft artillery was parked at Schofield Barracks, ammunition was still stored in caves, and projected battery positions had hardly been more than plotted on paper. So far as I know, this difference was never brought to official attention.

I had planned visits to ports in Central America and in Colombia and Venezuela as well as Peru, but this was not to be. Shortly after attending another inauguration, that of a new (and controversial) president of Panama, orders came to disband the Special Service Squadron as such, transferring most of its ships to the Commander, Fifteenth Naval District (Panama), and ordering me to the command of Cruiser Division Eight, attached to the Pacific Fleet. So, after less than three months in the Canal Zone, we found ourselves once more en route to the West Coast by steamer to Los Angeles. We had to sell our newly purchased tropical furniture and our electric refrigerator, which had been modified to the cycles required for Panama. Such is the Navy. However, I must say that the transfer to the command of the division of fine new 6-inch cruisers was highly pleasing to me.

My new flagship, the *Philadelphia*,[25] was awaiting me off San Pedro. There, in early November, I relieved Rear Admiral Forde A. Todd,[26] who, when I was head of the department of mathematics, had been commandant of midshipmen at the Naval Academy. The remainder of my cruisers, the *Brooklyn*,[27] the *Savannah*,[28] and the *Nashville*[29] were in Hawaii with the fleet.

Since the *Philadelphia* was due for some alterations at the Navy Yard, Mare Island, we proceeded there at once. The work involved the installation of additional anti-aircraft guns and ready anti-aircraft ammunition stowage and other items to improve our war readiness. While there, we received orders to "clear ship for action," which required stripping the ship of all non-essentials and reducing the flammables on board to a minimum. All uniforms, with the exception of service uniforms, were to be landed. So, into mothballs went all my new, expensive full dress uniforms, and there they have remained ever since. Note that all this was one year before the Japanese attack on Pearl Harbor.

Our work was completed in time for the *Philadelphia* to join the fleet in Hawaii shortly before Christmas. My wife, who had come out on the Matson Line, and I spent a very pleasant Christmas in the famous old Halekulani Hotel "on the beach at Waikiki."

I was glad to see the other ships of my division and their captains, all of whom I knew well. Besides Vance Chaplaine[30] in the *Philadelphia*, they were W. W. Smith[31] in the *Brooklyn*, A. C. Bennett[32] in the *Savannah*, and R. S. Wentworth[33] in the *Nashville*. My immediate "Chief" was Rear Admiral Husband E. Kimmel,[34] Commander, Cruisers, Battle Force, and the Fleet Commander in Chief was Admiral "Joe" Richardson.[35]

We were soon hard at work carrying out an intensive schedule of training under simulated war conditions. All ships were kept at a maximum state of readiness and full up with fuel, provisions, and other necessary supplies. No large ships ever put to sea without an anti-submarine escort of destroyers, and ships ran darkened at night and never anchored outside of Pearl Harbor, the only harbor in the area not open to submarine torpedo attack.

I am glad to be able to testify here that no one could have been more indefatigable than Admiral Kimmel in getting his cruisers ready to face what all felt sure was coming. We never knew what he was going to spring on us next. He was liable to come suddenly on board any ship of his command and hold any emergency of casualty drill that came into his head. For instance, with the ship at battle stations (general quarters), he might have one of his aides pull the power switch to a turret and see how long it took to get it operating again with jury-rigged connections. One time in particular, with my ships moored alongside each other in a nest, he directed me to sound "general quarters" and then watched to see how long it took to get up 100 rounds to each gun. These light cruisers had fifteen 6-inch guns as a main battery, mounted in five triple turrets. I called his attention to the regulation that only dummy or target practice ammunition, and not service ammunition, could be used for a drill. He ordered me to go ahead, nevertheless, which we did, to learn many a valuable lesson. We found bottlenecks in the ammunition supply, magazine stowage arrangements that needed altering, and changes in crew assignments necessary to maximize efficiency. All these were rectified as promptly as possible. When Admiral Kimmel later was censured by the Bureau of Ordnance for violating its regulation, his only comment was, "I don't give a d——, I found out what I wanted to know." It was too bad that some of this could not have been brought out later at one of the Pearl Harbor investigations.

NOTES

1. William T. Tarrant (1878–1972). Vice Admiral. U.S. Naval Academy, Class of 1898.
2. Joseph K. Taussig (1877–1947). Vice Admiral. U.S. Naval Academy, Class of 1899.
3. Thomas C. Kinkaid (1888–1972). Admiral. U.S. Naval Academy, Class of 1908.
4. USS *Chicago* (CA-29). Commissioned in March 1931, she was based on the West Coast with the fleet, 1932–1940.
5. Ernest J. King (1878–1956). Fleet Admiral. U.S. Naval Academy, Class of 1901. Chief of Naval Operations and Commander in Chief, U.S. Fleet, 1941–1945.
6. Charles P. Snyder (1879–1964). Admiral. U.S. Naval Academy, Class of 1900. President of the Naval War College, 1937–1939.
7. LeRoy Taylor (1913–). Captain. U.S. Naval Academy, Class of 1935. His wartime memoirs of Pacific battles are located in the Naval War College's Naval Historical Collection.
8. Mark Clark (1896–1984). General, U.S. Army. U.S. Military Academy, Class of 1917. He commanded U.S. Army forces in Europe during World War II and UN forces during the Korean War, 1952–1953.
9. Dwight D. Eisenhower (1890–1969). General, U.S. Army. Supreme Commander of the Allied Expeditionary Forces, 1943–1945. President of the United States, 1953-1961.
10. Louis Mountbatten (1900–1979). Naval officer, Royal Navy. First Earl Mountbatten of Burma. Supreme Allied Commander, Southeast Asia, 1943–1946; Governor General of India, 1947–1948; Admiral, 1953, and First Sea Lord, 1955–1959.
11. Isaac C. Kidd (1884–1941). Rear Admiral. U.S. Naval Academy, Class of 1906.
12. Raymond A. Spruance (1886–1969). Admiral. U.S. Naval Academy, Class of 1907. Commander, Fifth Fleet, Pacific Area, 1944–1945; Commander in Chief, U.S. Pacific Fleet, 1945–1946; president of the Naval War College, 1946–1948.
13. John W. Wilcox (1882–1942). Rear Admiral. U.S. Naval Academy, Class of 1905.
14. John W. Rankin (1886–1972). Captain. U.S. Naval Academy, Class of 1908.
15. USS *Erie* (PG-50). Commissioned in July 1936, she served as flagship of the Special Service Squadron.
16. USS *Charleston* (PG-51). Commissioned in July 1936, she served as flagship of the Special Service Squadron and made several goodwill cruises to Latin American ports.
17. Frank H. Sadler (1880–1962). Rear Admiral. U.S. Naval Academy, Class of 1903.
18. Daniel Van Voorhis (1878–1956). Lieutenant General, U.S. Army. He served in the Spanish-American War, World War I, and as colonel of the cavalry in World War II.
19. Sanderford Jarman (1884–1954). Major General, U.S. Army. U.S. Military Academy, Class of 1908. He served in World War I and as commander of the Coast Artillery and Anti-Aircraft Command, Panama Canal Zone, 1938–1941. In World War II, he commanded Anti-Aircraft Artillery Command, Eastern Defense Command, 1941–1944. He retired in 1945.
20. William Dawson (1885–1972). Foreign Service Officer. Educated at the University of Minnesota and École Libre de Sciences Politiques, he served as ambassador extraordinary and plenipotentiary to Panama, 1939–1941, and as political adviser to the U.S. delegation to the UN, 1946 and 1947.
21. USS *Tattnall* (DD-125). Commissioned in 1919, she joined the Special Service Squadron in 1938 and remained until it was disbanded in September 1940.
22. Charles Darwin (1809–1882). English naturalist. He served as naturalist in the HMS *Beagle* that circumvented the globe in 1831. His observations were the basis for his work on the evolution of the species.
23. Carlos A. Arroyo del Rio (1893–1969). President of Ecuador, 1939–1944. A lawyer, rector of the University of Guayaquil, a member of the Liberal Radical party and a senator. In 1944, he was removed from office because of Ecuador's defeat in a border war with Peru and went into exile.
24. Galo Plaza Lasso (1906–1987). President of Ecuador, 1948–1952. A diplomat, politician, and minister of defense, 1938–1940, he was ambassador to the United States, 1944–1946. A proponent of democracy, he served two terms as secretary-general of the OAS.
25. USS *Philadelphia* (CL-41) served with the Atlantic Fleet in neutrality patrols in 1941.
26. Forde A. Todd (1881–1971). Rear Admiral. U.S. Naval Academy, Class of 1904.
27. USS *Brooklyn* (CL-40). In May 1941, she joined the Atlantic Squadron. During the remainder of the year, she served as a convoy escort and in neutrality patrols.
28. USS *Savannah* (CL-42). In 1941, she served as flagship, cruiser divisions, and participated in neutrality patrols. In September of that year, she convoyed U.S. and British ships across the Atlantic Ocean.
29. USS *Nashville* (CL-43) was commissioned in 1938. In 1941, she served as an escort ship and in neutrality patrols. In 1942, she patrolled Alaskan waters and took part in the attack on the Japanese in the Aleutian Islands. Later, she took part in major operations in the South Pacific, including transporting General Douglas MacArthur to invasions at Morotai and the Philippines.
30. Vance D. Chaplaine (1887–1970). Rear Admiral. U.S. Naval Academy, Class of 1909.
31. William W. Smith (1888–1966). Vice Admiral. U.S. Naval Academy, Class of 1909.
32. Andrew C. Bennett (1889–1971). Rear Admiral. U.S. Naval Academy, Class of 1912.
33. Ralph S. Wentworth (1890–1979). Commodore. U.S. Naval Academy, Class of 1912.
34. Husband E. Kimmel (1882–1968). Admiral. U.S. Naval Academy, Class of 1904. Named Commander in Chief, Pacific Fleet, in 1941, he was relieved of command and found guilty of dereliction of duty after the Japanese attack on Pearl Harbor.
35. James O. Richardson (1878–1974). Admiral. U.S. Naval Academy, Class of 1902.

USS Savannah *(CL-42) was Hewitt's flagship from May to mid-October 1941 when he was on neutrality patrols. (National Archives)*

XI *Convoy Duty, 1941*

In the spring of 1941, the Pacific Fleet was acutely conscious of the possibility of an air attack on it while in Pearl Harbor. Consequently, frequent air raid drills were held with the ships in port. The various berths were divided into air defense sectors, with a flag officer in charge of each. The Naval District participated in these exercises, but, insofar as I know, the Army, which had the major responsibility for the defense of the fleet at its base, took no part. An Air Defense Board, headed by Rear Admiral P. N. L. Bellinger,[1] at that time in command of the Naval Air Force based on Oahu, prophetically suggested that an enemy carrier attack would be delivered shortly after dawn from the northward in a sixty-degree sector between 330 and 030. Assuming a high-speed run during the night, they said the attacking force could be at dusk the previous evening as far out as some five or six-hundred miles. The only American planes with sufficient range to meet such a threat were the Navy patrol planes, and there were only enough of these to cover the most dangerous sector for a limited time.

Presumably because of this air menace and also because of the realization that in the event of hostilities the fleet would have to draw its reserve personnel, ammunition, supplies, and other equipment from the mainland, the Commander in Chief, Admiral Richardson, was in favor of maintaining only an advance force in the Hawaii area. On the other hand, President Roosevelt felt that the presence of the entire Pacific Fleet in that advanced position would serve as a prime deterrent to Japanese aggression. Because of this disagreement, Admiral Richardson was detached on February 1, and relieved by Admiral Kimmel, who became as energetic in readying the fleet for war as he had been with his cruisers.

At the exchange of command ceremonies, after bidding farewell to Admiral Richardson, I shook hands with Admiral Kimmel, congratulated him, and wished him the best of luck. Looking me in the eye, he replied, "Well, Hewitt, I'm going to need it." Never shall I forget that; much as he deserved the best, his luck could not have been worse.

With the international situation constantly growing more grave, I became concerned about the presence of my wife in the Islands and endeavored to persuade her to return to the mainland. She would have none of it. However, since occasionally some ships would vanish into the unknown, I finally made her promise that if I did not turn up in a reasonable time after I was expected, she *would* take the ship.

In April or early May, I commanded a high-speed task force, which transported a detachment of Marines to Midway for its defense. We kept on the alert, ready for an attack—air, surface, or submarine. The mission was accomplished without event.

On May 19 the fleet went to sea for scheduled tactical maneuvers to last ten or eleven days. At the end of this period, my flagship, the *Philadelphia*, was to depart for overhaul at Mare Island, so, before leaving port, I shifted my flag to the *Savannah*. On the first day out, upon completion of the day's tactical exercises, when the fleet had resumed its normal cruising disposition with the cruisers forming a protective screen, a flag signal was hoisted by the Fleet Flag *Pennsylvania*, directing the *Savannah* to "Screen the *Mississippi*." Not understanding this signal, particularly as it was not also addressed to Commander, Cruiser Division Eight, and thinking my shift of flag might have been forgotten, I sent by the blinker to CINC, "ComCruDiv 8 is *Savannah*." The only reply was a repetition of the previous signal. I directed Captain Bennett to close the battle line at the center of the disposition, and soon we sighted the *Mississippi* steaming out toward us. Getting her course and speed, we swung in ahead. About that time a destroyer approached us flying a signal addressed to ComCruDiv Eight, "We have important mail for you." Taking her under our quarter, we shot a messenger line to her and hauled aboard a bag containing a heavily sealed envelope, "TO BE OPENED BY CCD8 ONLY." Opening this in the privacy of my bridge cabin, I found an order and another sealed envelope. The order directed me to take charge of the *Savannah*, the *Mississippi*, and certain destroyers, which were already gathering around me, to proceed at 15 knots on such and such a course until out of sight of the fleet, and *then* to open the second envelope.

The second envelope contained an order placing me in command of Task Force 7, composed of four groups of which I already had the first, the other three to be similarly detached at one or two-day intervals. Each group was to proceed independently to the Panama Canal, preserving strict radio silence, avoiding all contact with other shipping; to transit the Canal secretly at night, concealing as well as possible the ships' identities and holding no communication with the shore. Each group, upon arrival in the Caribbean, was to proceed to Hampton Roads, unless otherwise directed by the Commander in Chief, United States Atlantic Fleet. The Commander, Fifteenth Naval District, was directed to arrange for the night transit of the successive groups, which were to arrive off Tagoba Island after dark on the nights of June 2, 4, 6, and 8, respectively. The total force comprised my entire Cruiser Division Eight, Battleship Division Three (*Idaho, New Mexico,*[2] *Mississippi*), and thirteen destroyers. This constituted a sizable reinforcement to the Atlantic Fleet at a time when our British cousins were very hard-pressed.

During the movement of my group to the Canal, I disposed the destroyers as an advance screen at visual distance in order that I might be warned of contact with other shipping in time to maneuver the two larger vessels so as to avoid their being sighted. This I had occasion to do several times.

It was during this voyage that we heard over our radio the news of the search for the *Bismarck*[3] and its eventual sinking on May 27; also the proclamation by President Roosevelt of a state of emergency.

Task Group 7.1 approached the Canal on the evening of June 2, staying as far out as possible until after dark and still having time to clear the Caribbean entrance before full daylight. The final approach was made with the *Mississippi* at full speed, the *Savannah* going ahead to make the first transit. All ships had their names on the stern and the initials on the bows of boats covered over. Crews had been thoroughly briefed.

In spite of all precautions, however, our attempts at secrecy were not too successful. As the *Savannah*, darkened, started up the channel to Balboa, the Army signal station blinked an AA at us, "What ship is that?" For awhile we refused to answer. Finally, fearing some hostile action on the part of the fort and supposing the Army authorities had been informed about my orders, I replied, "Commander, Task Force 7." The Army reaction to that was to inquire, "What nationality?" My answer to that appeared to satisfy them for we continued on without trouble. However, as we crossed the ferry lane at Balboa, the headlights of an automobile on the ferryboat just leaving its slip were turned on us, illuminating us nicely by silhouette for a Japanese oiler moored at a dock close aboard on the opposite side. Furthermore, when we reached the first locks, we found that only one set was being used, the others being worked on night and day for the bomb-proofing of the lock machinery. Consequently, the lock immediately across from us, swarming with workmen of many nationalities, was brilliantly floodlighted. They could not read our name, but they could easily determine our type. Incidentally, one of the Canal employees, who called up from the lock wall to ask, "What ship?" was answered by a bluejacket wag on the forecastle, "The *Bismarck*. What the h—— do you think it is?"

During the passage to Panama, radio orders were received for Task Force Seven to rendezvous at Guantánamo, thence to proceed to the northward as a unit, with ultimate destinations of Hampton Roads for the battleships, *Philadelphia* for the destroyers, and Boston for the cruisers. Task Group 7.1, reassembling off Cristobal on the morning of June 3, reached the rendezvous on the 5th for a pleasant stay (my first visit to that familiar base in many years) while awaiting the remainder of the force. The other three groups, Rear Admiral Munroe[4] in *Idaho*, Captain Coman[5] in *New Mexico*, and Captain Chaplaine in *Philadelphia*, arrived on schedule in two-day intervals.

On June 11, Task Force Seven headed north, holding day and night exercises en route. It was my first experience handling a miniature fleet of my own. On June 14, the *Nashville* was ordered ahead to participate in the movement of U.S. Marines to Iceland. Shortly after daylight of the 17th, sending the *Philadelphia* and *Brooklyn* on in, *the Savannah* anchored off the Massachusetts Bay entrance to Cape Cod Canal for me to have an early morning conference on the flagship *Augusta*[6] with the Commander in Chief of the Atlantic Fleet, Admiral King. Thence the *Savannah* followed my other cruisers to a dock in the South Boston Annex of the Charleston Navy Yard. To our surprise, we found across the dock from us HMS *Rodney*,[7] fresh from delivering the *coup de grace* to the *Bismarck*.

The captain of the *Rodney*, Frederick Dalrymple-Hamilton,[8] who was shortly to be knighted and to become a rear admiral, called promptly in accordance with naval etiquette, and I returned his call. It was most interesting to hear from his lips a first-hand account of the search for and final sinking of the *Bismarck*. And it was surprising to see in the captain's cabin of a British man-of-war, which had just been in combat, many of the comforts of home, such as personal pictures, paintings of the captain's estate, etc., which we, not yet combatants, had landed months before.

The commandant of the First Naval District to whom I reported was none other than Admiral Tarrant, whose flag captain I had been on the *Indianapolis*. As soon as our official business had been completed, he arranged a call for me to my daughter in Brooklyn. The minute she recognized my voice, she almost jumped through the telephone, wanting to know where I was. I could not tell her directly, but when I told her that I had just been talking to Ruth's father, she knew. Then I asked her what news she had of her mother. To my amazement, she gasped, "Mother got here yesterday!" So it was that with my ships in the hands of the Navy Yard I was able to hop a train and spend a happy weekend with all my family.

Upon being attached to the Atlantic Fleet, I became Commander, Cruisers, Atlantic Fleet, by virtue of my seniority to the other cruiser division commanders, both classmates. But after my arrival in Boston, I was to see little of my own division or any of the others. President Roosevelt had declared a neutrality zone which extended well across the Atlantic, and naval task groups of mixed constitution were being formed to patrol it.

After a week at the yard, I set forth on the first of such patrols with the *Savannah*, *Philadelphia*, and destroyers *Wilson*[9] and *Lang*.[10] Our orders were to report any raiders or suspicious vessels sighted, and we were particularly warned to look out for vessels showing evidence of having altered their character at sea, such as newly painted names and newly painted wavy water lines. Furthermore, we were advised to look out for tentage or other canvas on deck which might conceal guns. Upon returning from this patrol, we were to base in Bermuda.

On July 2, at the extreme limit of our patrol, in 32° west longitude near the Azores, one of the destroyers sighted a northbound vessel flying Dutch colors which answered almost exactly the above description of a suspicious vessel. Its name, *Stad Arnhem*, was newly painted. It had a wavy waterline, and there was tentage on deck. When the *Savannah* closed to look it over, the master reported to me by signal that he had sailed from Freetown on June 18 in a large convoy under British escort, that the convoy had been attacked by a submarine on the nights of June 26 and 27, losing three ships. On the following day it had been ordered to scatter, proceeding independently to a rendezvous on July 9 in 52° 40' north latitude, 20° 00' west longitude. The master further reported that he had picked up on the previous day in 36° 46' north latitude, 30° 30' west longitude, fifteen survivors from the German MS *Elbe*, reported sunk by an unknown aircraft carrier on June 6 in 26° 30' north latitude, 41° 00' west longitude. He further added that these survivors were suffering from exposure and from scurvy.

A suspicious looking ship, admittedly with some Germans aboard! We were most anxious to have a closer look, but since we were technically non-combatants, we could not claim under international law the right of visit and search. But the report of illness on board gave us an excuse to offer medical assistance and a supply of citrus fruits. If the ship were a raider, the offer would be refused, as I thought it might be. But, really to my surprise, it was accepted with thanks. So off in a whaleboat went the doctor and his assistants, reinforced by the *Savannah*'s gunnery officer and first lieutenant disguised as hospital corpsmen. The boarding party did find sick Germans under canvas on deck, who were duly treated, and there were no signs of concealed weapons. The circumstances were promptly reported to Washington and London. The Admiralty confirmed that the *Stad Arnhem* was from a dispersed convoy out of Freetown and that they knew about one of the ships reported sunk, but had not had the news of the other two. So all was well.

My task group reached Bermuda on July 8, completing its first neutrality patrol without further significant event. We had a good chance to look over that beautiful island and to enjoy its swimming. As has been recorded, I had seen it twenty-three years earlier, but only through a porthole.

The foregoing was the first of a number of similar neutrality patrols from Bermuda to the eastward and return, most of which were without particular incident of note. The composition of these groups varied and sometimes included a fleet carrier, in which case the task group commander shifted his flag to the carrier, the better to observe and control the air operations.

During the first week of August, the newly formed Amphibious Brigade, which had been spending some time exercising in the Caribbean, carried out a major amphibious exercise on the North Carolina coast at New River. This brigade, which consisted of the First Marine Division and the First Army Division under the command of Major General Holland M. Smith, USMC,[11] embarked in attack transports of the Atlantic Fleet Base Force (Rear Admiral Randall Jacobs).[12] The transport commander was Captain R. R. M. Emmett, U.S. Navy,[13] who will figure later in this narrative. General Smith was an old friend and shipmate who had been Fleet Marine Officer when I was Pacific Fleet Operations Officer and had worked closely with me in operations planning.

Admiral King ordered all the available flag officers of the Atlantic Fleet to witness this exercise—a most farsighted move. So it was that on August 1, I proceeded westward from Bermuda to New River with my current task group, *Savannah* (F), escort carrier *Long Island*[14] (a converted freighter), and two destroyers, *Gwin*[15] and *Meredith*.[16] In order to get the best view of the landing, I decided to watch it from the air, which I did, in one of the Savannah's two-seater observation planes. It was a new and very strange sensation to be catapulted off a ship. After the beach landing was completed, I joined General Smith in his headquarters on shore to observe the purely military part of the exercise from there. It was all most interesting and rewarding. And, while I fully realized the future probability of such operations, I did not foresee my own close connection with them.

After the New River exercise, there was another patrol across the Atlantic, followed by a return to the area off the Virginia Capes for target practice. My final neutrality patrol in early September with Task Group 26, with flag carrier in *Wasp*,[17] with *Savannah* and destroyers *Gwin* and *Meredith*, proved to be rather exciting. Somewhat east of Bermuda, eastbound, we intercepted a dispatch from a Canadian man-of-war to the northward of us, reporting the sighting of what she thought to be a German cruiser proceeding on a southerly course at high speed. What she had seen had disappeared in the haze to the southward before positive identification could be made. Plotting the position given and the possible courses and possible speeds showed that the supposed raider could well come into our search area. Speed was increased and the group's course and aircraft search patterns were oriented accordingly. One plane, returning in the afternoon from the first search flight launched, made a message drop on the bridge before being recovered (strict radio silence, except in emergency, had been enjoined). His message stated that he had sighted a suspicious vessel at the extreme safe limit of his flight, but had to turn back before making a close approach. The silhouette sketch he drew bore a strong resemblance to one of the German cruiser types. The pilot's testimony after landing seemed to confirm this possibility, although he stated that he was far from sure.

By this time, the Atlantic Fleet had orders from the president to destroy any Axis raider found in the neutrality zone proclaimed by him. No time was lost, therefore, in launching another search flight to confirm the original contact. And a squadron of torpedo-bombers was brought up to the flight deck and armed in readiness. I began to wonder if it was to be I who, in carrying out my orders, would first involve the

United States in the war. However, the scouting planes returned at dusk without further contact.

The search was continued the following day without result. It was estimated that the raider, if there was one, might be making for British Guiana with the object of destroying some of the bauxite supply, so important to our own and the British aircraft construction program. This opinion was shared by the captain of HMS *Rodney*, which appeared on the scene and was granted permission to join my task group. Incidentally, when I sent a personal message of welcome to Captain Dalrymple-Hamilton, it was answered with appreciation by another captain, who added, "*Admiral* Dalrymple-Hamilton had left."

The high-speed fruitless search—later found to be based on a false alarm—drew us so far southward that it became advisable for us to put into Trinidad for fuel. There I encountered my classmate, Rear Admiral Jonas Ingram,[18] who, with his division of old 6-inch cruisers of the Omaha type, was covering the western South Atlantic. We had a pleasant visit, exchanging information and experiences.

Upon our return to Bermuda, about September 20, I received orders that directed me, in the *Savannah*, north to Argentia, Newfoundland, one of our new bases acquired under the Roosevelt-Churchill destroyer deal. Task Group 14.3 assembled under my command preparatory to undertaking the duty of convoy escort. It consisted of the carrier *Yorktown*,[19] the battleship *New Mexico*, the heavy cruiser *Quincy*,[20] and some twelve destroyers in addition to my flagship, the *Savannah*. As well as receiving all necessary convoy instructions at Argentia, we had an opportunity to look at the base facilities under construction and the air strips, as well as to get a little exercise by taking walks around the countryside. There was nothing to see except a few small villages, the hardy inhabitants of which earned their living by the sea. One interesting sight was an itinerant floating country store, a schooner which went from village to village, mooring with its stern close to the beach and providing for its customers one or two boats which they could haul back and forth themselves by cables.

By October 1, Task Group 14.3 had left to meet its first eastbound convoy, south of Newfoundland—a fast, small, but apparently very important convoy. At MOMP (the assigned Mid-Ocean Meeting Point, just a few hundred miles west of the British Isles) we exchanged it for a small westbound convoy, which we brought safely to port after experiencing considerable heavy weather—so much so that the *Quincy*, one of our treaty cruisers whose structural strength had been cut to a minimum with the object of getting as much armament and speed as possible into 10,000 tons, cracked a frame and had to be sent in under destroyer escort to the Boston Navy Yard.

After our return to port, about mid-October, the *Philadelphia* joined Task Group 14.3 to replace the *Quincy*, and I was able to return to my regular flagship for the first time since the preceding May. By the 25th, we were at sea again with another important eastbound fast cargo convoy. We arrived at the designated MOMP on November 2, and there took over a very large and important troop convoy carrying a British armored division to the Middle East via Halifax. I do not remember the number of this division, but I do remember very well the signal I received from the Commanding General, "The ——— Armored Division is immensely proud of your magnificent escort." Signed, Beckwith-Smith. Well they might have been, because four very tired-looking war-torn British destroyers were replaced by one large carrier, one battleship, two light cruisers and twelve destroyers.

British convoy instructions gave the convoy commodore in one of the ships of the convoy responsibility for the tactical handling of the convoy itself. I felt, however, that the safety of the heavy ships of the escort required that they be placed within the anti-submarine screen of destroyers, the carrier at the rear, where she could maneuver readily to launch and recover planes, and the battleship and cruisers each leading columns, a position from which they could move out promptly to meet any surface threat. With such a disposition, which I adopted, leading the center column with my flagship, I thought that it was incumbent upon me to take over the tactical handling of the entire convoy. I so advised the commodore, and he agreed. I continued this system throughout my convoy escort duty.

Early in the morning of November 8, we arrived at the approaches to Halifax, which were closely patrolled by local forces. Turning over the convoy to its commodore, the escort peeled off and proceeded to Casco Bay (Portland, Maine), newly established as a convoy escort base. Little did I realize what I would be doing exactly one year later!

Waiting in Halifax at that time was a force of U.S. naval transports, with escort, which, by Roosevelt's and Churchill's agreement, was to carry this armored division around the Cape of Good Hope to its ultimate destination. Who could have known that it would wind up in Singapore in time to become prisoners of the Japanese!

After fuelling and provisioning at Casco, Task Group 14.3 proceeded to Halifax, where I had the pleasure of meeting personally the commodore of the convoy we had recently brought in, a retired British admiral and a delightful gentleman. We established most cordial relations. By November 13, after a Canadian armored division had been embarked from Britain as a replacement, we sailed eastbound with the same convoy, which we delivered safely to British escort at MOMP, on November 18.

After delivering the return westbound convoy to Halifax on November 24, the escort again proceeded to Casco Bay. Unfortunately, on the way to Casco in a fog, the *Philadelphia* touched a rock in the narrow entrance, which necessitated her proceeding to Boston for docking. It was there that she and I were on December 7.

It so happened that my wife had taken an apartment in the Miles Standish Hotel in Boston to be nearby when I got into port, either in Casco Bay, Boston itself, or Narragansett Bay, or even New York. The *Philadelphia* being in dry dock in South Boston on that day, we had accepted an invitation for lunch with old friends, a retired naval captain and his wife, living in one of the Boston suburbs. In view of the increasingly tense situation, I never left the ship without giving my staff duty officer complete information as to where I could be reached in the event of emergency. Arriving at the home of our hosts, we found that we were being taken out to an inn instead of having lunch at the house. Returning there after a pleasant meal, we found waiting the following: one police car, one telephone emergency repair truck, and one Navy official car. The policeman asked if I were Admiral Hewitt and then informed me that I was to call my flagship immediately. The telephone truck had been sent to investigate the failure of the number to answer. Dashing into the house, I picked up the phone and called the flagship's number. The minute the operator heard it, she exclaimed, "Oh, are you Admiral Hewitt? It's terrible! The Japs have bombed Pearl Harbor!" That is the way I learned that we were at war.

Repairs to the *Philadelphia* were swiftly completed and she was back with the task group in time for all of us to spend Christmas in Casco Bay. My wife was joined in a Portland hotel for the occasion by our daughter Floride, whose husband, by then gunnery officer of an Atlantic destroyer, had not been heard from since Pearl Harbor Day.

NOTES

1 Patrick Niesson L. Bellinger (1885–1962). Vice Admiral. U.S. Naval Academy, Class of 1907.

2 USS *New Mexico* (BB-40). She left Pearl Harbor in May of 1941 to serve with the Atlantic Fleet on neutrality patrols.

3 *Bismarck*, German battleship. 42,000 tons; eight 15-inch guns. She was sunk on May 27, 1941 by British battleships *Rodney* and *King George V* on her way to attack Allied shipping.

4 William Munroe (1886–1966). Vice Admiral. U.S. Naval Academy, Class of 1908.

5 Robert G. Coman (1887–1963). Commodore. U.S. Naval Academy, Class of 1909.

6 USS *Augusta* (CA-31). Commissioned in 1931, she served as flagship of Admiral Ernest J. King, Commander in Chief, Atlantic Fleet, 1941. She took President Franklin D. Roosevelt to his meeting with Prime Minister Winston Churchill at Argentia, Newfoundland, in 1941 for the signing of the Atlantic Charter.

7 HMS *Rodney*. British battleship. 33,900 tons; length, 660'; beam, 106'.

8 Frederick H. G. Dalrymple-Hamilton (1890–1974). Admiral, Royal Navy.

9 USS *Wilson* (DD-408). She served in neutrality patrols in the Atlantic in the summer of 1941 and in the fall operated out of Bermuda where she served as an escort ship.

10 USS *Lang* (DD-399). She was an escort ship involved in carrier and anti-submarine training in 1941.

11 Holland M. Smith (1882–1967). Marine Corps general in World War II. Known as the father of amphibious warfare, he led his forces in attacks on the Aleutians, the Gilberts, the Marshalls, the Marianas, and at Guam and Iwo Jima.

12 Randall Jacobs (1885–1967). Vice Admiral. U.S. Naval Academy, Class of 1907.

13 Robert R. M. Emmett (1888–1977). Rear Admiral. U.S. Naval Academy, Class of 1907.

14 USS *Long Island* (AVG-1). Based in Norfolk, Virginia, she was involved in testing aircraft operations from converted cargo ships and was the Navy's first escort carrier.

15 USS *Gwin* (DD-433). Commissioned in January 1941, she was assigned to the neutrality patrol in the Caribbean and then in the North Atlantic out of Iceland.

16 USS *Meredith* (DD-434). Based in Boston in mid-1941, she was involved in patrol duty, then was assigned to Iceland on neutrality patrols.

17 USS *Wasp* (CV-7). She served as Admiral Hewitt's flagship from August 24, 1941, to September 2, 1941, and was assigned to neutrality patrols.

18 Jonas Ingram (1886–1967). Admiral. U.S. Naval Academy, Class of 1907.

19 USS *Yorktown* (CV-5). Served with the neutrality patrol of the Atlantic Fleet from May through early December 1941.

20 USS *Quincy* (CA-39). In 1941 she was assigned to neutrality patrols and convoy duty in mid-Atlantic, Icelandic, and South Atlantic waters.

Louis, 1st Earl Mountbatten of Burma (1900-1979) Vice Admiral, Royal Navy, and Chief of Combined Operations, hosted Admiral Hewitt during his visit to Combined Operations activities in England in June 1942. (Naval Historical Collection)

XII *Preparing for Operation TORCH, 1942*

Christmas afforded but a short respite. We were by now, of course, operating under full war conditions with all the rights of a belligerent. By December 27, Task Force 26, *Philadelphia*, CVE (Escort Carrier) *Long Island*, were at sea en route to Argentia, which was reached on New Year's Day after a pretty rough trip. The base at Argentia, together with that in Iceland near Reykjavík, was by now being used to furnish complete air cover for the central part of the northern transatlantic convoy routes. In charge of these activities and responsible for the safe conduct of convoys in that area was the Commander, Support Force, Vice Admiral A. L. Bristol,[1] with headquarters at Argentia. In Iceland, a large fjord on the west coast just north of Reykjavík, with the unpronounceable name of Hvalfjördur, was used as an assembly and dispatch point for convoys and their escorts bound to and returning from North Russia. Sections of convoys destined for Russia would break off from European-bound convoys south of Iceland and be escorted into Hvalfjördur to await the makeup of convoys for the particularly hazardous Murmansk run. Their escorts would pick up returning shipping and proceed south to join westbound transatlantic convoys.

During the first four months of 1942, my task group was involved in a number of convoy escort trips, several of which took us into Iceland and Argentia as well, although our main base for refueling, etc., remained Casco Bay. I found Iceland to be most interesting. Although in the midst of winter, its west coast was surprisingly temperate, warmed as it was by a branch of the Gulf Stream. This is what kept the Denmark Strait open and free of the ice that was banked up against the east coast of Greenland. But the weather was uncertain, and there were frequent blows, so that ships at their moorings, even in sheltered Hvalfjördur, had to keep steam up, and if one left his ship to visit Reykjavík, it was always uncertain when boating would permit his return.

Reykjavík was a pleasant modern city, and the Icelanders themselves fine, sturdy, and friendly people. Among other things, I had the pleasure of meeting and having tea with the head of their government at his private residence. The Sunday morning service for the British and American armed forces at the cathedral in

Reykjavík, a beautiful church, was an event worth recording. And last but not least, it was a pleasure to encounter once more my erstwhile friend of HMS *Rodney*, now Rear Admiral Dalrymple-Hamilton, as the British Flag Officer, Iceland. I enjoyed having tea with him and his delightful lady.

In late February 1942 Admiral King established the Amphibious Force, Atlantic Fleet, with headquarters at Hampton Roads. To it were assigned the previously mentioned Amphibious Corps, under Major General Holland M. Smith, U.S. Marine Corps, and all the attack transports that had previously been under the Fleet Base Force. It was realized that the assumption of the offensive against both the Axis Powers and Japan would involve major landings in the face of enemy opposition and that, therefore, the responsibility for the training and planning for these operations and the command of the special craft required for them should devolve on a commander having no other duty. Rear Admiral Roland E. Brainard[2] of the Naval Academy Class of 1906, who received this important assignment, established his headquarters in a small building in the Hampton Roads Naval Base, which was shared with the Fleet Base Force.

On April 20, Admiral Bristol, overburdened by his tremendous responsibilities, unfortunately, suffered a heart attack to which he succumbed. An immediate relief was a necessity, and Admiral Brainard was ordered to take his place. At that time, I was returning from Iceland in command of the escort of a westbound convoy. To my amazement, I received dispatch orders detaching me from command of Cruisers, Atlantic Fleet and Cruiser Division Eight upon arrival in port, directing me to proceed to Hampton Roads immediately to assume command of the Amphibious Force.

Early on April 28, the *Philadelphia* arrived at the New York Navy Yard, and at about 8:30 a.m., after a brief ceremony, Rear Admiral Lyal A. Davidson[3] relieved me of command of Cruiser Division Eight. I hated to leave my cruisers, my fine flagship, and my loyal staff personnel, but even more interesting work lay ahead. Accompanied by my flag lieutenant, I drove immediately to Floyd Bennett Field and took off promptly in a two-engine plane for the Naval Air Station, Hampton Roads. By noon, I was in command of the Amphibious Force, Atlantic Fleet. This was the quickest change of duty I ever made.

Having been established only two months before, my new command was in its infancy. But already its responsibilities were many and varied, with, initially, few means with which to meet them. Headquarters had been established in a small building near one of the Naval Base piers in a space which was reluctantly granted to us by the Fleet Base Force, which itself needed more room. The Commander, Transports, Captain Emmett, was afloat in his flagship *Leonard Wood*.[4] The Amphibious Corps Commander, my friend General Smith, had his headquarters in Quantico. His Corps had been dispersed, the Marine First Division to the Pacific and the Army First Division to Britain. But shortly, the Ninth Army Division, under Major General Manton S. Eddy,[5] based in Fort Bragg, North Carolina, was assigned to the Amphibious Force for training purposes.

AMPHIBLANT, to use the abbreviated title, was charged with training the assault transports, cargo ships, and the crews of the landing craft carried by them; the training of crews for the larger beaching amphibious craft—tank landing craft (LCT), infantry landing craft (LCI), and tank landing ships (LST), the construction of large numbers of which had already been initiated in the United States; and the training of assigned Army units in amphibious operations. The last included not only embarkation and disembarkation, but the principles of combat loading, of joint communications, and of joint handling of operations on assault beaches where there was Navy responsibility and Army responsibility. As may be grasped, this was a considerable task. To make matters worse, all our Marines, our amphibious experts, were detached to the Pacific, soon to be followed by General Smith himself—not, however, before I had been able to profit very greatly by his experience and wise advice.

Adequate training of naval crews in beaching and retracting their craft under surf conditions required the use of exposed beaches. These were available outside of Cape Henry, an area which could be reached by craft operating from Little Creek. But training of troops and of transport crews and boat crews in execution of landings from the open sea was not practicable without unjustified risk, due to the presence of enemy submarines off the Cape and the unavailability of escort craft, which were fully occupied in the protection of transatlantic and coastal convoys. Consequently, all training involving transports had to be carried out in the smooth waters of Chesapeake Bay, using beaches north of the mouth of the Patuxent at Solomons Island, and the Lynnhaven Roads beaches between Little Creek and Cape Henry. To meet the above needs, a training base was established on the west side of the Little Creek estuary and a smaller one at Solomons Island. There were several competing naval training activities already established at or near Little Creek, namely inshore patrol on the other side of the inlet and a SeaBee training area further east, on ground now part of the present amphibious base.

An efficient and successful amphibious operation, however, involves more than the mere loading of troops on a transport, embarking them and their equipment in landing craft in boats and setting them ashore on a selected beach. It includes the proper loading of transports so that weapons, equipment, and supplies may be unloaded in the order needed (combat loading). It involves the naval gunfire and its control needed to support the landing and the first advance inland to secure a beachhead. It includes a joint organization on the assault beach, where naval responsibility ends and Army responsibility takes over; the Navy Beachmaster to handle the beaching and retraction of landing craft, to repair and salvage craft that have been stranded or disabled, to maintain communications to seaward, and to take care of casualties for return to ships; and the Army shore party commander to prepare beach exits and route traffic forward, to unload loaded craft and dispose of their cargoes, to maintain communications forward to the front line, and to receive and turn over to the Navy the casualties to be returned seaward. There also had to be joint training for Navy radio and signal personnel and Army Signal Corps crews, because communication systems of the two services differed considerably, and they had to be brought into harmony.

The immediate need was for the establishment of joint schools, as strongly urged by General Smith, one for communications, one for gunnery, one for the study of beach organization problems, and one for the training of Army transport quartermasters and Navy transport cargo officers in the technique of combat loading. These schools were set up in hastily constructed wooden buildings in an area (a potato field when I first saw it) immediately adjacent to the landing craft piers already constructed at Little Creek. Fortunately, we were able initially to have considerable Marine Corps help and, on the Navy side, the assistance of many officers who had participated in previous major amphibious exercises. For guidance, there was a series of standard operating procedures which had been established as a result of Navy-Marine Corps experience—procedures which subsequent experience proved to be thoroughly sound.

Quite early in the game, I met in Washington the then Vice Admiral (Lieutenant General and Air Vice Marshal) Lord Louis Mountbatten, the son of Admiral of the Fleet Prince Louis of Battenberg, who, at the outset of World War I, had been removed from his post as First Sea Lord because of his German name, thus the subsequent anglicization of the name. In March of 1942, Lord Louis had been appointed as Chief of Combined Operations with the rank of vice admiral and, to emphasize the necessary cooperation of services, a corresponding rank in the other two. Thus, he was, in a sense, my transatlantic opposite number. He had come over to press the construction of the specially designed landing craft, to obtain allocation of as many as possible for British use, and to further Allied cooperation in planning for the future, particularly with regard to European landings. I found him to be a man of great personal magnetism, apparently very able, but considerably younger than I. This encounter resulted in a visit by me to Combined Operations activities in Britain a month or two later.

An important part of the gunnery program was the training of what we called "shore fire-control parties" to observe and direct naval gunfire. These were naval personnel familiar with naval fire control procedures, equipped with means of communicating with the fire support ships, who could direct and control naval gunfire from forward positions on shore in accordance with troop requests, just as if they were on board ship. This was important, because Army observation and Navy control methods were diametrically opposite, the former reporting error and the latter prescribing the correction to be made. With a shot falling 200 yards beyond the target, an Army observer would say "Over 200," while a Navy spotter would order "Down 200." In order to train these fire-control parties and the ships of the Atlantic Fleet, which might be called upon to conduct gunfire against land targets, a type to which they were unaccustomed, an island on the eastern side of Chesapeake Bay, Bloodsworth, occupied only by a duckhunter's camp, was found and converted into a target area. Here, destroyers and cruisers conducted practices as they became available.

The manifold duties connected with the organization and efficient execution of all this amphibious training manifestly could never have been satisfactorily carried out without the assistance of an able and fairly large staff. But, in addition to training, AMPHIBLANT was soon faced with an additional problem—that of planning actual operations against possible future objectives. One of these was for the seizure of Vichy French Martinique to prevent its use as a Nazi submarine base. Another was for the occupation of Dakar for the same purpose, a previous Anglo–Free French attempt at which had been frustrated by the loyalty of its governor to the Vichy government. In addition, there was at one time a project for the establishment of an advance base in the Azores, even against possible Portuguese resistance inspired by fear of Nazi reprisals. And, finally, beginning in July, the planning for the operation which was actually carried out, the landing in North Africa.

I was indeed fortunate in my staff, a wonderful team of dedicated, loyal, and hardworking officers of vision, some of whom I inherited from Admiral Brainard, one who came with me from my cruiser staff, and others who were later assigned to me. They deserve the greatest credit.

The chief of staff, to whose thoroughness and energy much is owed, was Captain Lee P. Johnson,[6] nicknamed Woolsey after a renowned mathematics professor who had served at the Naval Academy for many years. The operations officer was Captain E. A. Mitchell;[7] the gunnery officer, Commander T. F. Wellings;[8] and the communications officer, Commander D. S. Evans.[9] Commander L. A. Bachman,[10] who had been my cruiser flag secretary, came with me, and because of a recent directive that officers of the Regular Navy were no longer to be assigned as personal aides, either as flag lieutenant or flag secretary, I made him the intelligence officer. As his replacement as flag secretary, I was fortunate in being assigned Lieutenant Commander Julian Boit,[11] a Naval Academy graduate who had temporarily returned to civilian life. Of several young officers sent to me by the Navy Department from whom to choose a flag lieutenant, Lieutenant B. H. Griswold III, U.S. Naval Reserve,[12] was finally chosen. It was only after he had thoroughly proved his worth in carrying out this assignment that I found that it was his father who was the Baltimore owner of our new gunnery target, Bloodsworth Island.

Other important members of the staff were Commander Stephen R. Edson, SC, U.S. Navy, the supply officer; Lieutenant Commander H. B. Brookman, U.S. Naval

Reserve,[13] engineering and matériel; Commander R. W. D. Woods, U.S. Navy,[14] air; Commander B. S. Pupek, MC, U.S. Navy,[15] medical; and Commander R. A. J. English, U.S. Navy,[16] planning. The last, who had been my destroyer division engineer officer in 1931–1932 and who later was with some of the Byrd polar expeditions, came to me from the Naval War College to fill a very definite need.

A strictly naval staff, however, was not enough. The joint training and the planning for operations in which both the Army and Navy were concerned really required a joint staff. Upon my application to the War Department, several able Army officers were assigned to me, several of whom had had the advantage of a course at the Naval War College, and others who, with the First Army Division, had participated in the amphibious exercises of the previous fall. With these, I believe I organized what was the first joint staff, with a Navy division headed by my naval chief of staff, and an Army division headed by Colonel B. S. Johnson[17] as my Army chief of staff. Other prominent members were Colonel L. B. Ely[18] as G-2 (intelligence), Colonel E. C. Burkhart as G-3 (operations), Colonel T. H. Smyser, and Colonel N. E. McCluer.[19] The Navy division of the staff was organized along general staff lines, N-1 for personnel, N-2 for intelligence, N-3 for operations, etc. On matters pertaining particularly to their own services, the two divisions operated separately, under my direction, of course. On joint matters, however, they operated jointly, with the respective sections, N-2 and G-2, for instance, and N-3 and G-3, linked together. It seemed to work splendidly with little or no friction.

Colonel McCluer was placed in charge of the joint schools, which had been or were to be established, a duty which he carried out to the greatest satisfaction of all. Captain W. P. O. Clarke, U.S. Navy,[20] was detached from command of a transport division and given the very important duty of conducting the training of the crews of landing craft, not only of smaller craft carried by the large assault transports and assault cargo ships, but those for the larger sea-going and cross-channel types, the landing ship tanks (LST), the landing craft infantry (LCI), and the tank landing craft (LCT). This involved the assembly and instruction of officers and men drawn from all walks of life for the manning of craft which were still on the way when the program was initiated.

The later performance of these craft in crossing the seas with green crews and in subsequent combat operations manifested the thoroughness with which Captain Clarke accomplished his task. In fact, this gallant and able officer, in order to do what had to be done, gave of himself so unsparingly that he finally broke down in early 1943 and had to be hospitalized and later retired. He passed away in 1949, a victim of disabilities thus incurred. I consider him to have truly given his life for his country, to have been a real war casualty.

As the staff grew, the facilities which we shared with the base force became more and more inadequate and cramped. My own office was in a small bedroom, which I sometimes had to use as such, although I had been assigned quarters in the Navy-operated Hotel Chamberlin across the Roads at Old Point. Early steps were inaugurated to find a satisfactory location which would give us what our enemies would have called *lebensraum*.[21] Also, a fairly good size cabin cruiser or houseboat yacht was found in the Philadelphia area and assigned to me. This not only gave me an independent means of reaching the various training sites (such as Solomons) by water but made it possible to establish a flag mess and to offer fairly comfortable quarters to visiting generals and flag officers.

As may well be imagined, everyone kept pretty busy, and there was little or no time for rest or relaxation. The records show I was more or less constantly on the move, with trips at least once a week to Washington for conferences and appeals for needed matériel and personnel, a visit to the Army Ninth Division at Fort Bragg, and voyages up the bay to witness dawn landing exercises and target practices. And, of course, regular administration, the setting up of schools, and the aforementioned planning could not be neglected.

In early June, Admiral King, the Chief of Naval Operations and Commander in Chief, U.S. Fleet, decided to send me over to the United Kingdom to visit Admiral Mountbatten and make a tour of his Combined Operations activities in order that we in the Amphibious Force might gain what we could from British experience. Accompanied by two of my staff, Commanders Bachman and Wellings, I departed from Baltimore harbor via British Overseas Airways flying boat early in the morning of June 16.

At the last moment we were informed that, because we were to make a stop in neutral Eire, we must wear civilian clothes during passage. Since we had been wearing uniforms constantly since our entry into the war, this posed a bit of a problem—most of our other clothes were inaccessible, having been packed and stored. I finally got hold of an old dark blue suit which, having been made years before, fitted me rather closely. My two aides managed to find something suitable. We were, however, well dressed in comparison to certain other passengers on our plane who were clothed merely in khaki trousers and shirts with loud civilian ties.

There were a number of interesting civilian passengers on this plane. One, with whom I was to share a double-bunked stateroom in the tail, turned out to be a distinguished British jurist, Sir Norman Birkett,[22] who had just completed a visit to bar associations in the United States, a delightful and most interesting man.

Because of fog, we were unable to reach our first stop in Newfoundland that night. Instead, we were forced to put down at a small fishing port on the east coast of New Brunswick. There, rough accommodations for the night were found for us in a rather second-rate, unopened, and unheated summer hotel. We were warned to be at the dock shortly after dawn to reboard the plane. Arriving there breakfastless, after a night in which we had had to sleep in our clothes to keep warm, we had to wait while the plane was being readied. Unless its engines were turning over, our flying boat had no heating or cooking facilities, so we remained on the dock eating cold boiled lobster from a fisherman's shack—the first and only time, I may say, that I had such a dish for breakfast.

Finally, we took off and were able to sit down to a more orthodox breakfast. I imagine that we had tea rather than coffee, but, by that time, anything warm hit the spot. After refueling at our regular stop in Newfoundland, we took to the air again for our overnight transatlantic leg of the voyage to Foynes, a small harbor on the west coast of Ireland. I could have slept more easily in a pitching and rolling destroyer than I did bouncing up and down in the tail of that plane, but Sir Norman and I managed to get some rest.

At Foynes, we were all forced to pass an inspection by the Irish immigration and customs official, who scrutinized our passports carefully. These bore no indication whatever of any military status. Appearing alphabetically in accordance with the passenger list, I followed a number of the young men in khaki. I was asked if I was in the government service. Upon replying in the affirmative, my interrogator wished to know, further, if I was attached to the War Department. My efforts to evade this question failing, I finally admitted serving under the Navy Department. At this, the inspector looked at me with a smile, stamped my passport, and said, "My name is Hewitt, too."

Later the same day we arrived at Bristol, England, where we disembarked and boarded a special train for London. I had hoped to be able to shift into uniform, but this was impossible, as our baggage was transferred directly from the baggage compartment of the plane to the luggage van of the train. My friend, Sir Norman, with whom I sat, was most solicitous as to whether or not I was to be met and whether I had any British money. I had to admit that I did not have a farthing and that I did not know whether anyone would meet me but supposed that there might be someone from the U.S. naval attaché's office. He insisted that he would get a taxi and see me to my destination.

As we drew into Waterloo Station and were rising preparatory to leaving our car, I noted a large group of people on the platform in uniform. As I stepped out of the train in my rumpled and all-too-small suit, I found myself greeted by one exceedingly smart looking British vice admiral (Lord Louis), one British rear admiral (H. E. Horan),[23] one U.S. brigadier general (Lucian K. Truscott),[24] one U.S. naval attaché, and assorted aides and orderlies. It was a very pleasant, but under the circumstances somewhat embarrassing, welcome. Before we knew it, we were whisked off in official cars driven by very smart "Wrens"[25] drivers and established in a large suite in the Dorchester Hotel on the edge of Hyde Park. It was not until some years later that I again met my friend, Sir Norman, and that was at the Nuremberg trials, where he was one of the British judges. Lunching with him there and recalling the above incident, he laughed and said, "Yes, here I was, going to see you safely to a hotel, but instead you get carried off by all that rank, and I could not even find a taxi."

That Friday evening of June 19, once more suitably clad, I attended a small dinner with Admiral Harold Stark,[26] commanding our naval forces in Europe. It was interesting to be driven through the dark streets of completely blacked-out London. The cars had only dimmed lights, sufficient to prevent their colliding with each other, but not enough to light their way. How the drivers ever found their way, I would not know.

The weekend was occupied with conferences at Combined Operations headquarters, which was in a four-story building at 1 Richmond Terrace, formerly occupied by Scotland Yard. Here we learned the history of the Combined Operations organization, how it worked, and met its principal officers. We were given complete information as to its current activities and were even allowed to see hush-hush plans for a projected cross-channel raid on the Continent. We were also shown very interesting pictures of past raids.

Sunday afternoon my party and I, accompanied by Admiral Horan, who was to be our guide, philosopher, and friend throughout our visit, took a train for the Portsmouth Harbor station where we transferred to the *Sister Anne*, a yacht about the size of my old *Eagle*, which Lord Louis used as his flagship to visit Combined Operations activities, much as I used the *Carman* in the Chesapeake Bay. There we were greeted by Lord Louis himself and put up comfortably in small cabins. At dinner that night in the small messroom, the usual Royal Navy wardroom etiquette was carefully observed, that is, no smoking until after the King's health had been drunk to with the after-dinner port. During the dinner, Lord Louis, sitting at the head of the table with me on his right, asked me if I knew the custom. I replied that I did, that in the Royal Navy on board ship, the King's health was always drunk to while sitting, having been so decreed by King James, I believe, as a result of cracking his head against a deck beam when attempting to rise at dinner on a man-of-war of those days. The Admiral however, added an interesting story to that. He told us that when his father, Prince Louis of Battenberg, was First Sea Lord, a pamphlet on etiquette and customs in the Royal Navy was brought to him for his approval. When he read about the toast to the King, he declared that to be wrong, that he had never seen it done. "What my father did not know," said Lord Louis, "that the King's health was always drunk to while sitting, except in the presence of a member of the royal family, which he was."

At each end of the table, in front of Lord Louis and his aide at the foot, was a decanter of port. With dessert over, Lord Louis and the aide simultaneously removed the stoppers, held them up and then deposited them on the table. Then, each, without filling his own glass, passed the decanter to his left (the port must always go around clockwise). When each decanter had reached the opposite end of the table, and the Admiral's glass and that of the aide had been filled, the stoppers were ceremoniously replaced. Then Lord Louis stood and said, "To the President of the United States," to which we all drank while standing. Still standing, I raised my glass "To His Majesty, the King," then, having been assured that Lord Louis was not considered a member of the royal family to that extent, sat down with the others while drinking the toast.

After a pleasant night's rest, we found ourselves at anchor off Cowes on the Isle of Wight. There we visited two British assault transports which had just taken aboard Canadian troops preparatory to an exercise to be held the following day. There were few features differing from our own transports, except that they had heavier hoisting gear, permitting the landing craft they carried to be loaded at the rail, personnel and all—a most desirable feature. We also saw a tank landing craft, a prototype of the LCTs which was even then being manufactured in the United States. From there we went to the training base at Cowes, the headquarters of which was in the ordinarily sacred precincts of the Royal Cowes Yacht Club. After luncheon there, we went to Southampton in the Admiral's barge and thence by car to Lord Louis's estate at Broadlands for tea with Admiral and Lady Mountbatten.[27] We found them to be occupying only one small wing of the mansion, the remainder being given over to a hospital managed by Lady Mountbatten herself for the civilians injured from the German bombings.

From Broadlands, we rejoined the *Sister Anne* in Portland in time for dinner. On her, we met two new guests, Major General Eisenhower, recently sent to England to command U.S. Army Forces there, and Brigadier General Clark, with whom I shared a stateroom for the night. We finally tumbled to the fact that we had met at Fort Lewis some three years earlier. (As I mentioned previously.)

The next morning, Tuesday, June 23, we witnessed from ship and shore a landing exercise on the steep, shaley beach at Bridport and the simulation of the seizure of its harbor. Although we did not know it at the time, this was the rehearsal for the later successful but costly raid on Dieppe, carried out by the same Canadian troops. The British methods we found were quite similar to ours. Thence we visited a nearby combined operations training base, spent another night on the *Sister Anne*, looked over another base the following morning, Wednesday, June 24, and returned to London by car in time to board a night train for Glasgow. We certainly kept moving.

After a hasty early morning breakfast at the railroad hotel in Glasgow, we proceeded to Inveraray by automobile, skirting the beautiful Loch Lomand en route. It was my first sight of Scotland, and I enjoyed it immensely. At Inveraray, we visited the training establishment, then had lunch with Vice Admiral Hallett,[28] who was in command of the Combined Operations training organization. This was followed by two interesting lectures, partially illustrated, on the aspects of the amphibious assault problem and the lessons of past operations. In the interim, we managed to meet a very delightful gentleman, the Duke of Argyll, who invited us to visit his castle where we knew he had a magnificent collection of ancient arms and armor. Unfortunately, time did not permit us to accept. Lieutenant Colonel Campbell of the U.S. Marines, who had joined the party, was particularly intrigued by this encounter, since the Duke, "The Campbell," was the titular head of the Campbell clan. I should also mention that in front of the inn, the Argyll Arms, on the shore of Loch Fyne, we were entertained by the marching and countermarching of the bagpipe band of one of the highland regiments, which, of course, played, among other selections, "The Campbells are coming."

We boarded the transport *Ettrick*[29] just in time for dinner and after a little rest witnessed a night landing exercise at 3:30 a.m., which included a number of novel features. Thence, after breakfast on the *Ettrick*, we motored to another training center, Castle Toward, where we witnessed a demonstration of tanks landing under cover of smoke. Then we visited a train ferry converted for the carrying of landing craft, and the HMS *Tasajera*,[30] the prototype of all tank landing ships, the later well-known LSTs. This was what is called a Maracaibo-type oiler, a shallow draft tanker designed to carry raw petroleum from Lake Maracaibo to the refineries at Aruba. This craft had been converted by the installation of a deck to carry tanks, large bow doors and a ramp which could be let down on the beach. We witnessed a demonstration of its capabilities from the bridge and the tank deck. Then, since we ourselves were due to land, I was invited to go ashore in a tank, an invitation which I accepted with pleasure. Going down the ramp, hanging on to the tank turret, I was amazed to see three side boys on each side of me, and a boatswain's mate with his pipe. I am quite willing to wager that I was the first and very likely the last admiral ever to be piped over the side in a tank.

Next we visited the beach party training center at Inverkip and then Largs, the largest training center, where we spent the night. Both of these were on the Clyde. The following day, Saturday, was spent inspecting a number of other activities in the same general area.

On Sunday, June 28, we had an interesting drive across Scotland to Methyl on the Firth of Forth, where we visited HMS *Bulolo*,[31] a merchant ship converted into what the British called a headquarters ship from which forces engaged in a landing operation—naval, army, and air—could be effectively directed and controlled. She carried the necessary communications equipment, had a large war room with special plotting equipment, from which commanders and their staffs could watch the progress of the operation afloat, ashore, and in the air, and was well fitted with quarters for the necessary personnel—officer and enlisted. The British had early felt the need for such a ship because in several of their combined operations a combatant ship (cruiser or battleship) used as a flagship, was called away for combat duties, leaving the operation temporarily leaderless. Later, we were to adopt the same type of ship for our own amphibious operations.

Later that day, we flew to London. The following day, the 29th, we traveled from London to Plymouth by car, stopping at Salisbury for lunch with the commanding general of the Southern Army. On arrival at Plymouth, we were shown the underground headquarters of the Southwestern Naval Command. It was highly interesting to follow the plotting of all shipping and aircraft in the Channel area as carried out by busy Wrens receiving constant information from radar and other observation stations. The admiral and the watch officers of his staff were thus kept in constant touch with the situation in his area, day and night. We also inspected Admiral Forbes'[332] previous operations room constructed in the magazines and other underground spaces of Eggbuckland Keep, one of the ancient fortifications of Plymouth—this with the idea of its possible future use as an underground headquarters for a U.S. amphibious command in connection with a cross-Channel operation. Also inspected with an idea of possible future use as an American barracks was the nearby Bickleigh refugee camp, originally constructed to house civilians evacuated from bombed-out areas.

After a comfortable night as Admiral Forbes' guests at Admiralty House, we returned to London for further conferences at Combined Operations headquarters, during which, arrangements were made for close liaison between the Amphibious Force and Combined Operations, including full exchange of information and also of personnel. Several British officers with experience in previous landing operations were detailed to the Navy Department and thence to my Hampton Roads staff.

On the afternoon of July 1, we took a late train to Bristol where we spent a spooky night in a completely darkened hotel, amidst many of the ruins in that heavily bombed city. Fortunately, there was no raid that night. In fact, although we saw in the distance several night air raids, none occurred in our immediate vicinity throughout the trip.

Flying on the 2nd to Shannon airport in Eire, we drove to Limerick where we had a delightful meal at a fine Irish inn before continuing to Foynes. This afforded me my only real visit to Eire. That night we boarded a seaplane at Foynes for another transatlantic flight, this time via Newfoundland to New York. By the Fourth of July, we were back at Hampton Roads after a very interesting and productive, but strenuous, two-and-a-half week trip.

During my absence, the work of training, organizing and planning had been continued in high gear under the able direction of Captain Johnson. And it was about this time that we received secret information as to the possibility of landings in North Africa and some planning in that direction was initiated. N-2 and G-2 began the tremendous task of collecting all possible information about the Atlantic coast of Morocco, off-shore and on-shore, including weather and surf conditions, beaches, beach approaches and exits, adjacent terrace features, coast defenses and local defense forces, army and naval. This required probing all possible sources of information in a highly secret manner so as to give no inkling of the objective. Were this to leak to the enemy, a concentration of submarines could not only inflict heavy losses but very likely defeat the operation as a whole.

July was a period of intensive preparation, with a staff working in ever more cramped quarters. There was much travel back and forth for conferences with the high command in Washington, and there, on July 25, we received the go-ahead for TORCH, the North African landings. Our Army leaders had long favored a limited invasion of northern France, even in 1942. The British, who realized the difficulties and lack of readiness as they did not, were opposed. We, in the Amphibious Force, who also realized the problem, were greatly relieved at the final Anglo-American decision to undertake the North African alternative.

It was unfortunate that we could not have had an organization such as the British Combined Operations to coordinate the activities of all services in training, planning, and provision of matériel for the landing of ground forces against opposition on an enemy shore. We would have been spared such mistakes as the Army's purchase of wooden Chesapeake Bay Line steamers for prospective European use as cross-Channel transports. One was even fitted with special bulwarks and moved in convoy to Britain, where it was probably soon scrapped. No thinking seaman would have ever considered risking troops in such an unseaworthy and flammable craft where it might be subject to submarine or air attack or gunfire. Another mistake from the amphibious point of view was the training at Camp Edwards, Massachusetts, of Army engineer boat crews for surf landings. These crews were employed in the Algerian landings and performed efficiently, but they were engaged in what, to us, was properly a Navy function. After TORCH, they were soon drawn off for other engineer duties and were never used as boatmen in other Mediterranean operations. At a time when the Amphibious Force was exercising every effort to recruit *anyone* with marine experience for landing craft crews—fisherman, yachtsmen, etc.—it was distinctly annoying to read advertisements in leading newspapers addressed to the [same] sort of people, "Join the Army's navy." And it was still more annoying to have some of our best Coast Guard officers and surf men taken away from us to instruct these soldier crews. This was partly the Navy's own fault, for the Bureau of Personnel, depending on voluntary enlistment, did not feel that it could guarantee boat crews in what the Army thought was sufficient number. So the Army, having the benefit of the draft, went ahead on its own.

The decision to undertake TORCH resulted in the movement of one regimental combat team of the Ninth Infantry Division in Transport Division Eleven under Captain Campbell D. Edgar[33] to Britain. These, with the First Infantry Division, already there, were to participate with British forces in the landings in Algeria, inside the Mediterranean. About the same time, Captain A. C. Bennett, who had been my flag captain in the *Savannah*, was appointed a temporary rear admiral to establish an advance base in Britain. The Third Infantry Division, which had participated in some amphibious exercises on the West Coast, was brought east to become part of the Western Task Force, destined to land in Morocco. Of interest to me was the fact that this Third Division was the one whose guest I had been at field maneuvers in Camp Lewis, Washington, three years before. Also of interest was that it was commanded by a Naval Academy graduate, Major General Jonathan W. Anderson[34] of the Class of 1911.

Amphibious training of naval transports, boat crews, shore parties, and Army elements, when they became available, went on apace. Everywhere, we tried to instill the idea that no matter what uniform an officer or man wore, he was a member of one team working toward the same objective. To illustrate this, when later on we were able to establish our own headquarters in Ocean View, guarded by military police and bluejackets, the guard to honor a visiting dignitary was always paraded with alternate files of soldiers and sailors.

When active preparations for TORCH were added to the ever-increasing training load and staff requirements, the facilities available to the Amphibious Force at the Naval Base, initially cramped, became entirely inadequate. It was essential to find a site conveniently located and large enough to provide sufficient office space and where our work could be carried on undisturbed and in security. Such a locality was found in the Hotel Nansemond at Ocean View, on the beach front, near the boat and ferry landings on Willoughby Spit, not far from our budding Amphibious Base at Little Creek. There was some difficulty in getting it at first, because it had been preempted by some Army activity of lesser importance. Getting it was difficult because of secrecy requirements. We could not, of course, use immediate overseas operation requirements as an argument. However, after much effort and delay, we were finally able to move in on September 15. It was none too soon, because by that time a target date of November 8 had already been set for TORCH.

We had the whole hotel. Once again, my office was my bedroom, but I still managed to commute most of the time in my barge across the bay to the Chamberlin. A flag mess was set up, some officers were quartered in the hotel and others in adjacent beach cottages. A Nissen hut camp was established in a nearby park for the enlisted personnel attached to the headquarters. Then we really started to make progress, especially in the all-important planning.

Frequent visits by me and members of my staff to Washington continued. There, in about mid-August, as I remember, I first met General Patton,[35] who had been ordered in from training armor in the California desert to assume command of the Western Task Force. He and his staff who accompanied him were fine soldiers and fine gentlemen but, initially, at least, were handicapped by being almost completely ignorant of the technique and requirements of amphibious operations. I begged General Patton to set up his headquarters near me, where we and our staffs could have the daily contact which I considered to be so important to the necessary joint planning. But he felt that it was necessary for him to be at the War Department.

Exercises for continued training of the Third Division and the remaining elements of the Ninth Division, both of which came under my command for that purpose, were continued on the beaches near Solomons and Little Creek. For many of these, General Patton joined me, and we became very good friends, although of quite different temperament. Major General Ernest Harmon,[36] with some of his Second Armored Division from Fort Knox, also joined us for some time in August in the joint purpose of training his tank crews and our tank landing craft crews in the beach landing of tanks. Whenever they could be withdrawn from other duty, the cruisers, destroyers, and battleships which were expected to furnish our gunfire support, were sent into the bay for gunnery exercise on our Bloodsworth Island firing range. And our joint shore schools were all working full blast. There was little rest for one whose duty it was to supervise it all.

The worst task, however, was the planning, for there were so many uncertainties involved. Not until the end was it known just what naval units were to be available. Many transports reached us just in time for final rehearsals and had little or no other training. Any Navy plans and Army plans had to be closely coordinated.

By the time the Nansemond headquarters had been set up, the general features of the overall plan were beginning to take shape. The mission assigned to the Western Naval Task Force was: "To establish the Western Task Force on beachheads ashore near Mehdiya, Fedala, and Safi, and to support subsequent coastal operations in order to capture Casablanca as a base for further military operations." The plan had to be based on the assumption that the French forces would resist, although it was devoutly hoped that they would not. The strong fixed defenses of Casablanca, the presence of French naval forces in the port, and the absence of suitable landing beaches in the area ruled out any direct attack on that city. Fedala, a small port up the coast at the extreme range of the Casablanca batteries, had practicable beaches and only minor fixed defenses. It was chosen as the site of the main landing.

Since the British air facilities at Gibraltar would be fully occupied in supporting the Algerian landings, the only air support initially available to the Western Task Force and Naval Task Force was naval air. Therefore, the early seizure of an airfield was considered essential. Such a field existed at Port Lyautey on the Sebou River, some eighty miles up the coast from the principal objective. Not only was it an airfield but a French naval hydroplane base, since the windings of the river permitted smooth water landings into almost any wind. There were good beaches on both sides of the Sebou River mouth, at Mehdiya, and the fixed defenses there were minor. Port Lyautey would be one objective of the Northern Attack Group.

The relatively small tank landing craft carried by the assault transports and supply ships could handle only light tanks. Therefore, some other means had to be found for the landing of the fifty-four medium tanks of General Harmon's Second Armored Division, which General Patton considered essential to the success of a land attack on Casablanca. The small phosphate shipping port of Safi, about 140 miles south of Casablanca, had a dock which could accommodate an ex-Key West–Havana car ferry which was seaworthy and capable of carrying tanks. But there were no practicable beaches except inside the protective breakwaters, so an attack here presented a special problem. Of this, more later. Although hundreds of the big tank landing ships (LST) were under construction, unfortunately, none were yet available.

Thus it developed that the operation would have to be carried out by three main Attack Groups, the Northern at Mehdiya-Port Lyautey, the center at Fedala, and the southern at Safi. It had been agreed by the Joint Chiefs of Staff that unity of command would be exercised through a system by which the naval commander was to be in supreme command until the Army was firmly established on shore. Then the supreme command would pass to the Army commander and it would be the naval commander's duty to render all possible support to the operations on shore. With widely separated attack groups, this principle naturally applied also to their commanders.

Shortly after our move into Nansemond, General Patton and his staff did shift headquarters to Hampton Roads, thereby greatly facilitating the final planning. When it came down to details, many compromises between the military and the naval points of view became necessary. The point of landing best suited to future military operations was frequently impractical for surf landing of boats, where the best landing beaches often presented little promise to the military. Daily discussion of the problems between commanders and staffs soon resulted in joint solutions which were reasonably satisfactory.

Similar contact between naval and military command in the three attack groups was also essential to the formulation of their more detailed plans which involved the exact points of beaching, the number and size, and the timing of boat waves, and what units were to go in each. Accordingly, arrangements were made to effect this as early as possible.

General Harmon, who was to exercise the Army command in the Southern Attack Group, was already on the scene at Hampton Roads. Rear Admiral Davidson, who had relieved me in command of Cruiser Division Eight and whose division was to be assigned to the Western Naval Task Force, was made available to me as the naval commander of the Southern Attack Group. He and the general established contact as soon as his flagship, *Philadelphia,* could be spared from other duties and brought into Hampton Roads.

For the Army commander of the Northern Attack Group, my friend General Truscott, whom I had met in Britain the preceding June, was selected. He had the immense advantage of his experience with combined operations. His naval opposite number was to be Rear Admiral Monroe Kelly[37] who, with his flag in the *Texas*,[38] commanded the few battleships of the Atlantic Fleet available to support the operation. Admiral Kelly, General Truscott, and their staffs, and also their prospective transport commander, who would be responsible for preparing detailed plans for the boat waves, were also brought together.

There was no flag officer available, with the exception of myself, to command the Center Attack Group. But I had found from my past experience in fleet problems and maneuvers that it was most unwise for a commander of a force also to assume command of a unit of that force. To occupy himself with the details of operating a subordinate unit almost always meant that he would have to neglect the supervision of his command as a whole. Accordingly, I decided to give the command of the Center Group to Captain R. N. M. Emmett, Commander, Transports, Amphibious Force, Atlantic. Having been actively engaged in all the major landing exercises held during the past year or two, he was by all odds the most experienced amphibious officer in the command. In order to be centrally located and at the point of main attack, I intended to accompany the Central Group to be present there if needed. The troop commander for the Center Group would be Major General Anderson commanding the Third Infantry Division. Captain Emmett and General Anderson were able to start joint planning early.

The task of establishing the Western Task Force ashore in Morocco included not only its landing at the selected points but safeguarding of its movement to those areas against enemy attack—submarine, surface, or air. Axis submarine or raider attacks might be expected at any point during the passage. There were substantial French naval forces at Casablanca and also at Dakar; there were substantial French light forces and a number of submarines that had to be guarded against if the French decided to resist. Also there were two partially completed battleships of unknown mobility, the *Jean Bart*[39] at Casablanca and the *Richelieu*[40] at Dakar, which might be brought into play. The French also had a considerable number of air units at nearby fields whose opposition might have to be combated. To meet these threats required more than the cruisers, old battleships, and destroyers which were to be assigned to the various attack groups to furnish gunfire support and raider and submarine protection. Accordingly, two additional groups were formed: a support group consisting of the new battleship *Massachusetts*[41] and the heavy cruisers (with 8-inch guns) *Wichita*[42] and *Tuscaloosa*,[43] and an air group consisting of the carrier *Ranger,*[44] the light cruiser *Cleveland,*[45] and four auxiliary carriers (converted oil tankers), each with a submarine screen of destroyers. The former was to be commanded by Rear Admiral R. C. Giffen,[46] and the latter by Rear Admiral E. D. McWhorter,[47] both classmates and old friends upon whom I knew I could count for anything. In fact, I knew all my principal subordinate commanders well and had the utmost confidence in them—a most comforting thought.

Both Admirals Giffen and McWhorter reported to my headquarters as early as possible to be briefed as to the general plan and to discuss their roles in detail. To promote secrecy and deception, it was decided that the covering group would assemble at Casco Bay, Portland, Maine, and sail to join Task Force 34 from there. Similarly, the air group would be advanced to Bermuda, conduct preliminary training there, and join the Task Force later. In view of the security afforded by Bermuda, where all communications were under strict and effective British control, it was decided also to send there three old World War I four-stack destroyers to be fitted for special service in connection with the Mehdiya and Safi landings. They would accompany the air group in its sortie from Bermuda, acting as part of its screen, to the rendezvous with the main body of Task Force 34.

The special service these destroyers were designed to perform was of particular interest. The *Dallas*,[48] to be with the Northern Group, was to charge into the Sebou River after the boom protecting the entrance had been cut, and land a company of rangers for the seizure of the airfield at Port Lyautey. The other two, *Cole*[49] and *Bernadou*,[50] were to be used by the Southern Group to effect the initial surprise landing at Safi by dashing in through the breakwater entrance in darkness and going alongside docks to land their companies of specially trained rangers. All three vessels had their masts and stacks cut down at the Bermuda dockyard, so that they were very low in the water, making a minimum of silhouette, and the last two were provided with scaling ladders adjusted to the known height of the Safi docks at the state of the tide at H-hour of D-day.

The British, in some of their combined operations, had made good use of submarines to scout out landing areas to fix their position and then to act as beacons to lead transportation into the disembarkation area. This was of particular importance to us because we not only wanted the beaches marked, but a report of existing surf conditions was essential. Our intelligence indicated a probability of suitable conditions for landing of only one day in five in November and December on the Moroccan Atlantic coast. The Eastern and Center Task Forces in the Mediterranean would not have to be faced with such a problem. Accordingly, one submarine division of five boats was assigned to Task Force 34. This would give a beacon submarine for each of the three landing areas, one to observe Casablanca and one to watch Dakar for any reaction by the French forces there. The division commander, Captain Norman S. Ives,[51] would ride my flagship with me.

The only vessel with anywhere near adequate accommodations and communication facilities available to serve as my flagship was the heavy cruiser *Augusta*, which was or had been the flagship of the Commander in Chief, Atlantic. Accordingly, she was assigned to Task Force 34. Commanding her was Captain Gordon

Hutchins.[52] This powerful ship would add combatant strength to the force and, if present with the Center Group, would augment the gunfire support. But it suffered the disadvantage already noted by the British for this type of force flagship, the possibility of its being diverted to a necessary purely combatant role. As will be seen, such a diversion actually occurred, but, since it was for only a few hours, it had no serious effect.

Most of the transports originally assigned to the Amphibious Force, Atlantic Fleet had come from the old Army Transport Service in various degrees of matériel condition. All had to be converted to attack transports by being fitted to carry beaching craft for personnel, vehicles, and light tanks, and to be able to lower them in water which might not be entirely smooth. To obtain transports in adequate numbers to carry and land General Patton's Western Task Force, the Pacific Fleet had to be drawn on, and the conversion and manning of other merchant vessels had to be rushed. Not until very late was it possible to determine just how many would be available, and some reported barely in time to participate in a final rehearsal. Except for Coast Guard manned transports and the older naval transports, the training crews and boats left much to be desired, but the date set for the landing, November 8, 1942, was a must. We had to do the best we could with what we had.

The time had not yet come when the Army was to develop confidence in the accuracy of naval gunfire against land objectives. Consequently, the Supreme Commander, General Eisenhower, and other Army commanders were insisting on landings under cover of darkness and sufficiently before daylight to give reasonable time for the establishment of a beachhead. The zero hour for TORCH as a whole was set for midnight, at which time a message to the French from President Roosevelt was to be broadcast, announcing the landing and its purpose and asking that the Allied forces be received as friends. This hour was satisfactory for the Eastern and Center Attack Forces, which would be proceeding close along the Algerian coast as if en route to Malta. But this hour was entirely too early for the Western Task Force, which would be approaching its destination from seaward. Considering the state of training and the distance boats would have to travel from transport area to beach, it was estimated that at least four hours would be required between anchoring and beaching of the first waves. This would mean that transports would necessarily be anchoring at 8 p.m., and thus would be in sight of shore before dark. Thus the surprise considered so essential to success would be lost. As a result of urgent representations, a zero hour of 4 a.m. was authorized for the Western Task Force.

Submarines, French as well as Axis, were a great source of anxiety. In an effort to provide protection to anchored transports beyond that which could be afforded by a mobile destroyer screen, a mine detachment consisting of three large minelayers (named for old Navy monitors), five fast minelayers (converted from old destroyers), and several minesweepers were added to the force. The sweepers and fast minelayers would augment the anti-submarine screens underway. A fleet tug was also added to provide for possible breakdowns or other emergencies.

With the addition of five naval oil tankers to ensure adequate fuel supplies, the Western Naval Task Force would comprise a fleet of about one hundred vessels of all types, of which the most important were three battleships, three heavy and four light cruisers, one fleet carrier and four converted carriers, thirty-eight destroyers, twenty-three assault transports, and six assault supply ships.

With the exception of the covering group and the air group, which were to sortie from other points, the remainder of the shipping for Task Force 34 was gradually assembled in Hampton Roads during October for loading and for final rehearsals and training in Chesapeake Bay. The accommodation of such a large influx taxed the port facilities of Norfolk and Newport News, as well as the Naval Base, severely. Without the effective cooperation of the Army Port of Embarkation, the problem would have been well-nigh unsolvable. All those concerned were deserving of the highest credit, particularly as no one except those in the top echelon of command had any idea of what it was all about.

Considering the desirability of setting deceptive courses, the possibility of encountering bad weather, the possibility, if not the probability, of breakdowns in hastily readied ships with green crews, the necessity of conserving fuel and of refueling smaller ships en route, and the requirement to avoid areas of reported submarine concentrations, it was decided to set a departure date which would give ample leeway to meet these contingencies. October 24 was therefore selected for the main body of the force.

Off the Virginia Capes the shoal water of the Continental Shelf extends out about a hundred miles. To avoid mines which might be laid by enemy submarines, outgoing and incoming shipping was restricted to a long narrow channel constantly swept by Navy mine craft. The major shipping of the Western Naval Task Force proceeding out this channel single file, as it would have to do, would make a column some thirty miles long. In order to form a proper convoy disposition at the end of the channel, the leading ships would have to maneuver back and forth off the entrance for some two hours or more waiting for the rear ships to catch up. This would have provided such a rare opportunity for lurking submarines that it could not be accepted. It was decided to reduce this risk by dividing the force into two detachments, the advance detachment under Rear Admiral Kelly composed of Port Lyautey and Safi Groups, departing a day ahead, on the 23rd, to rendezvous later with the following detachment. In view of the submarine menace, it was not desirable to let the advance detachment proceed at slow speeds, so it was directed initially on a southerly course as if destined to the West Indies. To promote this deception, the Haitian government was asked for permission to hold amphibious exercises in the Gulf of Gonâve, in the hope that there might be some leak of information in Port au Prince.

Since the preservation of radio silence by all the force during the voyage to Africa would be of the utmost importance, rendezvous and alternative rendezvous were set in advance for the advance detachment, the covering group, and the air group. Hampton Roads and Amphibious Force headquarters at the Nansemond were centers of great activity throughout October, particularly toward its last week.

In the midst of this, on October 20, I received a secret dispatch directing me to report to President Roosevelt at the White House at 11:00 a.m. the next day. General Patton, already in Washington, was also to be present. There were so many last minute matters requiring my attention that I did not feel able to leave until the next morning. If flying weather was good, I could make the appointment easily by taking off not later than 9:00 a.m. Predictions were favorable. But since one does not arrive late for an appointment with the president of the United States, I decided to play it safe by having my car moved over to Old Point and directing that I be called at 5:00 a.m. with the latest weather report, in order that, if necessary, I might start for Washington in ample time by automobile.

The early morning report to my Hotel Chamberlin apartment convinced me that I could safely count on flying and encouraged me to roll over gratefully for a little more needed rest. But while having breakfast at the Nansemond, I received word that adverse visibility conditions were setting in, and if I wanted to get away, I had better get over to the airfield as soon as practicable. Mr. Griswold and I broke all records getting there, only to encounter considerable delay while my pilot awaited clearance. My feelings may be imagined. At last, to my relief, we were permitted to take off. But that relief was short-lived, because hardly had we passed over Fortress Monroe, when the plane winged over and headed back, the pilot reporting that he had been ordered to return. Why, he did not know. That was almost the first blow. But it developed that he had been called back merely to get his secret weather code, which he had forgotten. We were soon once more on our way.

Arriving over Washington with a low cloud ceiling, we were directed to circle while some plane in trouble was coached into a landing. I became more and more impatient. At long last we came down through the overcast. My delight at finally seeing Anacostia Field below me was somewhat indescribable. Whisked to the White House by a car with one of Admiral King's staff, we arrived just in time—a narrow escape.

General Patton and I were brought into the White House by separate entrances, in such a manner as not to be seen by any of the usually waiting reporters, who might have smelled a rat, meeting only in the anteroom of the president's office.

Ushered into the sanctum, I was able to greet the president as an old friend of *Indianapolis* days and then to present General Patton, whom he was seeing for the first time. We were greeted cordially and waved to seats. Then the president, leaning back in his chair with his cigarette holder in his hand, said, "Well, gentlemen! What have you got on your minds?" Whew! As if we did not have plenty! But I know that was said just to put us at our ease. Both the general and I discussed our plans at length and assured the president that we would carry through to the best of our ability. After a hearty handshake and a "Godspeed," we departed as we had come. By midafternoon I was back at my desk at the Nansemond, trying to tie up some loose ends.

A bit of a postlogue. Back in my apartment after a late dinner at the Chamberlin, I was sitting in a lounge chair, trying to catch up with the day's news in the paper when I suddenly caught myself falling out of the chair. Thoroughly alarmed, my good wife marshaled me into bed and, despite all my protests, insisted on calling up my medical officer who, in response, came dashing across the Roads in my barge to see me. After giving me numerous tests and finding that my eyes and other parts of my anatomy reacted properly, he merely prescribed more sleep.

NOTES

1 Arthur L. Bristol (1886–1942). Vice Admiral. U.S. Naval Academy, Class of 1906. Commander, U.S. Task Force 4, Argentia, Newfoundland.

2 Roland E. Brainard (1886–1967). Vice Admiral. U.S. Naval Academy, Class of 1906.

3 Lyal A. Davidson (1886–1950). Vice Admiral. U.S. Naval Academy, Class of 1910.

4 USS *Leonard Wood* (AP-25). Acquired by the Navy in June 1941, she was operated by the Coast Guard. In November, she transported troops to the Far East.

5 Manton S. Eddy (1892–1962). Lieutenant General, U.S. Army. He commanded the Ninth Division in the Tunisian and Sicilian campaigns in 1943 and took part in the Cherbourg campaign and the liberation of France. He commanded operations in France, Germany, and Luxembourg and was named commanding general of the U.S. Army in Europe in 1950.

6 Lee P. Johnson (1886–1964). Commodore. U.S. Naval Academy, Class of 1909.

7 Edward A. Mitchell (1895–1964). Rear Admiral. U.S. Naval Academy, Class of 1917.

8 Thomas F. Wellings (1898–1969). Rear Admiral. U.S. Naval Academy, Class of 1921.

9 Douglas S. Evans (1900–1965). Rear Admiral. U.S. Naval Academy, Class of 1922.

10 Leo A. Bachman (1902–1997). Rear Admiral. U.S. Naval Academy, Class of 1924.

11 Julian McCarty Boit (1900–1975). Rear Admiral. U.S. Naval Academy, Class of 1920. Flag secretary to Admiral Hewitt throughout the Mediterranean campaigns.

12 Benjamin H. Griswold III. Flag lieutenant to Admiral Hewitt. He remained with him throughout the Mediterranean invasions.

13 Harold R. Brookman (1898–1956). Rear Admiral. U.S. Naval Academy, Class of 1920.

14 Ralph W. D. Woods (1902–1982). Rear Admiral. U.S. Naval Academy, Class of 1923.

15 Bernard S. Pupek (1900–?). Captain, U.S. Navy, Medical Corps.

16 Robert A. J. English (1899–1969). Rear Admiral. U.S. Naval Academy, Class of 1922.

17 Bayard S. Johnson (1894–?). Colonel, U.S. Army.

18 Louis B. Ely (1899–?). Colonel, U.S. Army. U.S. Military Academy, Class of 1918.

19 Nathan E. McCluer (1892–?). Colonel, U.S. Army. He trained Army shore parties to unload landing craft. He retired in August 1945.

20 William P. O. Clarke (1893–1949). Rear Admiral. U.S. Naval Academy, Class of 1917.

21 *Lebensraum.* Living space.

22 William Norman Birkett (1883–1962). First Baron Birkett. Barrister and judge, he was knighted in 1941. He served as an alternate British judge at the Nuremberg war crimes trial in 1945.

23 Henry E. Horan (1890–1961). Rear Admiral, Royal Navy. CO, HMS *Leander*, 1940–1941; Combined Operations Headquarters, 1941–1943; Commander, Combined Operating Bases (Western Approaches), 1943–1946.

24 Lucian K. Truscott (1895–1965). General, U.S. Army. As a brigadier general in 1942, he commanded the troops of the Northern Attack Group of the Western Task Force in the landings in French Morocco, for which he was awarded the Distinguished Service Medal and promoted to major general. He led troops in the invasions of Sicily, Salerno, Anzio, and southern France. Later, in 1945, he commanded the Fifth Army in Italy. He was promoted to general in 1954.

25 Wrens, the acronym for the Women's Royal Naval Service. The service was established in 1917 during World War I and then disestablished in 1919. It was re-established in 1939 at the outbreak of World War II. More than 74,000 Wrens served in the war and 91 were killed in action. The Wrens became a permanent part of the Royal Navy in 1949.

26 Harold F. Stark (1880–1972). Admiral. U.S. Naval Academy, Class of 1903. Chief of Naval Operations, 1939–1942.

27 Edwina Ashley Mountbatten (1901–1960). Countess Mountbatten of Burma. She married Lord Louis Mountbatten in 1922.

28 John Hughes-Hallett (1901–1972). Vice Admiral, Royal Navy. Naval advisor to Combined Operations, 1941.

29 HMS *Ettrick* (1942). Frigate, River Class. 1,445 tons; dimensions 306' x 37 1/2'; speed 21 knots.

30 HMS *Tasajera*, built in 1938; 3,952 gross tons; carried six 20-mm guns; was requisitioned by the Royal Navy as a tank landing ship from May 1941 to February 1946.

31 HMS *Bulolo*. Built as a merchant ship in 1938 and converted to a landing headquarters ship in 1942.

32 Charles M. Forbes (1880–1960). Admiral of the Fleet, Royal Navy; Commander in Chief, Home Fleet, 1938–1940; Commander in Chief, Plymouth, 1941–1943.

33 Campbell D. Edgar (1889–1961). Rear Admiral. U.S. Naval Academy, Class of 1912.

34 Jonathan W. Anderson (1890–1967). Major General, U.S. Army. U.S. Naval Academy, Class of 1911.

35 George S. Patton (1885–1945). General, U.S. Army. He played a major role in Operation TORCH, commanding the ground troops in the 1942 invasion. He participated in the invasion of Sicily and the Battle of the Bulge.

36 Ernest Harmon (1894–1979). Brigadier General, U.S. Army. U.S. Military Academy, 1917; Commanding General, Second Armored Division, 1942; First Armored Division in the Tunisian campaign and at Cassino and Anzio, Italy, 1943–1944; Commanding General Second Armored Division, Battle of the Bulge, 1944–1945; first military governor of the Rhine, 1945; retired, 1948; president of Norwich University, 1950–1965.

37 Monroe Kelly (1886–1956). Vice Admiral. U.S. Naval Academy, Class of 1909.

38 USS *Texas* (BB-35). From 1939–1942, she served with the neutrality patrol and as a convoy and escort ship.

39 *Jean Bart* (1940). Battleship. Displacement 35,000 tons; Length 794'; Beam 108' 7"; Draught 26 1/2'.

40 *Richelieu* (1939). Battleship. Displacement 35,000 tons; Length 794'; Beam 108' 7"; Draught 26 1/2'.

41 USS *Massachusetts* (BB-59). She served as Admiral H. K. Hewitt's flagship during the invasion of North Africa, where she fired the first 16-inch shells against a European Axis ship.

42 USS *Wichita* (CA-45). In 1941, she operated in the North Atlantic and then sortied to Iceland where she engaged in patrol duty protecting U.S. shipping.

43 USS *Tuscaloosa* (CA-37). In April 1941, she was based at Bermuda in the neutrality patrol. Later, in August, she headed for Newfoundland for the meeting of Prime Minister Winston Churchill and President Franklin Roosevelt.

44 USS *Ranger* (CV-4). From 1939 to 1941 she was in the neutrality patrol operating between Bermuda and Newfoundland.

45 USS *Cleveland* (CL-55). Commissioned in June 1942, she was part of the task force that participated in the invasion of North Africa, November 1942.

46 Robert C. Giffen (1886–1962). Vice Admiral. U.S. Naval Academy, Class of 1907.

47 Ernest D. McWhorter (1884–1950). Rear Admiral. U.S. Naval Academy, Class of 1907.

48 USS *Dallas* (DD-199). In mid-1941, she served as a patrol, escort and convoy ship in North Atlantic waters.

49 USS *Cole* (DD-155). In 1939, she sailed with the neutrality patrol in Atlantic waters. She escorted convoys to Iceland and Newfoundland from 1941 to 1943.

50 USS *Bernadou* (DD-153). In 1939, she was part of the neutrality patrol and was on the Newfoundland-Iceland convoy run until 1942 when she took part in Operation TORCH, landing assault troops at Safi, Morocco.

51 Norman S. Ives (1897–1944). Captain. U.S. Naval Academy, Class of 1920.

52 Gordon Hutchins (1891–1952). Rear Admiral. U.S. Naval Academy, Class of 1913.

Unloading stores on Phosphate Pier, Casablanca, Morocco, November 1942 (Naval Historical Collection)

XIII   *The Voyage to North Africa, 1942*

And so the great day approached. At a conference held on shore, the details of the plans, Navy and Army, were gone over by General Patton and me and members of our staffs, with the principal commanders, many of whom were being let in on the secret for the first time. By October 22, the ships of the advance detachment had all moved out into Chesapeake Bay or Lynnhaven Roads, some holding last minute rehearsals. On the 23rd, Admiral Kelly and his group departed, as planned, ostensibly for the Caribbean. And on that day, General Patton and I, and those of my staff who were to accompany me on the operation, moved aboard the *Augusta*.[1]

As dawn broke on the 24th, a long column of ships, mostly transports with Army trucks on deck and soldiers hanging over the rail, started filing out past Fortress Monroe, bound beyond the Capes of the Chesapeake. The destroyers of the screen had already gone ahead to patrol the assemblage area off the entrance to the swept channel. In the midst of this sortie was the *Augusta*. As we passed the Hotel Chamberlin, I wondered what my wife and the other service wives there were thinking. I had merely told my wife that I had to go out on an exercise, and that it might be some time before I got back. Being a good Navy wife, she asked no questions.

We passed out of the channel, feeling well-protected, for the air overhead was well filled with Navy patrol planes and a guardian blimp, and our destroyers were all around us. By nightfall we were well on our way to the northeastward in five parallel columns of large ships—the *Augusta* leading the center one and the cruisers of my old Cruiser Division Eight heading the other four. We were off to a new adventure—the plans made and in the process of execution, one could only pray for the best.

General Patton was quite impressed with the orderliness and smoothness of a fleet sortie, something which he had not seen before, but the getaway was not entirely without a hitch and last minute problems required hasty solutions. The most serious was the breakdown of the *Harry Lee*,[2] an old transport taken over from the Army Transport Service, which had acquired the nickname of "Leaning Lena" from its tendency to assume a list and retain it. This casualty occurred after the ship had been loaded and the troops embarked. The transport *Calvert*[3] had to be hastily substituted. Although the latter was brought into a mooring across the dock from the *Lee*, the transfer was no simple matter. A combat-loaded transport must have on the top of its cargo all the equipment and supplies that will be needed first in an assault. Unfortunately, the items that had to be loaded to the top on the *Calvert* were on the top of the *Lee*'s holds. Thus, the *Lee* had to be fully unloaded before loading the *Calvert* could commence. It was impossible to get her ready in time to sortie with her group. The destroyers *Eberle*[4] and *Boyle*[5] were left behind as an escort, and she was given necessary rendezvous instructions. She actually sailed two days after the main body.

The other hitch was the acquisition of some craft to transport aviation gas for the use of Army planes to be based on the Port Lyautey airfield. This required a seaworthy vessel small enough and of sufficiently light draft to navigate the shallow Sebou River up to the airfield. A suitable ship was finally found in the SS *Contessa*, flying the Honduran flag and commanded by a valiant British seaman by the name William H. John. This ship, however, could not be made ready to sail with the convoy for the reason that she required some repairs, and for the more important one that when her crew of mixed nationalities learned that she was to carry a very flammable cargo to an unknown destination, most of them promptly jumped ship. The crew was ultimately filled out with volunteers of merchant seamen from the Norfolk city jails. The master of the ship himself had no idea where he was going. The only one on board who did know was the naval liaison officer, Lieutenant Commander A. V. Leslie, USNR, who was given sealed orders to be opened after departure. The story of the *Contessa* crossing the Atlantic all alone is a saga in itself. She got away all by herself on October 26.

After forming a cruising disposition before sundown on the 24th, the main body took up a cruising speed of 14 knots, which, with the zigzag, gave a speed of advance of about 12 knots. As darkness fell, destroyers in the rear of the screen dropped astern to drive down any submarine which might be trailing, and after dark, a change of the base course was made. These expedients became standard procedure throughout the voyage. In view of radio silence and the undesirability of using any light signals during darkness, signals were made by flag before dark, prescribing all course changes for the night with times of execution. The changes were then automatically made at the given time, with no signal other than a whistle blast by column leaders. Naturally, it was highly important that those signals be received and understood by each ship. Screening destroyers always acted as shepherds for lagging ships. Radar proved to be of utmost value in checking the positions of ships in the disposition.

Most of the first day out was spent in exercising the ships of the main body in maneuvering by flag signal, using the prescribed allied convoy signal book called Mersigs, and in the various set zigzags. One oil tanker, due to an engineering casualty, was forced to drop back, but was able to regain station well after dark. There were other similar casualties on the following day, the 26th, but, fortunately, all ships concerned were able to rejoin before dark.

In mid-afternoon of the 26th, contact was made with the covering group, as scheduled, approaching from the northward. This group maneuvered to take station in a protective position, some fifteen miles in advance of the main body. The cruiser *Brooklyn* was ordered ahead as a linking ship, halfway between, in order to maintain contact and repeat signals. It was her special responsibility to ensure that all maneuvering signals got through and that the acknowledgement of the commander, covering group was duly transmitted to the *Augusta*. Before dark on the same day, Admiral Kelly's advance detachment was sighted on the horizon to the southward. It was directed to take station fifteen miles astern and to join the disposition after daylight. That these contacts were duly made was a source of great satisfaction. During the day there had been one reported submarine contact, but it was probably false. Course was now altered more to the eastward.

After daylight on the 27th, the disposition maneuvered so as to permit Admiral Kelly's detachment to catch up. This was formed in four columns, with the Northern Group ships in two columns on the left, and the Southern Group ships similarly to the right. By opening out and moving up with two columns on each side of the main body, the task force disposition, as then formed, had nine columns of ships abreast in logical order, with the vessels for Mehdiya-Port Lyautey to the northward, those for Fedala in the center, and for Safi on the right. The flagship *Augusta* now took station well ahead of the center column to facilitate signaling and observation of the disposition as a whole.

All that was now lacking was the air group and the *Calvert*, which had been left behind at Hampton Roads. But Admiral McWhorter and his group turned up as scheduled, being sighted on the starboard bow about 10 a.m. of the 28th. The carriers took station astern of the main body, where they could readily maneuver to launch and recover planes. They promptly established a daylight anti-submarine air patrol over the disposition, relieving the float observation planes of the cruisers and battleships. Having reached a longitude to the eastward of Newfoundland, course was now altered to the southeastward to suggest Dakar as a destination. Happily, the weather so far had been fairly good.

On the morning of the 29th, five days out, the *Calvert* and her escort turned up, to my great relief. Now Task Force 34 was all present, except for the *Contessa*, which would be on its own until it reached the Northern Group attack area.

General Patton and his staff had little to do during the voyage except to amuse themselves as best they could. The general spent some time reading the Koran. He wanted to be thoroughly acquainted with the Moslem religion and customs so that neither he nor any of his troops would do anything to antagonize the native Berber population.

As for me, I spent all my time either on the flag bridge or in my bridge cabin. With plans all made and promulgated, there was little to do except to study the intelligence and weather reports broadcast to us, to watch for reported concentrations of submarines, to plan the changes of course necessary to avoid such danger spots and to throw off possible trailing submarines, and to be ready to take suitable action in the event of an emergency. Ships were still breaking down now and then, but, fortunately, resuming station after effecting repairs.

A good commander should always try to plan ahead what his action should be in the event of possible emergencies. With such advance decisions in mind, valuable seconds can be saved in taking decisive and sound action when the emergency actually arises. One decision which I tried to face was "in the event that a transport is torpedoed, how many destroyers do I dare to leave behind to pick up survivors, without weakening the screen so much as to unduly endanger the remainder?" Considering my responsibility for the lives of some 35,000 soldiers and as many more naval personnel, and the fact that the screen was none too strong as it was, it was a most difficult decision to make, and one that I never did solve to my satisfaction. I thank God that the occasion never arose where I had to implement it. There were occasional alarms but no actual attack throughout the voyage.

The smaller vessels of the task force, such as the destroyers, did not have sufficient steaming radius to complete the voyage. It was necessary to refuel them once to get them across, and it was highly desirable to top them off again a day or two before arrival in order that they might be capable of sustained high-speed steaming in the event of combat. The latter consideration also led to a decision to refuel the cruisers. The first fuelling was initiated in fairly good weather on October 30 and was completed the following day in a mid-Atlantic area. Since it required a steady course and a slow speed for the tankers and the ships being fuelled, it was a period of great vulnerability to submarine attack. The air patrols were doubled, and the vessels of the screen that were not actually fuelling maintained a high-speed patrol. General Truscott, desiring further opportunity to indoctrinate some of his subordinate commanders, asked and received permission to visit several ships of the Northern Attack Group during the operation, transferring via motor whaleboat. This was accomplished safely and to his satisfaction, and to my relief when he returned to his own ship.

Some ships, during the fuelling period for others, carried out anti-aircraft practices on targets towed by carrier planes.

By November 2, we were well south of the Azores—in fact almost between them and the Cape Verde Islands and still heading on southeasterly courses. We were warned of three submarines to the northwest of the Cape Verdes, four to the west of the Azores, and four more not far from our line of advance. There were several submarine sound contacts reported during the day, some of which may have been authentic, and a German shore station was overheard broadcasting what we knew to be a contact report. It looked as if we might have been spotted.

After dark that night, the night of November 2–3, several very radical changes of course were made, which, by the morning of the 3rd, found us heading to the northeastward so as to pass to the northward of the Azores. It may be difficult for the layman to appreciate, but large changes of direction during a fully darkened night by such a large body of ships in close formation is a tricky maneuver. That it was accomplished without untoward event is a testimonial to the training and skill of the officers primarily concerned.

The enemy submarine estimate received during the early morning of the 3rd indicated a possible concentration off Dakar, which led us to hope that our ruse of heading in that general direction might have been successful. These submarine position estimates were the result of Allied radio direction-finder bearings taken during the night, when the submarines habitually surfaced and reported by radio to their higher command. We were now moving toward the Strait of Gibraltar.

It was planned to start the topping off fuelling on the 3rd, but the weather became too rough, the convoy wallowing in the trough of a moderate swell from the North Atlantic. Even proposed anti-aircraft practices had to be called off. One of the planes from the carrier *Ranger* crashed, but the pilot and crew were picked up by the destroyer *Wilkes*.[6] One transport dropped back as the result of an engineering casualty, but rejoined.

The weather on the 4th, if anything, was worse, and the fuelling again had to be postponed. The auxiliary carrier *Suwannee*[7] had an engineering casualty, and the minelayer *Miantonomah*[8] was unable to keep up on the prescribed course due to an excessive roll. The latter was directed to proceed independently and given a rendezvous for the following day. We were having our troubles.

On the 5th, we still could not fuel, and some of the shorter ranged small craft were getting so dangerously low that the possibility of towing had to be considered. We were also approaching an area where we were liable to encounter north and southbound European-African traffic. In fact, after dark that night, an emergency turn had to be executed to avoid being sighted by a lighted vessel, which, upon being investigated by a screening destroyer, turned out to be a Portuguese passenger steamer bound for the Cape Verde Islands. She was directed to maintain radio silence for twelve hours. Other contacts were made on the following day, but none saw the convoy.

On the 6th, with somewhat more favorable weather, the scheduled refueling was carried out. By that time, it was a must. All weather reports were, by now, receiving more careful attention than ever. There was an alternative plan by which, if a Moroccan landing ultimately proved impracticable, the Western Task Force would be landed inside the Mediterranean in western Algeria near the Moroccan border.

However, this was an undesirable alternative since it would greatly delay, if not defeat, attainment of Casablanca as a supply port for the Allied armies of North Africa. After dark, a destroyer was detached to take station well to the southward for the transmission of important despatches to the beacon submarines, to the *Miantonomah*, which had not yet rejoined, and to the Supreme Allied Commander in Gibraltar. The beacon submarines were directed to report surf conditions. Transmissions by a single vessel well away from the convoy itself would not disclose the convoy position to enemy direction finders.

In order to effect a timely arrival in their assigned areas, it would be necessary for the various attack groups to begin breaking off shortly after daylight on the previous day. Therefore, a decision as to whether to carry out the attack on November 8, as scheduled, had to be made early on the 7th. All night long on the 6–7th, General Patton and I studied the incoming weather reports, and Lieutenant Commander Steere worked on his weather charts, covering all the North Atlantic. As previously mentioned, the latter had spent most of the summer studying the relationship between weather in the North Atlantic, where the swells which broke on the Moroccan coast were generated, and the actual surf conditions in that area. We were receiving independent surf predictions from both the War and Navy Departments, but from our knowledge of the backgrounds of the experts involved, we placed greater confidence in the latter.

There were many factors which had to be weighed. An attempted landing through over-rough seas might spell disaster, an entire failure, and/or undue loss of life. On the other hand, delay would undoubtedly mean loss of surprise, serious exposure to gathering submarines as the task force cruised up and down off the coast awaiting favorable weather, lowering of fuel supplies, and, finally, perhaps entire abandonment in favor of the alternate plan.

Army predictions were entirely unfavorable. The Navy report was slightly more optimistic but not too encouraging. Mr. Steere was of the opinion that the landing would be practicable. Furthermore, he felt that the conditions would be much less suitable on the following day, the 9th. I still had one ace in the hole. If, later on, unfavorable reports were received from the beacon submarines, I could halt the operation by radio. I decided to go ahead, and General Patton concurred. Divine Providence was with me, for it was one of the most important decisions of my life. Conditions for sixty days after the 8th were highly dangerous.

Several years later, a Russian general, with whom I became associated in connection with the United Nations and who had apparently been studying my background, told me that he was most interested in Professor Morison's[9] account of the foregoing incident. He said, "You decided to proceed with the attack without asking the general?" "Yes, General," said I, "General Patton was fully informed, but I was the seaman, and it was my responsibility to decide whether a landing would be practicable."

The Russian just shook his head in disbelief. Apparently, it was incomprehensible in the Russian army that an admiral should make a decision involving a general.

As soon as it was sufficiently light for signaling, the signal "Execute Attack Plan One" was transmitted to the task force by flag and by light. By 0700, the flag signal, "proceed on service assigned," was directed to the commander of the Southern Attack Group in the *Philadelphia*. Admiral Davidson immediately assumed charge of the ships assigned to his group and moved off to the southward toward Safi. He was joined by the auxiliary carrier *Santee*,[10] detailed to him from the air group to provide his air support. The destroyers assigned to the remainder of the main body realigned themselves as an anti-submarine screen and a change of course more to the northeastward was made.

Shortly thereafter, the airplane tender *Barnegat*,[11] which had come from Iceland to join the force as a tender for seaplanes at Port Lyautey, was sighted. And by 0800, to our relief, the little *Contessa* appeared, safe after a lonely and perilous voyage.

An hour after noon, the covering group and, a little later, the air group were detached to take up their assigned stations and duties. The auxiliary carrier *Sangamon*[12] joined the ships of the Northern Group to supply their air support.

At 1500, the Northern Group was detached and Admiral Kelly directed his course toward the mouth of the Sebou River. At the same time, command of the Center Group was turned over to Captain Emmett, the *Brooklyn* and *Augusta*, respectively, taking stations ahead of the left and right wing columns. From then on, Captain Emmett exercised tactical command of his unit.

The African coast was picked up on the radar, and somewhat before midnight coastal navigation lights were unexpectedly sighted, thus greatly facilitating navigation. Later it was learned that they had been turned on for the benefit of a French coastal convoy. They were, however, turned out before the arrival of the transports in the disembarkation area, which was reached slightly ahead of schedule, a few minutes before midnight, but not until after a number of radical maneuvers had been made to counteract the effect of an unexpected coastal current. There was a swell, but little wind and no rough sea. The beacon submarine had been sighted; no adverse reports had been received; landing craft were being hoisted out and loaded. The appointed beach was only seven miles away.

Broadcasts of President Roosevelt's message announcing the landings were intercepted from Washington and London. For better or worse, the operation was underway.

During the morning watch off Fedala on November 8, all was quiet ashore. In fact, no sounds other than that of slow-running, circling landing craft and the voice of Captain Emmett over the TBS (short-range ship-to-ship radio) giving orders to his transports were heard in the transport area. Unknown to me until later, all the other groups had arrived at their stations exactly on time. Quoting our eminent naval historian, Professor (Rear Admiral) Samuel E. Morison, "So closely was the timetable executed that the Northern Attack Group arrived at its planned position off Mehdiya at 2400, the Southern Attack Group made Safi at 2345, and the Center Group was in Fedala Roads at 2353. For precision planning and faultless execution, this on-the-minute arrival of a large, complicated Task Force after a voyage of about 4,500 miles merits the highest praise." These are kind words, but the planning was easy. Past experience (the *Indianapolis* presidential cruise, e.g.) indicated the desirability of always having ample "velvet" to reach a destination on time, regardless of weather, etc. Credit for faultless execution belongs to the various group commanders.

NOTES

1 USS *Augusta* (CA-31). Admiral Hewitt, General Patton and Rear Admiral Hall sailed to North Africa in her on October 23, 1942, where she participated in the fighting.

2 USS *Harry Lee* (AP-17). Originally a passenger ship, she was purchased by the U.S. Navy in 1940. Prior to 1943 and the invasion of Sicily, she served as a troop transport ship and conducted amphibious exercises in the Caribbean.

3 USS *Calvert* (AP-65). She participated in the North African invasion and successfully landed troops in Safi, Morocco.

4 USS *Eberle* (DD-430). She took part in the landings in North Africa in November 1942, and provided fire and bombardment support at Mehdiya, Morocco.

5 USS *Boyle* (DD-600). As part of Task Force 34, she took part in the landings at Fedala, Morocco, November 8–11, 1942, and fought the French at Casablanca.

6 USS *Wilkes* (DD-441). Assigned to Task Force 34, she participated in the attack on Fedala, Morocco, November 8–11, 1942, and fought the French at Casablanca.

7 USS *Suwannee* (ACV-27). Converted from an oiler to an auxiliary aircraft carrier, she took part in Operation TORCH as part of the Center Attack Group. Her planes engaged in bombing raids and in anti-submarine patrols.

8 USS *Miantonomah* (CMc-5). Part of Task Group 34.9 of the Western Naval Task Force, she sailed to Morocco where she laid a mine field outside of the transport area and escaped two submarine attacks in Fedala harbor.

9 Samuel Eliot Morison (1887–1976). Naval historian and professor at Harvard University, 1925–1955. He was designated official U.S. naval historian, holding the rank of lieutenant commander during World War II. He wrote the fifteen-volume *History of United States Naval Operations in World War II*.

10. USS *Santee* (ACV-29). Acquired by the Navy in 1940 as an oiler, she later was converted to an auxiliary aircraft carrier, later redesignated an escort carrier. As part of Task Group 34.2, she sortied to Safi, Morocco, where she took part in the landings, fueling ships, and launching planes.

11 USS *Barnegat* (AVP-10). She participated in the landings at Mehdiya and helped to establish the air station at Port Lyautey.

12 USS *Sangamon* (ACV-26). Originally an oiler, she was converted to an auxiliary aircraft carrier in 1942. As part of Task Force 34, she sailed to North Africa to support the landings near Port Lyautey.

French fishing trawler with American ensign and troops loading for transport ashore, Morocco, December 1942. (Naval Historical Collection)

XIV *Operation TORCH, 1942*

The details of the landings in Morocco have been so thoroughly covered by historians, both on the American and the French sides, that I shall endeavor in these reminiscences to limit myself to the events of which I was an eyewitness, or to those in which I, as the task force commander, was intimately concerned. At about 0130 our radio intercepted reports from both London and Africa of the midnight scheduled landings in Algeria. It was, of course, assumed that this information would be transmitted from Algiers and Oran to the French command in Morocco, which might result in a military alert. We were hoping against hope that when discovered, the searchlights on shore would be elevated to the vertical, the signal that there would be no resistance and that we were being received as friends. All of our units were under strict orders not to fire unless fired on or unless other positive signs of hostile reaction were shown. In each case an immediate report was to be made via the chain of command, and there was to be no general engagement except by order of the commander of the particular group concerned. In order to expedite such reports and orders, resort was had to American baseball terminology. "Batter Up" in plain language over the TBS meant "I am being fired on," and "Play Ball" from a commander was the order for the unit addressed to go into action.

The Center Group, on account of the depth that far offshore, could not anchor in the transport disembarkation area and had to heave to, occasionally maneuvering to counteract the effect of the current. This, coupled with the darkness and the unfortunate inadequate training of some transports, resulted in delays which early made it evident that the Zero Hour of 0400 could not be met. About 0300, Captain Emmett postponed H-Hour to 0430, and shortly thereafter set it back another fifteen minutes. Radar plotting showed the first wave of boats starting in about 0400, but they did not land until 0505, a little over an hour late.

As the first wave was approaching the beach, or just after it had landed, a searchlight was turned on from the Chergui or Pont Blondin battery on the northeast flank of the landing area and immediately turned upward. The hoped-for signal? No! It was immediately brought down to the water's edge, picking up the advancing boat waves. Then was heard the sound of machine-gun fire, apparently from ashore, immediately followed by a stream of tracer bullets from one of our scout or support boats directed toward the searchlight, which immediately went out—either shot out or turned off.

The destroyers assigned to the special duty of furnishing gunfire support were in position well inshore, clear of the boat lanes, and the cruiser *Brooklyn* was also on station to cover the Chergui battery on the left flank of the landing. The *Augusta* was in a position on the right flank, more toward Casablanca. The minesweepers and the destroyers of the screen were maintaining an active patrol on the flanks and seaward side of the transport area. It was about 0530 that a coastal convoy of two small French steamers, escorted by the small corvette *Victoria*, coming down the coast blundered into the left flank screen with unfortunate results. Not knowing what he was up against, the gallant little corvette, ignoring the minesweeper *Hogan*'s[1] warning to stop, opened fire and attempted to ram. The *Hogan*'s 20 mm return fire swept the *Victoria*'s bridge, killed the captain, and brought the little convoy to a halt. This gunfire was noted from the *Augusta* and the incident was promptly reported over the TBS. Boats returning from the beach reported, via Captain Emmett, that there appeared to be little opposition on shore, but that many boats had been damaged on landing.

By about 0600, faint outlines of the shore and heights above Fedala began to appear in the early morning twilight. This was followed by the flashes of gunfire from the shore batteries as they became able to distinguish the shipping offshore. By this time, there had been numerous reports of "Batter Up." With the gunfire support vessels under fire, "Play Ball" was soon given for the Center Group, and the action became general. The Brooklyn, delivering a rapid fire on Chergui with her fifteen-gun 6-inch battery, was a sight to behold, and that battery was soon silenced. The cruisers had launched their observation planes at daylight. It was not all one-sided, however, for the destroyer *Murphy*[2] received a hit in one engine room, which killed three men and disabled the engine.

The fire of the *Augusta* and right flank support destroyers similarly silenced the defenses on Cape Fedala, the tip of the little peninsula which, with its outlying breakwater, formed Fedala harbor. Unfortunately, one of the oil tanks of the tank farm there, which we had particularly planned to conserve for future use, was hit and set on fire. This silencing was only temporary, for these batteries came to life later and once more had to be taken in hand.

By 0800 firing between shore and ship at Fedala had died down, and the *Augusta* closed the transports again to be prepared to furnish anti-aircraft protection. It was well that she did, because about that time a few French planes flew in and strafed the Fedala beaches. Little or no damage was done, and no transports were hit. The planes of Admiral McWhorter's air group were already in the air—fighters, torpedo bombers, and scouting planes, furnishing air cover and information, and standing by to attack. The French submarines in Casablanca harbor constituted such a dangerous threat that the air group had been given orders that any attempt by them to sortie was to be considered hostile. This, however, was unnecessary, because the anti-aircraft fire against the planes circling over the harbor was sufficient evidence of French resistance. The submarines, the *Jean Bart*,[3] and the anti-aircraft batteries were accordingly bombed. French airfields in the vicinity were also worked over, but French planes took little part on the whole.

In the meanwhile, Admiral Giffen,[4] with his covering group, had similarly gone into action against the ancient Table d'Oukasha battery to the northeast of Casablanca, the *Jean Bart* with its one completed quadruple turret alongside a dock, and the modern El Hank battery to the southwest of the harbor entrance.

Reports of these actions reached me fairly promptly, but the anxiously awaited news of events in the north and south was slow in coming. Later it was learned that everything had gone well at Safi in accordance with the plan. A scout boat had found and marked the entrance buoy; the *Cole* and *Bernadou* had dashed in alongside the selected docks and landed their rangers successfully; other elements had landed on small beaches, one inside the little harbor, one at the entrance, and one to the southward. Surprise had been complete and resistance negligible. The *Lakehurst*[5] was soon disembarking her tanks.

In the north, however, things had not gone quite so well. Troops had been landed at or near the proper beaches, but with some confusion and errors similar to those at Fedala, where some troops had been landed northeast of Fedala and one group of boats had so lost its way in the darkness that searching along the coast for its beach it had found itself in Casablanca harbor, where crews and passengers were promptly taken prisoner. Also, surf conditions were bad and, as at Fedala, many boats were stranded and disabled. Furthermore, here, unlike at Fedala and at Safi, strong military resistance was encountered. (In the French defense organization, it is the Navy which usually mans coastal fortifications, and it was the Navy which was putting up the spirited fight at Fedala.) The ancient fort, called, the Kasba, at Mehdiya, high on a hill commanding the entrance to the Sebou River, was manned by a strong detachment of the famous Foreign Legion. The other defending forces in that area were also legionnaires and two regiments of the Moroccan *Tirailleurs*, the cream of the French colonial army. General Truscott, fearing that inaccurate naval gunfire would endanger his troops, had elected to carry the Kasba by storm. He wished naval gunfire to be used only when called for by the troops on shore. The *Texas* and the *Savannah* could have demolished the old stone fort in short order, but, unfortunately, they were not called on to do so. Consequently, there were serious delays in cutting the barrier net, and then it was accomplished only on the north side. The *Dallas*, with her French river pilot (secretly smuggled to the United States in time to join our convoy) ultimately reached its destination up river after ramming the net on D+2.

Returning to the Fedala story, as soon as it become light enough and the shore batteries sufficiently silenced, the transports moved closer in to the beach to reduce the boat run, and there they were able to anchor. The minelayers, as planned, proceeded to lay an anti-submarine minefield beyond torpedo range on the left (northeast) flank of the transport area, and the vessels of the screen continued their active patrol of the other two sides.

The Naval War College and staff experience during fleet problems had taught me that lack of adequate information from subordinate commanders was not only annoying to superior commanders, but often made sound decisions difficult. I had learned to ask myself what I would want to know were I in my superior's shoes. The whole world now knew where we were, so there was no further need for radio silence. Accordingly, I directed Captain Bachman, my intelligence officer, to prepare a situation report on the operation of the Western Task Force every two hours for transmission to the Supreme Allied Commander (General Eisenhower) and the CINC Mediterranean (Admiral Cunningham)[6] at their headquarters on the Rock. This was done religiously, so that I felt I was doing everything possible to keep those officers informed of developments as I knew them. It was not until three days later, when the SAC dispatched a staff officer to me from Gibraltar in a British destroyer to find out what was going on that I learned that none of these dispatches had been received. I have never been able to determine the reason. It is probable that the British communication and decoding facilities at Gibraltar were so overloaded that my reports were lost in the shuffle. There was no doubt of their having been broadcast from the *Augusta*.

As it happened, General Patton and I were to experience somewhat the same sort of difficulty with reports from the Northern Task Force, so much so that ultimately, at the request of General Patton, Brigadier General Cannon[7] of the Army Air Force, who was with us, was sent up to Mehdiya to investigate.

General Patton having expressed a desire to go ashore at Fedala, shortly after 0800 a Higgins personnel landing craft, being carried on the well deck of the *Augusta* for just such a purpose, was swung out by the aircraft recovery crane and lowered to the port rail. While some of the general's equipment was being loaded into it, a report was received from an observation plane that a number of French destroyers were sneaking close in along the coast, under cover of a smoke screen, toward the Fedala transport area. Since these immobile ships would soon be within torpedo range, no time could be lost in driving the destroyers off. The *Augusta*, the *Brooklyn*, and the two nearest destroyers swung into action—the two cruisers opening fire on their unseen targets on bearings and ranges given them by their observation planes. With a target sharp on the port bow, the blast of the *Augusta's* after

8-inch turret completely wrecked the fragile landing craft and it had to be cut away, contents and all.

The gallant little French ships were soon forced back toward their harbor, but not without loss. The covering group, firing at El Hank, had drawn too far to the westward to counter the sortie of these light forces and I had to call Admiral Giffen back. During this action and subsequent ones during the day, the two cruisers had to dodge torpedoes several times. Whether these came from the surface ships or from the French submarines that had escaped being sunk in the harbor and then succeeded in getting out has not been entirely established.

We finally succeeded in getting General Patton ashore about three hours late (not three days, as in some accounts). Instead of being annoyed at the delay, as charged, he stood alongside me at the bridge and watched the action with keen interest. But the incident did emphasize the undesirability of joint command being exercised from a flagship which might have to be diverted from that function. Steps were immediately taken by our Navy Department to convert a number of transports to command (or, in British terminology, headquarters) ships, and this was the last time a cruiser was so employed in one of our amphibious operations.

The day was not over before my subsequent good friend, Contre Amiral Gervais de la Fond, made repeated courageous and skillful attempts to torpedo the Fedala transports, in the course of which practically his entire command was either sunk, beached, or otherwise disabled, including the gallant little admiral himself, who was wounded. A *Ranger* plane had reported that the *Jean Bart*, as a result of bombing, had been gutted by fire.

Resistance at Safi having ended, and the *Massachusetts* and cruisers of the covering group having imposed considerable damage, the *New York*,[8] which had done little firing, was ordered up from the Southern Group as a reinforcement. During the 9th, very little happened from the naval point of view, except that unloading was continued from transports now moved well inshore but, as a result of the many casualties, with fewer boats. One cargo ship was moved to a dock in Fedala harbor, which could now be used instead of the open beach for discharging the landing craft. It was well, for a very heavy surf was now breaking. The nights of the 8–9th and 9–10th were spent by the *Augusta* and *Brooklyn* underway inside the minefield and destroyer screen, anxiously maintaining station near the transports. Anxiously, because news of the landing could be expected to bring German submarines into the area in spite of our offshore air patrols. Admiral Michelier, the Prefect Maritime at Casablanca, who had been ordered by Admiral Darlan[9] in Algiers to resume command of all French forces in Morocco, rejected all negotiations for an armistice. Our forces, thus, landed at Fedala and at Safi and closed in on Casablanca from both directions. (An interesting sidelight, illustrative of Army and Navy cooperation, was that General Harmon's advancing armored forces were refueled by some of Admiral Davidson's landing craft, which followed them along the coast.)

On the morning of the 10th, General Patton came out for a conference with me on the *Augusta*. Disembarking from a bobbing landing craft, he had to climb a rope embarkation net up the high side of the ship to the well deck. Although he was a well-known athlete, he was so slowed by fatigue and by the equipment he wore that I momentarily feared for his safety. If he had ever let go, he would have sunk like a stone. Captain Hutchins and I, who were waiting to receive him, got down on our knees, reached over the side, and as soon as we could, grabbed his arms and literally hauled him aboard. As we walked up to my cabin, I noted that the general did seem pretty well worn out, so, remembering an *Indianapolis* experience, I sent my orderly to summon the ship's medical officer. When he arrived, I said, "Doctor, I think the general is very tired, and I wish you would prescribe for him." "And," I added, "you might prescribe for me, too." He took the hint. Forever after, General Patton claimed that I had saved his life on that occasion.

Hardly had General Patton left the ship on his return to shore when there was a report from an observation plane that there were several small enemy vessels offshore, apparently firing into our troops advancing from Fedala. This naturally could not be allowed, so the *Augusta, Brooklyn,* and two accompanying destroyers took off once more down the coast. This was somewhat of a surprise, because we had been led to believe that all the light forces in Casablanca were, by this time, *hors de combat*. They were only two small corvettes, which were soon driven back into port, but not before we received a surprise of another sort.

As we came down the coast to close the range, our proximity to the *Jean Bart* caused us no concern, because we knew that she had received hits from the *Massachusetts* and had been heavily bombed. Her turret, trained toward the *Massachusetts* on the 8th, had not been moved since that day, according to reports from the air. Suddenly, two huge orange splashes rose, so close alongside the bridge of the *Augusta* that I and others on the flag bridge were doused with the spray. It was no place for the *Augusta* to be. We promptly rang up full speed, put the rudder full right, made smoke and zigzagged away, but not before we had been near-missed several times more by the *Jean Bart's* two-gun salvos. The French gunnery was excellent. It was a close call. Later I was to learn the French side of that episode from a rugged Breton, who, as her captain, was responsible for sneaking that half-completed ship out from under the noses of the Germans when France fell and who, promoted to *contre amiral*, was in command of the Casablanca defenses at the time of our landing. This was Pierre Jean Ronarc'h,[10] a gruff man with a keen sense of humor, who became a very good friend. Said he, "On Sunday (the 8th), the *Massachusetts* made a hit on the barbette, which jammed the turret in train. The crew, after working diligently for thirty-six hours, finally got it free. I ordered it left trained as it was.

So it happened, when you ran down the coast on Tuesday after our little corvettes, the gunnery control officer sat up in the top beckoning and saying, 'Come a little closer! Come a little closer!' And you came."

In the early evening of November 10, I issued the necessary orders for the naval participation in the final assault on Casablanca. This was to consist of the bombing and bombardment of targets, selected by the Army, by naval planes and the batteries of the *Augusta*, the *New York*, and the *Cleveland*[11] at long range, and four destroyers closer in, commencing at 0715. The *Cleveland,* which had been the cruiser escort for the air group, was brought in because she still had a full allowance of ammunition.

Shortly after midnight of the 10–11th, word was received from General Patton that Casablanca might capitulate at any time, and directing that we be prepared to suspend hostilities at short notice. This information was promptly passed on to the naval forces, and they were directed to be ready to cancel the proposed bombardment upon the receipt of a cease-fire broadcast *en claire.*

By 0700, the bombardment vessels were on station with their guns loaded and elevated, and bombing planes were in the air proceeding toward their targets. But at that very moment, the welcome word arrived from shore, and the cease-fire was broadcast to all stations. It was in the nick of time, because fingers were already on firing keys and bomb releases. Down came the guns and back went the bombers to their carrier. Fittingly, it was the twenty-fourth anniversary of the armistice day of World War I. That date now had a double significance for me.

Returning to our position off Fedala, we learned that there was to be an armistice conference with French officials that day at the Hotel Miramar in Fedala, and Admiral Hall[12] went ashore to get the details. He sent out word that General Nugues, the governor general, and other military officials would not arrive until afternoon, but that Admiral Michelier would lunch with General Patton at a Fedala restaurant (the hotel's kitchen having been put out of commission by a destroyer shell intended for the Batterie du Port). My presence was requested. I got ashore about 1230 and found quite an assemblage at a pleasant *brasserie,* some dozen in all, consisting of General Patton, Admiral Michelier, and myself, together with leading members of our staffs. Colonel Wilbur, who had attended the École de Guerre, and Marine Major Rogers of my staff were there as interpreters, but none was really needed because most of the French officers spoke excellent English.

I was a little uncertain how to approach Admiral Michelier, whom I found to be a fine-looking man of medium height. The desire to establish friendly relations was uppermost in my mind, so I put out my hand, which he took, and said that we had come as friends and old allies, and that it was with the greatest regret that we were forced to fire on the *tricouleur*. He looked me in the eye and said, "Admiral, you had your orders, and you carried them out. I had mine, and I carried them out. Now, I am ready to cooperate in every way possible." I am happy to testify that he kept his promise faithfully.

During the course of a very amicable conversation at the luncheon, the subject of our urgent need for the facilities of the port of Casablanca arose. Admiral Michelier replied, "You have not seen it! *C'est une cimitière*!" And so it was, as we later discovered.

The later conference at the Miramar was more formal and certainly stiffer. General Nogues was received with all the honors due his rank, by a guard of military police. General Patton, having succeeded to the overall command after establishing his headquarters ashore, presided. General Nogues, pending receipt of awaited orders from Admiral Darlan, would make no formal agreement other than the cease-fire then in effect and a release of prisoners by each side. In order to avoid loss of French prestige with the restive native Berber population and take advantage of the service of the French military in preserving order, this was a wise decision. The governor general sought permission to take disciplinary action against certain subordinates who, he claimed, had been guilty of insubordination. This was refused by General Patton, who had been informed that General Bethouart, one of the French officials secretly advised of TORCH in advance, had been placed under arrest by General Nogues in the early morning of the 8th for attempting to isolate the governor and forestall resistance to the landing. The impression was gained that General Nogues was one of those who had become firmly convinced of the ultimate success of the Axis and was afraid to offend the Nazis. It was 1700 before I was able to return to my flagship.

Contrary to some published accounts, there was never any thought of moving any of the Center Group transports into Casablanca harbor on this date. Not only is this my own firm recollection, recorded five years later, but it was amply substantiated by the testimony of my chief of staff, Admiral Hall. We still had little or no information of the readiness of the harbor to take any ships. Such a move would have been difficult in darkness and would have interrupted the landing of supplies such as provisions and fuel still being urgently demanded by the Army. Moreover, the presence of these transports there would interfere with the reception of the D+5 follow-up convoy, due within about thirty-six hours, by daylight of the 13th. Had there been any chance of moving any ship into port that night, I certainly would have taken the *Augusta* in, not only because she was a valuable ship then serving no useful purpose at Fedala, but because it would have expedited arrangements for future operation of the port.

There had been indications of gathering submarines, evidenced by unsuccessful attacks on vessels of the air and covering groups, either from French or Nazi submarines. This situation was naturally a source of worry, but was not unexpected. By now, the transports were anchored close in, one flank supposedly protected by an anti-submarine field with other approaches covered by what was thought to be an adequate screen composed of every available suitable vessel, destroyers, and minesweepers. After dark, the two cruisers (the *Brooklyn*, due to expenditure of its main battery ammunition, had been exchanged for the *Cleveland* of the air group) were anchored for their protection in inner berths. To have kept them underway offshore during the night would have necessitated weakening the transport screen by the withdrawal of two or more destroyers. Also, fuel was becoming a consideration.

Darkness closed in early on that evening of November 11, and, except for the loading and movements of boats, all was quiet with the totally darkened shipping in transport area. With some of my staff, I was on the flag bridge apprehensively looking at the blaze of light from the now illuminated Casablanca, the glare from which was certainly silhouetting my ships from eastward. Hardly had I drafted a message to the Army requesting action to obviate this hazard, when there was the boom of an underwater explosion nearby. It was the transport *Joseph Hewes*,[13] torpedoed on the port bow. The time was 1948. A few minutes later, the oil tanker *Winooski*[14] and the destroyer *Hambleton*[15] were hit on their port sides. All available boats in the vicinity were promptly dispatched to the *Hewes*, which was wildly signaling by blinker for help. Unfortunately, she sank in less than an hour, taking her gallant captain, Robert McL. Smith,[16] a splendid officer, a loss which grieved me greatly. Fortunately, her troops had been landed and the remainder of her crew, except for several killed by the explosion, were rescued. But a large part of her cargo was lost. The hit on the *Winooski* was in an empty fuel tank, and did not prevent the further discharge of her fuel, nor her return home for repair. The hit on the *Hambleton* was more serious. She was hit in an engine room and fire room and lost twenty of her crew. But the crew succeeded in keeping her afloat. She was towed into Casablanca the following morning, where, with French assistance, she was repaired sufficiently to enable her to return with a westbound convoy.

It having become a matter of urgency to discover what use could be made at once of Casablanca harbor, my operations officer, Captain Mitchell, was dispatched there with several others to survey the situation. He was not able to return with the necessary information until the following morning.

Rear Admiral Hewitt and Rear Admiral John L. Hall confer during Operation TORCH, 1942. Naval Historical Collection)

There were no further attacks that night. The guilty submarine was sighted and attacked by a screening destroyer, but succeeded in making its escape only to meet its fate several days later off Casablanca at the hands of other U.S. screening vessels.

After a sleepless night, I called a conference on the *Augusta* in the very early morning to discuss the new developments and get the ideas of my principal subordinates at Fedala. Present were Captain Emmett, the commanders of the screen and the minecraft, my chief of staff, Rear Admiral Hall, Captain Norman S. Ives, the commander of the submarine squadron from which came our beacon submarines, and other senior officers.

Three principal courses of action seemed to be open. They were:

a) To move all ships practicable into Casablanca at once;
b) To continue unloading during daylight at Fedala, getting them underway at dark and taking them to sea, returning to the anchorage in the morning;
c) Continue the unloading at Fedala day and night.

Course a) was discarded by me because it would mean delaying the entry of the D+5 convoy, as previously mentioned. When the Army first proposed this timing, we had strongly demurred, stating our conviction that we could hardy guarantee the readiness of Casablanca harbor before D+10. But the Army had insisted, maintaining that the arrival of the troops and equipment to be carried by that convoy by D+5 was a must. We had agreed only with many misgivings. It seemed preferable to me to risk transports close in to shore from which the troops had been disembarked and the cargo partially landed than it was to expose ships fully loaded with men and matériel cruising up and down well offshore to the mercies of a gathering submarine pack.

This left course b) or c). Captain Emmett insisted that it was of the utmost importance to keep the unloading going without interruption. The officers of the screen thought that the previous night's attack was a freak success and seemed to feel reasonably confident that they could prevent future ones. Captain Ives, the submariner, pointed out that anchored ships were sitting ducks, which was, of course, true. But I did have considerable faith in the screen and the minefield, in spite of what happened.

It was a difficult decision that I had to make—one for which I accept full responsibility—and one which, based on the existing premises and knowledge I then had, I would make again today. Influenced by a desire to ensure the safe and timely arrival in port of the following convoy, to avoid interruption in the delivery of supplies and munitions to General Patton's forces, and to expose only partially discharged ships to the major risk, I decided with reluctance to adopt course c). I ordered Captain Emmett to continue unloading day and night, but at the first sign of further trouble, to take his ships promptly to sea.

I then proceeded into port with the *Augusta*, where we moored with the help of French tugs, anchored by the bow and stern into the breakwater, called the jetée. As we passed in through the entrance, it was rather tricky to see the French sailors all standing by their anti-aircraft guns. Had there been any breach of faith on the part of the French, we would have been in for trouble.

There was, however, no cause for uneasiness. No one could have had more perfect cooperation than that which was shown us. The *Augusta*, with the aid of a French pilot and tugs, was placed port side alongside the phosphate pier, just inside the entrance along the northeast breakwater. Here we were able to survey the conditions in the harbor, which was indeed a *cimitière*. The hull of a capsized French destroyer lay just inside the entrance. Opposite us, alongside the main pier, was a line of sunken merchant vessels. On the other side of this pier, partially hidden by the damaged dock house, was the badly damaged *Jean Bart*, resting on the bottom. At the end of this pier was a capsized passenger vessel which had arrived from Dakar on the 7th, carrying women and children fleeing that port in fear of an attack there. Fortunately, they had been taken ashore before the shelling of the *Jean Bart* had started. The long-range bombardment on that ship had been responsible for all the surrounding damage.

Contact with Admiral Michelier's staff was established early through his chief of staff, Rear Admiral Missoffe, who came on board with the news that his chief had established a special *Bureau des Affaires Américains*, through which we could deal directly in obtaining needed services. Plans were made for the reception of the D+5 convoy the following morning, November 13—the French exerting every effort to clear a maximum number of berths.

A problem of protocol engaged my attention. We had defeated a gallant French resistance and were more or less taking charge. But Admiral Michelier was a vice admiral, and I a rear admiral. Furthermore, we had not come as conquerors but as friends and allies. It was important to restore that relationship. I sent my flag lieutenant to the *Amirauté* to inquire when it would be convenient for Admiral Michelier to receive my official call. After some delay, I received word that the admiral would be happy to welcome me at the Admiralty at 5:00 p.m. the following day. I sensed that the French were surprised and wanted time to prepare a proper ceremony.

This day of November 12, unfortunately, ended far from happily. At about 6:00 p.m., while it was still daylight, three transports at Fedala, the *Edward Rutledge*,[17] the *Hugh L. Scott*,[18] and the *Tasker H. Bliss*,[19] were torpedoed. The first two sank within a short time, but the *Bliss*, on fire, hung on until after midnight. It was a daylight attack, successful in spite of our minefield and our surface and air patrols. Unfortunately, there were no salvage vessels immediately available, but, with the exception of those killed in the explosion or trapped below by fire, most of the crews were safely brought ashore where they were well cared for by the Army, French civilians, and their own surviving medical personnel. Later, it was learned that this attack was the work of a U-boat which had sneaked down from the northeast, so close to shore that it passed safely inside the anti-submarine minefield.

In accordance with his orders, Captain Emmett promptly got the surviving vessels of his force underway and took them to sea. There was no question now but that the Center Group ships would have to be brought into Casablanca the next morning for final unloading, instead of the D+5 convoy due at the same time. Orders had to be radioed to rear Admiral Bryant,[20] in the USS *Arkansas*[21] to cruise with his convoy well off-shore out of sight of land until further orders.

Hardly had the above catastrophe occurred when a British destroyer, HMS *Welshman*,[22] arrived bearing Rear Admiral Bieri[23] and some Army members of General Eisenhower's staff seeking information about the situation in Morocco. As previously related, the Supreme Allied Commander had received none of my carefully prepared intelligence reports. We took them aboard the *Augusta*, the *Welshman* having come alongside. General Patton, whose headquarters had not yet been moved to Casablanca, was sent for and we conferred well into the night. At about 2:00 a.m., with the flames of the burning *Bliss* just being quenched as she finally went under, the visitors departed for Gibraltar to report the latest sad news. Our attention was then turned to the plight of the survivors. There was no rest for the weary.

The 13th was a busy day. The French port authorities having determined that five transports could be handled and berthed on that day, Captain Emmett was ordered to send in that many to arrive as early as possible. The *Augusta* was shifted to the southern jetty, the *jetée*, where she was moored at right angles, anchored by the bow with the stern to the jetty. Other vessels not requiring dock space for unloading, such as the auxiliary carrier *Chenango*, which had flown off her cargo of Army fighter planes to be based ashore and was now ready to act as an oiler, were similarly moored parallel to the flagship. Hardly had this move been made than the *Augusta* was called upon to take alongside the British destroyer *Venomous*,[24] carrying survivors from HMS *Hecla*,[25] sunk the previous night off the straits. These poor men were taken aboard and fed and clothed, some having little to cover their nakedness.

In the planning of Operation TORCH, it had been realized that the vessels of a convoy arriving off Casablanca could be moved into port only a few at a time and that a protected off-shore anchorage area would be necessary. This could only be provided by an anti-submarine minefield, which was the principal reason for the inclusion of a large mine force in Task Force 34. The planned field had now been completed, the entrance marked with a patrol vessel stationed off it, and due notice broadcast to allied shipping and the allied command. It is interesting to note, particularly in view of the Fedala events, that no ships were ever successfully attacked inside this field nor in subsequent similar fields off Oran, or at Sicily, or at Salerno.

Captain Emmett's first ships arrived in the early afternoon and were safely berthed as planned. Unloading was started at once, but there was confusion, for the Army had made insufficient provision for handling stores dockside.

My call on Admiral Michelier that afternoon was very pleasant. I was greeted by a very smart guard of honor of French bluejackets, dressed in blue coats and white trousers and white caps, topped by the traditional Pompon Rouge. As I passed down the line on my formal inspection, I studied their faces for signs of resentment, which I could well have pardoned, for many had lost friends and shipmates at our hands. But all was quite militarily correct.

As I proceeded up the steps to the entrance, I noted two major caliber projectiles, one mounted on each side. These, I later found, were unexploded shells from the *Massachusetts*, mounted especially for my benefit—truly a French touch. The many shells from the *Massachusetts* which failed to detonate indicated faulty fuses, which later became the subject of a Bureau of Ordnance investigation.

The Admiral welcomed me politely, and since his English was very good, we had no need for an interpreter. At first, I was a little uncertain of him, because I knew that he had once been the French naval attaché in Berlin and thus might have some Axis leanings, but I was soon disposed of this idea. Among other things, he urged me to take every possible precaution to combat air attack. Said he, "I know these Germans. I expect they will attack us with everything they have." The *Jean Bart* had an anti-torpedo net around her to protect her from an attack like the one at Pearl Harbor. He called my attention to this, and said, "*Le Jean Bart, c'est fini*. Let me place the net around your *Augusta*." In view of the way my flagship was moored, with other shipping close to her on each side, I felt that there was little danger. Moreover, the net would have interfered with very necessary boat traffic. So I declined this very thoughtful and kind offer.

Admiral Michelier returned my call very promptly the following morning, when he was received on the *Augusta* with all the honors due his rank (barring a gun salute, not customary in wartime). The basis for a lasting friendship had been laid.

This was D+6, the 14th, and scattered elements of the Western Naval Task Force no longer required were being started on their way home. Admiral Giffen and his covering group and Admiral McWhorter and his air group, needed elsewhere, and their Moroccan task completed, had already departed. Three vessels of Admiral Kelley's group were ordered south to complete unloading—two to Safi and one to Fedala's little port. The last, the *Electra*,[26] was torpedoed en route but put into Casablanca only slightly damaged. The remainder of the Northern Attack Group was directed to rendezvous off Casablanca on the 15th with the five Center Group transports from there and return to the United States.

The 15th saw the departure of the foregoing transports and entry of eleven more, some from the Northern Group. To accommodate them, many had to be docked two abreast. Only the inboard ship could be unloaded onto the dock; the outboard ones had to discharge into lighters provided by the French. The unloading situation became even more chaotic and was the subject of many conferences with the Army in an effort to get it cleared up. It is difficult for me to see how anyone could contend that all this shipping might have been handled on the 11th.

By the morning of the 16th, General Patton had established his headquarters in Casablanca in the midtown Shell Oil building. This made for more effective liaison, and I promptly visited him there. The *Brooklyn* and three destroyers, short of fuel and having been prevented by rough weather from fuelling at sea, entered port and were berthed at the *jetée* alongside tankers, of which the torpedoed *Winooski* was one. The British hospital ship *Newfoundland*,[27] arriving at nightfall to pick up the survivors of the *Hecla*, unaccountably failed to receive word of our minefield and, ignoring the frantic signals of our patrols, was damaged by a mine. Fortunately, since she was light draft and the field was deep-laid to protect against submerged submarines, the damage was minor.

Captain Emmett's Task Group 34.9 was now reorganized to include, with the exception of the *Augusta* and the mine squadron, all the remaining undamaged vessels of Task Force 34. At daylight of the 17th, this force began to sortie from Casablanca, a movement which was not completed until late afternoon. After assembling, course was laid for Hampton Roads. Admiral Bryant was directed to bring his ships in the next day.

On the 18th, the follow-up convoy, UGF-2, arrived early off the port. Its entry and berthing was not completed until well after dark. I was happy that no mishaps had befallen these ships, heavily laden with troops and stores. And it was somewhat of a satisfaction to note that this was D+10, the date for which we had originally argued and which the Army had maintained would be too late.

November 19 was devoted to picking up loose ends. Admiral Hall and his party moved ashore to establish the Moroccan sea frontier and the naval operating base, Casablanca. I lunched with General Anderson at the suburban villa which he had taken over for his headquarters and which later served as the scene of the January Casablanca Conference. After lunch, I went to General Patton's headquarters for a meeting with General Eisenhower, who had flown down from the Rock. Good-byes were said all around.

I had decided to return independently with the *Augusta*, depending on high speed and zigzag and the avoidance of usual convoy routes for her protection. Thus, all available destroyers could be used to screen returning transports and there would be no refueling problems for the *Augusta*. However, leaving on the morning of the 20th, we were screened until well out of sight of land by two of Admiral Bryant's destroyers. They then returned to port.

The following two dispatches received that morning and later duly transmitted to the Western Naval Task Force as a whole were sources of great satisfaction and pride, both to me and the splendid officers and men who were primarily responsible for the successful accomplishment of the task assigned. I quote:

> For Admiral Hewitt from Eisenhower x With successful completion of your task under Allied headquarters and your return to normal American command I want to express my grateful appreciation of the splendid services you and the officers under your command have rendered x I am making immediate official report to Washington to this effect but in the meantime I hope it is proper for a soldier to say to a sailor "Well done."

And this from General Eisenhower's Supreme Naval Commander, Admiral of the Fleet, Sir Andrew B. Cunningham, Royal Navy, to the commander of the Western Naval Task Force:

> On departure of WNTF I send you my congratulations on a fine job well done x The problems faced were in many ways the most difficult and I have admired the energy and resolution with which you and all under your command have tackled them x I send very good wishes to your Force for speedy passage and good landfall.

The first few days out were uneventful and we were able to proceed at about 23 knots—a higher speed was precluded by fuel considerations. But by the 23rd, we had run into heavy weather which forced a matériel and unsafe reduction in speed—unsafe that is as far as avoidance of submarine attack was concerned. But the ship, like her sister the *Quincy*,[28] with me on a previous occasion, cracked a frame forward while driving into a heavy sea. In order to get all the speed and armament possible into these ten-thousand-ton treaty cruisers, factors of structural safety had been somewhat slighted. With bad weather predicted for the remainder and enemy submarines operating actively off our coasts, I felt that it was not wise to risk this fine ship and its crew by finishing the voyage unescorted at reduced speed. Accordingly, I decided to proceed into Bermuda to await an escort, which I directed Captain Emmett to detach and send me.

On arrival at Bermuda, I received a pleasant surprise in a very funny way. At sea in a war zone, we never flew personal flags, but as we entered the Great Sound in Bermuda, my two-star was broken at the main. When an old friend, Rear Admiral James,[29] the commander of our Bermuda operating base came on board, he said, "What are you doing flying a rear admiral's flag?" "Why not?" said I, "I am a rear admiral." No, you are not," said he, "You are a vice admiral." I told him that it was the first that I had heard of it, but he insisted that it was true, that it was in all the news reports. However, since I could not well assume a new rank on the basis of a news report, my old flag continued to fly.

After two pleasant days at Bermuda, during which I was very pleasantly entertained by the governor general and his lady, Viscount and Viscountess Knollys,[30] and by Vice Admiral and Lady Curteis,[31] and with Rear Admiral James, I inspected the facilities of our naval base. Our escort had arrived and refueled, so we departed for Hampton Roads. We arrived there without incident, going alongside the pier at the base shortly after noon on November 30th. On the dock waiting for me was my chief of staff, Commodore Johnson, and my official car bearing bright new three-star plates. There seemed to be no longer any doubt as to my promotion. PHIBLANT had received the official word, but none had thought to pass it on to the commander of Task Force 34.

The three returning convoys—Admiral Davidson's, Admiral Kelley's, and Captain Emmett's—all reached their homeports without incident. All of these officers had performed splendidly. The mission of the Western Naval Task Force had been completed. Now it was time to return to the duty of COMPHIBLANT.

Settling back into the old routine, I found things at Ocean View and at our Little Creek amphibious base humming. Commodore Johnson and my joint Navy-Army Staff had carried on splendidly. The new landing craft—Landing Ship Tank (LST), the Landing Craft Tank (LCT), and the Landing Craft Infantry, Light (LCI [L]), all patterned after their British prototypes, developed by Lord Louis Mountbatten's Combined Operations organization—were coming off the ways in numbers, and their crews were being assembled and trained under the direction of the indefatigable Captain W. P. O. Clark. I had the pleasure of riding the first LST to report to the Amphibious Force in a first landing exercise off Fortress Monroe. These craft were of low speed, but very seaworthy; they could carry and discharge a large number of vehicles and their crews; and they had fuel capacity sufficient to cruise thousands of miles. The others, of far less endurance, could still carry vehicles and troops from nearby bases to assault beaches.

NOTES

1. USS *Hogan* (DD-178). A ship of the Western Naval Task Force, she was involved in minesweeping off Fedala. She forced the surrender of the French ship *Victoria* that attempted to ram her. *Hogan* continued anti-submarine patrols until she returned to the United States in December.

2. USS *Murphy* (DD-603) was commissioned in 1942. The destroyer was part of the Center Attack Group of the Western Naval Task Force that participated in Operation TORCH. The ship suffered damage in the attack on Point Blondin.

3. *Jean Bart*. French fast battleship built in 1940 with a speed of 30 knots, a displacement of 35,000 tons, and 15-inch armament. She was damaged by the USS *Massachusetts*' guns at Casablanca in 1942.

4. Robert Giffen (1886–1946). Vice Admiral. U.S. Naval Academy, Class of 1907.

5. USS *Lakehurst* (APV-3) transported equipment and supplies to Safi, Morocco for Operation TORCH. In December she returned to Casablanca with men and matériel.

6. Andrew B. Cunningham (1883–1963). First Viscount Cunningham of Hyndhope. Admiral, Royal Navy. During World War II, he was commander in chief of British naval forces in the Mediterranean, 1939–1942. In 1943, he was named Allied naval commander in the Mediterranean. He was First Sea Lord, 1943–1946.

7. John K. Cannon (1892–1955). Lieutenant General, U.S. Army.

8. USS *New York* (BB-34) was commissioned in 1914. She served during World War I on blockade duty and in World War II participated in Operation TORCH.

9. Francois Darlan (1881–1942). Admiral of the Fleet of Vichy, France, as well as the vice-premier, foreign minister, and minister for national defense during World War II. He was assassinated in Algiers following the armistice with the Allies.

10. Pierre Jean Ronarc'h (1892–1960). French naval officer who, as captain of the *Jean Bart*, was responsible for her escape from Saint-Nazaire before the German attack. The ship was still under construction and successfully made its way to Casablanca. Ronarc'h was promoted to rear admiral in 1941 and headed the Navy in Morocco until 1943. As a vice admiral, he commanded the French forces in the Mediterranean until the end of the war. He was head of the Navy in Algeria until 1947.

11. USS *Cleveland* (CL-55). Commissioned in 1942, she took part in Operation TORCH, covering the landing of troops at Fedala, Morocco. During the rest of the war she was in the Pacific theatre where she was involved in many major battles.

12. John L. Hall (1891–1978). Admiral. U.S. Naval Academy, Class of 1913.

13. USS *Joseph Hewes* (APA-22). Part of the Center Attack Group of the Western Naval Task Force, she was hit by a torpedo from *U-173* and sank in Fedala harbor.

14. USS *Winooski* (AO-38). She took part in the North African landing at Fedala. Despite the fact that she was torpedoed, she continued refueling operations.

15. USS *Hambleton* (DD-455). Part of the Western Naval Task Force, she was torpedoed off Fedala, towed to Casablanca, repaired, and returned to the United States for permanent repairs.

16. Robert McLanahan Smith Jr. (1896–1942). Captain. U.S. Naval Academy, Class of 1919.

17. USS *Edward Rutledge* (APA-24). Torpedoed by *U-130*, she sank in Fedala harbor.

18. USS *Hugh L. Scott* (AP-43). A ship of the Western Naval Task Force, she was torpedoed by *U-130* in Fedala harbor, foundered, and sank.

19. USS *Tasker H. Bliss* (AP-42). Torpedoed by *U-130* in Fedala harbor, she burned and sank.

20. Carleton F. Bryant (1892–1987). Vice Admiral. U.S. Naval Academy, Class of 1914. He assumed command of USS *Arkansas* in April 1941 and was relieved in May 1943. He served as Commander, Center Support Group, Western Naval Task Force during the landings in North Africa.

21. USS *Arkansas* (BB-33). Commissioned in 1912, she escorted convoys to Europe and Africa, including three to Casablanca, Morocco, during Operation TORCH.

22. HMS *Welshman*, British destroyer. Completed in 1940. Displacement 2,650 tons; length 410'; guns, six 4.7".

23. Bernard H. Bieri (1889–1971). Vice Admiral. U.S. Naval Academy, Class of 1911.

24. HMS *Venomous*. Admiralty modified. Weight 1,120 tons; 300, 312' x 29 1/2' x 10' draught.

25. HMS *Hecla* (Depot Ship). Built in 1940. 11,000 tons. She was lost during Operation TORCH.

26. *Electra* (AK-21) participated in the invasion of North Africa at Safi. She was torpedoed on the way to Fedala, but was beached at Casablanca and repaired.

27. HMS *Newfoundland*. Cruiser. Completed in 1942. Displacement, 8,000 tons; Length 549', Beam 62', Draught, 16' 5".

28. USS *Quincy* (CA-39). Ordered to the neutrality patrol in 1941, she remained on patrol duty until March 1942. She was sunk in the South Pacific in August 1942.

29. Jules James (1885–1957). Vice Admiral. U.S. Naval Academy, Class of 1908.

30. Edward George William T. Knollys, Second Viscount (1895–1966). Governor and Commander in Chief, Bermuda, 1941–1943; chairman, BOAC, 1943–1947; and director of various banks and insurance companies.

31. Alban T. B. Curteis (1887–1961). Admiral, Royal Navy. Promoted to Vice Admiral in 1941 as Commander, 2nd Battle Squadron and second in Home Fleet, 1941–1942; Senior Naval Officer, Western Atlantic, 1942–1944.

Secretary of War Henry L. Stimson presents Vice Admiral H. Kent Hewitt the Army's Distinguished Service Medal on January 6, 1943. Admiral Ernest J. King, Chief of Naval Operations, and General George Marshall are in the background. (Naval Historical Collection)

XV *Sicily and Anzio Invasions, 1943*

December and January passed all too quickly, with many and varied activities in addition to those connected with the major mission of my command. In a formal outdoor ceremony at Little Creek, I had the pleasure of conferring on several officers of the Amphibious Force, Army and Marine as well as Navy, the decorations well earned by them for especially meritorious conduct during the TORCH operation. And I was highly honored myself by receiving the Army Distinguished Service Medal from the hands of Secretary Stimson[1] at the War Department and the Navy Distinguished Service Medal from Secretary Knox[2] at the Navy Department.

Other matters which occupied much of my time were talks on Operation TORCH delivered at the Naval War College in Newport and at the Army War College in Washington, and frequent conferences at the Navy Department. All this, however, was interesting and pleasant and my journeys gave me an opportunity to see something of my scattered family.

At the Casablanca Conference in the latter half of January, President Roosevelt and Prime Minister Churchill, attended by their chiefs of staff, finally reached the decision that the occupation of Sicily was to be the next major step in the war against the Axis, commencing with an allied assault in July under General Eisenhower as the Supreme Allied Commander in the Mediterranean. Accordingly, a rapid buildup of naval amphibious and support forces in the Mediterranean, as well as land and air forces, was a requisite.

It was not long thereafter that I was called to Washington and informed that I was to be ordered to North Africa to command the U.S. naval forces in the Mediterranean theater and would be relieved of command of the Amphibious Force, Atlantic Fleet by Rear Admiral Alan G. Kirk,[3] who had been U.S. naval attaché in London. My new title was to be a long-sounding one—Commander, U.S. Naval Forces, Northwest African Waters—abbreviated COMNAVNAW.

Pursuant to these orders, I was detached from PHIBLANT on February 28, after a very heart-warming farewell reception the preceding day, given by the officers of the command. I would like to have taken with me all the officers of my fine staff who had done so much toward the establishment of the Amphibious Force and the success of the Moroccan operation. But this could not have been done, in all fairness to Admiral Kirk, without considerable loss of continuity in the extremely important amphibious training which was being carried on. Thus it was, with keen regret, that I had to leave Captain Johnson behind, a key man who was particularly wanted by Admiral Kirk as his chief of staff. The Navy Department made available to me for my new chief of staff the newly promoted Rear Admiral Spencer S. Lewis,[4] whom I knew then but slightly but who proved indeed to be a most fortunate choice. I did take with me my flag lieutenant and flag secretary and other key officers, including Commander Bachman for intelligence, Commander R. A. J. English for planning, and Commander Harold R. Brookman for engineering and logistics.

It was arranged that the senior members of my staff, my personal aides, and I would proceed to Algeria by air, while the remainder of the staff, with the enlisted personnel, necessary equipment, and stores would go to Oran via the assault transport *Samuel Chase*,[5] which had participated in the Mediterranean part of the TORCH operation. When I asked Admiral King where I should set up my headquarters, he left that decision entirely to my discretion. The port at Oran was being turned over to U.S. naval administration, and the *Samuel Chase* was ordered there to await further orders. Since the Supreme Allied headquarters had already been set up in Algiers, this was my natural initial destination in order that I might report personally to General Eisenhower and to the Supreme Naval Commander, Admiral Cunningham.

About the 9th of March, we departed from the North River, New York, via a flying boat of the American Export Lines, the ultimate destination of which was London, via a very circuitous route. The passengers included several civilians, among whom was a young Free French diplomat, M. Hervé Alphand,[6] who in later years was to become the French ambassador to the United States. The itinerary took us in comparatively short hops to Bermuda, Trinidad, Belém, Bathurst, and, finally, for us, Port Lyautey. At each stop we had brief layovers, which permitted us to see the sights or renew old acquaintances. In Bermuda, it was pleasant being the guest of Admiral James and revisiting the governor general and British admiral who had welcomed me so pleasantly just a few months before on my return trip from Morocco. At Trinidad, I had the opportunity of inspecting the new U.S. naval base. But the stop at Belém, where I had never been before, was of particular interest. This was the once thriving city of Pará, in the days when Brazil supplied most of the world's rubber. Here was a magnificent state theater or opera house, a library, and other beautiful buildings, constructed in the city's heyday and now little used. At Bathurst, I made a very pleasant official call on the British governor general of Gambia, being received by a guard of honor of fine looking black soldiers.

Approaching Port Lyautey in the early morning, it was interesting to pick up the beaches near Mehdiya, with some wrecks of landing craft still showing; to pass over the Kasbah, the old fortification which had caused so much trouble; and to land on one of the reaches of the winding Oued Sebou off the seaplane ramps at the airfield. It was this river, with its bends, which permitted Lyautey to be a seaplane base as well as a land-plane base, for a flying boat could always find a stretch of water where it could make a head-into-wind landing.

At Port Lyautey, we were met by Rear Admiral F. J. Lowry,[7] the newly appointed commander of the Moroccan Sea Frontier. Admiral Hall had already moved up to Oran to command the Amphibious Force, Northwest African Waters, which was in the process of being formed. Admiral Lowry, of course, gave me the latest news of naval affairs in Morocco. Port Lyautey had been established early as a U.S. naval air station, and naval patrol planes operating from there were busily covering the sea approaches to Casablanca and assisting the RAF in covering the Strait of Gibraltar and its approaches. Casablanca was being used extensively as a convoy turn-around port and as a refueling and repair base for escort and other shipping. All this was to form part of my command.

Looking west across Port Lyautey, Morocco (Courtesy of the Naval Historical Collection)

All the passengers on our plane were now given a medical examination to ensure that they had received all the inoculations required for the European-African theater. Those of us in the services had no trouble in this respect, but not so Monsieur Alphand, who had not been adequately warned. Although he had everything required for Britain, his destination, the Army quarantine authorities insisted that he would have to remain at Lyautey until other inoculations had been completed. To me, it was unthinkable that a friendly diplomat, travelling on official business should be so detained, but it took several calls to headquarters in Algiers before he was cleared to continue his journey in our plane to London. And this in a country which was a French protectorate.

Eventually, we secured air transportation to Algiers in a more or less rattletrap Army Air Corps plane, in which we were provided bucket seats with other passengers of lesser rank. No plush VIP treatment in this case.

When we made a stop at the airfield near Oran, Admiral Hall was there to greet and confer with us, as was Captain Francis T. Spellman[8] who had already been ordered to command the Naval Operating Base, Oran. Rear Admiral A. C. Bennett, who had commanded the advance amphibious detachment in the British Isles and who had participated in the Mediterranean part of TORCH, had been recalled.

After a short stop, we continued to Algiers' Maison Blanche airport, which we reached in the late afternoon of March 15. Here we were met by Captain Jerauld Wright,[9] who was then the U.S. naval representative on General Eisenhower's staff and who had previously figured in clandestine pre-TORCH landings on the Algerian coast and the abduction of French General Giraud from France. He conducted us to a small villa which had been prepared and manned for our accommodation by personnel from the USS *Thomas Stone*,[10] one of our transports torpedoed en route to the TORCH Algiers attack; towed to an anchorage in Algiers Bay, she ultimately had been driven hard and fast aground in a storm. (For the story of this gallant ship, see Morison, Vol. II.) That night Admiral Lewis and I dined with Captain Wright in the mess presided over by General Sir Humphrey Gale[11] of the Supreme Allied staff, in a villa just overlooking the Hotel Saint Georges, which had been taken over as Supreme Allied Headquarters.

Promptly the next morning, I reported to the Supreme Allied Commander at the Saint Georges and was heartily welcomed and introduced to his chief of staff, General Bedell Smith.[12] I then reported to Admiral Cunningham and received a similar welcome. I was assigned an office immediately adjacent to that of the admiral, my chief of staff being given a room in what was practically the same suite. My aides were also assigned nearby offices, and Captain Wright was transferred to my own staff as assistant chief of staff.

Oil storage area east of Port Lyautey, Morocco (Courtesy of the Naval Historical Collection

There seemed to be no doubt that my place was in Algiers, for it was only there that I could deal directly with the Supreme Commander and his overall naval commander. Accordingly, plans were immediately made to bring the *Samuel Chase* with the remainder of the staff personnel and equipment to Algiers. To accommodate the bulk of my staff and its activities, an *École des Filles* in the outskirts of Algiers was assigned to us. Here, after the arrival of the *Samuel Chase*, were established the quarters for our enlisted men; a radio station for direct communication with Washington as well as with Casablanca, Port Lyautey, Oran, and other U.S. naval facilities being established in North Africa; and office space for other staff sections which could not be quartered in the Saint Georges. All this, however, could not be accomplished until the first part of April. Our Seabees (construction battalion detachment), when they became available, set up several Quonset huts in the patio of the school and installed additional sanitary facilities.

In the meantime, however, the U.S. Naval Forces Northwest African Waters was officially established on March 16, 1943. Somewhat later on, this was made the U.S. Eighth Fleet, a much less unwieldy title, which also facilitated the assignment of call signs to its task forces. In the first operation order to this command, the following task forces were set up:

   a) Amphibious Force, Northwest African Waters, Rear Admiral J. L. Hall;
   b) Moroccan Sea Frontier, which included Casablanca and the Naval Air Station, Port Lyautey, Rear Admiral F. J. Lowry;
   c) Naval Operating Base, Oran, Captain Francis T. Spellman (later Commodore Charles M. Yates);[13]
   d) Salvage Force which, under Captain Sullivan (once of Merritt, Chapman & Scott), was already cleaning up Casablanca and Oran;
   e) Advance Base Force, which included detachments trained to administer new bases when they became available.

Under the Amphibious Force there were the following task groups:

   1. Landing Craft and Bases. This was to handle the new landing craft, which were beginning to arrive in numbers, and the small bases necessary for their accommodation. This was commanded by Rear Admiral R. L. Conolly,[14] newly arrived;
   2. Escort Sweeper Group, comprised of the destroyers and minecraft assigned to NAVNAW for the purpose of escorting convoys in the Mediterranean, minesweeping, and laying protective mine fields;
   3. Joint Amphibious Schools. These were established at and near Arzew, a few miles east of Oran. Here was a small port and a fine stretch of beach which had been the scene of one of the landings in TORCH for the seizure of Oran.

The movement of U.S. shipping, naval personnel, and naval matériel to North Africa, consequent to the decision of the Casablanca Conference, had been initiated early in February and was already well under way upon my arrival in the North African theater. The new landing craft, with crews hastily assembled and trained by Atlantic Fleet Amphibious Force, were already arriving in large numbers, and arrangements had to be made for their accommodation. In many cases, even the commanding officers of these craft had never been to sea before. Their safe arrival at their assigned destinations, even shepherded as they were by destroyers or other larger naval vessels, was a tribute to their courage and determination.

Algiers and other Algerian ports to the eastward had been placed under British control and were being fully employed for the prosecution of the Tunisian campaign. Consequently, it was necessary for the U.S. Navy to make use of every suitable port to the westward of Algiers, many of which were very small, for the rapidly arriving LST, LCT, LCI (L). Oran, the principal port, which, with its neighboring Mers el Kebir, had already been established as a U.S. naval operating base, was fully occupied in the handling of transports, supply shipping, and the larger combatant vessels and thus could not be utilized for the smaller craft. But this was the natural place for the Amphibious Force commander, Admiral Hall, to set up his headquarters, as he had already done.

A few miles east of Oran was the small breakwater-protected port of Arzew on the northern flank of a fine beach, which trended south several miles to the little fishing village of Port aux Poules. This had been the scene in the TORCH operation of one of the principal landings for the capture of Oran. Its proximity to Oran and to an excellent amphibious training area made Arzew, with its port facilities, a natural selection as a landing craft supply base. The Army Amphibious Training Command, moved from Camp Edwards, Massachusetts, boat battalions and all, had been established at Port aux Poules prior to the arrival of the U.S. Navy on the scene. It had been so chosen upon his arrival in the theater by Rear Admiral Richard L. Conolly, who in February had been ordered by Admiral King as Commander, Landing Craft and Bases, Northwest African Waters (abbreviated to COMLANCRABNAW). Admiral Conolly had wisely established his initial headquarters in an old winery at Demeane, overlooking the Arzew beaches, in close contact with his immediate chief, Admiral Hall, centrally located with respect to the initial landing craft bases and in a position where he could readily supervise the training of his landing craft and coordinate activities with the Army command at Port aux Poules.

The other ports available as landing craft bases were two to the westward of Oran—Nemours near the Moroccan border and Beni Saf—and three between Arzew and Algeria—Mostaganem just across a wide bay from Arzew, Ténès, and Cherchell. Of these, only two, Mostaganem and Ténès, were suitable for the accommodation of the LSTs, and these could not take care of all that were due. Accordingly, another LST base was established at Port Lyautey on the Sebou River to take care of the overflow. Nemours and Beni Saf were assigned as LCT bases, and Cherchell was given over to the LCI (L). Personnel for the establishment of these bases, composed mainly of retired or reserve officers and men, had been sent over with Admiral Conolly.

Naturally I was anxious to inspect all this activity as soon as possible, but other matters required my prior attention. In the first place, I found that planning for HUSKY on the Supreme Commander's level was already well underway, in spite of the fact that the Tunisian campaign was still in progress and a reverse had been suffered at the Kasserine Pass. It had already been decided that I would command a Western Naval Task Force to land the U.S. Seventh Army under General Patton in the western part of Sicily, while the British Eighth Army under General Montgomery[15] would be landed around the southeast corner of the island by an Eastern Naval Task Force under the British Admiral Sir Bertram Ramsay.[16] Commander English and others of my planning section were assigned as my representatives with the Supreme Commander's planners until a definite task was assigned to the Western Naval Task Force.

In the second place, it was necessary to get firmly established in suitable living quarters as well as in the office space assigned and to make the official calls required by custom and protocol in order to make friendly contacts and to further Allied cooperation. With respect to living quarters, the small villa originally allotted to me was entirely inadequate to the needs of my staff and me. All the better housing had already been assigned to the earlier arriving Army and Army Air Corps general officers, many of whom were much my juniors. No proper provision had been made by the Supreme Allied staff for any U.S. naval commander. While this was a matter with which I had no intention of bothering General Eisenhower, I was determined to defend the honor of my cloth. After calling the attention of the Supreme staff officer handling such affairs to the fact that my rank was merely that of a lieutenant general, I was finally assigned Villa Dar El Azizi, which was just being vacated by an Air Corps general who was moving up toward the Tunisian front. This was large enough reasonably to accommodate eight or ten of the senior officers of my staff in addition to the chief of staff and me. This added to efficiency as well as comfort, because it made possible a general discussion of current affairs at meals as well as in the large living room in the evening. I replaced the military police assigned for our security by a bluejacket guard as soon as I could. I wanted the other services to know that the U.S. Navy was on hand. We were able to move into these quarters just eight days after our arrival. (The owner of the villa, a wealthy wine grower of Danish birth named Sorensen, and his family had previously been moved into their chauffeur's apartment over the garage. We took pains to see that they were as comfortable as possible.)

General Bernard L. Montgomery, Head of the Eighth Army, with General George Patton, Head of the Seventh Army, as they plan the invasion of Sicily, 1943 (Naval Historical Collection)

In the meanwhile, I had made my call on General Giraud,[17] who, as one of the two heads agreed upon for the French Provisional Government, represented the Vichy side. General de Gaulle,[18] the Free French representative there, as I recall, was then still in London. As will be remembered, General Giraud had become a Nazi prisoner early in the war, had escaped to occupied France, and then just prior to TORCH had been spirited out of France to meet with General Eisenhower in Gibraltar. I found him to be a very fine figure of a soldier, very cordial and very correct, but above all else, a proud Frenchman whose one wish was to command an early landing in the northern Mediterranean to drive the hated "*Boche*" from his homeland. Unfortunately, he did not understand the many problems involved.

Another call which I made was on Vice Admiral Jacques Moreau, the prefect maritime or commandant of the naval district, whose jurisdiction extended from Oran in the west to Bizerte in the east and in whose house Admiral Darlan had been visiting at the time of his assassination the previous December. I found him to be a delightful gentleman and splendid officer whose hatred of the Axis powers and loyalty to the Allied cause was beyond doubt. Like most of the officers of the French navy, he had felt himself bound by oath to what he considered the legal government of France in Vichy. This contact was the beginning of a long friendship, lasting until his unfortunate death in 1962 as the result of an automobile accident in France. Incidentally, we needed no interpreter, because the admiral's English was very good.

Calling on me, and also needing no interpreter, was the little *Contre Amiral* Gervais de LaFond, who commanded French naval activities in Algiers. It developed that it was he who had commanded the French light forces at Casablanca and that he had been hospitalized as a result of a wound suffered when his flagship, the cruiser *Primauguet*,[19] had been put out of action by the forces under my command. In spite of that, we also became good friends. Upon returning his call, I found that his quarters were in the ancient palace of the Dey of Algiers on the waterfront. Mme de LaFond spoke English as well as I, having been born in Brooklyn, New York, of French artist parents.

Aerial view of Casablanca, Morocco, and its harbor (Naval Historical Collection)

By March 26, I was finally able to get away for my inspection of our landing craft bases. I was most anxious to see at firsthand what was going on. My car having arrived on the *Samuel Chase*, my flag lieutenant and I set out for Cherchell along the fine coastal road, arriving in time for lunch with Commander Jalbert, who was just in the process of establishing the LCI base there. Although he had been there only a few days, I found everything going well and that he had already formed a firm *entente cordiale* with the local French authorities. Not only did Commander Jalbert, whom I came to know well later on, have an excellent command of the French language, but he was possessed of great tact.

The walled town of Cherchell itself was extremely interesting, as it had been a Roman colony and still showed many traces of its origin, including a stadium in a good state of preservation, which reminded me of the Colosseum in Rome. Even parts of the breakwater which enclosed the little harbor were relics of Roman days.

From Cherchell we went on to Ténès, where we met Admiral Conolly who had come to meet us there. We spent the night at a delightful French inn. Ténès was another walled town. In fact, I was to discover that most of the old towns in Algeria were similarly walled, presumably to protect them from raids in earlier days.

The coastal drive along the Algerian coast was beautiful, a drive which might well rival the famous Corniche road of the French Riviera. It was a revelation to me, who had imagined all of North Africa to be more or less a sandy desert area. That part of Algeria near the Mediterranean shore has a climate much like southern California, with similar flora. It abounds in well-kept vineyards (or did in those days).

Seeing that all was well at Ténès and that its harbor was adequate for quite a number of LST, we went on to Mostaganem the following morning. There we lunched and viewed progress in the establishment of that LST base. By midafternoon we were in Port aux Poules, where Admiral Hall met Admiral Conolly and me to confer with General O'Daniel,[20] the commander of the Army Amphibious Training Command, on the program of joint amphibious training which lay ahead of us. After a quick look at Arzew, we went on to Oran for the night.

March 20 was spent in familiarizing myself with Oran and its facilities and the small U.S. naval repair base which had been set up in Mers el Kebir. It was remarkable to see how much had been accomplished in so short a time. Those were indeed busy days for all of us.

The next day was spent in a trip to Beni Saf and Nemours and back again to Oran. Progress was also good at these small bases. On the 30th there was an important military-naval conference at Port aux Poules, attended by Generals Clark, Truscott, O'Daniel, Wolf, and Taylor,[21] and Admirals Hall, Conolly, and myself. As I remember, it was most productive. On the 31st, I flew back to Algiers and returned to my headquarters desk, there to find other important matters awaiting me. But I had the satisfaction that much had been done in these first two weeks.

The Eighth Fleet, in my first operation order, was organized as follows:

Task Force 81, Eighth Amphibious Force, under which were the following Task Groups: The Landing Craft and Landing Craft Bases, the Escort Sweeper Group (destroyers and mine sweepers), the Joint Amphibious Schools, and the Beach Battalions. The Beach Battalions, under specially trained beach masters, were composed of naval personnel to handle beach boat traffic and repair, signalmen and radiomen to carry on shore-ship communications, and medical personnel to care for casualties and direct their evacuation from shore to ship. Initially, all combat shipping was assigned to the Amphibious Force, but upon the later arrival of more destroyers, larger combat units, such as cruisers and motor torpedo boat squadrons, other task forces and groups, responsible directly to the fleet commander, were formed.

Task Force 82, Moroccan Sea Frontier. This included the naval air station at Port Lyautey as well as the naval operating base at Casablanca. The commander of the Moroccan Sea Frontier was responsible for covering the sea approaches to Casablanca, and, in cooperation with the British air and naval command at Gibraltar, assisting in the coverage of the approaches to the Strait of Gibraltar and in denying passage of the Strait to enemy submarines.

Task Force 83, Naval Operating Base Oran. This included administration of the port facilities at neighboring Mers el Kebir and Arzew. Here was to be established the major supply depot for the Eighth Fleet.

Task Force 84, U.S. Naval Salvage Force. This was the remarkable unit which had cleaned up the harbor of Casablanca and moved forward to other ports as the campaign progressed. Its Algerian headquarters were in the small port of Dellys, adjacent to Algiers.

Task Force 85, Advance Base Force. This unit consisted of officers and men of various ranks and ratings, especially trained to take over the operation and administration of the ports that were taken from the enemy and were to be used as advance bases for the Eighth Fleet.

No mention is made in the foregoing of the ubiquitous Seabees, the invaluable construction battalions. These were assigned to the various task forces according to need and availability. Other miscellaneous small units, which were to be under the immediate command of the fleet commander, were assembled as Task Force 80 and given task group numbers thereunder. The headquarters group came under this category.

The month of April, as may be imagined, was an extremely busy one. It was occupied with planning, with many conferences with senior commanders, both Army and Navy, and with visits and inspections. General Patton's staff, which was to be the Seventh Army staff, had established itself in Mostaganem, about 200 miles from Algiers. His deputy, General Geoffrey Keyes,[22] called on me on April 6 to discuss future plans, and about ten days later General Patton himself, just released from the Tunisian front, did the same. (Incidentally, he regaled me with many interesting tales of the Tunisian campaign.) I urged both generals to move up to the vicinity of Algiers, where our staffs could be in intimate contact in order to facilitate the detailed planning for HUSKY. For some reason, in spite of their pre-TORCH experience, they did not feel this to be practicable.

One day I was called upon by Air Chief Marshal Tedder[23] and by General Spaatz[24] of the U.S. Army Air Corps, with the plea that I place the U.S. naval air units based in Port Lyautey directly under the Royal Air Force commander at Gibraltar. Their claim was that the Gibraltar air command had not been receiving the cooperation it should from the Port Lyautey air command. Asked to cite an instance, they were unable to do so. It developed that what they wanted was to be able to issue direct detailed orders to U.S. naval plans units rather than to assign a general task to the U.S. air commander. This was a system to which I did not agree, and I told them so. I was also quite sure that Admiral King, himself a naval aviator, would be of the same opinion, and if I were to consent to their demands, I would probably get fired. However, I said, if they insisted, I would refer the matter to my commander in chief for his decision. They did not, however, want me to do anything like that. They wanted no idea to reach Washington that Allied affairs were not going smoothly under General Eisenhower. So our naval air remained under the command of the Commander, Moroccan Sea Frontier, and I heard no further charges of non-cooperation. When I related this incident to Admiral King a year or so later, he roared with laughter.

The end of April found me on another trip to the westward, this time by plane. In addition to inspections and witnessing a landing exercise near Arzew, conferences with General Patton and others, I had the pleasure of conferring well-earned awards on Admiral Hall and other officers at Oran. At Port Lyautey there was a very special awards ceremony, with the entire station paraded and my newly arrived band in attendance. The honoree was none other than the gallant French pilot M. René Malavergne, who had, at the risk of his own life, brought the *Dallas* and later the *Contessa* into the river and to the air station during the TORCH assault. I felt it an honor to represent the president in pinning the Navy Cross on his breast. At the conclusion, the band played the "Star Spangled Banner" and then the "*Marseillaise*." His family and many of his friends, who were present, seemed to be much moved. I felt that this little ceremony did no harm to local Franco-American relations.

Downtown Casablanca, Morocco (Naval Historical Collection)

The arrival of the new landing craft at many scattered bases had emphasized the need for a suitable flagship for Admiral Conolly, both for administrative purposes and for future operations. Such a vessel was found at Port Lyautey in the small seaplane tender *Biscayne*,[25] a converted Coast Guard cutter. She had adequate speed and communication facilities, together with a small plotting room and an unusual number of quarters for a ship of that size. The development of the Port Lyautey naval air station had been such as to make her services as a tender no longer necessary. She was, accordingly, turned over to the Commander, Landing Craft and Bases, in which capacity she served admirably throughout the Mediterranean campaign.

One of the first naval combatant units to report to my command in the Mediterranean was Motor Torpedo Boat Squadron 15 under the command of the then

Lieutenant Stanley M. Barnes.[26] When asked how soon he would be prepared to operate, he emulated Taussig in Queenstown in 1917 by saying "We are ready now." Without loss of time, I walked into Admiral Cunningham's office next door and proffered the squadron's services. They were gladly accepted, Barnes being directed to report to the commander of the inshore patrol. The British torpedo boat unit, which was based in Bône, was even then wreaking havoc on the desperate Axis effort, first to reinforce and later to evacuate Rommel's desert army. The American squadron promptly became a highly effective member of the team. Many miniature fleet night actions were fought off the African coast and later off the Sicilian and Italian coasts, utilizing to the best advantage the characteristics of each—the larger, more heavily gunned, and somewhat slower British craft as a main body, and the lighter and faster American craft with their excellent radar and torpedo armament as scouts and flank forces. The young men of M. T. B. Ron 15, by their initiative, efficiency, and valor, and general cooperative attitude, did much to further the Allied cause and to promote friendly British-American naval relations. M. T. B. Ron 15 and the other squadrons which later came to join it were to distinguish themselves throughout the Mediterranean campaign.

By the end of April, the Supreme Commander's outline plan for the invasion of Sicily (Operation Husky) had taken shape, but this later was subject to considerable modification at the insistence of General Alexander,[27] greatly to the relief of the United States naval command, which did not fancy successively phased landings on the west coast of Sicily and near Palermo, far from adequate land-based air support. An early July D-day was planned on the assumption that the Tunisian campaign would have come to an end by April 30. This, however, proved to be optimistic, since Tunis and Bizerte did not fall until May 7, and the final surrender of Rommel's once proud desert army did not take place until the 13th.

In anticipation of its availability, the French naval air base adjacent to the city of Bizerte, just inside the narrow entrance to the Bay of Bizerte, had been allotted to the U.S. Navy. The British were to have the naval base of Ferryville at the southern end of the bay and the port of Tunis itself. Bizerte, with its piers and seaplane ramps, proved to be ideal as an amphibious base and was so utilized until the end of the Mediterranean campaign. The American advance naval party, under Captain R. M. Zimmerli,[28] arrived at this base only two days after its surrender and went to work promptly. So did the salvage parties under Commodore Sullivan, which performed

Fourth of July celebration, 1943, at Headquarters, Supreme Allied Commander, Mediterranean, Hotel St. Georges, Algiers, Algeria. From left to right, Admiral Andrew B. Cunningham, RN, General Dwight D. Eisenhower, USA, Vice Admiral H. K. Hewitt, USN and Major General Lowell W. Rooks, USA.
(Naval Historical Collection)

miracles in blasting a channel through the hulks of vessels which had been sunk by the Germans, one on top of another, like so many jack-straws, to block the narrow but deep entrance.

Throughout April and May, landing craft, destroyers, and minor combat units continued to arrive in considerable numbers. The landing craft all moved forward to Bizerte as soon as it was available, while other units of the Eighth Fleet were based on Oran.

On May 20, I had the pleasure of flying to Tunis with General Alexander and Admiral Cunningham for the purpose of witnessing the victory parade, which was reviewed by General Eisenhower and other high U.S., British, and French officials. It was an interesting and memorable sight. There was Montgomery's Eighth Army, which had fought its way from Egypt; Free French units which had fought their way from Brazzaville; native French Colonial Algerian, Moroccan, and Senegalese troops in their picturesque uniforms; and British, French, and American troops which had participated in the final campaign in Tunisia. The parade was followed by a large and splendidly appointed official luncheon given by the French governor general in the Government House. By late afternoon, I was back in Algiers working on plans for HUSKY.

The final outline plan for the invasion of Sicily was issued to the prospective task force commanders on the following day, May 21. In accordance with this, the British Eastern Naval Task Force, under Admiral Ramsay, would land the Eastern Task Force, Montgomery's Eighth Army, on the east coast and southeastern peninsula of Sicily, with the object of securing the ports of Syracuse and Augusta and advancing to Messina in order to cut off the Axis line of retreat to Italy. The Western Naval Task Force, under my command, would land the Western Task Force, General Patton's U.S. Seventh Army, on the south coast of Sicily in the adjacent Licata-Gela-Scoglitti area. These landings were to be simultaneous, and would insure the early capture of the main enemy airfields, which were in the south and were close enough to ensure prompt link-up. Furthermore, since the attack area was closer to Malta and to Pantellaria (which was to be seized in advance), prospects for effective air cover were much improved. The principal disadvantages appeared to be that the Gela beach area seemed less favorable and that the major supply for the Seventh Army would have to be effected over exposed beaches, even after the eventual planned release of the port of Augusta to the U.S. forces.

The proposed composition of the new Seventh Army included the First and Third U.S. Infantry Divisions, veterans of TORCH and the Tunisian campaign and thus already in Africa, and the U.S. Forty-fifth Infantry Division, which was receiving amphibious training in the Hampton Roads area with my old command, the Amphibious Force, U.S. Atlantic Fleet, and would be brought over by my relief, Rear Admiral Kirk, combat-loaded in assault transports. The First Division was commanded by Major General Terry Allen,[29] and the Third by Major General Lucian K. Truscott, who, in TORCH, had been the Army commander in the Northern Attack Force landing at Mehdiya and the Sebou River area near Port Lyautey, Morocco. The Forty-fifth Division was under the command of Major General T. H. Middleton.[30] Also included was the Second Armored Division, now under Major General Gaffey.[31] Both this division and its commander had participated in TORCH.

The period from the receipt of the Supreme Commander's final plan to the actual sailing for the invasion of Sicily had to be devoted to intensive preparation and training at all levels—Army and Navy. The corresponding commanders at the task force and assault force levels and their staffs were brought into close contact as early as possible.

During this May–June period, reinforcements for the Eighth Fleet continued to arrive in ever-increasing numbers: cruisers, destroyers, mine craft, patrol craft, and the LSTs, LCTs, and LCIs, which were to be used and prove their worth for the first time in a major operation. One most welcome unit was my old Cruiser Division Eight, under the distinguished officer who had relieved me of that command, Rear Admiral Lyal A. Davidson, who was to continue with me throughout the Mediterranean campaign and become an expert on naval gunfire support of landings.

Another welcome unit was Cruiser Division Thirteen, under another old friend, Rear Admiral Laurance T. Dubose.[32] CRUDIV 8 was now composed of the *Philadelphia, Savannah,* and *Boise*.[33] The *Birmingham*[34] and *Brooklyn* formed CRUDIV 13. These fine cruisers with their fifteen-gun 6-inch batteries were to prove their effectiveness. Admiral Kirk himself, with the Forty-fifth Division loaded in some eighteen assault transports and with his necessary screening and other supporting units, arrived in Oran in mid-June.

Since the enemy was in possession of the northern shore of the Mediterranean and of Italy and Sicily, Allied shipping passing along the African shores of Morocco, Algeria, and Tunisia was constantly subject to bombing, torpedo, and mining attacks. During June, in spite of all precautions, the U.S. Navy lost two LSTs (with heavy losses of life), a minesweeper, and a patrol boat to torpedoes and mines.

The Seventh Army plan called for the landing of the Forty-fifth Division on the right flank in the vicinity of Scoglitti, with the objective of capturing the airfields at Comiso and Biscari, extending the beachhead inland, and linking with the British on its right. The First Division was to be landed in the center near Gela, with the tasks of securing the important airfield at Ponte Olivo, extending inland, and linking with the division on each of its flanks. The Third Division, on the left, was to land on each side of Licata, capture that small port, cover the left flank, and establish control with the First on its right. The First and Forty-fifth were to be grouped under Major General Omar Bradley[35] as the II Corps.

Based on the above, the Western Naval Task Force Plan, as finally developed, called for the landing of the Third Division by a Left (JOSS) Assault Force composed entirely of the new LST, LCT, and LCI. Since these landing craft were all to come from Admiral Conolly's command, it was natural that this force should be commanded by him. These LSTs were equipped with davits to carry small personnel landing craft (LCP) like the assault transports, so that an assault wave could be embarked and sent ahead prior to beaching the mother craft. The LSTs were also fitted with a new feature developed in Admiral Conolly's Landing Craft command to overcome the disadvantage of the unsatisfactory Sicilian beach gradients, which would not permit these craft to beach close enough for their vehicles to discharge directly from the ramp. Pontoons which had been developed by the Navy Bureau of Yards and Docks for the construction of floating docks, bridges, etc., were placed together to form causeway sections wide enough to accommodate tanks and trucks. A section was attached to each side of the LST by an ingenious hinge device and then triced up so that it would be carried clear of the water. When the LST grounded, these sections were lowered into the water, disconnected, and slid forward. One section was then placed in position immediately under the bow ramp. The other, alongside the first, was moved forward until its ramp was grounded on the beach. Thus, vessels and personnel could be disembarked completely dry. This experiment was a great success and these causeways are standard equipment for the more modern LSTs of today. A few of the JOSS LSTs were fitted with little flight decks for the launching of small Army (Piper Cub) observation planes.

The commander of the Center (DIME) Assault Force, the duty of which was to land the First Division, fell to Rear Admiral Hall, the commander of the Eighth Amphibious Force, and a veteran of TORCH. This force was to be a mixture of assault transports and assault supply ships, LST and LCI. To it were eventually assigned also two British landing ships infantry (LSI), which were converted cross-channel passenger steamers.

The Right (CENT) Assault Force, to land the Forty-fifth Division, was naturally Admiral Kirk's, with the ships in which they had been transported overseas already combat-loaded. Unfortunately, when they were loaded in Hampton Roads in early June, no detailed plans for that division were available, so some reloading may have been necessary during their short stay in Oran.

I have never learned the genesis of the strange code names, JOSS, DIME, and CENT, assigned by the Supreme staff planners for the foregoing assault forces.

It was the urgency of the planning and other preparations for the coming landing on the Italian mainland that dictated my own early departure from the Sicilian theater, much as I should have liked to have remained for the follow-through. But as has been described, the further U.S. naval operations in that area were left in able hands. The major part of my staff, including the planning section, returned to

Algiers on the *Monrovia*,[36] while I departed on the following day, July 13, for a conference with Admiral Cunningham at his Malta headquarters, embarked on my relief flagship, the destroyer *McLanahan*.[37]

This, my very first visit in peace or war to that island of great historical interest, was an experience for me which I consider worth recording in these memoirs. I knew, of course, that the city of Valletta, with its Royal Naval dockyard and all the defenses of the island, had been the targets of repeated Axis air attacks and that the island had held out only because of the determination of the garrison, the spirit of its people, and the gallant efforts of the British navy, at the expense of grievous losses, to keep it supplied. But I was not prepared for the complete devastation which met my eyes when at first light of July 14 we entered Great Harbor and moored under the beetling walls of the ancient fortress established so many years before by the Knights of Malta.

After an early meeting with my British CINC in his underground office, which was entered through a tunnel in the cliff at the edge of the old town, the accompanying members of my staff and I were given a memorable tour. First, we visited the dockyard, or what was left of it. It was interesting to see with what ingenuity machinery and tools had been salvaged from the wreckage and re-established in caves dug out of the soft sandstone hillside. These underground shops were working at full blast and the employees, most of whom were Maltese, seemed in excellent spirits in spite of all their trials and hardships.

The city of Valletta itself was a mass of rubble, with much of the population living in underground caves. The splendid old opera house was badly damaged, but, surprisingly enough, Admiralty House, the official residence of the Commander in Chief, Mediterranean, stood alone amidst its neighbors, practically unscathed. Thus there was preserved a fine building which had originally been the *auberge* of the French Knights of Malta and which had subsequently become the home of the British Commander in Chief, Mediterranean. It was interesting to read on a commemorative plaque in the entryway that one of Admiral Cunningham's distinguished predecessors there had been Horatio Viscount Nelson.

Presentation of the Army flag made by the Navy to Lieutenant General George Patton, USA, by Vice Admiral Hewitt, July 1943, en route to Sicily.
(Naval Historical Collection)

In the afternoon, during a hasty trip through the countryside, we were taken to see one of the geological mysteries of the island. This consisted of a series of ruts in solid rock, looking as if they had been made by many wheeled vehicles all converging as if toward a ford in a stream, but not emerging from the other side. We were told that no one had yet offered a satisfactory explanation of this phenomenon.

My flag lieutenant and I were Admiral Cunningham's guests for the night in that historic Admiralty House. After a delightful dinner below, during which the king and the president were duly toasted with excellent port, we adjourned to the roof for coffee and liqueurs. Sitting there in the bright moonlight, looking out over the darkened and ruined city, it was interesting to speculate on the crusaders and the famous seamen who had been there before us. Had one been a believer in spirits and such things, it would have been easy to imagine that their ghosts were present with us.

After a restful night, uninterrupted by bombing, we were early on our way in the *McLanahan* to Algiers, ready to turn to the important task that lay ahead.

During October, in connection with the duty of supporting the operations on shore in Italy, the fleet suffered two very serious losses: the sinking of the destroyer *Buck*[38] on October 7 while patrolling in the Gulf of Salerno, and the destroyer *Bristol*[39] off the coast of Algeria on October 13, while escorting a follow-up convoy for Salerno. Both of these tragedies were due to enemy submarine action. The *Buck* lost nearly all of its officers and all but ninety-four of its complement of 260. She sank so rapidly that there was no time to set depth charges on safe, and several detonated, killing nearby swimmers. Since no message was gotten off, the survivors were in the water almost a day before help arrived. The *Bristol* was more fortunate, although sinking rapidly, because she was in company with others and a torpedoman was able to secure the depth charges. But even with that, she suffered a loss of five officers and sixty-seven men, nearly a quarter of her complement. Mediterranean convoys bound for the combat area and points farther east were constantly subject to submarine and air attacks by U-boats and planes based on the south coast of France.

Considerable reorganization of the Eighth Fleet took place after the completion of AVALANCHE. As a matter of fact, the small western Algerian bases at Nemours, Beni Saf, Ténès, and Cherchell had been decommissioned by October 1, and most of their personnel moved up to Bizerte or to Palermo. Rear Admiral Lowry had come from Oran to Algiers to assume the administrative command of U.S. Naval Forces, Northwest African Waters, during my absence in the Salerno operation, leaving the Moroccan Sea Frontier command to Captain C. L. Nichols.[40] On September 21, when Rear Admiral Hall reached Algiers in his flagship, *Samuel Chase*, he took over the administration. Admiral Lowry shortly thereafter proceeded to Salerno, and there, on October 6, relieved Rear Admiral Conolly, who was then under orders detaching him for duty in the Pacific theater. In early November, when Admiral Hall and his staff departed for Britain to assume command of the newly formed Eleventh Amphibious Force there, Admiral Lowry succeeded to the command of Eighth Amphibious Force, and the Landing Craft and Bases was abolished as a separate command. Commodore B. V. McCandlish[41] ultimately came to Casablanca from the United States to assume command of the Moroccan Sea Frontier. I was sorry to lose both Admirals Hall and Conolly, but their experience was needed elsewhere.

Another change was due to the establishment of an Allied Control Commission in early October, the naval section of which was to deal with the Italian navy. This was headed by Captain Morse of the Royal Navy, but I was asked to detail an American deputy. The ideal selection was the captain of the *Brooklyn*, Captain H. W. Ziroli,[42] an able officer of Italian descent, who spoke that language like a native. To relieve him on the *Brooklyn*, I took Captain Carey out of the *Savannah*, which was out of action and being made seaworthy at Malta for a return trip to the United States. The *Savannah* ultimately went home under the command of her executive officer.

Besides losing officers to other theaters, the Eighth Fleet now began to be reduced by the detachment of landing craft and other shipping to the United Kingdom and the Indian Ocean. By mid-October, a large group of LSTs had departed to join Lord Louis Mountbatten's command for planned operations against Burma.

The unfortunate death of the British First Sea Lord, Admiral Sir Dudley Pound,[43] resulted in another loss to the Mediterranean. My esteemed naval chief and good friend, Admiral Sir Andrew B. Cunningham, was ordered to London to succeed as the seagoing head of the Royal Navy, a logical choice. Before he left, at a colorful ceremony at Admiral Cunningham's villa, attended by the principal members of our respective staffs, he and I were invested with the burnoose of a *Spahi d'honneur de premier classe* of the Seventh Algerian Regiment, a pleasant token of friendship from our French allies. On the following day, October 16, there was a very impressive farewell ceremony for the admiral outside the Hotel Saint Georges, Allied Forces Headquarters, led by the Supreme Allied Commander, General Eisenhower himself. But that was not all. When Admiral Cunningham went to the Maison Blanche airport the following afternoon to board his plane for London, he found, to his surprise, honor guards from all the services of the Allies and a large assemblage of his friends and colleagues there to bid him an affectionate good-bye and to wish him well. I think that he was quite overcome.

It was too bad that Admiral Cunningham had to miss the regimental dinner given by the Seventh Spahis on November 1 in honor of their new honorary members. This was held at the headquarters of the regiment, a short distance outside Algiers in the open patio of a Moorish-type building. For one uninitiated in Arab-type dinners, it was a novel and interesting experience. Fortunately, I had been tipped off as to proper procedures and customs. The *piece de resistance*, of course, was a sheep, roasted whole and carried in on a pole by two stalwart Spahis. It was set down in the center of the table within reach of all, but one waited until the senior Arab officer picked out, with his right hand, what he considered to be the most delectable morsel and offered it to the senior guest, which, in this case, was I. It was really very good, but I was rather unused to eating a full meal with no implements, using only my right hand and fingers. There were other special native dishes, such as couscous. Glancing up at the balconies overlooking the patio, one could see veiled women of the regiment in the moonlight looking down at the feast. I was given to understand that they later dined on the remains, and what they left fell to the dogs.

While I was absent in Washington, Admiral Davidson exercised temporary command of the Eighth Fleet from the Algiers headquarters. It was during this period, on January 22, that the unfortunate Anzio landing took place. Unfortunate, not because the initial landing, ably commanded by Rear Admiral Lowry, was not a success, but because the objective of the operation, the severance of the line of enemy communication west of the Apennines to his front lines, was not attained. Nor did it lead to the early capture of Rome. Instead, losses suffered by both ground and naval forces in holding and supplying this narrow beachhead until final breakout at the end of May were most severe. In December, when the idea of the Anzio leapfrog operation was first broached, both navies, British and American, were reluctant to accept it. The soldiers were told that January was a period of bad weather and that supply of the troops ashore over beaches could not be guaranteed. It was implied, however, that it would only be necessary to land one division with sufficient supplies for three days, with the inference that by that time it would be joined by the advancing Fifth Army. How wrong that estimate was!

Lieutenant General Mark Clark, USA, and Vice Admiral Hewitt confer prior to the invasion of the Italian mainland at Salerno, 1943. (Naval Historical Collection)

I returned to my Algerian headquarters on January 25, and by January 30 I was in Naples. That night I took passage on HMS *Delhi*,[44] which was proceeding to the Anzio area to relieve my own *Brooklyn* as a standby gunfire support ship. After inspecting the situation at Anzio with Admiral Lowry, I returned to Naples on the *Brooklyn*. There was considerable damage in the harbor, which was within easy reach of enemy artillery, but nothing happened during my visit. After an inspection of Eighth Fleet activities in the Naples area, I flew to Taranto for my first visit there, conferred with the Allied Control Commission, then returned to my headquarters in Algiers.

The failure of the Anzio operation to accomplish its purpose, with the consequent delay in the capture of Rome, and the drain on naval resources in supporting an isolated beachhead, soon made it evident that troops could neither be withdrawn from the Italian front in time to prepare for a Mediterranean operation concurrent with OVERLORD, even if delayed to June, nor could adequate amphibious forces be made available that early. This situation developed at a time when demands were being made in the north for the expansion of the proposed Normandy operation to a five-division assault.

NOTES

1 Henry Stimson (1867–1950). American statesman and lawyer. Secretary of War, 1940–1945.

2 Frank Knox (1874–1944). Journalist and secretary of the Navy, 1940–1944. He worked to rebuild the U.S. Navy, making it the most powerful in the world.

3 Alan Kirk (1888–1963). Admiral. U.S. Naval Academy, Class of 1909.

4 Spencer Lewis (1888–1952). Vice Admiral. U.S. Naval Academy, Class of 1910.

5 USS *Samuel Chase* (APA-26). She served as a convoy ship and then supported the Allied invasion of North Africa, landing a complement of troops near Algiers.

6 Hervé Alphand (1907–1994). Diplomat. Director of Economic Affairs, French National Committee, 1941–1944; ambassador to the United States, 1956–1965.

7 Frank J. Lowry (1888–1955). Vice Admiral. U.S. Naval Academy, Class of 1911.

8 Francis T. Spellman (1895–1972). Rear Admiral. U.S. Naval Academy, Class of 1917.

9 Jerauld Wright (1898–1995). Admiral. U.S. Naval Academy, Class of 1921.

10 USS *Thomas Stone* (APA-29). She served as a troop transport during the invasion of North Africa, carrying British troops to Algiers. Hit by a torpedo and adrift, her troops were off-loaded to HMS *Spey* and carried to Algiers.

11 Humphrey Gale (1890–1971). Lieutenant General, British Army. Chief administrative officer to General Eisenhower during the North African campaign, 1942. Deputy chief of staff, Sicily and Italy. Advisor to General Eisenhower during the Normandy landings, 1944.

12 Walter Bedell Smith (1895–1961). General, U.S. Army. In 1942, he served as chief of staff of the Allied North African campaign. In 1944, he was appointed chief of staff of SHAPE and of U.S. forces in Europe. He thus became the chief architect of the European war. He served as ambassador to Russia, 1946–1949, and director of the CIA, 1950–1953.

13 Charles M. Yates (1884–1964). Commodore. U.S. Naval Academy, Class of 1908.

14 Richard L. Conolly (1892–1962). Admiral. U.S. Naval Academy, Class of 1914. President of the Naval War College, 1950–1953.

15 Bernard Montgomery (1887–1976). First Viscount Montgomery of Alamein. He was knighted and promoted to general in 1942 after defeating Rommel's force in North Africa, the first major defeat inflicted on the Germans. He played a singular role in Europe at Sicily, Normandy, and the Netherlands. He was promoted to field marshal in 1944.

16 Bertram Ramsay (1883–1945). Deputy naval commander, North African landings, 1942; Commander, Eastern Naval Task Force, Sicily, 1943; Allied Naval Commander, Normandy, 1944.

17 Henri-Honoré Giraud (1879–1949). He escaped from prison in 1942 and tried to establish an army to fight the Germans. Spirited from France to North Africa by the Americans, he was appointed commander in chief of Free French forces in North Africa, then, in December 1942, high commissioner.

18 Charles de Gaulle (1890–1970). General, French Army. President of the Fifth Republic. Leader of the Free French forces during World War II.

19 *Primauguet.* French Cruiser. Built in 1928. Displacement 7,249 tons; Length 575'; Beam 57 1/2'; Draught 17 1/4'.

20 John W. O'Daniel (1894–1975). Major General, U.S. Army. He participated in the landings in North Africa, 1942; Sicily and Salerno in 1943; and Anzio and Southern France in 1944; and commanded the Third Infantry Division, 1944–1945.

21 Maxwell Taylor (1901–1987). General, U.S. Army. U.S. Military Academy, Class of 1922. Commanding general of the 82nd Airborne Division, which he led in the invasions of North Africa, Sicily, and Italy, and of the 101st Airborne Division during its landings in France. In 1949, he was chief of staff of American Forces in Europe; he led the American military government in Berlin, 1949–1951; chief of staff of the U.S. Army, 1955–1959. He retired in 1959 but returned to government service as Chairman of the Joint Chiefs of Staff, 1962–1964; in 1964 was appointed U.S. ambassador to South Vietnam.

22 Geoffrey Keyes (1886–1967). General, U.S. Army. He was a deputy commander of the Second Armored Corps in North Africa in 1942–1943 and the Italian campaign, 1943–1945.

23 Arthur W. Tedder (1890–1967). Air Marshal, RAF, 1945. Commander in chief, Mediterranean Air Command, 1943; Deputy Supreme Commander, Allied Air Forces in Europe, 1943–1945.

24 Carl Spaatz (1891–1974). Army Air Force General. In 1942, he took command of the Eighth Air Force, then became Commander of the Allied NW African Air Forces and the Twelfth Air Force, which took part in the landings in Africa and Sicily. He became the first head of the U.S. Air Force in 1947.

25 USS *Biscayne* (AVP-11) was part of the Atlantic Fleet on patrol and plane guard missions. She arrived at Casablanca in November 1942 where she serviced patrol squadrons.

26 Stanley M. Barnes (1912–1996). Captain. U.S. Naval Academy, Class of 1933. Commander, Motor Torpedo Boat Squadron 15 stationed in the Mediterranean.

27 Harold R. Alexander (1891–1969). British Army General. Commander in Chief of British forces that defeated Rommel's Afrika Corps. In 1943, Eisenhower named him Deputy and field commander of the Allied North Africa Forces. In 1944, he became a field marshal and was appointed Supreme Commander of the Mediterranean theater.

28 Rupert M. Zimmerli (1898–1979). Rear Admiral. U.S. Naval Academy, Class of 1921.

29 Terry Allen (1888–1969). General, U.S. Army. He led the First Infantry Division in the North African campaign through the occupation of Tunis and in 1943 took part in the invasion of Sicily. He led the 104th Division in battles in France and Germany in 1944.

30 Troy H. Middleton (1889–1976). General, U.S. Army. Leader of the 45th Infantry Division in Sicily and in Salerno in 1943. He headed the VIII Corps which fought in France at the Battle of the Bulge.

31 Hugh Gaffey (1895–1946). Major General, U.S. Army. He commanded the Second Armored Division during the landings in Northwest Africa and Sicily, 1942–1943.

32 Laurence T. DuBose (1893–1967). Admiral. U.S. Naval Academy, Class of 1913.

33 USS *Boise* (CL-47) was commissioned in 1938. After action at the Battle of Guadalcanal, the *Boise* participated in the invasion of Sicily and the landings at Taranto and Salerno. In late 1943, she returned to the Pacific theater.

34 USS *Birmingham* (CL-62) was commissioned in 1943. She joined the Atlantic Fleet in the Mediterranean and supported the invasion of Sicily, then was transferred to the Pacific Fleet where she participated in the major invasions there.

35 Omar Bradley (1893–1981). General, U.S. Army. U.S. Military Academy, Class of 1915. During World War II, he commanded the First Army at the D-Day landings, the Second Corps in North Africa and Sicily in 1943. In 1949, he was named Chairman of the Joint Chiefs of Staff and in 1950 was promoted to five star General of the Army.

36 USS *Monrovia* (APA-31). In June 1943, she docked in Algiers, taking Admiral Hewitt and General Patton aboard. On July 6, she sailed to Sicily.

37 USS *McLanahan* (DD-615). She made several convoys to Algeria in the spring of 1943. Taking part in the invasion of Sicily at Gela, she served in the anti-aircraft and anti-submarine screen for invasion forces.

38 USS *Buck* (DD-420). She was assigned to convoy duty in 1941–1942 as part of the Atlantic Fleet. In 1943, she conducted patrols off Tunisia and Algeria before participating in the invasion of Sicily.

39 USS *Bristol* (DD-453). She served as a patrol and convoy ship and participated in the landings at Fedala, Morocco, in November 1942.

40 Charles L. Nichols (1892–?). Captain.

41 Benjamin V. McCandlish (1886–1975). Commodore. U.S. Naval Academy, Class of 1909.

42 Humbert W. Ziroli (1893–1979). Rear Admiral. U.S. Naval Academy, Class of 1916.

43 Sir Dudley Pound (1877–1943). Admiral, Royal Navy. Named First Sea Lord and Chief of the Naval Staff, 1939–1943.

44 HMS *Delhi.* Cruiser. Built in 1918. Displacement 4,850 tons.

King George VI presents Vice Admiral Hewitt the insignia of the Order of the Bath, July 1944. (Naval Historical Collection)

XVI   Operation ANVIL-DRAGOON and Aftermath, 1944

My personal movements during the final phases of Operation ANVIL-DRAGOON[1] were too numerous and varied to describe in detail here. Suffice it to say that, afloat by PT boat and destroyer relief flagship, I followed the operations of Admiral Davidson's support group to the westward, including the bombardments of St. Mandrier and the defenses of Marseilles, and inspections of the harbors of Toulon, Marseilles, and Port du Bouc as soon as they could be entered. On shore, I kept in touch with General Patch[2] and his division commanders and also the French Army command. With my friend Admiral Lemonnier,[3] I visited the cities of Toulon and Marseilles as soon as they fell and made a special trip to the rocky fortress of St. Mandrier on August 29, the day after it fell. It was particularly interesting to view the above-ground damage there and the chaotic condition of the underground tunnels, where most of the German naval garrison had been enduring a miserable existence for nearly two weeks.

On September 3, in the destroyer *Plunkett*,[4] I effected a rendezvous off Marseilles with the Commander in Chief, Mediterranean, who was flying his flag in HMS *Ajax*.[5] Admiral Cunningham's intention was to have a look at that city and harbor, but there were no large vessel berths available inside, and the mistral blowing that day made it too rough for boating. Both ships, therefore, proceeded to the sheltered Gulf of St. Tropez, where the usual courtesies were exchanged, and some of the assault beaches were inspected from the shore side.

Both Admiral Cunningham and I made the trip by auto to Toulon and Marseilles on the following day, lunching with Admiral Lemonnier and returning to our respective flagships at St. Tropez by nightfall. This visit gave me an opportunity to check on the U.S. naval detachments which had been established in each of those large cities to handle our naval affairs there.

By September 7, the U.S. Seventh Army and the French First Army, forming General Devers'[6] Army Group, were well on their way up the Rhône Valley and flanking routes, and everything was quiet along the Riviera. To the eastward, our troops had gained nearly to the Italian border with little opposition. Taking advantage of the opportunity, and accompanied by some of my staff, I journeyed by car along the coast as far as Nice, visiting the newly established U.S. PT boat base on the Golfe de Juan and seeing Cannes and Antibes for the first time. Nice seemed little changed from what I remembered of it in 1914, except for the camouflaged concrete gun emplacements and pill boxes along the *plage*. Returning, we detoured through the perfume manufacturing center of Grasse, finding large quantities of that commodity available but none of the usual fancy bottles. I often wondered whether Chanel #5 in Navy medicine bottles, as it was later acquired by some, was as much appreciated at home.

On September 9, in the *Catoctin*,[7] we got underway from St. Tropez and proceeded into Toulon, mooring in the outer harbor. This gave me an opportunity to check the wonderful work our Navy Seabees (Construction Battalions) were doing in assisting with the clearance of the devastated naval dockyard there, and for a second visit to St. Mandrier. I also seized the opportunity to revisit Marseilles on September 11 to get firsthand information on the progress of the salvage work in the harbor and the mine clearance, inside and out. An interesting side event on the way to lunch with the commander of our naval detachment was a call on Madame Monde, the sister of Edmund Rostand, in her delightful villa overlooking the sea. She was a most charming lady, well on in years.

As is well known to historians, Toulon is considered more or less the "Cradle of the French Navy." September 13 and 14 were to be red letter days for that ancient city, for they were to be marked by impressive ceremonies celebrating *Le Retour de la Pompon Rouge*— the *Pompon Rouge*, of course, being the little red tassel at the top of a French sailor's hat.

The festivities began with the arrival of the French fleet and its entry into the port at 1100 on the 13th—an impressive sight, the ships were dressed (their largest ensigns at the gaff and others at the fore and main mastheads), flying long homeward-bound pennants, and their crews were at quarters in immaculate uniforms. They were led by the cruiser *Georges Leygues*,[8] flying the flag of the chief of staff of the French navy, my friend Vice Admiral Lemonnier. Next was the old battleship *Lorraine*,[9] which had been so effective in the bombardment of St. Mandrier. Following her was the Third Cruiser Division consisting of the *Emile Bertin*,[10] flagship, and the *Duguay-Trouin*,[11] commanded by Rear Admiral Auboyneau,[12] the "Free French Opposite Number" for Admiral Lemonnier, who, as a captain, had been present with Admiral Muselier[13] at the seizure of Saint Pierre and Miquelon in 1941. Admiral Jaujard's Fourth Cruiser Division, the *Montcalm*,[14] flagship, and the *Gloire*,[15] brought up the rear of the larger vessels. Finally came the light forces consisting of the destroyer leader *Malin*[16] and the destroyers *Le Fortune*,[17] *Forbin*,[18] and *Basque*.[19] All the traditional passing honors were exchanged between these ships and the *Catoctin*, so that the strains of the "Star Spangled Banner" and the "*Marseillaise*" were intermingled.

Admiral Cunningham, wearing his flag (as the British say) in HMS *Sirius*,[20] and Admiral Davidson in the *Philadelphia*,[21] arrived and moored shortly after the formal entry of the French. From then until mid-afternoon there was a round of official calls between all the principal dignitaries. The evening was marked by an official dinner given by Admiral Lemonnier on *Georges Leygues*, attended by all the senior flag officers present—a most pleasant affair, with all the niceties of cuisine and wine for which the French are noted.

The 14th of December, however, was the big day for the citizens of Toulon. Officially, it began with a reception given by the city of Toulon at the *mairie* or *hôtel de ville* in which the senior officers of the Allied navies present were included. This took the form of the French counterpart of an American cocktail party, a *vin d'honneur*. I have a nice picture of myself signing the Golden Book of Toulon with Admiral Lemonnier looking on.

Then came a *déjeuner* at the Naval Club, given by the minister of marine, Monsieur Jacquinot—another meal doing full justice to the fame of French cuisine.

The afternoon ceremonies, I think, must have been viewed by every man, woman, and child in Toulon, for I have seldom seen more dense nor, may I say, more orderly crowds. The whole occasion was most impressive and heartwarming.

In the center of Toulon there is a large public square bordering the broad Boulevard Strasbourg on its northern or shoreward side. In the middle of this square is a beautiful sculptured monument dating from World War I, dedicated to the citizens of Toulon who have fallen for their country. The inscription reads *Aux Toulonnais, Cris pour la Patrie, 1914–1918, 1939–1941*. Drawn up on three sides of a rectangle were the representatives of all the Allied naval services, British bluejackets and Marines on one side, Americans on the other, and the mass of French bluejackets in the middle. Also, in varied garb but in military formation, were units of the French *maquis*, the underground or so-called FFI (*Force Francais d'Interieur*). Immediately facing the monument were the principal dignitaries, French and Allied. With solemn ceremony and the playing of the French national anthem, M. Jacquinot, the minister of marine, laid a wreath at the foot of the monument. Then occurred an incident, completely unscheduled, which was somewhat embarrassing to me. A French woman, probably a war mother, approached me bearing a large wreath and indicated that I was to place it at the monument. I demurred and motioned that she should do it. But she was insistent, so there was nothing for me to do but to carry out her wishes.

Then followed the grand parade or *defilé*, down the Boulevard Strasbourg. It was an impressive sight with the happy crowds watching it. It was reviewed by officialdom from the sidewalk in front of the square. My picture shows us all standing at salute, probably as some national color passed. In the center, bareheaded, is M. Jacquinot. To his right, in order of rank, are the French: Admirals Lemonnier and

Lambert, M. Sari—the civilian prefect of the war, Admirals Auboyneau and Jaujard, and an engineer or construction officer of the French navy—probably the commander of the Toulon dockyard. On M. Jacquinot's left were the Allied Admirals John H. D. Cunningham, Hewitt, and Davidson. So ended a memorable day.

General de Gaulle himself arrived on the following day, September 15, and marked the occasion by inspecting the shipping in the harbor from a small French naval craft. All men-of-war were full-dressed in his honor, and the customary special honors were rendered as he passed. The strains of the "*Marseillaise*" were heard from every ship having a band. It was pleasant to receive the following signal:

"*Le General de Gaulle addresse ses féliciations à l'Amiral pour le succesès de sa flotte et pour la belle présentation de ses bâtiments.*"

Thus, one month after the initial landing, Operation DRAGOON was formally concluded.

It was on this same day of September 15 that Lieutenant General Devers assumed command of the U.S. Seventh Army, the French First Army, and all ground forces in Southern France, thus establishing the Sixth Army Group. His initial headquarters was set up in Lyon, where I decided to visit him in order to determine what further assistance the Army desired from the Eighth Fleet.

Accordingly, I left Toulon by car on the 18th, accompanied by Captain Brookman of my staff and a French naval aide who also acted as guide and interpreter. It was an interesting ride through Aix en Provence to Avignon, where we spent the night, but still more interesting to be able later to see the ancient city, which was once, for a short time, the home of the popes. I enjoyed seeing the *Pont d'Avignon*, famed in song and history.

Our route the following day followed the east bank of the Rhône, on a road that had sides littered with bombed, burned-out, and abandoned German vehicles and other vestiges of war. The American bombing of bridges across the Rhône tributaries ahead of the retreat had forced the fleeing Germans to abandon much of their equipment. Our own progress was slowed by the many damaged bridges on the route, hastily repaired by the Army engineers.

We did reach Lyon in time for a pleasant lunch with the general. After settling inter-service affairs at a very satisfactory conference, we took off for Grenoble where we planned to spend the night. This was a delightful drive to Grenoble by the Isere River, beautifully situated among mountains. It is on the route that Napoleon followed upon his return from Elba. The city itself had been little touched by the war, and we were made most comfortable in an excellent hotel with superb cuisine.

We left Grenoble with regret the following morning, September 20, and reached the *Catoctin* at Toulon by mid-afternoon. The next five days were spent in final inspections of the U.S. naval detachments at Toulon and Marseilles to make sure that they were functioning well in caring for naval units visiting those ports and in rendering required assistance to Army elements. The only combat unit of the Western Naval Task Force still employed in active operations was a flank force commanded by the French Admiral Jaujard in the *Montcalm.* This was composed of one or two cruisers and three or four American destroyers engaged in covering the western advance of a small detachment of the Seventh Army toward the Italian border.

On September 25, the *Catoctin,* with admiral and staff embarked, departed from Toulon, arriving Naples early on the 27th. There I returned to my villa in Alto Posillippo and resumed direction of Eighth Fleet affairs from our shore headquarters down by the harbor.

The Mediterranean campaign, as far as the Navy was concerned, seemed about over. No further major operations were planned. Our mine vessels were busily engaged in sweeping enemy mines off the French coast. In this they were receiving the valuable assistance of a U.S. Navy lighter-than-air detachment of blimps, which had originally been flown over in stages from Lakehurst to Port Lyautey to aid British anti-submarine forces in denying the Strait of Gibraltar to enemy submarines. They were commanded by Lieutenant Commander Presley M. Rixey, Jr.,[22] a resourceful and energetic officer, the son of a Marine Corps colonel and the grandson of the very Chief of the Bureau of Medicine and Surgery who had made possible my admittance to the Naval Academy. These blimps were, of course, most vulnerable to enemy air attack, but by the time they became available in the Gibraltar area, this was no longer a threat. By hovering over the Strait with their magnetic detectors, they made undetected submarine passage of that narrow body of water virtually impossible. It was also discovered that over quiet water and with the right light they were very good at spotting submerged objects such as mines. To move them to the coast of Provence, it was merely necessary to transfer their portable mooring masts and other equipment to a convenient airfield. They saved the sweepers much time and effort.

Outside of the foregoing operations, naval requirements were minor. Some amphibious forces were retained to provide general army support and to assist in any leapfrog landings that might be planned in connection with the final campaign in Italy. A few cruisers, destroyers, and motor torpedo boats were also retained to provide support services. With those exceptions, active units of the Eighth Fleet were transferred for service elsewhere. Escort forces were no longer needed, because the threat of submarines and air attack had been eliminated from the Mediterranean, and thus, shipping was able to proceed singly and to burn navigation lights at night.

In view of the above, it was now necessary to begin the reduction of the Eighth Fleet shore activities and, as they could be spared, to plan their gradual closing out. These still included the Moroccan Sea Frontier with Casablanca and Port Lyautey; supply, hospital, and repair facilities at Oran; the amphibious base at Bizerte; the Palermo repair and recreation facilities; and lesser activities in the Naples area,

Corsica, and the south of France. Personally, I had hoped that my Mediterranean experience might make some contribution to final operations in the Pacific, but this was not to be the case. I was to remain in the Mediterranean almost until the final surrender of Germany. Meanwhile, several events of interest occurred, and I was to have some pleasant personal experiences.

The routine of the Naples headquarters was quietly resumed on September 28, and on the following day I made a quick trip to Rome for a call on the U.S. ambassador to Italy, Mr. Alexander Kirk,[23] and also Mr. Myron Taylor, President Roosevelt's representative to the Vatican. The latter took me for a very pleasant private audience with the pope,[24] who seemed much interested in my account of our operations. I was able to assure him, in response to an inquiry, that the men of his faith had done their full part in our armed forces.

In addition to the considerable administrative detail involved in the gradual reductions in the Eighth Fleet, the first half of October was taken up with many pleasant official and social activities, and with the award of decorations earned by officers and men during the summer's operations. I was firmly of the conviction that to be effective and fully appreciated, recognition of extraordinary services should be prompt and the presentation made with due ceremony. This I tried to accomplish as far as was in my power.

Among the social activities were several dinners given by senior officers of the English-speaking Allied forces, and some occasioned by the visits of a number of high-ranking Brazilian officers. There was also a visit from our congresswoman, Edith Nourse Rogers,[25] whom I found to be most interesting and pleasant. She made a most thorough inspection of our U.S. naval dispensary in Naples and added much to the cheer of the patients.

An anecdote which I like to relate illustrates the pleasant relationship which existed at that time between the British and American services, and particularly the two navies. It was the custom at official dinners for the senior American officer to toast the king of England, and the senior Britisher to toast the president of the United States. One day Admiral Sir John Cunningham[26] suggested to me that too many words were being used. He said, "I know that, between us, there is only one king and one president." I agreed. So, thereafter, when we happened to be the seniors, he would rise, raise his glass, and say "To the president," and I similarly would say, "To his majesty, the king."

The campaign in Italy was still on, and the flank of our forces in France, moving toward the Italian border, was being supported by a small Franco-American force of cruisers and destroyers, the command of which, after the departure of Admiral Davidson, had devolved upon Contre Amirals Jaujard and Auboyneau. Admiral Davidson, at this time, was detached from the Eighth Fleet and ordered home to Washington to await orders. Personally, I was sorry to see him go, but for his sake, I was glad. He had served in the Mediterranean without a break since early 1943 and had participated in TORCH before that. He was tired and needed the rest which he so well deserved. Unfortunately, his leave was all too short, and he was called to duty in the Navy Department. A stroke, not long thereafter, forced his retirement in 1946 and led to an untimely death in 1950. He was truly a war casualty.

By mid-October, it was time for me to have another look at my far-flung naval empire, preparatory to the closing out of many of its activities, to confer awards, and to get a firsthand view of the situation. Accordingly, I embarked on the *Brooklyn* on October 17 for an overnight run to Palermo, which by now had not only become a major repair base but a recreation center for the Eighth Fleet. I was received there not only by a bluejacket guard but by one of the MPs and Italians as well. The shipyard, dispensary, and personnel quarters were thoroughly inspected, as well as the ammunition depot about to be discontinued, which had been established to provide for the requirements of naval gunfire support for Salerno and the south of France.

Bizerte was reached early the following morning, October 19. This was the major base of the Amphibious Force, Eighth Fleet, and a very full day was spent in company with Admiral Lowry and Captain Jalbert, the base commander, inspecting all of its activities and many of the amphibious craft present. Also inspected was the fleet repair ship *Delta*[27] (the envy of our British friends) and an LST which had been especially fitted as a repair ship. At 1100, the personnel of the Amphibious Force present and an attached beach battalion were paraded for the presentation of awards and an address as to their probable future duties. After a very pleasant luncheon with Contre Amiral Longhaud, the French naval commander at Bizerte, there was an afternoon conference with all the U.S. naval officers at the base.

At Algiers, the U.S. Navy was now represented by Captain Robert Morris,[28] who had done splendid work throughout the Mediterranean campaign in amphibious training and operations. He was occupying my old villa of Villa dar el Azizi. He came aboard the *Brooklyn* upon its arrival in the harbor about 0900 on October 20. He was followed shortly thereafter by British Vice Admiral Miles,[29] whose title was Flag Officer, Western Mediterranean, and by the French Admiral Sol, who was the current prefect maritime. This call was primarily to revisit my old headquarters and to see some of my old friends, whom I was able to entertain on board the *Brooklyn* at dinner in the evening. These naturally included Amiral and Mme Moreau, who had not yet been able to return to their home in France. I was able to give them news of their home in Le Mourillon, a naval residence section of Toulon, which I had taken pains to visit in their behalf. It was not good news, for it had been occupied by some German non-commissioned officers who had more or less wrecked it prior to their hasty departure.

An overnight trip on the *Brooklyn* brought us to Mers el Kebir. Here, in company with Commodore Yates, commanding the Naval Operating Base Oran, and

Commodore Edgar, the Eighth Fleet transport commander, a quick visit was made to ship and shore activities, including the naval supply depot and naval hospital, where the party lunched with Captain Tyler,[30] MC, USN, the commanding officer. In the early afternoon, my aides and I emplaned for Casablanca to spend the night of October 21 with Commodore McCandlish, the commander of the Moroccan Sea Frontier and the Naval Operating Base Casablanca.

On the morning of the 22nd, I proceeded to Port Lyautey by car, pausing for a moment in Rabat to greet my friends, Amiral and Mme de la Fond, who had been exiled there the preceding December by General de Gaulle as a result of holding an official memorial mass for Admiral Darlan. The U.S. naval air station at Port Lyautey was reached in time for an inspection of the blimp base and lunch with Commodore Owens, the air station commander. After luncheon, there was a ceremonial presentation of awards, following which I boarded my plane for Oran. After dinner there with Commodore Yates, I returned aboard the *Brooklyn,* having completed the round of Eighth Fleet activities, except for those in Corsica and the south of France.

An eventful five days of the following week were spent in France. The *Brooklyn* moored in the harbor of Toulon at 0800 of October 24, upon which Commodore Dougherty, the commander of our Toulon-Marseilles naval detachment, came on board. Shortly thereafter, I received calls from Admirals Jaujard, Auboyneau, and Lambert. The latter, who had been the commander of the battleship *Richelieu* (sister ship of the *Jean Bart*), was now the prefect maritime at Toulon. He presented me formally with a posthumous Croix de Guerre for an American bomb disposal officer, Lieutenant (j.g.) Lewis, who had lost his life in clearing enemy obstructions at La Ciotat. This I accepted on behalf of the next of kin.

Later the same morning, acting for President Roosevelt, I conferred the Legion of Merit on Admirals Jaujard and Auboyneau, each on their respective flagships, the *Montcalm* and the *Emile Bertin.* These ceremonies were followed by a *Vin d'Honneur* on the *Montcalm* and a luncheon on the *Emile Bertin.* Admiral Jaujard presented me with a handsome wooden plaque in which were inset the badges (each French man of war has one) of the *Montcalm,* of the *Jeanne d'Arc,* the *Duguay-Trouin, Emile Bertin, Georges Leygues,* and the *Gloire,* as a souvenir of the five large French ships which served under my command during DRAGOON.

In the afternoon of the 24th, with Commander English and Lieutenant Commander Griswold, I proceeded by car to Aix en Provence to join General Devers on his private train (previously used by Nazi high command) for an overnight trip to Dijon, and thence to the headquarters of the Sixth Army Group at Vittel. Never had I traveled in such comfort and, since there were a number of high-ranking Army friends aboard, the occasion was very pleasant.

At Dijon the following morning, I accompanied General Devers on an inspection of the Army's 36th General Hospital and a French military hospital (the French First Army was part of General Devers' army group). Thence, we departed by car to Vittel, a pleasant drive through the French countryside, arriving just in time for lunch. That afternoon I received at the hands of General Devers an Oak Leaf Cluster for my Army Distinguished Service Medal. Among those present was Lieutenant Colonel Henry Cabot Lodge[31] of General Devers' staff, brother of Commander John Davis Lodge,[32] the Eighth Fleet's liaison officer with the French.

On the morning of October 26, in a military car kindly loaned by General Devers, we went on to the Seventh Army headquarters at Epinal for a call on General Patch and the presentation there of an Army Distinguished Service Medal to my planning officer, Commander English. From there we had another beautiful drive to Paris, which we reached in time to be greeted at the U.S. Navy's Royal Monceau Hotel by Admiral Alan Kirk (now commanding U.S. naval activities in northern France) and by Admiral Lemonnier, by now fully established at the Ministère de la Marine as chief of staff of the French Navy. Incidentally, this was my first sight of Paris since passing through it en route to Brest during World War I.

The day of the 27th was fully occupied, first in a pleasant call on my old chief, General Eisenhower, at his headquarters in Versailles, and on his chief of staff, General Bedell Smith, and then on our ambassador Caffrey[33] at the U.S. embassy, and on the minister of marine, M. Jacquinot, at his ministry. I dined with Alan Kirk at his chateau.

Thus concluded an enjoyable interlude in France. We flew back to Marseilles the next day, motored to Toulon, boarded the *Brooklyn*, and on the 29th were back in Naples.

There is little to relate for the month of November in 1944, during which, officially, I was primarily occupied with the handling of multitudinous administrative details. Socially, there was a staff celebration of the second anniversary of the TORCH landing and the observance of the American Thanksgiving holiday. On the 14th, there was a pleasant reception at the Allied headquarters at Caserta, given by the British political representative, Mr. Harold Macmillan[34] (later the prime minister of Great Britain). December, however, was a more eventful month.

The Germans having been driven north of the Arno, I decided to do a little sight-seeing, taking with me as a guide an officer of my staff who in civil life was an architect, and as a student had become thoroughly familiar with the architectural wonders of Italy. Driving to Rome on December 2, I was put up in the royal suite of the Albergo Grande, and entertained at dinner by Commodore Ziroli, who, by now, was well established as the U.S. liaison officer to the Italian Navy.

After a marvelous drive up the coast the following morning, we reached Livorno (Leghorn) early in the afternoon, in time to inspect the U.S. PT boat base there, newly established for coastal operation along the enemy western flank. The British Admiral Morse[35] (Flag Officer, Italy) was our host, and we spent the night at his villa.

Early on the 4th, we departed for Florence via Pisa, those renowned points of interest. Since it was the first time I had ever seen them, my pleasure may well be imagined. We had to cross the Arno into Florence by a military bridge, the enemy having, in his retreat, blown all the bridges except the ancient Ponte Vecchio. Apparently the Germans had some respect for its architecture and history. Anyway, it was not a bridge which could have supported any appreciable military traffic. It was a busy day of sight-seeing, during which the American military government was my host. I was invited to sign the Golden Book of Florence and also had the unusual pleasure of tea with a delightful Italian countess in her ancestral home.

Naturally, I would have liked to make a longer visit, but official matters were pressing, so we had to return to Rome on the 5th. We took the higher route via Siena, where we lunched in the famous square, noted for its annual horse race. To me, Siena was fascinating and is one of the places which I would like most to revisit. The numerous old fortified hill towns through which, or past which, our Fifth Army had had to fight its way were of extreme interest to me. After another night in Rome, and remaining for an official luncheon given by Commodore Ziroli in honor of the Italian Admiral de Courten, I reached Naples again in time to become involved in what my friend Admiral John Cunningham later on jocularly called the Hewitt Mutiny. The Germans, in their hasty evacuation of Greece, had left a political vacuum which the Greek communists, the ELAS, were seeking to fill and to seize the reins of government. This movement was being opposed by the Greeks loyal to their government in exile, King George. The British, under Churchill's direction, were landing considerable forces to restore order and protect the interests of the legal government. At this juncture, Secretary of State Stettinius[36] made an address in which he said, in effect, that the matter of the Greek government was something for the people of Greece themselves to settle, and that the United States would render *no assistance whatever* to either party to the controversy.

When I read this announcement in our radio press, I realized that some action on my part was necessary, because LSTs of my Eighth Amphibious Force were actively engaged at that moment in ferrying large numbers of British troops with their equipment and supplies from the south of Italy into Greece. Accordingly, I despatched a message in secret United States code to the Chief of Naval Operations, citing Mr. Stettinius's declaration and calling Admiral King's attention to the fact that the U.S. Navy actually was rendering considerable assistance to the British military intervention. It was not necessary to state that I, naturally, was highly in favor of all the British were doing to defeat the communists.

Admiral King's reply was an order to me that none of our naval craft would be used further to aid the Greek operation. I immediately called on Admiral

Cunningham to advise him of this order and my personal regret, and issued the necessary instructions to my own forces. Admiral Cunningham was very much concerned, particularly as a large British force had already embarked on several U.S. LSTs at Taranto that were about to sail. He at once advised the Supreme Allied Commander, Field Marshal Wilson,[37] who immediately called an Allied conference at his Caserta headquarters.

When the conference, composed of the senior officers of the British and American three services, convened, I stated the situation and informed them regretfully of my orders. To my amazement, my own Army colleague, General McNarney,[38] who, after the departure of General Devers, had become the deputy Allied commander, turned to Field Marshal Wilson, informed him that the Mediterranean Allied Forces of all services had been allotted to him to employ as he saw fit, and advised him to direct me to continue with the operation of ferrying the British troops. Containing my indignation as well as I could, I said quietly (I hope), "Sir, you may issue any order you wish, but not one of my ships will move until my orders from Washington are changed." With that, my friend Admiral Cunningham jumped in and said, "Of course, General, you cannot issue any such order. You would be putting Admiral Hewitt in an impossible position." With that, the conference broke up, with a decision to refer the matter to the prime minister. The Washington side of the story is told in Robert Sherwood's *Roosevelt and Hopkins.*

The situation was temporarily so tense, and I was so fearful that some Allied official might give contradictory orders to my ships at Taranto, that I got their U.S. naval commander on the telephone, and after being assured that he recognized my voice, I directed him that he was, under no circumstance, to move unless otherwise directed by me. Fortunately, Admiral King was able to rescind his order shortly thereafter and normal operations were resumed. It is an interesting sidelight in our change of policy that the protection of Greece from the communists ultimately devolved upon the United States.

Hardly had this controversy been resolved when there was a round of farewell parties for General Wilson, who was being relieved as the Supreme Allied Commander by General Alexander. We saw "Jumbo," as General Wilson was nicknamed, off to England on December 12.

The following day the House Military Affairs Committee arrived at the air field near Caserta, where they were met by the principal commanders of each U.S. service. One of the members was Congresswoman Clare Boothe Luce,[39] whom I found to be a very interesting as well as attractive person. At a reception for the Committee that afternoon at Caserta, to which our allies were invited, Admiral Cunningham told me, on his arrival, that he was particularly anxious to meet the famous Mrs. Luce. Naturally, I took him over and presented him. During the course of the conversation, Mrs. Luce asked what her committee was supposed to do that evening. When I told her that they were being entertained by the Army in Naples and taken to some play or opera, she showed extreme lack of interest. Thereupon, in almost the same breath, Admiral Cunningham and I invited her to dine at our villas. Having to defer to my senior, a compromise was reached by which she was to come to me for cocktails and to meet my staff, and that I would then drive her on for dinner at the Villa Emma. She and Admiral Cunningham got on so well and had such an absorbing discussion about world affairs that it was quite late when we delivered her to her hotel. Later on, we learned that the Army was furious with the Allied navies for shanghaiing the only worthwhile member of their committee.

The year 1944 was finished off with the traditional naval Christmas observances, a trip by air to Casablanca to meet the Senate Meade Committee, a visit with the Committee to our air station at Port Lyautey, and a return to Naples on New Year's Eve. The U.S. Navy on Christmas makes a particular point of entertaining poor children on board ship and at shore activities. This was no exception and was made especially joyful this year, because Italian children throughout the preceding war years had known little of Christmas. I was kept very busy, both on the 24th and 25th, visiting the patients at our Army hospital, naval dispensary, Italian children's hospital, and the various naval children's parties. I would not have missed any of them. At the children's hospital I was happily greeted in each ward by a shout of "*Buon Natale, Amiraglio.*" Our own hospitals were visited by a choir of little Italian boys dressed in sailor suits made for them by our sailors from cast-off uniforms. The choir serenaded the patients with well-known carols—"O Sole Mio," and "God Bless America" in an English which they probably did not understand. It was all most heartwarming.

As we toasted the arrival of the New Year at the senior U.S. naval officers' mess, there were hopes for a peace soon to come.

NOTES

1 Operation ANVIL-DRAGOON. On August 15, 1944, the invasion of Southern France commenced on the coast of Provence, backed by pre-landing bombardment by naval forces commanded by Admiral Hewitt in USS *Catoctin*. This was the largest amphibious invasion Hewitt led and one that was eminently successful on all counts. General Alexander M. Patch's Seventh Army landed in daylight to make its way up the Rhône Valley to secure the liberation of France and Germany.

2 Alexander Patch (1889–1945). General, U.S. Army. He was in command of the Seventh Army during the invasion of Southern France on August 15, 1944.

3 André G. Lemonnier (1896–1963). Admiral, French Navy. He headed the Free French Navy in 1943 and was in charge of landings in Corsica and Provence in 1943 and 1944.

4 USS *Plunkett* (DD-431) participated in the invasion of Southern France where she transported military leaders to the beaches and performed screening activities, bombardment, and fire support at various ports.

5 HMS *Ajax*. Cruiser (March 1, 1934), 6,896 tons displacement; length 530'; Beam 55' 2"; draught 16'.

6 Jacob L. Devers (1887–1979). General, U.S. Army. He served as commanding general in the North African theater in 1944 and deputy commander-in-chief, Mediterranean theater. In September 1944, he took command of the Sixth Army that fought in France and secured the surrender of Germany in Bavaria and western Austria.

7 USS *Catoctin* (AGC-5). Flagship for the Commander, Eighth Fleet, in Algiers, 1944, then sailed to Naples, Italy. The invasion of southern France was

planned on her decks and she took part in the assault in August 1944, serving as the command and communications post for the invading forces.

8 *Georges Leygues*. French Cruiser (*Gloire* Class). Built in 1936. Displacement, 7,600 tons; length, 548'; beam, 57 1/2'; draught, 17 1/3'; complement, 540.

9 *Lorraine*. French Battleship. Built in 1913. Displacement, 22,189 tons; length 541 1/3'; seam 88 1/2'; draught, 32'; complement, 1,133.

10 *Emile Bertin*. French Cruiser/Minelayer. Built in 1933. Displacement, 5,885 tons; length, 548'; beam, 51 3/4'; draught 17 3/4', complement, 567.

11 *Duguay-Trouin*. French Cruiser. Launched in 1923. Displacement, 7,249 tons; length, 575'; beam, 57 1/2'; draught, 17 1/4'; complement 577.

12 Philippe Auboyneau (1899–1961). French naval officer, was appointed commander of the Free French naval forces and merchant marine in 1943. He was general-major of the Navy in Algiers in 1943 and took part in Operation DRAGOON in 1944. He was promoted to admiral in 1957.

13 Emile H. Muselier (1882–1965). French naval officer, was named commander of the Free French naval forces and merchant marine in 1940 by General De Gaulle. After conflicts with de Gaulle and instances of insubordination, he was removed from his post in 1942. In 1943, he was named prefect of police for Algiers.

14 *Montcalm*. French Cruiser (*Gloire* Class). Built in 1935. Displacement, 7,600 tons; length 548'; beam 57 1/2'; draught 17 1/2'; complement, 540.

15 *Gloire*. French Cruiser (*Gloire* Class). Built in 1935. Displacement, 7,600 tons; length 548'; beam 57 1/2'; draught 17 1/2'; complement, 540.

16 *Le Malin*. French Destroyer. (*Fantasque* class). Launched in 1933. Displacement, 2,569 tons; length 411 1/2'; complement, 220.

17 *Le Fortune*. French Destroyer (*Alcym* class). Launched in 1926. Displacement, 1,378 tons; dimensions, 330.9' x 33 1/4' x 9 1/2'; complement, 142.

18 *Forbin*. French Destroyer (*Alcym* class). Launched in 1928. Displacement, 1,378 tons; dimensions, 330.9' x 33 1/4' x 9 1/2'; complement, 142.

19 *Basque*. French Destroyer (*Alcym* class). Launched in 1929. Displacement, 1,378 tons; dimensions, 330.9' x 33 1/4' x 9 1/2'; complement, 142.

20 HMS *Sirius* (Cruiser). Sept. 18, 1940. Displacement, 5,450 tons; length, 506'; beam 57 1/2'; draught, 14'.

21 USS *Philadelphia* (CL-41) took part in the invasion of Southern France, closing the beaches at the Gulf of St. Tropez and providing counter-battery gunfire. She provided gunfire support for troops in Toulon and Nice.

22 Presley M. Rixey (1911–). Lieutenant Commander, U.S. Navy.

23 Alexander C. Kirk (1888–1979). Ambassador to Italy, December 8, 1944 March 5, 1946.

24 Pope Pius XII (1876–1958) held the Holy Office, 1939–1958. He made diplomatic efforts to end World War II. During the war, he established relief agencies for civilian victims of the war.

25 Edith Nourse Rogers (1881–1960). Congresswoman from the 5th District, Massachusetts, 1925–1959.

26 John Cunningham (1885–1962). Admiral, Royal Navy. He was named Chief of the Levant prior to Operation TORCH in 1942, was appointed Commander-in-Chief, Mediterranean, 1943, and First Sea Lord in 1946.

27 *Delta* (AR-9) was commissioned in 1941. In 1943, she arrived in Oran, Algeria, then was detailed to Bizerte, Tunisia, and later to Italy, where she prepared landing craft for return to the United States.

28 Robert Morris (1901–1984). Rear Admiral. U.S. Naval Academy, Class of 1923.

29 Geoffrey John Audley Miles (1890–1986). Vice Admiral, Royal Navy. Served in World War I; Captain of HMS *Nelson* for two years; Rear Admiral, 1941; head of military mission, Moscow, 1941–1943; Vice Admiral, 1944.

30 George Tyler (1888–?). Captain, U.S. Navy, Medical Corps.

31 Henry Cabot Lodge, Jr. (1902–1985). U.S. Senator and public servant. A member of the Army Reserve, he went on active duty in 1941 and served in Army operations in France, Germany, and Italy in 1944 and 1945.

32 John Davis Lodge (1903–1985). Brother of Henry C. Lodge; governor of Connecticut, 1951–1955.

33 Jefferson Caffrey (1886–1974). U.S. ambassador to France, 1944–1949.

34 Harold Macmillan (1894–1986). English statesman and scion of the Macmillan publishing company. He stood for Parliament in 1924 as a Conservative. During World War II, he served as British resident minister in North Africa, 1942–1945. He was prime minister, 1957–1963.

35 John Anthony Vere Morse (1892–1960). Vice Admiral, Royal Navy. He served in World War I and was head of the British naval mission to China, 1934–1937. After World War II, he was a flag officer, Malaya, 1945–1946.

36 Edward R. Stettinius (1900–1949). American Statesman. He left U.S. Steel, where he was chairman of the board, in 1940 to enter government service. He served as under-secretary of state in 1943–1944 and Secretary of State, 1944–1945. He was the first U.S. representative to the U.N. in 1945–1946.

37 Henry Maitland Wilson (1881–1964). Field Marshal, British army and 1st Baron. Educated at Eton, he served in World War I, was promoted to general in 1941, Commander-in-Chief, Middle East, in 1943, and Supreme Allied Commander, Mediterranean, and Field Marshal in 1944.

38 Joseph T. McNarney (1893–1971). General, U.S. Army. In October 1942, he held the post of deputy supreme commander in the Mediterranean area and commander of U.S. forces there.

39 Clare Boothe Luce (1903–1987). American politician, diplomat, and playwright. A Republican, she entered politics in 1940 and served as a Congressional representative from Fairfield County, Connecticut, 1943–1947. From 1953 to 1956, she was U.S. ambassador to Italy.

Joseph Stalin, Franklin D. Roosevelt, and Winston Churchill at the Yalta Conference, February 1945 (Naval Historical Collection)

XVII *War's End and Twelfth Fleet, 1945*

During the month of January 1945, one of the principal concerns of the Eighth Fleet, in addition to preparing most of its remaining amphibious units for transfer to the Far East, was to assist in preliminary arrangements for President Roosevelt and the U.S. delegation at the Yalta Conference[1] to be held at that Black Sea resort early the following month. Lieutenant Commander Griswold,[2] my flag lieutenant, was sent ahead by air with others to survey and report on the situation there. It was proposed to provide for the necessary rapid communication to Washington by sending my amphibious flagship, the *Catoctin*, to Sevastopol, about thirty-five miles west of Yalta, which was the nearest port to which the Russians would guarantee mine clearance. The *Catoctin* had adequate communication equipment for the purpose and, in addition, was well provided with quarters for staff, and even for the president, should the accommodations provided ashore prove inadequate. The old cruiser *Memphis*[3] arrived to act as my flagship, and the *Catoctin* was sent down to Palermo, our now flourishing shipyard, to have its flag quarters specially fitted to care for the president should they be required. Fortunately, my experience on the *Indianapolis* eight years previously enabled me to advise on just what was needed. I made an overnight trip in the *Memphis* on January 18–19 to look her over, shortly after which the *Catoctin* departed for the Black Sea, being the first vessel flying a U.S. Navy commission pennant to pass through the Bosporus in many, many years.

The quarters assigned to the president and his party at Yalta were in an old and long unoccupied palace of the czars. The Russians had done a pretty good job of getting it ready, but the *Catoctin* personnel, arriving early, were able to do much to assist in the extermination of insect life and to provide the comforts and facilities to which their countrymen were accustomed.

I took the opportunity of this two-day visit to Palermo, with Admiral Lowry, who was also there, to inspect many of the landing craft (LST and LCT) there. Such inspections, in my opinion, did much to keep officers and crews on their toes, particularly when the incentive of imminent combat operations was lacking. I was pleased with what I found. I was further greatly impressed with the children's soup kitchens, which I inspected at the invitation of Captain Nichols, the Palermo base commander, and Commander Hoffman,[4] his executive officer. These had been set up largely through the initiative of the latter by our enlisted men themselves. The Sicilian economy had been badly hit by the war, and the people, particularly the poor, had suffered accordingly. Many of the children were emaciated and badly undernourished. To remedy this situation as far as possible, the cooperation of the church, which operated the schools, was first secured. Then it was arranged to save the leavings from the naval messes in a sanitary manner instead of discarding them. These remnants were boiled up into a good soup and rushed out hot in Navy trucks to the various schools, where they were served to the children under the supervision of the sisters. The requirement for a child to get his ration was a clean face and hands and a clean container of some kind. Not only did this procedure act as an incentive to cleanliness, but it did much for the welfare of the children and friendly relations with the populace. This idea soon spread to other of our bases.

The president and the prime minister and the Combined Chiefs of Staff, with their aides, were to meet in Malta at the end of January, preliminary to the Yalta Conference. Malta, as a result of war damage, was rather hard put to suitably quarter the high-ranking officers, most of whom were to arrive by air, and auto transportation was at a premium. Accordingly, we sailed an LST from Naples, loaded with Army cars, to serve as a floating garage at Malta and to provide accommodation for the more junior personnel needing it. This proved to be a happy arrangement. Water, particularly hot water, being a scarcity in Malta at the time, many of the senior members of the delegation availed themselves of the ship's facilities.

Admiral Stark from London joined me in Naples on January 27, and together we proceeded to Valletta in the *Memphis* that night, berthing in the great harbor the following morning. We were entertained at tea that afternoon by the Vice Admiral, Malta, and dined with Admiral John Cunningham at Admiralty House, the history of which I have previously related.

On the 29th, the various members of the Combined Chiefs began arriving. Admiral King and his chief aides were met at Luca Airfield by Admiral Stark and me, as well as by CINCMED and the Vice Admiral, Malta. A U.S. naval conference was held with Admiral King as soon as we had escorted him to his quarters at Tigue House.

The governor of Malta, Lieutenant General Schreibner, gave a resplendent dinner on the 30th at the Governor's Palace, to which I was fortunate enough to be invited. Among those present were Field Marshal Maitland Wilson, both Admirals Cunningham (John and Andrew), Admiral Somerville,[5] Lord Leathers,[6] and General Ismay;[7] and on the American side, Admiral King, General Marshall,[8] Admiral Stark, General Bedell Smith (representing General Eisenhower), and Admiral Land[9] (representing the War Shipping Board).

The days of January 30, 31 and February 1 were fully occupied by meetings of the Combined Chiefs in which I, of course, had no part. But during the social occasions connected therewith, it was pleasant to meet so many old friends. I was particularly happy to see once more my old chief, Andrew Cunningham. At another dinner at Admiralty House on January 31, Admiral King casually mentioned to his British opposite number that I was being considered for promotion—something which was news to me. Admiral Andrew himself stood up and said, "Why, of course! Hewitt must have his fourth star." That certainly was a forceful recommendation. On the evening of the 1st, I was able to get General Marshall and General Bedell Smith aboard the *Memphis* for dinner.

On the morning of February 2, President Roosevelt came in on the new USS *Quincy*[10] with my old *Savannah*, now fully restored and reconditioned after her severe damage at Salerno as escort cruiser. Admiral Stark and I were able to call on him about 1100 and were greeted by him as old friends. With him on the *Quincy* were his chief of staff, Admiral Leahy;[11] his naval aide, Admiral Wilson Brown;[12] and his naval medical officer, Doctor McIntyre, the one who had been with him on the *Indianapolis* eight years before.

Actually, Prime Minister Churchill had arrived from London by plane early on January 30, but since he was slightly indisposed, he was transferred promptly to HMS *Orion*,[13] and there put to bed by his physician. He recovered sufficiently, however, to join the president on the *Quincy* sometime after his arrival.

The night of the 2–3rd was a busy one at Luca Airfield. British and American planes took off at short intervals, ferrying the prime minister, the president, the Combined Chiefs of Staff, and their various aides and secretaries to the Crimea. Thereafter, Malta settled back to normal, and I returned on the *Memphis* to Naples. Until mid-February, there was nothing special to remark, except that my staff gave me a delightful party to celebrate my fifty-eighth birthday. That happened to be the day President Roosevelt, the Yalta Conference having been concluded, flew to Alexandria to rejoin the *Quincy*. The *Quincy* took him through the canal to the Bitter Lake where, by invitation, he received visits from Ibn Saud,[14] Haile Selassie,[15] and Egypt's King Farouk.[16] The *Quincy*'s crew later had many a tale to tell of being boarded by King Saud and his retainers and of a special Arab meal being cooked for him, desert style, on the *Quincy*'s fantail. By the 14th, the *Quincy* was back in Alexandria, where the president and the prime minister had a final meeting, the latter having embarked in a British cruiser after a visit to Athens.

The *Quincy* was scheduled to stop in Algiers, where a meeting with General de Gaulle had originally been planned. Feeling my duty to make a final call on the president before he departed from my area, I left Naples on February 15 aboard the *Memphis* and arrived in Algiers the following day. With me, in addition to the principal members of my staff, was Judge Rosenman, one of the president's assistants, who was joining the presidential party in order to assist in drafting the report of the conference during the return voyage.

Since the *Quincy* did not arrive in Algiers until February 18, I had an opportunity to entertain and be entertained by several old friends, including Admiral and Mme Moreau, and Admiral and Mme Ronarc'h. Early on the 18th, Ambassadors Kirk from Rome and Caffrey from Paris joined me on the *Memphis* and were on deck with me when we rendered presidential honors as the *Quincy* passed in. Official calls were made about 1100 and later I had the honor of having an informal luncheon with the president and his daughter, Mrs. Boettiger,[17] who was with him. He looked very tired, and she was obviously taking especial care of him. He had not long to live.

It was evident that my tour in the Mediterranean was drawing to a close. So I decided to make a final visit as well as inspection of the Eighth Fleet's African activities. Leaving Algiers in *Memphis* on the evening of the 18th, we docked at Mers el Kebir the next morning. That day and part of the next were spent inspecting the shipping that was present, the base, the receiving station, the supply depot, and the naval hospital.

On the 20th, we flew to Casablanca and spent the night with Commodore McCandlish at his villa. On the 21st, we had a most interesting trip by car through Rabat and Meknès to the old capital of Fez. This was my first opportunity to see the latter two. We put up at a beautiful modern hotel outside of the old city, the Palais Jamis, but we made a trip on foot through the medina, the native town, and the market. Indescribably smelly and crowded, but intensely interesting. Even in the casbahs of Oran and Algiers, I had never seen such narrow streets where one had to brush the passers-by to get through. The *Memphis'* doctor, a Baltimore dermatologist in civilian life, who was with the party, remarked that he would like very much to stay and study some of the great variety of skin diseases which he had noted.

After a flight from Fez back to Oran and an inspection of the amphibious training base and construction battalion (Seabee) center at Arzew, I proceeded in the *Memphis* to Bizerte for a two-day stay for final inspections and exchange of social courtesies with local French commanders on February 24–26. On the 25th, I had the pleasure of attending a luncheon given in my honor by General Mast at the residence in Tunis of the governor general, after which I was invested with the Tunisian order of Nichan Iftikar, rank of grand officer. Much had happened since I had been present at a victory luncheon at the same residence nearly two years before to celebrate the surrender of the Axis armies in Africa.

The next stop was Palermo. February 27 found me back at my desk in Naples. A few days later, Lieutenant Commander Griswold, who had served me so faithfully and efficiently as flag lieutenant during the preceding three years, departed for duty in Washington and to be nearer his home in Baltimore. I was very sorry to see him go, but our naval war in the Mediterranean was over and he deserved the opportunity to see something of his family. His place was taken by Lieutenant Peet,[18] who had been "breaking in" during Griswold's absence at Yalta and during the just completed North African trip.

The first half of March was spent in handling routine administrative affairs and in an inter-Allied exchange of pleasant social events. But mid-month found me at sea again on the *Memphis*, headed for another round of visits to the south coast of France via the Strait of Bonifacio, where, on the morning of March 16, we anchored off La Maddalena for a call on the Italian admiral there and a brief inspection of our PT boat repair facility which had been established at that base. Arriving at Ajaccio in the afternoon, calls were exchanged with the senior French naval officers there, who were later entertained at dinner on board. Departing that night, the *Memphis* moored in Toulon harbor early the next morning.

March 17 was a very busy day. The morning was taken up with exchanges of official calls between old friends—Admiral Lambert on shore and Admiral Jaujard on the *Montcalm*. Also, it was my pleasure to be able to confer the Legion of Merit on Captain Laurin aboard his own ship, the *Georges Leygues*. In addition, I was greeted by my son-in-law, Commander Taylor, who had just arrived in command of the destroyer *Parker*.[19] He had been serving in the Pacific and I had not seen him since sometime in 1941.

After a delightful luncheon given at their villa by the senior U.S. naval officers stationed at Toulon, and at which the French admirals were present, I proceeded by car to inspect our blimp detachment at Cuers, a small French airfield on the coast. Our blimps had been found to be so valuable in spotting minefields that part of Commander Rixey's squadron had been ordered up from Lyautey to assist in the operation of clearing mines off the coast of Provence. The day ended with a dinner given by Admiral Lambert at his villa.

On the 18th, I drove by car to Marseilles to inspect the U.S. naval detachment there and a number of landing craft which were present, and also to meet Admiral Kirk, who came down from Paris to meet me. While his title was Commander, U.S. Naval Forces, France, this did not include our forces on the Mediterranean coast, which naturally came under the Eighth Fleet. After a night in Marseilles as guests of Commander Carr, the detachment commander, Admiral Kirk joined me for a drive along the shore via Cassis and La Ciotat to the *Memphis* at Toulon. After a luncheon on board for him, attended also by Admirals Jaujard, Lambert, and Battet, and the U.S. naval detachment commanders at Marseilles and Toulon, Admiral Kirk departed for Paris and I for an inspection trip by car eastward as far as the Monacon border.

The night of the 19–20th was spent at the Hotel Carlton at Cannes. To support the flank of our army during its advance eastward, our PT squadron had established an operating base in the Golfe de Juan. This base, plus the PT boats present, I inspected on the morning of the 20th with their commander, Lieutenant Commander Dressling,[20] who had replaced Commander Stanley Barnes. From there, I went on to Beaulieu to meet General Tobin,[21] the commander of our eastern flank, and to dine with him.

I reached the *Memphis* at Toulon again in time for a dinner in my honor given by Admiral Jaujard aboard the *Montcalm*. This was my final fling in France as commander of the Eighth Fleet. By the morning of the 23rd, I was once more back in Naples. The remainder of the month was spent in routine duties, particularly in connection with the further reduction of U.S. naval activities in the Mediterranean. I was already under orders detaching me and ordering me home, and Vice Admiral Glassford,[22] who had been serving as our naval representative at Dakar, had been ordered as my relief.

April began with a beautiful Easter sunrise service on the steps of the Army Seventeenth General Hospital, a beautiful location on high ground on the outskirts of Naples. This was followed later by an Episcopal communion service on board the *Memphis*.

On the 3rd of April the Senate of the United States confirmed my promotion to admiral, and Admiral Glassford arrived from Dakar. On April 6, with all due ceremony, I broke my four-star flag on the *Memphis* and put on my extra stripe, naturally a happy occasion for me. For the next few days I was the recipient of congratulatory and farewell calls from the senior commanders of all services in the area. One of them was the new Supreme Allied Commander, Field Marshal Alexander, who, busy as he still was prosecuting the land campaign against the Germans, came all the way in from Caserta to see me. On April 10 there was a farewell dinner and dance for me, given by all the officers of my staff.

For me, April 11 was a day of mixed emotions. I was glad to be going home but sorry to leave my command and all those who had served their country so faithfully under my command. On board the *Memphis*, at 0930, I read my orders to the assembled staff and officers and crew. After a few words of farewell, I turned over the command to Admiral Glassford and directed that my flag be hauled down. With that ceremony, my Eighth Fleet went out of existence and our forces in the Mediterranean became a detachment of the U.S. Naval Forces, Europe, under Admiral Stark in London. I had been directly under Admiral King, the Chief of Naval Operations and Commander in Chief, U.S. Fleet.

The Navy Department had kindly sent a transport plane to bring me home, large enough not only to carry me and all my baggage, but some of the members of my staff, who were also being detached. When I arrived at the airfield about 1100, I found, to my surprise, not only a large gathering consisting of many of my immediate subordinates and staff who were not accompanying me but also Admiral Cunningham, his chief of staff, and others of the British staff. In addition, there was a guard of honor and my Eighth Fleet band. After shaking hands all around and receiving departure honors from the guard and band, I was piped through eight sideboys onto a platform on a fork lift truck, which had been rigged by the Seabees, instead of the usual plane ladder. As the platform was slowly hoisted to the level of the plane door, the band played "Auld Lang Syne." What could have been more heartwarming?

The plane arrived at our naval air station in Port Lyautey at 1830, and I was promptly whisked off to dinner with Commodore Owens, the station commander, and with Commodore McCandlish, who had come up from Casablanca for the purpose. At midnight we departed for a night flight to Lajes Airport in the Azores. This was uneventful except for being awakened in mid-flight by the pilot with the information that due to a low ceiling the Army Air Force authorities at Lajes had advised him to turn back. The pilot stated that he knew the field well and considered the ceiling sufficient for a safe landing. He wanted my instructions. I was not happy about turning back. I told the pilot that I wanted to get home as soon as possible, safely, that he was in command of the plane, and that I had faith in his judgement. We went on and made our landing without trouble about 0530.

During the refueling and check-up period, we had the pleasure of meeting many interesting personages in the airport lounge, including T. V. Soong[23] and Leon Henderson,[24] who were also westbound by commercial airliner.

Taking off from Lajes shortly after daylight on April 12, we reached Stephenville, Newfoundland, about six hours later. There we lunched, refueled, and again took off for our final destination, Quonset Point, Rhode Island, across Narragansett Bay from Newport, Rhode Island. We were over our destination about 1:00 p.m., but were unable to land on account of fog and were told to keep on to a final landing at the Navy Air Field at Patuxent, Maryland, which we did, and landed there about 10:00 p.m. This was a disappointment, but we were comfortably accommodated for the night and were able to take off for a return to Quonset at 9:00 a.m. At Patuxent, we received the news of President Roosevelt's death.

The commanding officer at Quonset, Commander Ben Wyatt,[25] an old associate and friend, had kept my family informed. In the morning, he sent a boat across the bay for them. So when I landed, I was greeted with open arms by my whole family—wife, both daughters, and my name-sake grandson.

It was during this period of deliberation that Secretary Forrestal[26] informed me of his plan of assigning me to relieve Admiral Stark as commander of the U.S. naval forces in Europe. This was an attractive post, but, as I told the secretary, I had been overseas and separated from my family for so long that I had hoped for some duty in the United States, such as superintendent of the Naval Academy or command of a sea frontier where I could have my family with me. The war still being on, insofar as Japan was concerned, no families had yet been permitted to go to Europe. To my surprise, Mr. Forrestal told me that I could have them with me.

On July 11, the day before I submitted my final report and left Washington, I, with other officers, had the honor of receiving the Legion D'Honneur and the Croix de Guerre at the hands of Admiral Fenard at a ceremony at the Army and Navy Club. On July 28, after a short leave in Newport, I was en route by air via Quonset, Patuxent, Lajes, and Orly (Paris) to London. I was met at the airport by my old Mediterranean chief of staff, Rear Admiral Lewis, who had become Admiral Stark's chief of staff in anticipation of my arrival. Admiral Lewis, a widower, had married a Wren (WRNS) officer in Algiers the preceding year and was delighted to have London duty. And I was glad to have him with me again.

I reported to and was welcomed by Admiral Stark, another old friend. But since he was not due to depart until mid-August, I did not relieve him at once but took advantage of the opportunity to acquaint myself with Twelfth Fleet affairs and visit some of its activities, which were in the process of being closed out or reduced. Also, the large staff which had been attached for the prosecution of war activities was being cut down. My family was to follow me by ship, arriving about the time Admiral Stark's quarters would become available to us. These consisted of an apartment in the headquarters building at 20 Grosvenor Square in London and a delightful country place called "Romany" on the Wentworth Estate in Virginia Water, near Windsor Great Park.

On August 15, the French were planning an elaborate celebration of the first anniversary of the landing in Southern France, or, as they called it, Provence. Naturally, I was anxious to accept their official invitation to attend, and Admiral Stark kindly agreed. The intervening period gave me an opportunity to have a look at the U.S. naval activities in Northern France, Belgium, and Germany, all of which came under the Twelfth Fleet command. Admiral Kirk had returned home, and our commander in Paris was Commodore McManes.[27] Admiral Ghormley[28] was in charge of our naval interests in Germany, while in the Bremen area, Commodore R. E. Robinson, Jr.[29] was in command. Vice Admiral Glassford, who had relieved me in the Mediterranean, had in turn been relieved by Rear Admiral Jules James, who, in Bermuda in 1942, had broken the news to me that I had become a vice admiral.

To carry out this program, I flew to Paris on August 5. There I called on and lunched with Ambassador Caffrey, inspected our naval setup there, and saw many old friends. On the 7th, I flew to Le Havre, detouring over the Normandy beaches and Cherbourg. After seeing Le Havre and its port activities, I went on to Brussels where I became the guest of Ambassador and Mrs. Sawyer,[30] and our naval attaché, Commander Boaz.

The next day was occupied by an auto trip to Antwerp, a boat tour of that harbor with the U.S. representative there, and a flight to Frankfurt where I was welcomed by Admiral Ghormley. There I called on my old Chief, general Eisenhower, and saw the headquarters offices of all the U.S. Forces, Germany. This was the day, August 8, that Russia belatedly declared war on Japan. Bob Ghormley and I celebrated the event suitably at his quarters.

On the 9th, Ghormley and I flew to Berlin, landing at Tempelhof Airfield. We called on General Lucius Clay[31] and lunched with him, after which I was given a personally conducted tour of the war-ruined city. I was impressed not only by the ruins and by the site of Hitler's suicide but by the swarms of women engaged in cleaning the streets of accumulated rubble. The catastrophe into which *Der Fuhrer* had led his people was all too evident. The night was spent in Admiral Ghormley's attractive villa on a lake on the outskirts of Berlin, in the American sector.

Bad weather and flooding of the airfield prevented a flight to Bremen on the 10th, so we proceeded there by car via Hanover. I was rather glad of this, for it gave me a chance to see something of the German countryside and the manner in which the Russians checked traffic in and out of the autobahn. I had never been in Germany before.

Saturday, the 11th, was spent touring the Bremen-Bremerhaven enclave with Commodore Robinson. I boarded the SS *Europe*,[32] which was being readied to be turned over to the United States. I also saw the full-rigged training ship which had been acquired by the U.S. Coast Guard for its Academy at New London. The submarine assembly sheds and the large number of submarines in various stages of completion along the Weser were most interesting. By the end of the day, I was en route to Paris for a quiet Sunday at the Royal Monceau.

My departure for Marseilles had been delayed until after a call on General de Gaulle, which had been scheduled for Monday morning. It was a pleasant call, for he received me most graciously as an old friend. At Marseilles on the evening of the 14th, I found my old flagship, the *Memphis*, awaiting me and I was delighted to break my flag on her once more. She had been sent up by Admiral James to accommodate me. Also present was my old friend, the Commander in Chief, Mediterranean, Admiral Sir John Cunningham in the HMS *Ajax*. I dined with him that evening.

Preparatory to the ceremonies for the 15th, the *Ajax* and the *Memphis*, plus three attending U.S. destroyers, proceeded to St.-Tropez on the 14th and thence to the Gulf of Frejus, anchoring off San Rafael, which had been so stoutly defended by the Nazis only a year before. There we met Admiral Lemonnier in the *Lorraine* and other French cruisers.

It was a long day on the 15th, but an interesting one, beginning at Cap Drammont where the Thirty-Sixth Division had landed, where a beautiful monument was dedicated in the presence of the local French officials. The French VIPs attending were M. Jacquinot, the minister of marine, Admiral Lemonnier, and General Lattre de Tassigny[33]. The British were represented by Ambassador and Lady Diana Duff Cooper[34] and Admiral Cunningham, the United States by Major General Dahlquist[35] and myself. Owing to seniority, it was the United States which brought up the rear, and, of course, it was Lady Diana (the beautiful Diana Manners of *The Miracle*) who received the bouquets from the little flower girls. Thus, the local populace was given the impression that it was the British who had been the principal participants in the DRAGOON operation. I had sensed that this would happen and had begged Ambassador Caffrey to attend in order to lend proper U.S. prestige to the occasion, but he had not felt able to leave Paris at that time.

Be that as it may, all concerned were well acquainted with each other, and all went off most pleasantly. The second stop, following the coast to the westward, was the beach near St. Maxime, where the major assault of the Forty-Fifth Division had landed and where, the year before, I had landed Admiral Lemonnier once more on his native soil. After dedicating the monument there, we proceeded on to the town square of St. Maxime for some ceremonies and speeches. There, on my instigation, Admiral Lemonnier managed to find the young girl who had fallen off her bicycle the year before in her excitement on recognizing a French admiral who had overtaken her in a jeep. She seemed excited to meet us once more and the incident provoked quite a little amusement in the crowd.

There was another ceremony in the little pipe manufacturing town of Cogolin, near the head of the Gulf of St.-Tropez, the very town where, the year before, Admiral Lemonnier, General Patch, and I had practically been engulfed with proffers of wine. Just outside St.-Tropez itself, the official party lunched in style at the Hotel Latitude 43. After that, there were exercises in St.-Tropez, and the dedication of a monument at Cavalaire Beach, where the Third Division had landed to form the left flank of the Seventh Army. Then, back to the ships, which meanwhile, had been anchored once more in the Gulf of St.-Tropez.

First anniversary parade (1945) commemorating the landings in Southern France in 1944. (Naval Historical Collection)

The day was climaxed by a magnificent dinner given by M. Jacquinot on the *Lorraine* at 11:00 p.m. Formal, but also informal, because the principal guests knew each other so well, and with a cuisine and wines which only the French can provide. Truly a day to remember! Especially as it also marked the day of the Japanese capitulation. My one regret was that more of my principal naval commanders for DRAGOON could not also have been present.

After hauling down my flag on the *Memphis* the next morning, the 16th, I took the beautiful drive along the coast to the airfield at Hyères, stopping at Cap Nègre to view the monument there. After a direct flight to Hendon, I reached Romany just prior to Admiral Stark's departure for home, and officially assumed command of the U.S. Naval Forces, Europe and the Twelfth Fleet. This command, as far as forces afloat were concerned, was composed only of a few cruisers and destroyers in northern Europe, mostly based in Southampton, and a like number in the Mediterranean detachment. But it also included numerous shore activities, both in the British Isles and Europe, and naval representatives in Scandinavia and other European countries. The headquarters staff in London and many other details were gradually being reduced in accordance with demobilization and the lesser responsibilities of the post-war period. The ships, except for carrying on regular training, were primarily engaged in visits of courtesy and showing the flag.

I was, of course, in immediate contact with our ambassador, Mr. Winant,[36] with the First Lord of the Admiralty, Mr. A. V. Alexander, and the First Sea Lord, my old chief, Admiral of the Fleet, Sir A. B. Cunningham (soon to be Viscount Cunningham of Hyndhope). I became almost as much at home in the Admiralty as I was in my own headquarters in Grosvenor Square. And soon I had a private audience with His Majesty, King George, an audience which ran so long overtime that our respective sides became worried. His Majesty was discussing past experiences and Anglo-American naval matters in which he was particularly interested. From Admiral Stark I inherited two Royal Naval liaison officers, Vice Admiral Sir Geoffrey Blake[37] and Captain Reginald Errington.

My first visit to St. Paul's Cathedral was at an inspiring service there, attended by the King and Queen, on Sunday, August 19, to give thanks for the ending of the war with Japan. On the next day, my wife and daughter, who had left New York on V-J day, were due in Southampton on the *Queen Elizabeth*, so I had that to be thankful for in addition.

The *Queen Elizabeth*, since her completion during the war, had been employed exclusively as a troopship and had never before entered her home port of Southampton. Thus it happened that I was able to accompany the Lord Mayor and a special welcoming party and board the ship ceremonially in the outer roads. It was an all-around welcome. After docking and the completion of the festivities, we drove direct to Romany, where my wife and daughter found themselves enchanted with their new country home.

In order to accompany her mother, Mary Kent had had to give up her summer course at the Middlebury College Spanish Language School which, if completed, would have won her an M.A. degree. This she was reluctant to do, but it was finally decided that the experience of a year or so overseas would be something that she should not forego. While regretting the loss of the M.A., she has never been sorry for her decision.

The next few weeks were devoted primarily to settling down, by me officially, and by the family at Romany and in our flat at 20 Grosvenor Square. There was much sight-seeing and the making of new friends. We did give a dinner party housewarming at Romany at the end of the month at which the principal guests were the First Lord and First Sea Lord of the Admiralty and their wives and principal members of the staffs and their wives. It turned out to be a very pleasant Anglo-American affair which led to enjoyable social relationships later on.

One of the great tourist attractions in London is the daily changing of the guard at Buckingham Palace. When I mentioned to Captain Errington that I would like to take the family to witness it one morning, he promptly vetoed the idea, saying that it was necessary for him to make special arrangements. The special arrangement proved to be an invitation for us from the Colonel Commanding at Wellington Barracks to come to the Guard's Officer Mess for a sherry prior to the assembly of the "new" guard. This proved to be a privilege in itself, for the room was filled with priceless trophies and relics from the Napoleonic wars on up. The British are great on tradition. I could have spent a day there, but we were soon called to the door to watch the sergeants forming up their details and reporting them to the "Captain of the Guard," something which was done with the military precision for which the guards are famous. I was informed by the Colonel that it was custom for the Captain of the Guard to ask the permission of the senior officer present to march the guard off by approaching and saluting and that, in this case, I was the senior officer. Permission was given by returning the salute. Thus, I found myself gravely authorizing the King's guard to march over to the Palace. As they marched out of the barracks gate, arms aswing and bands playing "The British Grenadier," we followed, entered the palace yard by a special gate and were given a splendid stand to watch the whole ceremony, something which has to be seen to be fully appreciated.

While the details of the new guard were effecting the relief of the sentry posts of the old guard, and the assembly of the old guard was being completed, we were escorted back to the barracks for further refreshment. With the return of the old guard to Wellington Barracks, its Captain, in similar fashion, obtained my permission to dismiss the guard. I think that this is an experience few Americans have been permitted to enjoy.

September passed off quietly, with the exception of a few social engagements, one of which included a luncheon at Grosvenor Square for Mrs. James F. Byrnes, wife of the secretary of state, and Mr. and Mrs. John Foster Dulles.[38] Toward the end of the month, in connection with an inspection of our supply base at Exeter, which was being closed out and returned to the British, we visited Stonehenge and went on to Torquay, at the Imperial Hotel. There we had to leave Floride for a day, since she was indisposed. Mary Kent and I drove to Plymouth via the Cotswolds, met Viscount Astor,[39] and had lunch with Vice Admiral and Lady Dowding.[40] The underground war room, which I was permitted to inspect, was most interesting. Our return to Torquay was via Dartmouth, the British Naval Academy. The return to Romany on the 26th was via the Cotswolds and Salisbury, giving us a chance to see the magnificent Salisbury Cathedral.

My diary shows that on October 3 Admiral John Cunningham and his flag secretary, who were on a short visit to the Admiralty from the Mediterranean, dined with us at Grosvenor Square and that on the following day Admiral Andrew Cunningham and Lady Cunningham, and Admiral and Mrs. Kennedy-Purvis[41] had luncheon with us. It was Admiral and Mrs. Kennedy-Purvis who had often been my hosts, both formally and informally at Admiralty House in Bermuda during the summer of 1941 when I was conducting so-called neutrality patrols back and forth across the Atlantic.

Admiral Kennedy-Purvis now was the Deputy First Sea Lord, Admiral Cunningham's right-hand man in the Admiralty. One day Admiral Kennedy-Purvis gave the Hewitts a memorable trip in his barge down the Thames from the Westminster stairs to the Royal Naval College at Greenwich. It was interesting to see the observatory and straddle longitude 0, to visit the College, which was once a Royal Naval Hospital, and to visualize the banquet in the famous Painted Hall given to Admiral Stark as the farewell tribute of the Royal Navy.

SCANDINAVIAN TRIP

Copenhagen

It had been intimated to me by the U.S. naval representative in Scandinavia, and also by our diplomatic representatives in those countries, that a visit there by me would be a tactful gesture and productive of good will. And I was most anxious to see those countries for myself. I had no suitable ship available at this time, so I decided to go by air, taking with me Commodore Shelly,[42] my intelligence officer, and Lieutenant Commander Cragg, my flag lieutenant. Copenhagen was to be the first stop.

Some years after we were married, Floride and I had received an invitation to the wedding of a New York cousin whom I had never met. She was to be married to Prince Viggo of Denmark. Unfortunately, we were too far away to attend. The princess to be, Eleanor Hewitt Green, was a granddaughter of my great uncle, Abraham S.

Hewitt. So, when Commander Steeholm, our naval representative in Denmark came to London to arrange the details of my visit, I asked him if he knew the prince and princess. He did not, but knew of them, and promised to advise the princess of my hope of meeting her during my stay. Little did I realize the welcome that would await me on the Copenhagen airfield. As I got out of my plane on October 10, there to greet me was the American minister, Mr. Monnett Davis, whom I had met in previous years; the first secretary, Mr. Garrett Ackerson of Hackensack, whose mother had once given me piano lessons and whose father had been in Christ Church choir when I was a choir boy; Vice Admiral Lundsteen, the commander in chief of the Danish navy; and Prince and Princess Viggo. I was quite overwhelmed.

The princess, as soon as we met, said, "Call me Peggy. I am going to call you Kent." Then she added, "Even if you had not been identified by the uniform, I would have known you were a Hewitt." I soon found that she was a very fine and really genuine person.

We were whisked off to the legation as the guests of Mr. and Mrs. Davis, who gave a dinner that evening in my honor. Present were the Viggos, Admiral and Mrs. Lundsteen, the famous Danish scientist Professor Niels Bohr[43] and his wife, Garry Ackerson, Commander Steeholm, and my two aides. It was one of the most interesting evenings I ever spent. There were many interesting tales of the Nazi occupation during which Prince Viggo had gone underground. The princess, known to be an American, but unsuspected even by her most intimate friends, carried on circumspectly in her villa, quietly cooperating with the underground. The only news she had of the outside world was by clandestine radio. She told me how excited she had been when she had heard my name mentioned in connection with Casablanca.

The following day, October 11, was a full one. First, I called on Admiral Lundsteen at the Danish Admiralty and then on the prime minister. After that, I was taken on a visit to the Danish house of parliament, a beautiful building and beautiful chambers. Later in the morning, I had the very great honor of an audience with His Majesty, King Christian X,[44] whom I found to be a delightful gentleman as well as a most interesting man. He received me seated at his desk in his study. Alongside him was a window with two bullet holes in the pane. He told me that during the occupation he had been shot at one evening but luckily was missed. He had just left the holes in the window as a sort of memento.

During the war, he was permitted by the Nazis to come and go at will, and it was his daily practice to visit his people, sometimes on horseback and sometimes on foot. Apparently he was much beloved by the Danes, one of whom told me the following anecdote. It seemed that the Germans were astounded that royalty should mingle with the people unguarded, and one curious Nazi asked a citizen who protected his king. The terse reply was, "We all do."

After lunch with the Davises, I had the privilege of going through the factory where Royal Copenhagen porcelain was made and was presented with a beautiful souvenir of the work. Then I made a call on Professor Bohr. I had a dim idea that he had some connection with "heavy water," about which I had heard, but had no realization of his part in the development of atomic energy which led to the bomb that destroyed Hiroshima. Prince and Princess Viggo entertained me at a dinner that evening. The guests included Her Majesty the Queen, the crown prince and princess, and other prominent people—truly an unusual occasion.

It was about this time that I heard the disturbing news that my mother in Hackensack was very ill. Naturally, my first thought was to fly home to her. I would have requested the Navy Department's permission to do that except for the fact that the situation was in the capable hands of daughter Floride, who had advised that mother would not know me if I came, and that I was on an important diplomatic mission, the details of which had been scheduled well in advance. I reluctantly decided to carry on.

Oslo, October 12–13

After another morning of sight-seeing in Copenhagen, I took off for Oslo. At the plane to see me off were my host, Mr. Davis, the Viggos, and Admirals Lundsteen and Vadel. At Oslo, which was reached after a short but beautiful flight along the Swedish coast and up the Oslo Fjord, I was greeted by Mr. Osborn,[45] the U.S. ambassador, Admiral Corneliessen of the Norwegian navy, and Captain Bergesen,[46] U.S. Navy, our naval attaché. As in Copenhagen, one of the first things was a conference with the local newsmen, who were anxious to know the purpose of my trip and other matters of interest to their country. I think that all Scandinavians, even at that time, were fearful of their powerful neighbor across the Baltic and wished to be reassured of U.S. support.

At dinner that night, Mr. Osborn entertained all the Norwegians who had been connected with the recently completed Quisling[47] trial. I was taken to see Quisling's house the next morning and to the museum where there was an exhibit (in an excellent state of preservation) of an actual Viking ship which had lain buried for centuries. Then I had an audience with King Haakon,[48] a tall, fine-looking, very impressive man, who received me most cordially.

Stockholm

On the afternoon of the 13th, I boarded my plane for Stockholm, and after another beautiful flight was met by our naval attaché there and Mr. Herschel Johnson,[49] the American minister. After a quick trip around the city, I was put up at the Grand Hotel—really a grand hotel—overlooking the beautiful harbor and the Royal Palace in the distance. That evening Captain Wright, the naval attaché, held a dinner at the hotel, with guests who included Mr. Johnson, the military attaché, the senior Swedish admirals, and several other important people.

The next day was Sunday, but by invitation of the admiral commanding, I had the pleasure of visiting and inspecting the *Sverige* (Sweden), a small battleship, flagship of the Coastal Fleet (Kustflotten). She looked as a man-of-war should look, and her fine looking crew gave the appearance of being well-trained and well-disciplined, something always to be expected of Scandinavian seamen. The rest of the day was spent in a drive out to a beautiful resort hotel for lunch, seeing more sights, and, after cocktails with Captain Chandler, a quiet evening at the hotel.

Germany and Holland

For some reason, which I have forgotten, I made another quick trip to Berlin on the 15th, flying from Stockholm via Copenhagen. After a night with Admiral Ghormley, and meeting General Clay again, I flew to The Hague for my first visit there. I was met by Captain Frothingham and put up at the Hotel Witteburg, which was the Royal Netherlands Navy Mess. At dinner that night with Ambassador Hornbeck,[50] I met Mr. Boaz, the minister of marine, Admiral Stoewe, and General Frejtag Drabbe, the commander of the Netherlands Marines.

Wednesday, October 17, found me on a trip to Amsterdam through the canals with Admiral Stoewe as my host. After viewing the harbor of Amsterdam by boat, we went to the Amstel for an official luncheon given me by Admiral Stoewe. During this otherwise pleasant luncheon, I was called to the telephone for a trans-Atlantic call. It was my daughter Floride advising me of the death of my mother. She had made the necessary arrangements for services at the church in which I was brought up and for interment in the family plot. It was hard to carry on, but I had to. When my hosts gathered the nature of my news, they were most sympathetic.

After lunch, we were taken to see a wonderful collection of paintings by old Dutch masters that had been looted by the Nazis, including Goering,[51] but which had recently been recovered and returned from Germany. Then we returned to the Hague in time for an official dinner by the minister of marine, Mr. Boaz, which, having been long planned, I had to attend.

On the following day, I was scheduled to attend a diplomatic reception by Queen Wilhelmina,[52] and to be presented. The court of the Netherlands was reputed to be the most formal in Europe, and so I found it. But the Queen greeted me most graciously when I was introduced by Mr. Hornbeck. Prior to that reception, I was able to make a quick trip to Delft, and immediately afterward I took off for London. En route, we flew over still flooded Walcheren Island—flooded as a means of defense during the war by opening the dikes. I was met at the field by my younger daughter, her mother being in bed with a slight illness. I drove with her at once to Romany.

Not two days later, General Frejtag Drabbe of the Dutch Marines, with two aides, arrived in London to take passage to the United States in the carrier USS *Lake*

Champlain,[53] which was at Southampton. They called at my office. Since it was Saturday, and Romany was more or less on the way to Southampton, I took them out there for lunch and then sent them on their way in my official car. They were so appreciative that they sent Floride a bunch of orchids. The rest of October was quiet except for a visit to Hampton Court Palace, instigated by Captain Errington, who wanted us to miss nothing worthwhile in England.

Paris

Early November found me in Paris again, primarily for a celebration of the third anniversary of the North African landing on the 8th. I participated in a solemn procession up the Champs Elysées to the Arc de Triomphe, and in company with others, French and American, who were involved in that operation, laid a wreath on the Tomb of the Unknown Soldier. Among those attending was General Bethouart, who on that fateful morning had tried to convince the governor general of Morocco that he should not oppose the landing and had been placed under arrest in consequence (probably thereby being saved from execution by General Patton). After the ceremony, I greeted General Bethouart and mentioned to him how pleasant the present was as compared with 1942. "Yes," said he, "I was in jail then." "I know you were," I replied.

The day was finished by a reception at the Royal Monceau to which I gathered all those I could find, particularly of the Navy, who were concerned with TORCH, among them Admiral Moreau, Gervais de la Fond, Barjot,[54] Missoffe, and Sablé. Admiral Michelier, unfortunately, was in the south of France.

During November, Viscount Knowles, who, as governor general of Bermuda, had been my host upon my return from Casablanca and had been the first to help celebrate my promotion to three-star rank, turned up in London. Admiral James was up from the Mediterranean at the same time. So I was able to have a Bermuda luncheon at 20 Grosvenor Square with Viscount and Lady Knowles, the Kennedy-Purvises, and Jules James. Lots of fun reminiscing.

The outstanding event of November, however, was the special service in Westminster Abbey to celebrate the American Thanksgiving. This was attended by officers and men of all our services, by the American colony, and by leading British dignitaries, including Viscount and Lady Astor. Ambassador Winant, the senior general present, and I were ushered to seats in the choir where we could observe the whole impressive ceremony. When the bluejacket, soldier, and Marine color guard marched up the aisle into the chancel, and the officiating clergyman reverently draped the Stars and Stripes across the altar, everyone—certainly all of our countrymen—in that crowded Abbey were deeply moved.

December passed quickly. Christmas was celebrated quietly at Romany with a few of the staff as houseguests, and attendance at a quaint village church nearby. New Year's Eve was also celebrated there with a few of our good British neighbors in to help us see the New Year in. So ended an eventful and interesting year.

NOTES
1. The Yalta Conference was held in February 1945 in the Crimea with wartime leaders Winston Churchill, Franklin D. Roosevelt and Joseph Stalin participating. Agreement was reached on the unconditional surrender of Germany, on support of post-war European governments, on a conference establishing the United Nations, and on Russian demands in Poland and the Far East, in an exchange for the Soviets entering the war in the Far East.
2. Wait R. Griswold (1918–). Lieutenant Commander, Medical Corps.
3. USS *Memphis* (CL-13) was Admiral Harold Stark's flagship prior to the Yalta Conference. She was present at the first anniversary commemorating the allied invasion of Southern France in 1945.
4. Josiah Hoffman (1889–1967). Commander, U.S. Navy.
5. James Somerville (1882–1949). Admiral, Royal Navy. Commander in Chief, Eastern Fleet, 1942–1944; Combined Chiefs of Staff, 1944–1945; Admiral of the Fleet, 1945.
6. Lord Frederick James Leathers (1883–1965). British industrialist and government official. During World War II, he served as minister of war transport and attended the major Allied conferences, including Yalta and Potsdam.
7. Hastings L. Ismay (1887–1965). British Army General. During World War II, he served as chief of staff to the Ministry of Defense and deputy secretary to the War Cabinet.
8. George C. Marshall (1880–1959). American army officer and statesman, graduated from Virginia Military Academy in 1901. During World War I, he served at General Headquarters in France, then from 1919 to 1924 was aide to General John Pershing. In 1939, he was promoted to general. During World War II, he was chief military strategist for the Allies and as secretary of state drafted the Marshall Plan to rebuild Europe. He served as secretary of defense, 1950–1951, and received the Nobel Peace Prize in 1953.
9. Emory Land (1879–1971). Vice Admiral. U.S. Naval Academy, Class of 1902.
10. USS *Quincy* (CA-71), commissioned on December 15, 1943, was named to honor CA-39, sank at Savo Island on August 9, 1942.
11. William D. Leahy (1875–1959). Fleet Admiral. U.S. Naval Academy, Class of 1897. Chief of Naval Operations, 1937–1939. He was chief of staff to President Franklin D. Roosevelt, 1942–1945, and to President Harry S. Truman, 1945–1949.
12. Wilson Brown (1882–1957). Vice Admiral. U.S. Naval Academy, Class of 1902.
13. HMS *Orion*. Built in 1932. Displacement 7,215 tons; Length 530'; Beam, 55' 2"; Draught 16'.
14. Abdul Aziz ibn Saud (1880–1953). King of Saudi Arabia, he unified the Bedouins and drove Sherif Hussein from Mecca, founding the kingdom in 1932 on the religious teachings of Mohammed ibn Abdul-Wahhab, an 18th-century itinerant preacher who rejected Sufism and called for a return to the original teachings of Mohammed.
15. Haile Selassie (1892–1975). Emperor of Ethiopia from 1930 to 1974. After Italy invaded Ethiopia in 1935, he was driven into exile for two years, then he returned to rout the Italians. Though an absolute ruler, he introduced modernizing reforms in the 1950s and helped to establish the Organization of African Unity in 1963.
16. King Farouk (1920–1965). King of Egypt who was forced to abdicate after an armed revolt in 1952.
17. Anna Roosevelt Boettiger (1906–1979). Only daughter of Franklin D. and Eleanor Roosevelt. She accompanied FDR to the Yalta Conference in 1945.
18. Raymond E. Peet (1921–). Vice Admiral. U.S. Naval Academy, Class of 1943.
19. USS *Parker* (DD-604). She took part in Operation TORCH and the invasions of Sicily and Southern France. In 1945, she supported U.S. forces in the Mediterranean.
20. Richard J. Dressling (1916–). Lieutenant Commander. U.S. Naval Academy, Class of 1939.
21. Ralph C. Tobin (1890–1957). Brigadier General, U.S. Army. He joined the New York National Guard in 1916 and became its commander in April 1941. He was promoted to brigadier general in 1942.
22. William A. Glassford (1886–1958). Vice Admiral. U.S. Naval Academy, Class of 1906.
23. T. V. Soong (1894–1971). Chinese Statesman and Financier. Named foreign minister of China in 1941, he became premier and president of the Executive Yuan in 1944. He was China's chief delegate to the UN Conference in 1945. He resigned the premiership in 1947 when his anti-inflationary programs failed and in 1949, when the communists took over, he fled China for the United States.
24. Leon Henderson (1895–?). Economist and public servant. He served in the National Recovery Administration, the Works Progress Administration, the SEC, and the OPA during FDR's administration. After the war, he was an economics consultant.

25 Ben H. Wyatt (1893–1968). Commodore. U.S. Naval Academy, Class of 1917.

26 James Forrestal (1892–1949). Appointed secretary of the Navy in 1944 and named first secretary of defense in 1947.

27 Kenmore M. McManes (1900–1973). Rear Admiral. U.S. Naval Academy, Class of 1922.

28 Robert Ghormley (1883–1958). Vice Admiral. U.S. Naval Academy, Class of 1906.

29 Robert E. Robinson (1898–1977). Commodore. U.S. Naval Academy, Class of 1920.

30 Charles Sawyer (1887–?). U.S. Ambassador to Belgium, 1944–1945.

31 Lucius Clay (1897–1978). General, U.S. Army. U.S. Military Academy, Class of 1918. During World War II, he took charge of procurement for the U.S. Army, then served as deputy director of the Office of War Mobilization. From 1945 to 1949, he was military governor of the U.S. zone in Germany.

32 Now called barque *Eagle*.

33 Jean Lattre de Tassigny (1889–1952). French Army general, he commanded the 14th Infantry Division, known as the Iron Brigade in 1940. His troops barred the Germans from entering unoccupied France in 1942, and he was sentenced to prison by the Vichy government. He fled to England, then joined the Free French Army in Algeria and in 1944 participated in the liberation of France. In 1950, he was commander of French forces fighting the Viet Minh in Indochina.

34 Alfred Duff Cooper (1890–1954). British political leader and writer. Educated at Eton and Oxford, Cooper served the government in various capacities, including secretary of state for war, 1933–1937; First Lord of the Admiralty, 1937–1938, from which he resigned after the Munich Agreement was signed; minister of information in the Churchill government, 1940–1941, and ambassador to France, 1944–1947. In 1919, he married the renowned beauty and actress Lady Diana Manners.

35 John E. Dahlquist (1896–1975). General, U.S. Army. He commanded the 36th Infantry Division in Europe that participated in the invasion of Southern France in August 1944. In August and September, his division fought the German army at the battles of Montelimar and Vosges.

36 John Winant (1889–1947). U.S. ambassador to Great Britain, 1941–1946.

37 Geoffrey Blake (1882–1968). Vice Admiral, Royal Navy. Served in World War I; deputy director, Royal Naval Staff College, 1925–26; director, 1926–27; chief-of-staff, Atlantic Fleet, 1927–29; fourth sea lord, 1932–35; retired 1938. Flag officer liaison with U.S. Navy in Europe, 1942–1945.

38 John Foster Dulles (1888–1959). Lawyer and secretary of state, 1953–1959. He was U.S. delegate to the San Francisco conference that organized the UN and U.S. representative to the UN, 1946–1947 and 1950.

39 Viscount Waldorf Astor (1879–1952). British publicist and public servant. He served in parliament from 1910 to 1919 and in 1915 became publisher of the *Observer*. He was a leader of the Cliveden set that favored the appeasement of Hitler.

40 Hugh C. T. Dowding (1882–1970). Air Chief Marshal, RAF, during World War II.

41 Sir Charles Edward Kennedy-Purvis (–1946). Admiral, Royal Navy. Lord commissioner of the Admiralty and deputy first sea lord since 1942; president, Royal Naval College, Greenwich, and vice admiral, commanding, 1938–1940; commander-in-chief, America and West Indies, 1940–1942.

42 Tully Shelly (1892–1966). Rear Admiral. U.S. Naval Academy, Class of 1915.

43 Niels Bohr (1885–1962). Physicist and scientist from Denmark who developed the theory of atomic and molecular structure and contributed to the theory of nuclear structure.

44 King Christian X (1870–1947). King of Denmark from 1912 to 1947. He was taken prisoner by the Germans in 1943 and released in 1945.

45 Lithgow Osborne (1892–?). Ambassador to Norway, 1944–1946.

46 Alfred O. Bergesen (1897–1986). Captain, U.S. Navy. U.S. Naval Academy, Class of 1920.

47 Vidkun A. Quisling (1887–1945). Norwegian Army officer, politician and traitor. He collaborated with the Germans to invade and occupy Norway during World War II and in 1942 he was appointed premier. He was arrested and shot as a traitor in 1945.

48 King Haakon (1872–1957). King of Norway, 1906–1957. During World War II, he headed a government-in-exile in London.

49 Herschel Johnson (1894–1966). Foreign Service Officer. Ambassador to Sweden, 1941–1946; deputy U.S. representative on UN Security Council, 1946–1948; deputy chief, U.S. mission to UN, 1947–1948; ambassador to Brazil, 1948–1953.

50 Stanley K. Hornbeck (1883–1966). Diplomat. Special assistant to secretary of state, 1944; ambassador to the Netherlands, 1944–1947.

51 Hermann Goering (1893–1946). German statesman and supporter of Adolf Hitler who, from 1933 on, held positions of importance in the government. Hitler named him as his successor in 1939. After 1943, his influence waned. He was arrested, tried, and convicted at the Nuremberg trials.

52 Queen Wilhelmina (1880–1962). Queen of the Netherlands, 1898–1948. The queen spent the war years in London and returned to Holland after its liberation in May 1945. On the fiftieth anniversary of her reign, she abdicated in favor of her daughter Juliana.

53 USS *Lake Champlain* (CV-39). Commissioned in 1945, she sailed to England to bring returning servicemen home.

54 Pierre Barjot (1899–1960). French naval officer who joined the resistance in 1940. He worked as a journalist in Algeria until he was reinstated in the Navy in 1944, where he served on the staff of the ministry of defense. He was promoted to admiral in 1958.

King Umberto of Italy and Admiral H. K. Hewitt aboard USS Missouri *(BB-63) during the visit of the Twelfth Fleet to Naples, 1946. (Naval Historical Collection)*

XVIII *Twelfth Fleet, 1946*

1946

January 1946 in London was marked by the first session of the United Nations, which convened on January 10 and brought together leading statesmen and representatives from the principal nations who had been allied against Germany during the war. From the United States there were Secretary of State James F. Byrnes,[1] Mrs. Franklin D. Roosevelt, Mr. John Foster Dulles, Senator Tom Connally,[2] Mr. James C. Dunn, and, later on, Mr. Adlai Stevenson.[3] As naval advisor to the U.S. delegation and prospective U.S. naval member of the United Nations Military Staff Committee, there was Admiral Kelly Turner,[4] fresh from the Pacific. I had the opportunity to entertain all of them in one form or another at 20 Grosvenor Square.

It was about this time also that the ban against having wives overseas had been lifted, and we had the pleasure of giving a little party in order to welcome the newly arrived wives of some members of the staff and permit them to become acquainted.

Germany and Austria
I was able to attend a number of the initial meetings of the United Nations which were of interest, in spite of Soviet obstructionism which was already beginning to develop. But by the end of the month, I departed for a quick trip to Germany and Austria in order to confer U.S. Navy Distinguished Service Medals on Generals Clark and Truscott. The former was in Vienna and the latter in Bad Tolz, Germany. The trip to Vienna from Munich was made in style in what had been Hermann Goering's special train. During the passage from Linz through the Russian occupied zone, Russian guards rode with us.

The railroad trip was comfortable and interesting, giving me an opportunity to see something of the countryside and the people at the rail stations along the way. And the two or three days spent in Vienna as the guest of General Clark gave me my first and only view of that once delightful city. It was sad to see so much of it in ruin, but it was not too hard to visualize it as it must have been in the days of Johann Strauss. Well might the beautiful blue Danube have inspired him. And I would not have missed our trip out to the Vienna Woods. Russian soldiers encountered around Vienna seemed very friendly and particularly interested in the American naval uniform.

From Munich, we travelled south to General Truscott's headquarters, and thence with him to the Army recreation area at Garmisch-Partenkirchen, where we spent a night and were royally entertained. I had several bobsled runs with the general himself, and at dinner that night a tremendous cake was placed in front of me, decorated in honor of the Eighth Fleet with my four stars on it. The Navy Distinguished Service Medal was later conferred on General Truscott at Bad Tolz, with his headquarters detachment duly paraded.

Before returning to London, we had a highly interesting day at the Nuremberg trials. This was my first experience with simultaneous translation. With headphones on, one could switch as desired to any of the four languages being used—English, French, Russian, or German. I have always marveled at how these interpreters could listen to one language and, at the same time, speak what was said in another. I was told that German, in which the verb is always at the end of the sentence, was particularly difficult.

To see the accused, of whom one had heard so much, and to watch their reactions to what was said, was an unforgettable experience. For big fat Hermann Goering, who was directly responsible, as Hitler's right-hand man, for so many of the war crimes, I could feel no sympathy. But for some of the military, particularly for Admirals Raeder[5] and Doenitz,[6] I felt somewhat differently. As I have said elsewhere, if a military man were required to decide for himself the international legality of orders received from above before executing them, the result would be inefficiency and chaos in any defense establishment.

On this occasion, I had the pleasure of lunching with the distinguished British jurist Sir Norman Birkett, the alternate British judge at the trial, whom I had first met on a transatlantic flight in early 1942.

February 8 found me back in London, engaged in administrative work and in social affairs connected with the UN Assembly. In mid-month, I had a visit from the assistant secretary of the Navy, Mr. R. Struve Hensel.

During March, just prior to his relief by Mr. Averell Harriman[7] and his departure for home, Ambassador Winant held an investiture at the embassy for the purpose of conferring on the principal British leaders the American decorations which had been awarded to them. To this ceremony, he kindly invited me. Unfortunately, however, Admiral Andrew Cunningham had been stricken with a heart attack and was unable to attend. Mr. Winant did a very thoughtful thing. Knowing my close association with Admiral Cunningham, instead of turning the admiral's decoration over to Mr. Harriman, he sent it to me with the request that I confer it myself at the first opportunity.

I have neglected to mention that earlier in the year Admiral Cunningham had been made Viscount Cunningham of Hyndhope, and Field Marshal Alan Brooke[8] and Air Chief Marshal Portal[9] had been similarly elevated to Viscount. At the invitation of the admiral, my wife, our daughter and I had the unusual privilege of witnessing their introduction (or initiation) to the House of Lords from a position on the floor of the House itself, directly opposite the lord chancellor, the presiding officer, sitting on his woolsack. It was a remarkable ceremony conducted according to ancient tradition and too long for me to describe here. Suffice it to say that they, in their official robes, were marched around the chamber three times, bowing low to the chancellor each time and offering their credentials. He never deigned to notice them until the final time, when he lifted his hat in response to their obeisance. Then, and only then, were they members of the House. The official who led them around, called, for some reason, "The Black Rod," was none other than Vice Admiral Blake, my erstwhile chief liaison officer.

Istanbul

In the latter part of March, the Turkish ambassador in Washington, M. Ertegun, died. Wishing to do him especial honor and to cultivate friendly relations with the Turkish government, his remains were embarked on the battleship *Missouri*, which had been returned to the Atlantic after the Japanese peace treaty had been signed on its deck in Tokyo Bay. It was suggested to me that I join the ship at Gibraltar and, hoisting my flag on her, go with her to Istanbul. I left Southampton on the *Houston*[10] on March 20 and proceeded to Gibraltar to await the *Missouri*, which arrived on April 1. At Gibraltar, incidentally, I received my first seventeen-gun salute, the peacetime routine of salutes having again become effective. On transferring to the *Missouri*, which was commanded by Captain R. H. Hillenkoetter,[11] I found Ambassador Alexander W. Weddell,[12] who was accompanying the remains as the representative of the State Department, and a representative of the Turkish embassy.

The voyage eastward from Gibraltar was most enjoyable and gave me a chance to become acquainted with that fine ship, which, at the captain's invitation, I went over rather thoroughly. Also, by invitation, I had a meal with each of the officers' messes, even the chief petty officers' mess. The chiefs, having heard a rumor that I sometimes played acey-deucey, a seagoing form of backgammon, challenged me to a game with their mess champion. I accepted, and with considerable luck with the dice, managed to win—thereby making considerable character with the chiefs.

South of Sicily, we were joined by Rear Admiral James in the USS *Providence*[13] with several destroyers, the whole detachment proceeding as a unit toward the Aegean. As we approached the Dardanelles on the evening of April 4, we were met by a very smart division of Turkish destroyers, which promptly took up escort stations on each bow. Coming aboard with the pilot, and reporting to me as my Turkish aide for our visit, was a fine young submarine officer, Captain Ozduz, who spoke excellent English.

It was rather exciting to enter the strait through the bit of water which was the scene of the vain effort of the allied British and French navies in World War I to force a way into the Sea of Marmara, to see the crumbling Turkish fortifications with well-known names on each side of the strait, and to view the heights of Gallipoli where so many brave soldiers bled and died.

We dropped anchor off the Golden Horn near the Turkish flagship *Yawuz* early on the following morning of April 5, having passed a large lighthouse on which was painted in huge letters "Welcome *Missouri*." It was evident that the Turks were going to make much of our visit. The *Missouri*, of course, was the largest man-of-war to enter the Bosporus, and the first naval vessel to carry the stars and stripes there in many years. The *Yawuz*, incidentally, was none other than the ex-German battle cruiser *Goeben*, which eluded the French and British naval forces so successfully in August 1914, and whose entry into the Sea of Marmara contributed so much to the decision of a wavering Turkish government to join the German-Austrian alliance.

No sooner was the anchor down than we were boarded by Turkish officials and some of our own representatives in Turkey, including Ambassador Wilson[14] (whom I had known previously in Algiers) and our naval attaché, Captain Webb Trammel.[15] The first order of business was arranging for the transfer of Ambassador Ertegun's remains to shore, and the subsequent ceremonies. This was quickly accomplished and most successfully carried out about noon of the same day.

With the *Missouri*'s crew at quarters, the Marine guard at "Present," and the band playing the Turkish national anthem, the casket was slowly lowered into one of the *Missouri*'s boats, where it was received by the chief petty officer body bearers. It all reminded me of my own experiences many years before in landing the remains of Whitelaw Reid from the HMS *Natal* in the North River, New York. The Bosporus, however, by contrast, was unruffled. As the boat left the side, an ambassador's salute was fired with the Turkish ensign at the fore. Passing honors were rendered by all the men-of-war as the boat proceeded slowly to the landing.

At the landing, the casket was solemnly turned over to Turkish hands and placed on the traditional artillery caisson. The funeral procession through the streets of Istanbul was preceded by a military escort composed of Turkish army and naval units, and detachments of U.S. Marines and bluejackets from the ships present. Then came the caisson with the body bearers, officers of the various Turkish services as honorary pallbearers, and on the flanks in single file, an honor guard of Turkish soldiers with rifles carried at the reverse. Following all, also on foot, were the official mourners, among whom Ambassador Weddell, Admiral James, and I were included.

Once the obsequies were out of the way, our Turkish hosts proceeded to make every effort to make our stay in their waters an enjoyable occasion for every officer and man. For me, the remainder of the 5th, and part of the following day, was occupied primarily in making official calls and receiving return calls. All the Turkish officials, from the local vali (governor of the province) on down, were extremely cordial, and my aide, Captain Ozduz, was assiduous in looking out for my wants and making all arrangements. And the Turkish commander in chief, Admiral Ali Ulgen, and I soon became very good friends. In between visits, I was able to take in many of the sights, including an auto trip along the Bosporus, a call at Robert College, and visits to Saint Sofia and other beautiful mosques.

It had been arranged that our official party was to spend a day in Ankara, travelling to and from by the night train from Scutari, on the Asian shore, immediately across the Bosporus from Istanbul. We left on the evening of the 6th, crossing the Bosporus in Admiral Ulgen's barge, to be received at the dock by a very smart guard of Turkish bluejackets. Proceeding to the train side and our special private car at the end, we encountered another guard of honor of Turkish soldiers. I must say that I was extremely impressed by the appearance of the Turkish military. All appeared smart, well disciplined, and extremely hardy. I decided that I would not want to have to meet them as enemies.

Our private car was fitted with every comfort, and we dined in state with the finest of Turkish cuisine and wines. Our comfortable sleep was broken only by the cheers of crowds at the various stops, who had gathered to welcome the passage of the car bearing the Stars and Stripes. We did not mind, because it was pleasant to realize that such tokens of friendship for our country could occur in the middle of the night in the plains of Anatolia.

As we rolled into the handsome station in Ankara after breakfast on the morning following, we saw another large honor guard on the platform in three ranks, extending the full length of the train. After receiving the honors and inspecting the guard, we were whisked off to Ankara's very finest hotel. I should mention here that during the ceremonies incident to the remains of M. Ertegun, Ambassador Weddell very properly received honors as the senior. Thereafter, however, he insisted that his status as an ambassador had ceased and that I was the senior.

Our day in Ankara was an extremely busy one. In the morning, there were calls on leading Turkish officials from the premier and the minister of defense on down to the senior military commander, and the laying of a wreath on the tomb of Mustafa Kemal Atatürk.[16] Then there was an official luncheon with accompanying speeches on each side, followed by attendance at an interesting football game (British type). The final event was a call on the president of the Republic, Ismet Inonu,[17] who was extremely cordial. He showed us the magnificent view of the countryside about Ankara from the balcony outside his office and presented me personally with a beautiful golden cigarette case with his signature engraved on it. Although I do not smoke cigarettes, I preserved this as a priceless token of Turkish-American friendship and a personal souvenir of my only visit to Ankara. At this writing, over seventeen years later, M. Inonu, as premier this time, is again serving his country.

We returned to Istanbul as we had come, with military honors again at the station in Ankara, and another the following morning at Scutari. And, once more, there was a bluejacket guard to render honors as we boarded the barge for my return to the *Missouri*. With no official events scheduled during the day on Sunday, advantage was taken of the opportunity to see the sites of Istanbul, to take the drive out to the Black Sea entrance to the Bosporus, and to call at the famous Robert College where most of the modern leaders in the Middle East were educated. I would have liked to have had more time to give to Saint Sofia and the beautiful mosques, but it is a privilege to be able to see them even once.

No account of our visit would be complete without mention of the magnificent evening reception given at the Dolmabache Palace, an ancient residence of the Sultans on the shore of the Bosporus, the highlight of which was a remarkable exhibition of traditional Turkish dances in costume.

An afternoon reception was given on the *Missouri* on the 8th, the last day of our visit, in an effort to return in a small way some of the bountiful hospitality we had received. Most of the elite of Istanbul were present. Admiral Ulgen and I exchanged autographed photographs, he and I having become very good friends. As a last gesture, we were presented with a large number of Turkish rugs to be distributed later among the officers and men of the visiting fleet.

April 9 saw us on our way out of the Sea of Marmara and the Dardanelles. I was really sorry to say good-bye to my Turkish aide who, with the pilot and our Turkish destroyer escort, left us when we reached the Aegean Sea.

Athens

As we entered Greek waters, we were welcomed by the Greek Navy. Early on April 10, the *Providence* and the U.S. destroyers entered Piraeus, but the *Missouri*, being too long to be accommodated there, anchored offshore in Falirou Bay, midway between Piraeus and Athens. There we were able to land in our boats at the piers of the Royal Naval Yacht Club, honorary membership in which was extended to our officers.

The first day in port, as usual, was taken up with the customary official visits. With Ambassador K. L. Rankin, with whom I later had lunch, I called upon the leading dignitaries in Athens, including the Regent, the head of the Greek Orthodox Church, Archbishop Damaskinos, a giant of a man who towered over everyone, even without his tall headdress. It will be remembered that he had been accepted by the Greek people as temporary head of their government pending the results of a plebiscite then in progress to decide upon the return of the constitutional monarchy.

April 11 was proclaimed U.S. Navy Day in Piraeus, with a parade and a luncheon by the city fathers, all of which I had the pleasure of attending. At the luncheon, we were entertained by a chorus of charming young ladies in native costume, some of whom might well have served as models for reproductions of the ancient statuary.

Friday, the 12th, was marked by an official luncheon at the Hotel Gran Bretagne. In my remarks, in reply to the welcoming speeches of our hosts, I could not resist the temptation to observe that my only previous visit to the beautiful city of Athens had been a little over forty-seven years before, also in the battleship *Missouri*—but a very different *Missouri*—and wearing but a very narrow single stripe on my sleeve.

One of the memorable occasions of the visit was attendance at a memorial service for the war dead at the cathedral in Athens—a service conducted by the Regent himself.

The Archbishop Regent returned my official call by visiting the *Missouri* in person, during which he went over the topside from stem to stern and interviewed a few members of the crew who were of Greek extraction. He, as well as all others who visited the ship, appeared much interested in the plaques marking the site of the Japanese surrender ceremony.

On Saturday, our last day, in the presence of a landing force of U.S. Marines and bluejackets, I laid a wreath on the tomb of the Greek Unknown Soldier, so constantly and ceremonially guarded by two kilted evzones. That afternoon we received our Greek hosts and their ladies on the *Missouri* in a farewell party.

I cherish two personal mementos of that visit to Athens: the Order of King George I, with swords, conferred on me by the Greek government, and a beautifully sculptured head of an ancient goddess, presented to me by the Hellenic-American Society.

Before departure, the *Missouri*, with its long-range radio equipment, was able to transmit in code directly to Washington the confidential result of the United Nations plebiscite which was favorable to the return of the Greek monarchy.

Naples

Our next port of call was Naples—so long my headquarters in 1944–1945. There being no longer an Allied Naval Command there, Admiral Sir John Cunningham had returned to his regular Admiralty residence in Malta as CINC Mediterranean. Admiral James, as commander of the U.S. naval detachment in the Mediterranean, had succeeded in the occupancy of the famous Villa Emma. Since there was plenty of room in my mail plane, which was to bring my official correspondence from London, my wife and young daughter flew down on it to join me and be Admiral James' guests at the villa. The plane, before landing on the airfield under the shadow of Vesuvius, circled over the *Missouri* as she was entering the port on April 15. There my family was promptly met by Admiral James and brought out to the ship for lunch.

During the war period, I had had little contact with the Italian officials, but now the situation was quite different and the usual peacetime official calls were in order. These, however, were quickly disposed of in the afternoon, and I was soon able to relax on the beautiful terrace of the villa in the spot where, two years earlier, I had been invested with the Order of the Bath by King George. And from that terrace, it was interesting to watch the former Italian monarch, King Victor Emmanuel,[18] and his Queen out in a small boat fishing, watched over by an Italian Navy motor boat. The Italian government, the final status of which was still undetermined, was being presided over temporarily by Prince Umberto[19] as Regent. The deposed monarchs, under a security guard, were housed in a villa neighboring the Villa Emma.

As official duties would permit, I spent the next few days showing my family not only my old haunts but all the sites of Naples and vicinity, or as many as we could work in during the time we had. On the very first day we took in Pompeii, and then went on through the pass to the Gulf of Salerno, and then along the Amalfi Drive to that interesting ancient port. From there, we climbed the winding road to my favorite luncheon spot in picturesque Ravello. Passing a buxom native lass balancing a basket of lemons on her head as she climbed the steps of a footpath, we stopped and bargained for the whole basketful, with the intent of sending it by mail plane to citrus-starved London.

The visits of the *Missouri* to Athens and Naples were planned, primarily, with the object of giving the officers and men of that ship and its accompanying escorts a maximum opportunity to see the sights of those famous cities and of Rome as well. In Istanbul, also, all possible leave and liberty were granted during the more limited time available there. Without the longer nine-day stay in the Bay of Naples, many of the personnel would have had to miss the Eternal City. Therefore, it was not only the senior officers who were able to enjoy this cruise.

My old Villa Hortensi in Alto Posillippo, which was very comfortable and enjoyed a remarkable view, had been rather cheaply constructed during the Fascist era and was now in some disrepair, with its beautiful garden neglected. However, it was being used as a club for the few officers of the U.S. military services still stationed in Naples. So I was able to show my wife and daughter where I had lived during the latter part of the Mediterranean campaign.

Admiral James entertained us with dinner one night at Villa Emma, and I returned the compliment two evenings later on the *Missouri*. They were the occasions for renewing contact with many old associates, including the consul general at Naples, and Major General John C. H. Lee,[20] who had been active in the service of supply and was now the senior U.S. Army officer at the old Allied force headquarters at the palace of Caserta.

On Good Friday, April 19, with my family and flag lieutenant, I took the drive around the south side of the Bay of Naples as far as Sorrento, intending to lunch at the Hotel Vittoria there, known to me since my very first visit there in 1914. The hotel, however, had been taken over by the Fifth Army and bore a sign to the effect that it was closed to all others. Nevertheless, when I represented that, while I was not attached to the Fifth Army, I might have had some connection with its presence in that area, we were admitted and given a fine table on the terrace. It was a beautiful sunshiny day, and the outlook over the bay toward Capri, Ischia, Positano, Naples, and Vesuvius was at its best. After an excellent luncheon, we continued over the mountain to the south side of the Sorrento Peninsula and back through Amalfi once more. One cannot take the Amalfi drive too often.

In the evening, with our bags in the car, we drove to Caserta for dinner with General Lee, after which we boarded a special railroad car there for a night trip to Rome. Arriving, we were met by Commodore H. W. Ziroli, U.S. Navy, who had been assigned in September 1944 as U.S. naval liaison officer with the Italian navy. Soon we found ourselves established in the royal suite of the Grand Hotel, preparing for an audience at 11 a.m. in the Quirinale Palace with Prince Umberto. This was the beginning of another memorable day.

After being saluted at the palace by a smart honor guard, Commodore Ziroli, two senior members of my staff, and I were ushered up a wide flight of marble stairs to the audience chamber where we were greeted most cordially by the prince, who spoke perfect English. To my surprise, at the conclusion of the audience, the prince conferred upon me the Order of Saints Michael and Lazarus, with the rank of Knight Grand Cross. The insignia consisted of a broad green sash with pendant medal, and a large silver star worn on the left breast. Other officers present with me received the same order but with lesser rank.

From the Quirinale, joined by my wife and daughter who had been supplied with proper veils by Mrs. Ziroli, I went to the Vatican for a private family audience with Pope Pius. Since the decoration which I had just received was originally a papal order, I was advised to keep the insignia on for this occasion, which I did.

To reach the Pope's private study, we were led by a Vatican official through a long series of connecting rooms, each with many beautiful art treasures to observe, and each—so it seemed—with a Swiss guardsman or member of the Noble Guard on duty. Finally, we reached the presence and were warmly greeted by His Holiness, who had us sit down in front of his desk and engaged each of us in turn in conversation. Of me, he asked many questions about the war and whether the men of the Roman Catholic faith had compared well with others in the performance of their duty. When it became Mary Kent's turn, he inquired of her in French whether she spoke that language. She replied in French that she did to some extent but understood Spanish much better. With that, he launched into an animated conversation in that language, which I was able to follow. I was amazed at the facility with which he switched from one language to another. His English was impeccable.

At the close of our private audience, we moved with His Holiness into a larger audience room, where he received a large delegation of officers and men of the fleet who were on leave in Rome—a great occasion for them. My Filipino steward, a devout Roman Catholic, was quite overwhelmed at the honor. They all received rosaries or medallions, which had been especially blessed for them.

In the evening, we all attended a dinner given by the Italian minister of marine, Admiral de Courten and his wife. From where we sat, enjoying the delicious Italian food and wines, we had a wonderful view of the Tiber and the throngs along its banks. Previously, the Zirolis had given us a large reception at their apartment where we met many friends.

The weather on Easter Day was perfect and the sight of the crowds at Saint Peter's Square on that holy day was a memorable one. Easter is really a day to be in Rome. Unfortunately, I had to return to the ship by auto that evening. Prince Umberto had expressed a desire to see the *Missouri*, and I had to prepare for his visit. Floride and Mary Kent, however, remained at the Grand Hotel for several days of sightseeing with the Zirolis.

Speaking of the Zirolis, I should hark back to the spring of 1941 when the Commodore (then a commander) was the executive officer of my flagship, the *Philadelphia*. After many years of caring for an invalid wife, he had been a widower for some years when he met in California an attractive widow from one of the Latin-American countries. They became engaged and she came out to Hawaii to be married. Unfortunately, each time the wedding was scheduled, the *Philadelphia* was sent off on special duty and there had to be a postponement. On about the third time, the wedding was set for noon on Saturday, following what seemed like a certain fleet return to port on Friday. When we went out for maneuvers that week, my wife charged me to get Tony, as he was called, back in time, or she would not speak to me. What happened? On Friday afternoon, my division was ordered to scout to the eastward for some missing vessel. There was nothing to do but grant Tony leave, crowd him, sword, baggage and all into the back seat of an observation plane, catapult him off, and fly him into port. Thus, he was finally married, and I avoided domestic difficulties. But his best man and his shipmates were unable to be present. Thus, our interest in the Zirolis and theirs in us.

Prince Umberto was received on board the *Missouri* in the Bay of Naples with all the honors due to the head of a state that fine Monday morning. He was accompanied by his aide, General Infante, and by Admiral de Courten. Commodore Ziroli had previously joined me on board to assist in greeting the Italian guests. Both of us wore our Italian decorations for the occasion. The prince, as had Archbishop Damaskinos, went over everything topside very thoroughly, and he and Admiral de Courten obviously were much interested. Unfortunately, due to our regulations, the only liquid refreshment I could offer them in my cabin was coffee. And this was not the espresso to which they were probably accustomed.

Algiers

After the royal party was seen off with parting honors, the *Missouri* got underway for its next port of call, Algiers, at which we had been invited to stop. Here again, I looked forward to meeting old friends and revisiting former haunts. I knew that my friend Admiral Ronarc'h, who had shot at me two and a half years previously off Casablanca, from the *Jean Bart*, was still the prefect maritime at Algiers.

As we approached the harbor entrance during forenoon of the 23rd, we noted the cruiser *Jeanne d'Arc* inside, flying Ronarc'h's vice admiral's flag. This was the ship which I had first encountered at Trinidad in 1936 when I was on my way south with President Roosevelt, and which, overhauled and modernized in the United States, had participated in the DRAGOON operation under my command. As the *Missouri* passed in through the breakwater, it fired the customary twenty-one-gun national salute with the *Tricolore* at the main. After this had been answered by the Army shore battery, the *Jeanne d'Arc* fired seventeen guns with the Stars and Stripes at the fore—my second salute as an admiral. In accordance with international custom, this was answered, gun for gun.

As soon as the *Missouri* was moored, Admiral Ronarc'h came out in his barge to pay his official call and was piped over the side and then given the ruffles and flourishes due his rank. As I shook hands with him and thanked him for the salute, I could not resist saying that I appreciated the reception accorded me by the *Jeanne d'Arc* much more than that by the *Jean Bart*. Having an excellent sense of humor, he roared. So started a very pleasant four-day visit, during which I exchanged visits with the governor general, M. Yves Chataigneau, General Henri Martin, and the American consul general, all old friends, and, in a ceremony with a guard of American bluejackets and Marines and the *Missouri* band, laid a wreath on the Tomb of the Unknown Soldier in Algiers. When I first called on the governor general, he showed me with pride his appointment as a corporal in the First U.S. Army Division, with which he had served as a liaison officer in World War I. I was able to return the compliment by showing him my credentials as a *Spahi d'honneur* in the Seventh Algerian Regiment. After that, I never went anywhere officially without a clattering mounted escort of Spahis in their colorful full dress uniform.

We still had a U.S. naval representative in Algiers, Captain Robert Morris, who throughout the Mediterranean campaign had taken a leading part in the Eighth Fleet amphibious training and had participated in all the operations. He was occupying my old villa. Thanks to him and General Martin, I was able to take a pre-breakfast ride through the adjacent vineyard country as I so often used to do.

I had intended leaving the *Missouri* at Gibraltar and returning to England as I had come, but I was called to Paris to act as naval advisor and senior military advisor to the U.S. delegation to the foreign ministers' conference about to meet there. Accordingly, I hauled down my flag on the *Missouri* on April 27 and boarded my plane at the familiar Maison Blanche Air Field. When I arrived at the field, I found a whole troop of my Spahi regiment drawn up to see me off. Through the kindness of someone there, I have a splendid color photograph of them. I cannot help but wonder what has happened to that fine regiment now that Algeria is no longer French.

The conference was held at the Invalides and lasted until about May 13. It was interesting, but seemed to accomplish little, due to Russian obstructionist tactics to which we were already beginning to become accustomed. The leading light in their delegation at the time was the inscrutable Molotov,[21] who has since disappeared from view.

One of the memorable social affairs connected with the conference was a magnificent reception on April 30 at the Quai D'Orsay, given by the foreign minister, M. Bidault.[22] By that time, my family had joined me from Rome and we were able to spend considerable time seeing many of my French friends from Algiers days. Mary Kent was invited to visit a young cousin of Admiral Lemonnier's and his wife, M and Mme Gillet, at their beautiful country place near Paris. There, she was able to play tennis with friends near her own age and to soak in more of the French language firsthand.

We returned to London in time to attend the funeral of Admiral Kennedy-Purvis at St. Martin's in the Fields. Unfortunately, he had just succumbed to a short illness. It was a sad occasion, but a happier one was soon to follow. That was the delayed conferring of the Navy Distinguished Service Medal upon Admiral of the Fleet, Lord Cunningham. He had recovered to some extent from his attack, and he had expressed his willingness to attend a quiet after-luncheon ceremony in my Grosvenor Square quarters.

Since the president's chief of staff, Fleet Admiral Leahy, was in London at the time, I felt that it was my duty to invite him to make the presentation. He, however, knowing my feelings, insisted that I should do it. Then he made a suggestion of which I had not thought—that is, that we should each wear our insignia of the Bath for the occasion. I gladly agreed.

Present with Admiral Cunningham were Lady Cunningham and one or two members of his staff. With me were Fleet Admiral Leahy; my chief of staff, Admiral Lewis; my liaison officer, Captain Errington, Royal Navy; my flag lieutenant; and, of course, my wife. With Admiral Lewis also wearing his insignia, three ranks of the Order of the Bath were represented—the Knight Grand Cross, the Knight Commander, and the Companion. This was a touch which Admiral Cunningham seemed to appreciate greatly.

In June, there were a number of events of interest to record. On the 4th, I had the pleasure at my Grosvenor Square headquarters of presenting to a number of British officers of all three services the American decorations which had been awarded to them by authority of the president and of entertaining these gentlemen at luncheon.

On the 5th, my family and I were invited to view the races at Ascot from the Royal Enclosure—the first time we had seen that famous track. Never had we seen race spectators dressed in the traditional top hats, etc. Britain was returning to normal. But on the same day Admiral Cunningham retired and left the Admiralty for the home which he had recently purchased, the Palace House, Bishops Waltham, near Southampton. Admiral Sir John Cunningham thereupon became the First Sea Lord.

Saturday, June 8, 1946, was a big day in London, for it was the occasion of the Great Victory Parade, participated in by all the British services, including their female branches who marched as smartly as any. Also included were detachments of U.S. Army and Navy, both Marines and bluejackets, looking very well. Everyone participating, except the very senior officers, was on foot. General McNarney, who came over from the continent to represent the Army, Brigadier General F. A. Hart,[23] U.S. Marine Corps, and I rode in one car, following the senior officers of the British services.

The parade started in the vicinity of the Tower of London and wound around many of the principal streets in order to give as many as possible a chance to see it. It terminated beyond the Saluting Point on the Mall, where it was reviewed by the king and queen and the principal dignitaries. After rendering our salute to Their Majesties, those who were riding, drew out, alighted, joined the others on the royal stand and saw the parade from there. My family, at the invitation of Mrs. Alexander, the wife of the First Lord of the Admiralty, witnessed the parade from a splendid viewpoint on the roof of the Admiralty in Whitehall.

The crowning event of the victory celebration was a remarkable display of fireworks on the Thames which we were privileged to witness from a vantage point on the embankment near the Houses of Parliament.

It was about this time that Admiral Stark came back to London preparatory to receiving an honorary degree at Oxford. Mrs. Stark, who had not been with him in England during the war, of course, saw beautiful Romany for the first time when we had the pleasure of entertaining those old friends there for luncheon.

Another notable event of that period was a reception given by the king and queen at the palace of Hampton Court. We had visited Hampton Court previously, but under different circumstances. We now saw it in all its glory with the gardens in full bloom.

Our British friends love their traditions and a certain amount of pomp and circumstance, which I think is a fine thing, commemorating history as it does. At the instance again of Admiral Cunningham, Floride and I had the privilege of attending an official luncheon given by the lord mayor at the Guild Hall, during which Admiral Cunningham, Field Marshal Alan Brooke, and Air Chief Marshal Portal, whom we had seen made lords, were presented with the Freedom of the City of London and made honorary citizens. How much had happened in the world since that day so many years before when I, in an oversized ensign's frock coat, had sat immediately across the table from the lord mayor and Admiral Sims, when the latter had made his "Blood is Thicker Than Water" speech! And how true the admiral's prophecy had been!

By the middle of the month, I had to slip over to Paris once more for another week with the conference of foreign ministers, but I was back in time to see both Admirals King and Stark awarded their honorary degrees in a traditional and interesting ceremony at Oxford.

NOTES
1. James F. Byrnes (1879–1972). A Democratic senator from South Carolina in the 1930s, he supported Franklin D. Roosevelt's New Deal, served on the Supreme Court and as head of the War Mobilization Board during his administration. He was secretary of state, 1945-1947.
2. Thomas T. Connally (1877–1963). U.S. senator from Texas, 1929–1953. He supported U.S. participation in the UN.
3. Adlai Stevenson (1900–1965). Politician and diplomat. Involved in government work during World War II, he joined the State Department in 1945 and took part in conferences to establish the UN where he served as a delegate in 1946 and 1947. He ran unsuccessfully for president of the United States in 1952 and 1956. In 1961, he was appointed permanent ambassador to the UN.
4. Richmond Kelly Turner (1885–1961). Admiral. U.S. Naval Academy, Class of 1908.
5. Erich Raeder (1876–1960). German Admiral. He was appointed head of the German navy in 1928 and promoted to Grand Admiral in 1939. He was arrested in 1945 by the Soviets and charged with war crimes. In 1946, he was sentenced to life in prison but was released in 1956 because of deteriorating health.
6. Karl Doenitz (1892–1980). German Admiral and head of the German navy from 1943 to 1945. He negotiated the surrender of German forces to the Allies in May 1945.
7. William Averell Harriman (1891–1986). Democrat and statesman, he served as ambassador to the Soviet Union, 1943–1946, and to Great Britain in 1946. For the next twenty years, he took on many diplomatic assignments for U.S. presidents.
8. Alan Brooke (1883–1963). First Viscount and British Field Marshal during World War II. He served as Churchill's military advisor and helped to devise the Anglo-American strategy that resulted in Germany's defeat.
9. Charles Frederic Algernon Portal (1893–1971). First Viscount Portal of Hungerford. Royal Air Force officer. He directed the RAF in World War II and was named Marshal of the RAF in 1944.
10. USS *Houston* (CL-81) was commissioned in 1943 and saw service in the Pacific at the Battle of the Marianas and engaged in strikes on Okinawa and Formosa. In 1946, she was sent on a goodwill tour of European ports.
11. Roscoe H. Hillenkoetter (1897–1982). Vice Admiral. U.S. Naval Academy, Class of 1920.
12. Alexander W. Weddell (1876–1948). U.S. ambassador to Spain, 1939–1942.
13. USS *Providence* (CL-82). Commissioned in May 1945, she departed for the Mediterranean in November 1945, visiting Greece, then in April 1946, Istanbul, and in May, Alexandria, Egypt.
14. Edwin C. Wilson (1893–1972). U.S. ambassador to Turkey, 1946–1948.
15. Webb Trammel (1887–1970). Captain. U.S. Naval Academy, Class of 1910.
16. Mustafa Kemal Atatürk (1881–1938). Founder and first president of the Turkish Republic in 1923. A member of the Young Turks who opposed the Sultanate, he fought and won victories against the British and Russians in World War I and in 1921 drove the Greeks out of Anatolia. As president, he began the development of Turkey as a modern, secular westernized state.
17. Ismet Inonu (1884–1973). Turkish statesman. He negotiated the peace treaty with Greece which won recognition of an independent Turkey. He became prime minister of Turkey in 1923, and with Mustafa Kemal Atatürk began the process of westernizing his country. He served as president, 1938–1950.
18. Victor Emmanuel III (1869–1947). Son of King Umberto I and King of Italy, 1900–1946. He appointed Benito Mussolini as premier in 1922 and only disassociated himself from fascism when Italian defeat became evident. He negotiated with the Allies and fled to the south of Italy under their protection. He retired when Rome was liberated and abdicated in favor of his son in 1946.
19. Prince Umberto (1904–1983). King of Italy for thirty-five days in 1946. Once the republic was proclaimed, he went into exile in Portugal.
20. John C. H. Lee (1887–1958). General, U.S. Army. Graduate, U.S. Military Academy, 1909. He served in World War I and World War II and was in command of the Mediterranean theater of operations, 1946–1947.
21. Vyacheslav Molotov (1890–1986). One of the leading communist figures in Russia, he was instrumental in planning the 1917 revolution and held the office of deputy prime minister in 1941 as well as foreign minister. He headed the Soviet delegation to the UN until 1949.
22. Georges A. Bidault (1899–1983). French statesman and prime minister, 1946, 1949–1950, 1958. He served as foreign minister in 1944, 1947 and in 1953–1954. Charged with plotting against the state, he was exiled in 1962.
23. Franklin A. Hart (1894–1967). Major General, U.S. Marine Corps. He served as assistant naval attaché in London in 1941, special naval observer, liaison officer, Chief Combined Operations, 1941–1942, and participated in the raid on Dieppe in 1942. He led Marine divisions in major battles in the South Pacific, including the assaults on Tinian, Saipan, and Iwo Jima.

Admiral H.K. Hewitt and King Haakon of Norway during the visit of the Twelfth Fleet to Oslo in June 1946. (Naval Historical Collection.)

XIX Twelfth Fleet and Return to USA, 1946–1947

The end of June found me en route to Oslo in the *Houston*, accompanied by the *Little Rock*[1] and four destroyers, for a visit of courtesy to Norway. With me, as a passenger, was the commander in chief of the Norwegian Navy, Admiral Horne. He was a most congenial guest who seemed as delighted to be on board as we were to have him.

Oslo

Our stay in Oslo was a rather short one, but there was time for the usual calls and a royal visit to the *Houston* by King Haakon. Also, there was a luncheon at the palace given by His Majesty for the senior officers of U.S. ships. It was on this occasion that I learned the "skoal ceremony" for which I had fortunately been tipped off. The king, seated, catches your eye and raises his glass slightly. You immediately rise, hold your glass close to the left breast, and bow slightly. Then the toast is drunk. Of course, if the one offering the toast is other than royalty, he rises and bows. This custom is general throughout Scandinavia, the Swedes doing it more formally than the others.

Copenhagen

The next visit was Copenhagen, which my little squadron reached on the morning of July 4. As we moored, we full dressed ship, which means that we ran up dressing lines with signal flags from the bow up over the masthead and down to the stern, and broke the Stars and Stripes at each masthead. Every other man-of-war in the harbor followed suit, with the exception that they flew their own colors at the fore. The presence of our ensign at the main indicated that the full dress was in honor of the United States. One of the ships was the British cruiser HMS *Frobisher*,[2] whose captain, I was amused to discover when he called, was also named Hewitt. He was an Australian, and we were unable to establish any close relationship.

Since moorings for the men-of-war were too close to the city to permit the firing of salutes, we were unable to fire the customary national salute at noon. But the Danes accorded us unusual honor. By special order of the king, the Danish shore battery fired it for us.

It was a gay five days for all hands at Copenhagen. The family arrived by plane from London on July 5, Prince and Princess Viggo going with me to the airfield. We were established in great comfort in Copenhagen's finest hotel, the Angleterre. How pleasant it was to relax on the broad terrace overlooking the water and the main thoroughfare, consume luscious strawberries in thick Danish cream, and watch the Copenhagen world go by, principally on bicycles in a steady stream.

Admiral Vedel and Mrs. Vedel entertained for us at a grand dinner at the Royal Naval Club, which was graced by the presence of the crown prince and princess. As the senior officer guest, I had the honor and privilege of escorting her charming Royal Highness into dinner. (I was beginning to learn proper court procedure and terminology. Princess Viggo, not being of royal blood, was merely Her Highness!)

Except for a dance Saturday evening given by the American legation, the weekend of July 6–7 was spent primarily in sight-seeing Copenhagen and its surrounding countryside. On Sunday, we had a beautiful drive by automobile out to the ancient castle of Helsingor (Elsinore), such a perfect example of medieval days and so full of history and romance. I re-read my *Hamlet* as soon as I could after seeing it.

Returning, we had luncheon at a pleasant country inn, full of Danish families enjoying the holiday. In one obvious family party, we were amused to observe a young grandson get up and go around the table with a match to light his grandmother's cigar.

Monday, the 8th, was our last day in Copenhagen, and it was a full one. Mary Kent, Floride, and I were invited to lunch in the wardroom of the destroyer *Cone*.[3] I believe the captain extended the invitation fearing that the admiral would not deign to accept. However, I was always happy to go aboard a destroyer. I little realized that the executive officer, the then Lieutenant Commander Norton,[4] was to become my son-in-law. There was the usual reception on board the flagship in the afternoon as a farewell gesture to our Danish hosts which was attended by some of the royalty and also by Mrs. James C. Byrnes and Mrs. Lucius Clay, who happened to be in Copenhagen at the time. But the crowning event was a garden party, dinner, and dance given for the officers of the visiting squadron by Prince and Princess Viggo at their lovely estate, Stor Mariendal, in Hellerup, a suburb of Copenhagen. The next morning the squadron departed for Stockholm.

Stockholm

On July 9, the squadron got underway for Stockholm. It was the first time that I had ever entered the Baltic, and I enjoyed the trip, particularly up through the beautiful archipelago to Stockholm's beautiful harbor, which we reached on the 10th. We moored near the *Sverige*[5] and in plain sight of the Grand Hotel. With the exchange of official calls, it was a pleasure to renew my previous acquaintance with Admiral Ekstrand, the commander in chief of the Swedish Navy, and with Rear Admiral Samuelson, commanding the Coastal Fleet. The family flew on out from

Copenhagen the next day, in time for an official dinner given us by Mr. Voght, the Swedish minister of marine.

The next few days were taken up with sight-seeing and visiting Stockholm's wonderful shops. An extraordinary sight for us was the big orderly piles of firewood stacked along the streets between curb and sidewalk. It was the custom, we were told, to bring this fuel down from the northern forests during the summer in preparation for the long hard winter. Our naval attaché, Captain W. O. Wright, was host one evening at a reception and dance at the U.S. legation, which was enjoyed by all. A visit to the naval shipyard at Stockholm was very interesting, and on Sunday, July 14, we had the pleasure of a trip out into the Swedish countryside and of lunching on Swedish fare at a prosperous farm.

Luncheon on Monday with Admiral and Mrs. Ekstrand in their quarters at the Skeppsholme Ship Yard gave us a chance to see a real private home. And that evening we attended a large official dinner at the famous Hasselbacken. The Hasselbacken is a beautiful restaurant on a hill outside of Stockholm, with a wonderful view overlooking the harbor. With its beautiful gardens, it is arranged in a number of levels (or stories). The higher the level, the higher the prices, and the more select the company. We were on the highest level.

On the occasion of our visit, the Swedish papers had published an outline of my biography, including my date of birth. At the dinner at the Hasselbacken I was told by a retired naval officer, Commodore Forsell, that they had in Sweden a society composed of men who had been born in 1887, and he wondered whether I would consent to becoming an honorary member. Naturally, I replied that I should be honored. So, some months later I received a handsomely inscribed diploma which stated in Swedish that due to Divine Providence and the wisdom of his parents, having been born in the year 1887, Admiral H. Kent Hewitt had been admitted to the Society of the "87 Ärsmän." A year later, when the members became sexagenarians, I was asked to contribute an anecdote for their annual publication. They were so pleased with my story of an ensign stopping the fleet for a man-overboard drill that they sent me a beautifully inscribed cup with the hope that it would sometimes be used for the purpose for which it was intended. Accordingly, I now on my birthday make it a habit to get out my cup and drink a solemn skoal to my Swedish contemporaries.

There had been no audience with royalty, because the king and queen were at their summer palace up-country somewhere. But the regular palace was on an island near where our ships were moored, and the guard, when it marched across the bridge to the daily guard mount while we were there, did so to the tune of "Anchors Aweigh," a very delicate compliment. On our last day in port, a member of the royal family, Prince Bertil,[6] came aboard on an official visit, being received, of course, with the usual honors. The *Houston* had to salute with her 5-inch anti-aircraft battery, the starboard mounts of which were almost above the starboard gangway. The poor prince winced when the first bang went off right over his head, and I did not blame him. But he stood it like a man to the end of the twenty-one.

Our farewell reception on the *Houston* was attended by Prince Bertil and all the leading dignitaries in Stockholm, including most of the diplomats. Notably absent were the Russians, who had boycotted all the official affairs in our honor. I learned later that they had expressed great displeasure at our presence in the Baltic.

About this time, Secretary Forrestal turned up unexpectedly on a westbound flight around the world. I joined him for the flight to London, leaving my ships to proceed to Antwerp on July 18 without me.

My family returned with me on Mr. Forrestal's plane, and Mrs. Forrestal was unexpectedly in London to greet her husband. So, on July 19, the day after our return, we gave a dinner in their honor at our Grosvenor Square apartment. Present were Mr. Forrestal's British opposite number, the First Lord of the Admiralty, Mr. A. V. Alexander[7] and Mrs. Alexander; the First Sea Lord, Admiral Sir John Cunningham and Lady Cunningham; and up from the Mediterranean, Rear Admiral and Mrs. Jules James.

Mr. Forrestal having completed his visit, I flew to Antwerp the next day to rejoin my squadron, breaking my flag once more on the *Houston*. Again there was the usual round of calls and return calls, one of which gave me particular pleasure and amusement. This was to receive on board Alan Kirk, in top hat, cutaway, and striped trousers instead of uniform, with the honors due an ambassador rather than a vice admiral. He, too, enjoyed it, for it was the first time he had been accorded those honors, to say nothing of getting them from an old friend with whom he had served. Ambassador and Mrs. Kirk invited the Hewitts to visit them at the embassy during the ship's stay, but Floride did not feel well enough, having been somewhat exhausted by all the activities in Copenhagen and Stockholm. Mary Kent, however, flew over and had a grand time.

Belgium and Holland

With Alan Kirk, I called in audience on Prince Baudouin[8], who graciously conferred on me the Order of Leopold and the Belgian Croix de Guerre.

On July 23, we had the customary farewell reception on the *Houston*, and on the following day the ships departed for Holland. I myself seized the opportunity to drive overland by automobile to The Hague in order to see something of the intervening country. It was a thoroughly interesting and enjoyable drive. Walcheren Island, which we crossed, was still endeavoring to recover from the wartime saltwater flooding of its fertile fields from which the population drew its livelihood.

The ships were divided into two detachments, the *Houston* and two destroyers going to Rotterdam, while the *Little Rock* and the other two destroyers went to Amsterdam. Thus, no favoritism was shown between those two rival ports. The Hewitts went to the Hotel des Indes in The Hague to be in between and at the center of government. Mary Kent drove with me from Antwerp, and Floride recovered sufficiently to join us in the Netherlands.

The five days of our visit to the Netherlands, July 25–29, were very full and enjoyable ones in which I oscillated back and forth between Rotterdam, The Hague, and Amsterdam, making and returning the customary official calls and, with my family, attending many receptions and dinners. One high spot was a luncheon with Queen Wilhelmina at the summer palace, upon conclusion of which she invested me with the order of Orange-Nassau. In this ceremony, my wife and daughter were not included. Her Majesty had the most formal court in Europe and conducted affairs of that sort as if she were king, leaving out the ladies entirely.

Rotterdam and its burgomaster entertained the visiting ships royally, commencing with a beautiful reception and dance at the Town Hall. It was remarkable to note how the industrious Rotterdamers had already cleared away most of the rubbish of the terrible destruction which had been visited on their city and were beginning to rebuild.

On the *Houston* in Rotterdam on a pleasant Saturday morning, July 27, I had the great pleasure, in the name of the president, of conferring U.S. decorations on a number of distinguished Dutch officers. The first of these was the Navy Distinguished Service Medal to the commander in chief of Her Majesty's Netherlands Navy, Admiral Helfrich. This was particularly moving to that fine officer and gentleman, since it had been under his command in the East Indies that the first *Houston* had been lost. At the close of the investiture, in another little ceremony, the admiral made a personal presentation to the new *Houston* of a beautiful plaque in memory of the old.

After the luncheon that day on the *Houston*, the Hewitt family was treated by the Dutch navy to a most interesting trip through the canals from Rotterdam to Amsterdam, stopping at Delft en route. At Amsterdam, the official party was installed at the Amstel Hotel and entertained royally at dinner. On the next morning, Sunday, our naval hosts took us on a thorough water tour of that quaint city and then out to see the Zuyder Zee. We returned to The Hague by automobile in the afternoon with a new knowledge of what it meant to preserve the lowlands from the encroaching sea and respect for the people who had accomplished it.

Monday, the 29th, was marked by the customary farewell reception on the flagship. This was followed by a dinner at the embassy at The Hague, given by Ambassador Hornbeck. The 30th saw the ships en route to Southampton, and I by plane to London to catch up with some of my administrative duties. Two weeks later, however, I was again on the move.

Portugal

Earlier in the year, units of the British fleet had made an official visit to Portugal. It appeared to be desirable that a similar visit should be made by a detachment of the U.S. fleet, a proposal which was enthusiastically supported by the American ambassador at Lisbon, Dr. Herman Baruch[9] (brother of Bernard Baruch) and welcomed by the Portuguese government. The dates of August 16–20 were mutually agreed, and the Navy Department detailed a task force consisting of the new carrier *Franklin D. Roosevelt*[10] and attendant destroyers under Rear Admiral Cassady[11] to report to me for the occasion, rendezvousing off Lisbon in time for a joint entry.

Ambassador Baruch very kindly invited my wife and daughter to be his guests for the occasion. Unfortunately, Floride was rather tired after all the festivities in Scandinavia and Holland and fearful of the heat of Portugal in August, and so she regretfully declined. Mary Kent, however, accepted with alacrity.

With my flag in the *Houston* once more, and accompanied by the *Little Rock* and four destroyers, I departed from Southampton on Wednesday, August 13, and headed south for Lisbon, carrying out training exercises en route. These included, on Friday, an air search and attack exercise with the *FDR* group approaching from the westward.

Having effected a rendezvous in the early morning of the 16th, the squadron entered the Tagus on schedule, arriving off Lisbon about 0700. The carrier moored in mid-stream, while the other vessels went alongside the dock, where they were more readily available to visitors and could best be seen by the crowds on shore. Having the visit start on a weekend, or at least include a weekend, made it possible for the maximum number of people to view the ships and their personnel.

The making of "colors" at 0800, following the motions of the nearby Portuguese flagship *João de Lisboa*,[12] was the signal for the start of an extremely busy day. With the Portuguese ensign at the main, the *Houston* fired a twenty-one-gun salute in honor of its host country. The fort that returned the salute, Fort Bom Suceso (Fort Good Luck), may well have been the very one which saluted Prince Henry the Navigator upon his departure and return from his voyages of discovery. No sooner was this completed than the *João de Lisboa* opened up with a seventeen-gun salute with the Stars and Stripes at the fore in honor, of course, of the visiting U.S. admiral. The *Houston* immediately returned the salute, gun-for-gun, in accordance with international custom, although the *João de Lisboa* was only flying the flag of vice admiral. Before the day was over, a large amount of black powder was expended.

To anyone unfamiliar with the courtesies and ceremonies involved in an official visit of this sort to a friendly state, a description in detail of just what happened thereafter may be of interest.

Promptly at 0900, the American consul, Mr. Charles E. Dickerson, accompanied by Commander McLallen, the naval attaché, came aboard. At their heels was

Commander Moreira Rato, reporting to me as my Portuguese naval aide for the visit. The consul left the ship ten minutes later, receiving a parting consular salute of seven guns.

At 0945, I left the ship officially, with all the usual side honors, to pay my official calls. I was accompanied by Rear Admiral Cassady; my acting chief of staff, Commodore Shelley; the naval attaché; Commander Rato; and my flag lieutenant, Lieutenant Gaffney. The first call at 1000 was on the ambassador, Dr. Baruch, who thereupon joined the party.

The next call, at 1030, was on the Portuguese minister of marine, followed fifteen minutes later by a call on Vice Admiral Sousa Ventura, who had the strange title of Major General of Home Fleet.

At 1130, the party was received by the president of the council of ministers and minister of foreign affairs, none other than Dr. Antonio de Oliveira Salazar,[13] the real head of government. Then at 1230 we made our call on the president of Portugal, His Excellency, General Antonio Oscar de Fragosa Carmona.[14] We were received everywhere with great cordiality.

By 1450, the party was back on the *Houston* just in time to meet with about forty members of the Portuguese press at 1500. I presume that we must have had some lunch in between, but I do not remember how or when. The press conference gave us an opportunity to express our delight at visiting Portugal and the hope that our stay would serve to promote understanding and the traditional friendship between our peoples.

At 1600, Ambassador Baruch came on board to return my call. He was received with ambassadorial honors and on his departure was given a salute of nineteen guns, with the Stars and Stripes at the fore. Half an hour later, at 1630, Vice Admiral Sousa Ventura came aboard to return my official call and was duly saluted upon his departure. Next, at 1700, the minister of marine, Captain Rodriguez Tomaz, representing Dr. Salazar as well as himself, arrived to return my calls. He received a nineteen-gun salute with the Portuguese ensign at the fore upon his departure. The *Houston*'s guard, band, and side boys, as well as the senior officers, had a busy afternoon.

Fortunately, there was a gap of three hours until, at 2030, Admiral Cassady, Commodore Shelley, the captains of all U.S. ships present, and I became guests of Ambassador Baruch at a banquet at the embassy—a banquet honored by the presence of President Carmona and Dr. Salazar, as well as many other high Portuguese officials. The evening ended by the ambassador's and my looking in on a supper dance given by him and two hundred officers of the fleet. So ended the first day.

Saturday, August 17, began with a call at 1000 by the commodore of the Portuguese Home Fleet, Captain Pereira da Fonseca. He was given a commodore's salute of eleven guns upon his departure. His call was promptly returned by me at 1100. This more or less completed the exchange of official visits. Sometime during this morning, Mary Kent arrived on my mail plane and was met and taken to the embassy. It was there that I joined her and the ambassador en route to a magnificent luncheon at the Castelo de Pena, Sintra, given by Dr. Salazar in honor of the commander and officers of the Twelfth Fleet, which was set at 1430.

The old castle of Pena was perched on the top of a high hill, a short distance outside of Lisbon. The drive to it was beautiful and the view from it of the surrounding countryside on that perfect summer day was marvelous. The luncheon was attended by top Portuguese officialdom and their ladies, as well as by all the senior officers of the fleet. In the absence of my wife, and there being no ambassador's wife, Mary Kent was given a place of honor alongside Dr. Salazar. I have a picture of that table showing her there.

Being a recent college graduate and raised in a free society, my daughter was strictly against all dictators, such as those of Spain and Portugal. Salazar, a bachelor, was reported to take little interest in women. But apparently Mary Kent was able to hold up her end so well that a later picture taken on the castle terrace after the luncheon shows her and Dr. Salazar seated on a bench very evidently engaged in a serious discussion of mutual interest, probably world affairs. I was very proud of her.

That evening, about 2000, our naval attaché gave a strictly naval dinner in my honor, attended by the ambassador, the Portuguese minister of marine, and the senior officers of the Portuguese Navy and the Twelfth Fleet. This was a very pleasant affair which conduced to the further cementing of friendships already made.

Evening social affairs in all Latin countries seem to start very late. So it was not until 2230 that we arrived at the memorable diplomatic reception given in our honor by Dr. Baruch in the embassy garden. This was attended by most of the diplomatic corps and their wives, as well as by Portuguese officialdom. I had just met the Spanish ambassador, without catching his name, when Mary Kent came along. As I presented him to her, I said to her, "*Habla español con el embajador.*" With that she launched into an animated conversation with him, her command of the language being far more fluent than mine. Then I was called off to speak to someone else. Mary Kent finished by receiving a very special invitation to visit Madrid. It was not until later that she found that she had been talking with the brother of the hated dictator Franco.

It was too bad that the uncertain status at that time of our relations with Franco made it impracticable to let Mary Kent visit Spain. She was very anxious not only to see it but to take advantage of the opportunity to improve her knowledge of the language.

With some eight hundred officers and men of the fleet, I attended a special mass for the visiting Americans in the great Lisbon cathedral at 1000 on Sunday, the 18th. This was most impressive. On the conclusion of the service, the senior officers received a special welcome from the bishop. I returned to the ship for a quiet luncheon, but by 1500 the ambassador and I were at the Zoological Gardens where a large crowd was listening to a concert given for them by the Twelfth Fleet band.

The big event of that Sunday was the special gala bullfight given in the large Lisbon bullring for the benefit of the officers and men of the fleet. And that requires a special preliminary description, because a Portuguese bullfight is entirely different from the traditional Spanish one, and does not involve the mangling and killing of horses, nor the killing of the bull itself. The bull has cut-off padded horns, and the toreadors are all mounted on beautiful highly trained horses. The game is to prance around the bull and lead him on, and then plant a *banderilla* in his neck without letting the horse get hit. If he is, he is not injured. It involves a beautiful exhibition of riding and control of the horse, and there is none of the cruelty of the Spanish ring. When the bull appears sufficiently tired, a number of bravos in tam-o'-shanter caps appear and approach the bull single file. The first man grabs the bull between the horns and tries to twist his neck, but usually gets thrown himself for his trouble. And so does the second and maybe a third. But, finally, they manage to wrestle the bull down to the ground. With that, a herd of oxen is driven in to surround the tired bull and lead him off. Then another bull is introduced for another *corrida*.

The Lisbon bullring is a large one, really a slightly elliptical form. I would not be able to estimate its capacity for spectators, but the seats rise tier after tier as they would in a football stadium. The presidential box, in which sat President Carmona and Premier Salazar and their party, was at one end of the ellipse. Immediately opposite, on the other side of the ring, was a solid mass of white—bluejackets from the fleet. The ambassador's box, in which my party and I sat, was halfway around the ring. The president's box and other boxes were marked with beautiful hanging tapestries with coats of arms and other insignia denoting the occupants or the ancient family to which the box originally pertained. Our box, of course, had the Stars and Stripes. Every seat in the ring was taken, and gay flags flew everywhere. It was quite a sight.

Because it was a gala affair, all the participants were dressed in the traditional costumes of the eighteenth century. The toreadors were driven into the ring in a procession of ancient coaches of that era, drawn by gaily caparisoned four-horse teams driven by coachmen in three-cornered hats, wigs, knee breeches, etc. And behind them were led the mounts which were to be ridden. After duly saluting the president and circling the ring at least once for all to see, the coaches were withdrawn. Then the first team of toreadors mounted, again saluted the president, and received his permission to proceed. He then awaited the first bull, which soon appeared.

I personally love horses and love to see beautiful riding, but never before had I seen such a beautiful exhibition of horsemanship as that to which we were then treated. I have seen Spanish bullfights and hated them, but this I enjoyed to the utmost. After the first bull was driven out, another group of young horsemen appeared to take on the second bull.

Near the end of the third *corrida*, a splendid young gentleman in a three-cornered hat, silk and lace, unexpectedly appeared at our box to inquire if the *Signorina* Hewitt would deign to come down into the ring and make the presentation of prizes for best performance to the winners. The *Signorina* Hewitt, naturally, accepted. So, at the proper time, she was escorted down into the ring, immediately in front of the presidential box. There, in front of all the crowd, she did her part very gracefully. Again, I had reason to be very proud of her. Incidentally, helped by her knowledge of Spanish, she had picked up enough Portuguese to make a few congratulatory remarks, which apparently went over well. After the presentation, she was escorted up into the presidential box where we joined her.

As we left to join our cars, there was a tremendous throng around the entrance to see all the officialdom. When the *Signorina* Hewitt, instead of getting into the ambassador's car with me, went off in another direction in a destroyer jeep, driven by young Lieutenant Commander Norton, there was sort of a gasp of surprise. Probably no Portuguese young lady of her age would have been permitted such a liberty, especially unaccompanied by a *duenna*.

This day was climaxed by a splendid dinner at the Aviz Hotel given by the Portuguese Navy to the U.S. Navy, the minister of marine, Captain Tomaz, acting as host. This was attended by the senior officers of both services present in Lisbon and also by Dr. Baruch. At the end of the dinner, which was well toward midnight, we were escorted to an open air show at what was called the *Feira Popular*, or Peoples' Fair, in one of Lisbon's parks. We were given seats well forward from which we could enjoy the entertainment, mostly singing and dancing, very much.

President Carmona and Dr. Salazar had been invited to spend a day at sea on the *Franklin D. Roosevelt* in order that they might get an idea, firsthand, of carrier flight operations, and, to our gratification, they had accepted. The exercise was arranged for Monday, the 19th, so at 0845 that morning Ambassador Baruch and I shifted my flag from the *Houston* to the *Franklin D. Roosevelt*. We were followed aboard by representatives of the press and certain lesser officials who had been invited. At 0915, out came Dr. Salazar, the minister of marine, and the commander-in-chief of the Portuguese Navy, to be welcomed aboard with the honors due their rank. Finally, at 0930, General Carmona arrived and was accorded the full honors due the head of a nation—rail manned, twelve side boys, and a national salute.

At 1000, the *Roosevelt*, with her plane guard destroyers, got underway and headed out to sea. The period until she gained sufficient sea room to launch planes was devoted to showing the distinguished visitors around the ship a bit.

To my mind, there is no finer example of teamwork than that exhibited on the flight deck of a carrier when it is launching and taking on planes. Beginning at 1100, the *Franklin D. Roosevelt* put on a beautiful show which impressed the visitors tremendously. The first squadron of carrier planes that was launched passed overhead in regular formation and then returned in another formation, making the initials FDR. The planes then flew in toward Lisbon to make a similar demonstration over that city. During their absence, the *Franklin D. Roosevelt* fired an anti-aircraft practice against a towed sleeve. Upon their return and upon completion of the firing, the carrier's planes made a simulated attack on their mother ship, coming in from many different directions. They were then all recovered aboard the carrier without a hitch.

While the ship was returning to port, the president, Dr. Salazar, and the senior officials were entertained by Admiral Cassady and me at luncheon in the admiral's cabin, while other visitors lunched in the wardroom. The *Franklin D. Roosevelt* anchored punctually at 1600, and before his departure President Carmona, at his own request, made an address to all hands on the flight deck in which he expressed his great interest and his appreciation, and extended his congratulations on the efficiency which they had shown. His speech, of course, was in Portuguese, but it was well and promptly translated. The usual honors were given to the departing officials and the air was again full of powder smoke.

That evening, at 2000, I seized the opportunity to return some of the Portuguese hospitality by giving a dinner on board the *Houston* to Captain Tomaz, the minister of marine, and the senior officers of the Portuguese Navy. Admiral Cassady, of course, the commanding officers of the ships present, and the senior officers of my staff assisted me as host.

The last day of the visit, Tuesday, August 20, as compared to previous days, was relatively quiet. But Admiral Cassady and I and the senior members of our staffs were given a most pleasant luncheon at a nearby summer resort by the Royal British Club. And in the late afternoon, a large reception was held aboard the *Franklin D. Roosevelt* to return some of the hospitality which we visitors had received on shore. It was estimated that about 1,000 guests attended.

The real noteworthy event of the day, however, was a memorable reception given by the president of Portugal in the Grand Ballroom of the ancient palace of Queluz. The assemblage of itself was notable, consisting as it did of the elite of Portuguese society and officialdom. A woman would undoubtedly spend much time describing the gowns worn by the ladies, but that is beyond me. They were modern, as were the uniforms and evening dress of the gentlemen. But otherwise the setting was that of the eighteenth century. The musicians were dressed as they would have been then, and the illumination was by thousands of candles in the large chandeliers with their myriad of mirror-like pendants. There was no electric lighting in the entire castle. This was the grand finale of a never to be forgotten event in my career. And it was one of the final ones of major import.

By this time, my administrative duties were calling once more, so early the following morning I hauled down my flag on the *Houston*, said farewell to Ambassador Baruch, and with my daughter and staff took off by plane for London, which we reached in the late afternoon. The ships departed the Tagus under Rear Admiral Cassady, and then dispersed on their normal occasions.

My return to London on August 21 gave Floride and me a suitable opportunity to celebrate properly our thirty-third wedding anniversary at Romany two days later. To assist us, there was quite a galaxy of visiting admirals from the United States as well as some of the senior officers of the Twelfth Fleet and Twelfth Fleet staff. The visitors from home included Admirals Walter Anderson,[15] Forrest Sherman,[16] Marc Mitscher,[17] and my efficient subordinate in the Sicilian and Salerno operations, Dick Conolly.[18] It was a pleasant evening but somewhat marred by the news which the last name brought me.

Conolly, I knew, had orders to replace me as naval advisor to the foreign ministers' conference, just about to meet in Paris once more. The surprise was that he also had orders later to relieve me in command of the Twelfth Fleet. It seems that I was to be ordered home to appear before a board of medical survey, the official reason for which was a slight hypertension which had shown up on my annual physical examination and which my staff medical officer had considered to be of no consequence. I strongly suspected that a desire on the part of some for an additional vacancy on the upper flag list was more of a factor in this action than concern for my health or ability to carry out my duties. Also, I rather resented the strange manner in which the information reached me. My feeling, however, was that if that was the way those responsible decided I should be treated, then I was not going to dignify their action by any protest.

Austria

As a consequence, I decided to take the maximum advantage of the little time remaining to me in Europe to do a little more sight-seeing. So on August 27, with my family and two aides, I took off from Hendon Field for Salzburg, Austria, to attend the music festival there as guests of General Mark Clark. Arriving in the early afternoon, we were met by a Colonel McCrary and escorted to the *Schloss*, an old Habsburg castle just outside the city, which at that time was maintained by the U.S. Army as a guest house for VIPs.

The feature that evening was a magnificent concert given by the Vienna Boys Choir, which was thoroughly enjoyed by all those fortunate enough to be present. We were in a box with Mrs. Patterson, wife of the then American ambassador to Yugoslavia and with Brigadier General and Mrs. Tate.[19] The general, who was the deputy commander of U.S. forces in Austria, represented General Clark, who was in Vienna.

At 0900 the following morning, the Forty-second Division honored me by parading a guard and band for me in the city square of Salzburg. The band was the division's famed bagpipe unit. Passing in review after the completion of my inspection, the troops marched to the tune of "Anchors Aweigh."

After this ceremony, we were taken on a trip to Berchtesgaden with Colonel Hume as our escort. There we were met by Colonel Craft, commanding the Berchtesgaden recreation area of the U.S. Army. The first part of the trip was made in ordinary army sedans through beautiful country to the lower level area where Hitler and Goering had their houses and where their schutzstaffel guards were quartered. These houses and the barracks of the SS had all been badly damaged by RAF bombing and by last minute attempts at German demolition.

On account of the grades and the narrow winding roadway along the mountainside, interspersed with tunnels, the latter part of the journey had to be made in command cars and jeeps. This was quite a thrill, especially for the ladies. And it certainly gave one an idea of the tremendous amount of human labor which had been expended all for the pleasure and whim of one vain man. Arriving at a small parking area, about 420 feet below the summit of the "Eagle's Nest," one entered a small tunnel which led to a double-decked steel-caged elevator, which quickly carried one up to this remarkable aerie. We were told that the lower deck of the elevator was for the SS guards, who could thus always accompany *Der Führer* without intruding on his privacy.

The building at the top had been burned out, but otherwise was not too much damaged, except for the vandalism of visiting souvenir and treasure hunters. A marble fireplace had been badly chipped, and many beautiful oak panels had been torn out in an apparent search for secret passageways and hiding places. The view from the large picture window at one end of the main living room was indescribable. One could imagine the "Eagle" sitting there, brooding, and planning mastery of a world, so much of which lay before his eyes.

Returning from the heights to Berchtesgaden itself, we were entertained at luncheon at the Berchtesgaden Hof, a hotel which had formerly been reserved exclusively for the use of Nazi party members. My wife and daughter were presented with swastika embroidered napkins for souvenirs.

Switzerland

Returning to Salzburg, we took off about 1500 for Geneva. I had been particularly anxious to see Switzerland before leaving Europe and had arranged for a short visit there. We were met at the Geneva airport by U.S. Vice Consul Phillips and by a message of welcome from the Swiss chief of military personnel. There being no hotel accommodations available nearer than Montreux, we proceeded there by train after a quick look around Geneva. This was a fortunate circumstance, because it gave us a lovely trip along the shores of beautiful Lake Lucerne, and our hotel suite in Montreux with its fine view of the mountains and the lake could not have been beaten.

We had planned to fly to Berlin the next day in order that Floride and Mary Kent might have a look at that historic city, but our flight had to be cancelled on account of bad weather. So we had another pleasant, relaxed day at Montreux. Returning to

Geneva as we had come on Friday, the 30th, we did a little more sight-seeing in Geneva, visiting the League of Nations building among other points of interest. After luncheon, we returned by plane direct to Hendon Airfield.

With the advent of September, my duty with the Twelfth Fleet was drawing to a close, and I became busy in winding up my official affairs. Socially, we became involved in many farewells, particularly at or near Romany, with our good Wentworth neighbors. Between the 10th and 12th, we made a quick trip to Paris, during which we said good-bye to our friends there and dined with Mr. and Mrs. Caffrey at the embassy. On the 19th, at 20 Grosvenor Square, we gave a farewell reception for my staff, my senior associates in the Royal Navy, and other London friends.

Monday, September 23, was a sad day. With my wife and daughter accompanying me, I drove to Southampton, and there on the deck of the *Houston* formally turned over command of the Twelfth Fleet to Admiral Conolly, and lowered my four-star flag for the last time.

Knowing full well from his own experience how I would feel, my dear friend Andrew Cunningham had invited us to lunch with him and Lady Nona at his delightful retreat, the Palace House, at nearby Bishop's Waltham. It was there that we went immediately upon leaving the *Houston*. He did much to bolster my morale and show me how pleasant retired life really could be.

That night we dined in London at the Hotel Dorchester with another old British navy friend and his wife, Admiral and Lady Troubridge.[20] And on the evening of the 24th, my old staff gave a wonderful farewell party for the Hewitts. The memento of our service together, which they presented to me on that occasion, is another of my most valued possessions.

On October 3, there was to be a celebration in the city of Edinburgh in honor of General Eisenhower to which both Floride and I had been invited. Naturally, I was anxious to go, both on account of our personal association and because I felt that I was the one who should represent the U.S. Navy on this occasion. Admiral Conolly, who was taking up quarters in 20 Grosvenor Square and whose wife had not yet arrived, very kindly invited us to remain at Romany until it was time for us to leave for home. This we were only too glad to do.

Consequently, my wife and I boarded the night train for Edinburgh on the evening of October 2, arriving the following morning and going directly to the hotel accommodations which had been arranged for us.

At the University of Edinburgh we witnessed the impressive ceremony of the bestowal of an honorary degree on "Ike" and had the pleasure of meeting Mrs. Eisenhower for the first time. Then we went to the Town Hall and there saw the general made an honorary citizen of the city of Edinburgh. The final function was a magnificent luncheon given by the lord mayor and aldermen. It would require my wife to describe the magnificent and historic silverware and chinaware which was used for the table.

In the afternoon, we had enough free time to see some of the sights, in particular visiting Holyrood Castle, and magnificent Edinburgh Castle on its eminence, which serves as one of the most inspiring war memorials I have ever seen. We said good-bye to General and Mrs. Eisenhower later in the evening at a reception which was held for them at the hotel. They were returning to Germany.

On the next morning, October 4, we started our return to Romany by car, driven by Tims, the cockney chauffeur who had been Admiral Stark's and my official driver. Since at that time there were no "thruways" or autobahns in that part of Scotland and England, merely narrow highways which passed through village after village, we could not make much time—nor did we wish to. Consequently, we stopped for the night at a country inn, The Bull at Barnby Moor, where advance reservations had been made for us. This was quite delightful and an interesting experience, for the inn had been a stage stop for centuries probably. Incidentally, advance reservations were at that time necessary to secure overnight accommodations almost anywhere in England.

We were back in Romany on the 5th, and immediately became busily occupied in completing our packing, for on the 7th we were en route by motor to Southampton, there to board the SS *Washington* for New York. All three of us had a pleasant, relaxing week's voyage on the ship.

United States

Upon arrival in New York, we spent a few days in Hackensack visiting old friends and taking care of various business matters in connection with my mother's estate, and visiting her and my father's side-by-side graves. I had, at my own request, been ordered to Newport, where young Floride was living with her children and where I could have my medical board at the naval hospital there. I was assigned to the Naval War College as a consultant or advisor to the president, so that I could report for temporary duty to my friend and classmate, Admiral Raymond Spruance, which was fine as long as I was not to have regular duty of my own.

Having been overseas for so long, with an official car always available, I possessed no private car and now needed one badly. But the war was just over and private cars were not yet being turned out in sufficient quantity to meet the demand. All the dealers had long waiting lists of prospective customers. But my Hackensack hostess went to the local Buick dealer, whom she knew well, and managed to convince him that a native son, such as I, returning from the wars, should not be left without transportation. So thanks to her, Mary Kent, Floride, and I were able at the end of the week to drive to Newport in a brand new black Buick sedan. Floride and I were able to secure an apartment in a well-known cottage hotel there, and Mary Kent went to live with her sister.

Newport, Rhode Island

In Newport, we had a quiet four months or so until the Navy Department, despairing of getting me found unfit for active duty, finally ordered me as U.S. naval representative on the United Nations Military Staff Committee in March 1947. The board of medical survey at Newport had cleared me and so had a subsequent one, either in Washington or New York. The president of the first board confided to me that he could not find the things wrong with me that the Bureau of Medicine and Surgery apparently wanted him to. My duties at the War College were purely perfunctory, and I spent a lot of time in the library there and in swapping experiences with Raymond Spruance.

NOTES
1. USS *Little Rock* (CL-92) was commissioned in 1945. She served with the Sixth Fleet in Europe during the summer of 1946.
2. HMS *Frobisher*, Hawkins Class Cruiser, was built in 1924 and fitted out as a flagship. Displacement, 9,860 tons; Length 505'; Beam 58'.
3. USS *Cone* (DD-866) was commissioned in 1945 and joined the Atlantic Fleet. She visited ports in Europe on a goodwill tour in 1946.
4. Gerald S. Norton (1916–2001). Captain. U.S. Naval Academy, Class of 1939. He retired from the Navy in 1970.
5. *Sverige*. Swedish battleship. Launched on May 3, 1915. Displacement 6,800 tons; Length 392 3/4'; Beam 62'; Draught 20 1/2'; Complement, 450.
6. Prince Bertil (1912–1997). Third son of King Gustav VI of Sweden. He was chairman of the Swedish Olympic Committee and was chairman of the National Sports Federation for four decades.
7. Albert V. Alexander (1885–1965). British public official, served in World War I, in Labour administrations in the 1920s and as first lord of the admiralty in 1929. In 1940, he again was appointed first lord of the admiralty, a position he held throughout the war. From 1947 to 1950, he served as minister of defence. In 1955, he was leader of the Labour peers.
8. Prince Baudouin (1930–) became king of the Belgians in July 1951 upon the abdication of his father, King Leopold.
9. Herman Baruch (1872–1953). Ambassador to Portugal, 1945–1947.
10. USS *Franklin D. Roosevelt* (CVB-42) was commissioned in 1945. She was sent to the Mediterranean during the summer of 1946 where she visited Athens as a show of support during the civil war.
11. John H. Cassady (1896–1969). Admiral. U.S. Naval Academy, Class of 1919.
12. *João de Lisboa* (Sloop). Built in 1936 at the naval arsenal in Lisbon; displacement, 1,091; length, 234 1/3'.
13. Antonio de Oliveira Salazar (1889–1970). Prime minister of Portugal from 1932 to 1968. He ruled as a dictator, repressed the opposition, and improved the country's finances. He kept Portugal neutral in World War II. In 1968, he suffered a stroke and resigned.
14. Antonio Oscar de Fragosa Carmona (1869–1951) was president of Portugal from 1926 to 1951.
15. Walter S. Anderson (1881–1981). Vice Admiral. U.S. Naval Academy, Class of 1903.
16. Forrest Sherman (1896–1951). Admiral. U.S. Naval Academy, Class of 1917. He was appointed Chief of Naval Operations in 1949 and died while negotiating U.S. base rights in Spain.
17. Marc A. Mitscher (1887–1947). Admiral. U.S. Naval Academy, Class of 1910.
18. Richard L. Conolly (1892–1962). Admiral. U.S. Naval Academy, Class of 1914. Conolly served as president of the Naval War College, 1950–1953.
19. Ralph H. Tate (1899–?). Brigadier General, U.S. Army. A 1939 graduate of the Army War College, he served as G-4, chief of staff and deputy commander, Atlantic Base, Africa, 1942–1943. During the Italian campaign, he served as assistant chief of staff, G-4, Headquarters, Fifth Army and G-4, Headquarters, Fifteenth Army Group. In July 1945, he was sent to Headquarters, U.S. Forces in Austria, where he was named deputy commanding general.
20. Thomas Troubridge (1895–1949). Vice Admiral, Royal Navy. He commanded the naval force under Sir Bertram Ramsay during the 1943 invasion of Sicily; took part in the landings at Anzio, 1944, and commanded the carrier force during the invasion of Southern France, 1944. He served as fifth sea lord (air), 1944–1946.

Admiral H. Kent Hewitt being inducted into Le Confrérie du Tastevin as a chevalier, May 14, 1947, New York, New York. (Naval Historical Collection.)

XX   *The United Nations, 1947*

The Military Staff Committee of the United Nations is established under Article 47 of the Charter of that organization, with the duties of advising and assisting "the Security Council on all questions relating to the Security Council's military requirements for the maintenance of international peace and security, the employment and command of forces placed at its disposal, the regulation of armaments, and possible disarmament." Its membership is defined as consisting of the chiefs of staff of the permanent members of the Security Council (that is, the United States, United Kingdom, France, the Union of Soviet Socialist Republics, and China), or their representatives. The article goes on to state that "the Military Staff Committee shall be responsible under the Security Council for the strategic direction of any armed forces placed at the disposal of the Security Council." Since the chiefs of staffs, with their manifold other duties, could not be expected to be in constant attendance on this committee, it was their representatives who constituted the working membership.

Admiral Kelly Turner had been the representative of the Chief of Naval Operations on the committee when it was organized in London in February 1946. In the meantime, the headquarters of the United Nations had been moved to temporary quarters at Lake Success in Long Island. The U.S. delegation, headed by Ambassador Warren Austin,[1] which included the representation of our three services on the MSC, had offices at 2 Park Avenue in New York City and had to travel out to Long Island for all meetings of the organization. In addition to their duties as members of the MSC, the representatives of the U.S. chiefs of staff served as military advisors to their own civilian delegation.

Admiral Turner's relief was necessitated by his prospective retirement for physical disability, and I, with suitable rank and footloose, was perhaps a natural choice. The relief took place on the 1st of April 1947. There being no adequate naval quarters available for assignment to me, Floride and I took up residence in a small suite in the Drake Hotel at 56th Street and Park Avenue, while Mary Kent remained with her sister in Newport. Although I was given a special allowance, this arrangement involved quite a little additional personal expense. My Army and Air Force opposite numbers, however, were assigned pleasant quarters at the old Army post of Fort Totten, which in bygone years had constituted part of the defenses of New York City.

I found a great deal of serious work going on in the Military Staff Committee, at least insofar as the delegations of the three Western powers and China were concerned. But there was also a considerable amount of social activity devoted to the commendable aim of establishing friendly international relationships. Between the British, the French, the Chinese, and ourselves, there was no question as to this. The Soviet delegation, however, was proving to be an unknown quantity, although many members individually seemed to be quite amicable.

Admiral and Mrs. Turner kindly gave a large welcoming reception for us. There, Floride and I were able to meet the members of the Military Staff Committee delegation and their wives as well as many members of the civilian delegations to the Security Council. The senior member of the Russian Military Staff Committee delegation was Lieutenant General Vasiliev, who was reputed to have been an officer of the Imperial Guard prior to the Russian Revolution. He was a highly educated, very intelligent, and exceedingly quick-witted gentleman—quite a different type from his colleagues of the other services. But all three were quite affable. Vice Admiral Bogdenko, more of a peasant type, proclaimed that he "liked Manhattan because he lived in Manhattan." I never became sure whether he knew which end of a ship went first. The Russian airman, General Sharapov, seemed rather colorless, but had the redeeming feature of possessing the only Russian wife who could speak any English. We soon learned that none of the Russians ever accepted a social invitation unless it included a comrade. They always had to travel in pairs. And a junior officer wearing an army or a naval uniform might really be a member of the MVD, the secret police.

It was evident on the occasion of that first reception that our Russian opposite numbers had been studying my background. General Vasiliev told me that he had been reading about the landing in Morocco and stated that he was particularly interested in my decision on the morning of November 7, 1942, to proceed with the landing as scheduled, in spite of the reports of rather unfavorable weather. He said, "Did you decide that without asking General Patton?" "Yes, General," said I. "I, of course, informed the general, but I was the seaman and it was my responsibility to weigh the risk of landing under the prophesied surf conditions against the disadvantage of a delayed landing and the very serious risk of submarine attack while cruising off-shore awaiting better weather." My new friend shrugged his shoulders almost in disbelief. It was apparently incomprehensible to a Russian general that an admiral could make a decision that would affect a general.

The Chinese delegation was very interesting to me. With the exception of General of the Army Ho, a gentleman of the old Mandarin class, they were almost all quite fluent in English. Not being a "China sailor," I had not realized the difference in Chinese dialects until we later discovered that the pretty little English-speaking

Cantonese wife of the general's aide could not act as interpreter for her husband's chief at a dinner party, because she neither spoke nor understood Mandarin. The naval representative was a pleasant young captain named Chow, who was promoted to rear admiral in 1948, and then relieved by a Commodore Kao. The air representative was a Lieutenant General Mow, a colorful personality who entertained lavishly and was on a first name basis with many of our own air officers. I well remember a magnificent Chinese style dinner which he gave for our delegation. Toward the end of my tour, he disappeared from the delegation without relief. It was reported that he had been charged by Chiang Kai-Shek's government with some misappropriation of official funds, but this was hard to believe.

The French delegation, throughout my tour, was headed by the very able and affable Général de Division, Pierre Billotte, whose father also, in World War I, had been a distinguished officer of the French army. Initially, the naval representative was the rather junior but capable Capitaine de Frégate, Commander Marchal. In 1948, his place was taken by the delightful Contre Amiral Wietzel.

The British and the U.S. delegations were, rather naturally, the most closely linked of the Western allies. The British naval representative, who also doubled in brass as the Royal Navy's representative in Washington on the Joint Chiefs of Staff Committee, was Admiral Sir Henry Moore,[2] the hero of the North Cape action. He had to commute back and forth to attend the Military Staff Committee meetings which were held at least once each week. Later, when he was relieved of his Washington duty by my friend of *Rodney-Bismarck* fame, Admiral Sir Frederick Dalrymple-Hamilton, Rear Admiral William B. Slayter[3] took over the Military Staff Committee duty. Admiral Slayter was relieved in August 1948 by Rear Admiral Lord Ashbourne.[4] Both of those gentlemen and their wives became close personal friends. Admiral Moore, a widower, before he returned to Britain, was married in Washington to the widow of Vice Admiral Wilkinson,[5] who, as a commander, was the executive officer of the *Indianapolis* at the time I assumed that command.

The British army was represented at first by General Sir E. L. Morris,[6] and later by General Sir R. L. McCreery,[7] whom I knew well from Salerno days. He was the commander of the British Northern Attack Group in that operation. Naturally, we often seized the opportunity to reminiscence. Air Chief Marshal Sir Guy Garrod[8] was my genial Royal Air Force opposite number for my first year. He was followed by Air Vice Marshal Gibbs.[9]

My first U.S. Army opposite number was another old friend, Lieutenant General Matthew B. Ridgway,[10] the air-borne general who had ridden my flagship with me to Sicily where a detachment of his division was to fly in overhead. When he was transferred in July 1948, Lieutenant General Willis D. Crittenberger[11] took his place.

When I first reported, Brigadier General Charles Cabell[12] was the representative for the U.S. Air Force, but when my erstwhile Italian and European colleague,

General McNarney, reported a few months later, General Cabell stepped down to the assistant's position. In October 1947, General McNarney was succeeded by Lieutenant General Hubert R. Harmon,[13] who had distinguished himself in the Pacific theater. Naval air was well represented by my own successive chiefs of staff, Rear Admirals Ballentine,[14] McMahon,[15] and Harrill.[16]

Article 46 of the UN Charter states that "plans for the application of armed force shall be made by the Security Council, with the assistance of the Military Staff Committee." At the time I reported to the Military Staff Committee, it was operating under a directive from the Security Council to submit a general plan covering the availability, organization, and employment of UN armed forces when such became necessary for the maintenance or restoration of international peace and security. In order that the reader may understand the problem with which the Military Staff Committee was faced, it is necessary to quote or paraphrase the pertinent articles of the Charter by which all members of the UN are supposed to be, and are, legally bound.

Paragraph 1 of Article 43 reads: "All Members of the United Nations, in order to contribute to the maintenance of international peace and security, undertake to make available to the Security Council, on its call and in accordance with a special agreement, or agreements, armed forces, assistance, and facilities, including rights of passage, necessary for the maintenance of international peace and security." The paragraph following states that these agreements shall govern the numbers and types of forces, their degree of readiness, and the nature of the facilities and assistance to be provided. The Military Staff Committee is also called upon to recommend the nature of the aforementioned agreements.

Meetings of the Military Staff Committee were held originally at least once a week, and sometimes, at the call of the chairman, more often. As in the Security Council, the chairmanship rotated monthly between the member delegations. As senior officer of the U.S. delegation, this responsibility devolved upon me when it became our turn. These meetings were usually very long and tiring, because we lacked the equipment for simultaneous interpretation, and one had to listen to each item under discussion in each of four different languages. We were thankful that the British and ourselves spoke a common language. The French was not difficult to follow, and I even picked up a bit of Russian, particularly the often used "nyet," and "Amerikanski delegazi," which, when I heard it, alerted me to our being "taken apart." The Chinese, of course, was entirely beyond my ken.

Our time between meetings was taken up in preparing our proposals for the accomplishment of the Security Council directive, in attendance on meetings of the Security Council as advisers to our delegation to that body, and in conferences with our civilian delegation. We similarly attended meetings of the General Assembly during the annual meetings of that body. We worked hard on plans for a UN force until, at last, after an expenditure of much time, thought, and effort, it became plainly evident that the Soviet delegation had no intention of agreeing to anything that would make practicable the establishment of an effective UN force.

It was clear that no UN force that was organized as provided by the Charter could hope to cope with any threat to the peace involving one of the great powers. Therefore, the problem appeared to be the establishment of a force or forces which could be brought quickly into action for the prevention or control of minor conflagrations or brushfire wars in any part of the world. This led to the concept of a fire brigade sort of organization, whereby a military force of about division strength, with appropriate naval and air support to afford prompt movement and ability to land against opposition, would be in constant readiness. As in the case of a municipal fire department, quick action to meet an emergency would require distribution of units throughout the area to be covered—in this case, the world. And, following the fire department parallel still further, a unit initially employed could be reinforced as necessary from other areas.

This idea received approval of the Western allies in the Military Staff Committee and also of the Chinese delegation. It was thought that the military, naval, and air units made available for this UN assignment would normally be maintained in their home lands, but when called into action could utilize the most convenient bases in member nations, as provided by the Charter.

The above ideas were drafted in the form of general principles for discussion and hoped-for adoption by the Military Staff Committee, and ultimate submission to the Security Council for approval. No attempt was made to go into details other than a consideration of the general areas in which it might be desirable and practicable to establish the proposed peace-keeping units—for instance, the Americas, Europe, the Near East, and the Far East.

It soon became apparent that in the Military Staff Committee, where a unanimous vote was mandatory, the Soviet delegation was to be the stumbling block. The proposed draft of principles governing the organization and employment of UN peace-keeping had to be taken up and discussed, and adopted or rejected, paragraph by paragraph. Arguments were often lengthy, and in view of the repetitions in various languages, time-consuming and frustrating. Sometimes a paragraph agreed to at one meeting would be rejected by the Russians at a following meeting, after they had had time to get the word from higher authority. They were quite impervious to logical arguments. For instance, at one meeting, unanimous agreement had been obtained for a paragraph that member nations should make available bases necessary for the support of UN peace-keeping forces. At the following meeting, the Soviet chairman withdrew the assent of his delegation, stating as a reason that the Charter said nothing about bases. In vain did I argue that the Charter specified facilities and what was a base if not a facility. The only answer I got was "Nyet! The Charter says nothing about bases." So naturally those who were trying to make the Military Staff Committee an effective body got nowhere.

The Military Staff Committee gradually degenerated into nothing but a debating society. It is still in existence but does nothing but meet perfunctorily every two weeks and promptly adjourn. It is interesting to speculate what might have been the effect on the history of the world during the last fifteen years had a plan such as the one proposed been approved and put into effect.

The most rewarding features of my two-year assignment to the United Nations were the contacts gained with leading participants in world affairs, the experience of attendance at sessions of the Security Council and two annual sessions of the General Assembly, and the pleasant relationships with colleagues in our own and other delegations to the UN. Furthermore, it led to many pleasant events of personal interest.

During one of my visits to Paris in 1946, my erstwhile friend of Algiers, Admiral Moreau, who came of a Burgundy family and who, after the liberation of France, had sent to me in Naples two cases of very fine wine, told me of a society they had in Burgundy called *Le Confrérie du Tastevin*, or the Brotherhood of the Winetaster. He asked me if I would be willing to accept honorary membership. I said that I would be honored, but having in mind that I might be asked to pass judgment on samples of wine, I doubted my ability to meet the test. His reply was that my only test would be to go down into the cave and know to enjoy what you drink. Unfortunately, I had to return to the United States before there was a meeting at which I could be invested with my *tastevin*. The *tastevin* is a shallow silver cup used by wine tasters in testing wine drawn from casks in cellars, which in the old days were lighted only by flares. The shallowness and shining silver permits the taster to judge the color of the wine. Then, bringing the cup toward his lips, he tests the bouquet, another important factor. Finally, he sips the contents. The badge of the *Confrérie* is one of these *tastevins* hung around the neck by a red and gold ribbon, colors representative of the red and white wines.

It happened that there was a branch chapter of the *Confrérie* in New York City, which was holding a dinner at the Hotel Pierre that spring of 1947 for the initiation of several American wine connoisseurs. When it became known that I was to be in New York, my *parrains* (godfathers), Admiral Moreau and his brother-in-law Baron Thenard, proprietor of one of the finest vineyards, arranged that I should be included. It was quite an affair, presided over by the grand chancellor in the United States and other officials of the order in their picturesque robes, and attended by such dignitaries as the French ambassador to the United Nations and the French consul general.

Before entering the banquet hall, the members and guests gathered in a large anteroom for an aperitif—no cocktail! That would spoil the taste for the food and the wines to follow. For the same reason, *on ne fume pas* until after dessert. The dinner was a magnificent example of French cuisine of many courses with a different burgundy wine for each one. It should be understood that all this did not give one any feeling of alcoholic exhilaration, merely the pleasant feeling of enjoying to the utmost what one ate and what one drank. At the close of the meal, the chef was called up from the kitchen to be congratulated and kissed on each cheek.

The ceremony of initiation for the new chevaliers consisted of being called up to the dais at the head of the room and, after swearing to defend the wines of Burgundy, being dubbed on each shoulder with the root of a Burgundy grapevine and, finally, having the ribbon with his *tastevin* hung around his neck. This was a thoroughly enjoyable occasion, and I could not help but feel greatly honored at being thus accepted into an ancient order.

Not long afterwards, on June 21, 1947, I had the pleasure of escorting daughter Mary Kent up the center aisle of historic Trinity Church in Newport and giving her in marriage to the fine young man she had selected to become her husband, none other than the Lieutenant Commander Norton she had first met in Copenhagen. The wedding reception was held at the officers' club at the naval base. The get away was distinctly nautical and a bit unusual. The bridegroom, who at the time was the aide to the rear admiral commanding the base, had secretly parked his car across the bay at Jamestown. But I had a car standing at the club entrance, which looked out on the water. When the bridal couple finally made their departure under the usual shower of confetti, instead of getting into the waiting car, they dashed down the dock and into the admiral's barge, which promptly took off across the bay under full power, thus defying all pursuit.

The summer and fall were pleasantly spent in New York, where we found much to do. It was fun—as long as we were condemned to hotel life—to poke around on foot and try new places for dinner. Doing so, we found a number of "holes in the wall"— little French or Italian cafes where the food was good and inexpensive and the clientele interesting. Also, we were able to do a bit of theatergoing, especially as I was in somewhat of a favored position to obtain tickets. I particularly enjoyed taking Admiral Dalrymple-Hamilton to see *Mr. Roberts*, out of which we both got a tremendous kick. We viewed it from the second row, center, and between the acts were invited in to meet the star.

Our stay in New York also gave me a splendid opportunity to become better acquainted with my New York Hewitt relatives and to see something of my father's youngest and only surviving brother, my favorite bachelor uncle, who resided at the near-by University Club, which, under his sponsorship, I had joined. Unfortunately, one evening that summer I had to have him taken to the hospital where he died a few days later.

When Christmas rolled around, we were unable to get to Newport to spend that holiday with the rest of the family as we had planned, because of a severe blizzard that tied New York City up tight, making automobile traffic in and out of the city impossible, and we had too much baggage to attempt to go by train. However, we did get away a couple of days later to spend a week or ten days in Newport in a friend's house, which we were able to sublet for the purpose. We were able to entertain not only our own families but both of our daughters' mothers-in-law.

The dean of the Hewitt family in New York was my father's first cousin, Edward R. Hewitt, an eminent engineer, chemist, and inventor, and also an author of several very readable books. He was a widower who lived alone in the old family house in Gramercy Park, which was full of gadgets which he had devised to make life easier for himself. He was an extremely interesting personality who could converse knowledgeably on almost any subject. As a grandson of Peter Cooper, he had always taken an interest in Cooper Union and was a member of its board of directors. In the spring of 1948, he gave a reception at the Cooper Union to which he invited all the Hewitt and Cooper kin who could be located. Some two hundred attended, and it was a lot of fun. Both my daughters and their husbands came. All the in-laws seemed to enjoy the occasion as much as those of us who were meeting relatives for the first time and seeing those with whom we had been out of contact for years. The diagrams of the different branches of the families, prepared by Edward R.'s brilliant daughter, Candace, and posted on a side wall, drew the attention of all. It was indeed a memorable and unusual occasion.

NOTES
1. Warren R. Austin (1877–1962). Diplomat, politician, lawyer and senator from Vermont, 1931–1946. He was appointed permanent U.S. delegate to the UN in 1946 and held that position until he retired in 1953.
2. Sir Henry Ruthven Moore (1886–1978). Vice Admiral, Royal Navy.
3. William R. Slayter (1896–1971). Admiral, Royal Navy. CO, HMS *Liverpool*, 1941; CO, HMS *Newfoundland*, 1942; Chief of Staff, Home Fleet, 1943; CO, HMS *Excellent*, 1945; naval representative, Great Britain, UN Military Staff Committee, 1947; Commander-in-Chief, East Indies States, 1952–1954.
4. Edward R. Ashbourne, Third Baron (1901–1983). Vice Admiral, Royal Navy. He served in World War I and in World War II where he took part in the invasion of Sicily. He was CO, *Ariadne*, 1943–1945, and Third Submarine Flotilla, 1945, and British naval representative on the UN Military Staff Committee, 1949–1950.
5. Theodore Wilkinson (1888–1946). Vice Admiral. U.S. Naval Academy, Class of 1909.
6. Edwin L. Morris (1889–1970). General, British Army. He was chief of the general staff in India, 1942–1944, Commander-in-Chief, Northern Command, 1944–1946, and British army representative on the UN Military Staff Committee, 1946–1948.
7. Richard L. McCreery (1898–1967). General, British Army. He served in World War I in France and in World War II as chief of the general staff, Middle East, 1942; Commander, Eighth Army, Italy, 1944–1945, and Commander-in-Chief, British Occupation Forces, Austria, 1945–1946. He was the British army representative on the UN Military Staff Committee, 1948–1949.
8. Sir Alfred Guy Roland Garrod (1891–1965). Air Chief Marshal, RAF. He was Commander-in-Chief, RAF, Mediterranean and Middle East, 1945, and head of the RAF delegation, Washington, DC.
9. Gerald E. Gibbs (1896–1992). Air Vice Marshal, RAF. Director of Overseas Operations, Air Ministry, 1942–1943; senior air staff officer, HQ, Third Tactical Air Force, SE Asia, 1943–1944; senior air officer, HQ, RAF Burma, 1945; senior air officer, HQ, RAF Air Transport Command, 1946–1948; RAF member, UN Military Staff Committee, 1948.
10. Matthew Ridgway (1895–1993). General, U.S. Army. He graduated from the U.S. Military Academy, Class of 1917. During World War II, he served in Italy, France, and Germany and was commander of the European theatre. From 1946 to 1948 he was the U.S. representative to the UN's Military Staff Committee. During the Korean War, he was Supreme Allied Commander and later held the same post in Japan. In 1952, he was Supreme Allied Commander, NATO. He served as Army Chief of Staff prior to retirement in 1955.
11. Willis D. Crittenberger (1890–1980). Lieutenant General, U.S. Army. He graduated from the U.S. Military Academy in 1913; served in World War II in command of the IV Army Corps in the Italian campaign that successfully drove the Germans north of Rome and led to their surrender in Italy in April 1945. After heading the Caribbean Command for three years, he was named principal military advisor to the U.S. delegation to the UN in 1948.
12. Charles B. Cabell (1903–1971). General, U.S. Air Force. He graduated from the U.S. Military Academy, Class of 1925. He served in the European theatre during World War II. In December 1945, he was assigned to the UN Military Staff Committee, where he remained on duty as deputy and representative until 1947.
13. Hubert R. Harmon (1892–1957). General, U.S. Air Force. He graduated from the U.S. Military Academy in 1915 and served in the South Pacific theatre in World War II. He was the U.S. Air Force representative on the UN Military Staff Committee.
14. John J. Ballentine (1896–1970). Admiral. U.S. Naval Academy, Class of 1918.
15. Fred W. McMahon (1898–1986). Vice Admiral. U.S. Naval Academy, Class of 1920.
16. William K. Harrill (1892–1962). Vice Admiral. U.S. Naval Academy, Class of 1914.

Vice Admiral Bernard L. Austin, president of the Naval War College, General Mark Clark, USA (Ret.) and Admiral H. Kent Hewitt, USN (Ret.) at the College, ca. 1961. (Naval Historical Collection)

XXI The United Nations and Retirement, 1948–1949

The old United States Naval Hospital, adjacent to the Brooklyn Navy Yard at the time, was being transferred to a new and larger establishment at St. Albans on Long Island. This made the buildings of the old hospital, including the quarters of the medical officer in command, available for another naval purpose. In consequence to my repeated demand for quarters, the commanding officer's fine house was being assigned to me upon completion of certain repairs and renovations which were expected to be completed in the latter part of the summer.

In view of this prospect, I gave up my apartment at the Drake and rented the residence of a Hackensack friend who was to be away until my Brooklyn quarters were ready. Thus, I had a pleasant summer in old familiar surroundings, commuting back and forth to my office in my official car. We were able to occupy our Brooklyn quarters in time to celebrate our thirty-fifth wedding anniversary happily in our garden there with many old Hackensack friends and relatives, with whom I had many friendly conversations.

France

Hardly had we gotten settled in Brooklyn when I learned that I would be going to Paris in connection with the annual meeting of the General Assembly, which was to be held there that year. I left New York by ship with others of the U.S. delegation and some of the Secretariat in time to be on hand for the opening. The session convened in early October at the beautiful Palais de Chaillot on the right bank of the Seine, immediately across from the Eiffel Tower. The U.S. delegation was put up at the Hotel Crillon. The meetings of the Assembly were colorful, with its representatives from all over the world, many in their native costumes. I particularly remember Prince Faisal,[1] a fine looking Arab with whom I had several friendly conversations. However, in spite of all the deliberations, as usual, little was accomplished.

The social events connected with the Assembly were too many to be recounted here, but I enjoyed them and also seeing again my friends of Algiers days. Floride joined me shortly after my arrival, having decided to come over on her own. The embassy loaned me a car so that I could meet her in Le Havre and drive her, bag and baggage, back to Paris. What a good time we had once more in that beautiful city!

Being able to take a few days away from the Assembly by permission of Ambassador Austin, we were able to take advantage of a very thoughtful invitation extended to me by the French Navy, given to me at the time I made my official call on its chief, Amiral Lemonnier, at the Ministère de la Marine. This was a trip to Provence in order that Floride might see for the first time the scenes of our landing and that I might revisit them.

Floride not wishing to fly, we took the night train to Marseilles, where we were met in the morning by a fine-looking English-speaking naval aide with two cars, one for us and one for our baggage. After breakfast with the senior naval commander there and seeing the principal sights of the city and harbor, we journeyed slowly east along the coast toward Toulon. There we became the guests at the Amirauté of the Prefect Maritime, Contre Amiral Lambert, the bluff old sea dog who in 1943 had commanded the battleship *Richelieu*. It was tremendously interesting to me to see how Toulon had been restored and to scale once more the heights of St. Mandrier, the fortified island which had given us so much trouble.

After two comfortable nights at the Amirauté, we continued east along the beautiful Riviera coast, seeing the battle monuments dedicated in my presence at the first anniversary and the city of St. Tropez and its gulf, which had been the scene of so much of our activity. After having lunch at a pleasant café in St. Maxime, we drove on through Cannes to Nice where we were put up for the night in a fine hotel on the beach front. Gone were the concrete pillboxes camouflaged as bars and restaurants, which I had encountered there four years before.

The following day we drove on through Villefranche where in 1914 I had witnessed the mobilization for World War I, and thence to Monte Carlo where we spent the next night. In my opinion, except for the Amalfi drive, there is no drive that can compare with the one along the Upper Corniche.

We returned to Paris more or less as we had come, and there I resumed my duties with our UN delegation. Among others at the Crillon were Mr. and Mrs. John Foster Dulles, whom we had met in London in February 1946 when the UN was just getting started. They were delightful persons who had become most congenial friends, and we saw quite a bit of them. What a surprise it was to us all in our own and other delegations when the news of the presidential election that November reached us! Everyone, regardless of his political persuasion, seemed confident that Dewey[2] would be elected. We attended a luncheon that Wednesday in honor of Mr. Dulles, given by Carlos Rómulo[3] of the Philippines, at which I am sure the host planned to congratulate him as the prospective secretary of state. Nevertheless, that party was thoroughly enjoyed.

One of the outstanding events of our stay in France was a weekend visit to the Burgundy country and our participation in a grand reunion of the *Confrérie du Tastevin* at the Clos de Vougeot, the headquarters of the order. We were to be the guests of the Baron and Baroness Thenard at their beautiful chateau in the country near Dijon. Admiral and Madame Moreau accompanied us in the car which drove us to Dijon, but they stayed with friends in the city.

The ancient chateau, magnificent and indescribably beautiful, was approached through a stately tree-bordered lane. We were received with great cordiality by our host and hostess, who made us feel very much at home, or at least as much at home as we could feel amidst all that magnificence. We found both the baron and the baroness to be very real people. Among the many stories they told us was that of their only son, whose grave was shown us. He had been in the underground and, through the treachery of an informer, had been caught and killed by the Nazis as he was trying to reach his home one dark night. His body was deposited on the doorstep for his parents to find the next day. Later, the chateau was occupied by a German general and his staff, and the family was forced to live in an upper floor. The baroness showed me with pride the homemade American flag which had been secretly pieced together in the attic with whatever materials could be found by her servants and herself, in expectation of the eventual arrival of the Americans. It was ready and hung out when they did come. It made me happy to realize that the liberating troops were undoubtedly from the Seventh Army, in whose landing I had had a hand.

I am glad that I am one of those who has had the honor and experience of attending such an affair as was the reunion at the Clos de Vougeot. It was very special because ladies were invited—not even Madame Moreau had been to one before. We arrived in the yard just at dusk to be greeted by a crowd of gentlemen wearing *tastevins*, and swarming around the entrance to the ancient building which housed the cave and the wine-making apparatus. Fortunately, I had brought my *tastevin* with me from America and now had it on. But one of the welcoming committee insisted on taking it away from me and substituting another, implying that there was something wrong with mine. This seemed strange, since mine was inscribed with my name and the date of my initiation, but I could not demur.

We were finally ushered into the ground floor or cellar of the building which proved to be a large, dimly lighted room with sawdust on the floor. At one end there was a large dais, and around the side were ancient winepresses and wooden wine casks. There were several long rows of narrow tables made of planks on saw horses, so arranged that all the guests seated at them on wooden benches could observe the dais. Our *parrains* and their wives and Floride and I were seated as a group, three each on opposite sides of the table so that we could converse readily. In front of us at each place was an imposing array of wine glasses, from short to tall. We were attended by waiters costumed as workers in the vineyard, which they undoubtedly were. And on the dais, similarly costumed, was a chorus called the *Cadettes de Bourgogne*, who entertained us throughout the meal with what we would call the old songs of ancient Burgundy.

I would hate to say how many different courses we had, each one fit to have been prepared by Escoffier[4] himself. And the wines—a different one for each course—were exquisite. After the dessert, I found myself with one or two others, including the Swedish ambassador to France, called to the dais which was now presided over by the grand chancellor of the order, with his robed assistants. To my surprise, my *tastevin* was removed, I was again dubbed with the root of a vine, and my original *tastevin* was returned and hung around my neck, but with a broader ribbon. I had been promoted from *chevalier* to *grand officier*.

After the pleasant ceremony and a little more music, we listened to a discussion by a panel of experts as to which of the wines served were worthy of special mention. Madame Moreau asked Floride which of the wines she preferred. She replied that she knew little of wines, but she picked two which she thought were particularly delicious. To her amazement and that of the others, these were the very two that had been picked by the experts as being particularly noteworthy. My wife certainly "made character" with our French friends.

The General Assembly adjourned early enough for us to reach New York by ship in ample time for Christmas. Although it was the season when bad weather can begin to be expected in the North Atlantic, we had a very pleasant trip. As interesting deck-chair neighbors on the promenade deck, Floride and I had Senator and Mrs. Robert Taft,[5] who were returning from a trip abroad.

A happy Christmas was spent in our Brooklyn quarters, made particularly so by the presence of several members of our immediate family.

1949

Since I was reaching the statuary retirement age on February 11, my retirement was set for the first of March. I was then to be relieved of my duty with the Military Staff Committee by Vice Admiral Bernard H. Bieri. Consequently, much of January and February was spent in preparing for that event. There were final physical examinations at the naval hospital at St. Albans, a trip to Washington to appear before the Naval Retiring Board, and a hasty trip to Vermont to check on the remodeling work being done on the old farm house we had purchased the previous fall as a future home.

The meetings of the Military Staff Committee went on as usual, but also, as usual, nothing of importance was being accomplished. But at my last meeting, I was the recipient of a number of kind remarks from each of our fellow delegations. Even the Soviet delegation, in the person of General Vasiliev, expressed its pleasure at our past association and its regret at my departure.

The final event was a reception and dinner given in my honor by General Crittenberger at the officers club at Fort Totten, to which all the delegates to the Military Staff Committee and their wives were invited. Although it was after sunset when Floride and I arrived at the club, I received the unusual honor of a guard and band paraded after dark. After the rendering of the honors and the inspection of the guard by me, I was serenaded with "Anchors Aweigh," a particularly thoughtful touch. As I have mentioned before, that tune is not only the Naval Academy march, but that of my own Class of 1907, to which it was originally dedicated. As a memento of the never-to-be-forgotten occasion, I have a handsomely bound volume containing the signatures and good wishes of the guests.

Thus ends the account of my formative years and my forty-six years of active service in the Navy. As I look back at them, I realize how fortunate I have been in having parents who endeavored to bring me up to respect the principles which were theirs and to have been able to enter a naval career which I have loved from start to finish. While far from lucrative, it has been deeply rewarding in many other ways, which to me, at least, seems of greater import. And there are many other matters in which I deem myself very, very fortunate, not the least of them being my marriage and the success of the major war operations in which I became involved.

So long as I can be "on deck" and able to "navigate," I look forward to a continued happy life in retirement.

NOTES

1 Prince Faisal (1905–1975). Crown prince of Saudi Arabia, he became king in 1965. He represented Saudi Arabia at the San Francisco Conference establishing the UN and at meetings of the General Assembly.

2 Thomas E. Dewey (1902–1971). Politician, lawyer, and governor of New York, 1942–1954. He ran for president on the Republican ticket in 1944 and 1948 and lost both elections.

3 Carlos Rómulo (1899–1985). Philippine diplomat. His newspaper articles predicting Japanese actions in World War II won him a Pulitzer Prize in 1941. He served as an aide to General Douglas MacArthur during the war and rose to the rank of brigadier general in 1944. He was appointed a delegate to the UN in 1946 and became president of the General Assembly in 1949. From 1953–1961, he was ambassador to the United States.

4 Georges A. Escoffier (1846–1935). French chef and author of several cookbooks. He was chef at the Savoy and Carleton hotels in London where he earned a worldwide reputation for his cuisine.

5 Robert Taft (1889–1953). U.S. senator from Ohio. He opposed U.S. entry into the UN.

INDEX

Abbett, Henry J., 86–87, 91, 98
Aix en Provence, France, 202, 206
Alexander, Albert V., 223, 252, 264
Alexander, Harold R., 188–189, 197, 209, 218
Alexandria, Egypt, 215
Algiers, Algeria, 29, 178–181, 184–186, 188–189, 192–197, 205, 210–211, 215–216, 220, 272, 277
Allen, Burrell C., 70
Allen, Terry, 190, 197
Alphand, Hervé, 178–179, 196
Althouse, Albert, 70–72
Amoy, China, 28
Amsterdam, Holland, 228, 252–253
Anderson, Edwin A. G., 59–61, 63–64
Anderson, Jonathan W., 138, 141, 147
Anderson, Robert, 1, 11
Anderson, Walter, 260, 264
Andes Mountains, 24, 108
Andrews, Philip, 64, 72
Ankara, Turkey, 237–238
Annapolis, MD, 3–8, 16, 31, 41–42, 44–45, 62, 83, 85–86
Antibes, France, 200
Antwerp, Belgium, 220, 252–253
Anzio, Italy, 147, 177, 179, 181, 183, 185, 187, 189, 191, 193, 195, 197, 264
Argentia, Newfoundland, 121, 123, 125, 146
Argyll, Duke of, 135
Arroyo de Rio, Carlos, 108
Aruba, 135
Arzew, Algeria, 181–182, 185–187, 216
Ashbourne, Edward R., 269, 275
Astor, Viscount Waldorf, 225, 229, 231
Atatürk, Mustafa Kemal, 237, 247
Athens, Greece, 29–30, 215, 264
Atlantic City, NJ, 44
Auboyneau, Philippe, 200, 202, 204, 206, 211
Auckland, New Zealand, 18, 26
Austin, Warren, 267, 275
Avignon, France, 202
Azores, 67–68, 119, 129, 152–153, 219

Bachman, Leo A., 129, 131, 146, 162
Baja California, 24

Badger, Oscar, 86–87, 89, 98
Balboa, Panama, 70, 107–109, 117
Ballentine, John J., 270, 275
Baltimore, MD, 42, 85–86, 129, 131, 216
Barjot, Pierre, 229, 231
Barnes, Stanley M., 188, 197, 218
Bartlett, Owen, 66, 72
Baruch, Herman, 254–256, 258–259, 264
Bastedo, Paul H., 92, 98
Bathurst, Gambia, 178
Batista, Fulgencio, 55, 61
Battet, Robert, 217
Baudouin, Prince (of Belgium), 252, 264
Bellinger, Patrick Niesson L., 115, 123
Beni Saf, Algeria, 182, 185, 193
Bennett, Andrew C., 110, 112, 116, 179
Berchtesgaden, Germany, 261
Bergesen, Alfred O., 227, 231
Berlin, Germany, 197, 221, 228, 261
Bermuda, 68–69, 118–121, 123, 142, 147, 178, 220, 225, 229
Berrien, Frank D., 13, 17
Bertil, Prince (of Sweden), 251–252, 264
Bidault, Georges A., 244, 247
Bieri, Bernard, 170, 175, 280
Birkett, Sir Norman, 131, 147
Bizerte, Tunisia, 184, 188–189, 193, 203, 205, 211, 216
Blake, Geoffrey, 223, 231
Boettiger, Anna Roosevelt, 216, 230
Bohr, Niels, 226–227, 231
Boit, Julian, 129, 146
Bonaparte, Napoleon, 202
Bône, Algeria, 188
Boston, MA, 17, 30, 35, 107, 117–118, 123
Boston Navy Yard, 14, 121
Bradley, Omar, 190, 197
Brainard, Roland E., 126, 129, 146
Bremen, Germany, 220–221
Bremerton (WA) Navy Yard, 102–106
Brest, France, 65–68, 72, 207
Bridport, England, 134
Bristol, Arthur L., 125–126, 146

Bristol, England, 132, 136
British Guiana, 17, 121
Brooke, Alan, 234, 245, 247
Brooklyn Navy Yard, 277, 280
Brookman, Harold R., 129, 146, 178, 202
Brown, Wilson, 215, 230
Brownson, Willard H., 5, 11
Brussels, Belgium, 220
Bryant, Carleton F., 170, 172, 175
Buchanan, Franklin, 4, 11
Buenos Aires, Argentina, 22, 86, 93–94, 96, 98
Byrnes, James F., 225, 250

Cabell, Charles B., 269–270, 275
Caffrey, Jefferson, 207, 211, 216, 220, 222, 262
Cairo, Egypt, 29
Callao, Peru, 23–24, 31, 109
Camp Edwards, MA, 137, 182
Cannes, France, 200, 217, 278
Cannon, John K., 162, 175
Cape Verde Islands, 152–153
Capri, Italy, 241
Caribbean Sea, 59, 66, 72, 107, 116–117, 119, 123, 149, 156, 275
Carmona, Antonio Oscar de, 255, 257–259, 264
Casablanca Conference, 177, 181
Casablanca, Morocco, 139–142, 148, 154, 156, 177, 179–181, 184, 186–187, 194, 197, 203, 206, 210, 216, 219, 226, 229
Casco Bay, ME, 122–123, 125, 142
Cassady, John H., 254–255, 259–260, 264
Castro, Fidel, 55, 61
Cavite, Philippines, 27
Chaplaine, Vance, 110, 112, 117
Charleston, SC, 11, 39, 47–48, 86, 97, 107, 112
Charleston (SC) Navy Yard, 39, 118
Cherbourg, France, 33–34, 37, 146, 220
Cherchell, Algeria, 182, 184–185, 193
Chesapeake Bay, 85–86, 127, 129, 133, 137, 144, 149
China, 28, 211, 230, 267–268
Christian X, King (of Denmark), 226, 231
Churchill, Winston, 121–123, 147, 177, 208, 212, 215, 230–231
Civil War, U.S. (1861–1865), 1
Clark, Mark, 104, 112, 134, 185, 195, 260, 276
Clarke, William P. O., 130, 147
Clay, Lucius, 221, 228, 231, 250
Cleaves, Willis E., 97–98
Colombo, Ceylon, 28–29
Coman, Robert G., 117, 123
Conolly, Richard L., 181–182, 185, 187, 191, 193–194, 196, 260, 262, 264
Connally, Thomas T., 233, 247
Connecticut College, 83, 106
Conrad, Anna (grandmother), 1, 11
Cooper, Alfred Duff, 221, 231
Cooper, Lady Diana Duff, 221
Copenhagen, Denmark, 225–228, 249–252, 273
Corbesier, Antoine J., 5, 11
Corcovado Mountain, 22, 31

Coronado, CA, 24, 81
Corregidor, 27
Corsica, 204, 206, 210
Cowes, England, 134
Cristobal, Panama, 107, 117
Crittenberger, Willis D., 269, 275, 280
Cuba, 37, 46, 48–49, 51–52, 54–61, 64
Cunningham, Andrew B., 178, 180, 188–189, 192–194, 199, 201, 214–215, 223, 225, 234, 244–245, 262
Cunningham, John H. D., 202, 204, 208, 209–211, 214–215, 218, 221, 225, 239, 245, 252
Curteis, Alban T. B., 173, 175

Dahlquist, John E., 221, 231
Dakar, Senegal, 129, 141–142, 151, 153, 218
Dalrymple-Hamilton, Frederick H. G., 118, 121, 123, 126, 269, 273
Damien de Veuster, Joseph (Father Joseph), 25, 31
Darlan, Francois, 163, 166, 175, 184, 206
Darwin, Charles, 108, 112
Davidson, Lyal A., 126, 140, 146, 155, 190, 195, 199, 201–202, 204
Davis, Charles H., 15–17
Dawson, William, 107–108, 112
De Gaulle, Charles, 183, 197, 202, 206, 211
Devers, Jacob L., 199, 202, 206–207, 209–210
Dewey, George, 27, 31
Dewey, Thomas, 278, 281
Dieppe, Raid on, 134
Dijon, France, 206–207, 279
Doenitz, Karl, 234, 247
Dressling, Richard J., 218, 230
Dubose, Laurence T., 190
Dulles, John Foster, 225, 231, 278
Dunkirk, France, 105
Dunn, James, 233

Eastport, ME, 8
Eddy, Manton S., 127, 146
Edgar, Campbell D., 137, 147, 206
Edinburgh, Scotland, 262–263
Edson, Stephen, 129
Edward VIII, King (of England), 96
Eisenhower, Dwight D., 104, 112, 134, 143, 177–178, 180, 183, 187–189, 194, 196–197, 207, 214, 220, 262–263
ELAS, 208
Elba, 202
Ely, Louis B., 130, 147
Emmet, Robert R. M., 120, 123, 126, 141, 155
English, Robert A. J., 130, 146, 178, 182, 206–207
Escoffier, Georges A., 280–281
Evans, Douglas S., 146
Evans, Robley D., 5, 11, 20–21, 23, 25, 31

Faisal, Prince (of Saudi Arabia), 277, 281
Farouk, King (of Egypt), 215, 230
Farragut, David, 6, 11
Fedala, Morocco, 139–140, 156, 197
Fez, Morocco, 216

First World War, 17, 35, 70, 72, 78, 102, 107, 112, 128, 142, 147, 165, 175, 201, 207, 211, 230–231, 235, 243, 247, 264, 269, 275, 278
Florence, Italy, 208
Fond, Gervais de la, 184, 206, 229
Forbes, Charles M., 136, 147
Forrestal, James, 219, 231, 252
Fort Bragg, NC, 127, 131
Fort Lewis, WA, 104, 134
Foynes, Ireland, 132, 136
Franco, Francisco, 256
Frankfurt, Germany, 220

Gabbett, Cecil M., 64, 72
Gaffey, Hugh, 190, 197
Galápagos Islands, 107–108
Gale, Sir Humphrey, 180, 196
Galo Plaza, Lasso, 109, 112
Galveston, TX, 61
Garrod, Alfred Guy R., 269, 275
Geneva, Switzerland, 261–262
Gennerich, Gus, 95
George I, King (of Greece), 29, 31, 208, 239
George VI, King (of England), 96, 198, 223, 239
Ghormley, Robert, 220–221, 228, 231
Gibbs, Gerald E., 269, 275
Gibraltar, 30, 44, 139, 153–154, 179, 183, 186, 203, 235, 243
Gibson, Hugh, 90, 98
Giffen, Robert C., 141–142, 147
Giraud, Henri-Honoré, 180, 183, 197
Glasgow, Scotland, 134
Glassford, William A., 218, 220, 230
Goering, Hermann, 228, 231, 261
Gómez, José Miguel, 51, 61
Graf Zeppelin, 88
Grasse, France, 200
Great Britain, 105, 207, 231, 275
Green, Eleanor Hewitt (cousin), 225–226
Greenland, 125
Grenoble, France, 202
Griswold, Benjamin H., 129, 145–146
Griswold, Wait R., 206, 213, 216–217, 230
Guantánamo, Cuba, 14–16, 37, 39, 47–50, 54, 58–59, 63, 69, 117
Guayaquil, Ecuador, 108–109, 112

Haakon, King (of Norway), 227, 231, 248–249
Haas, Nelson B., 2–4
Hackensack, NJ, 1, 3–4, 9, 30, 40–41, 44, 59, 76–77, 106, 226–227, 263, 277
Hague, The, Netherlands, 228, 252–253
Haiti, 46, 49–50, 61, 144
Halifax, Nova Scotia, 122
Hall, John L., 165–168, 172, 175, 179, 181–182, 185, 187, 191, 193–194
Halsey, William F., 6, 11, 39
Hampton Roads, VA, 16–17, 19, 21, 30–31, 40, 42, 86, 116–117, 126, 136, 140, 144–145, 151, 189, 191
Harding, Warren G., 75, 83
Harmon, Ernest, 139–140, 147

Harmon, Hubert R., 270, 275
Harrill, William K., 270, 275
Harriman, William Averell, 234, 247
Hart, Franklin A., 245, 247
Hart, Thomas, 82–83
Havana, Cuba, 49, 60–61, 63, 140
Hawaii, 25–26, 31, 71–72, 76, 79, 101–102, 109–110, 115
Henderson, Leon, 219, 230
Hepburn, Arthur, 85, 98
Hewitt, Abraham S., (great uncle), 226
Hewitt, Charles (grandfather), 1, 2
Hewitt, Edward R. (cousin), 1, 274
Hewitt, Floride Hunt (wife), 41–42, 44–45, 86, 225, 229, 242, 245, 250, 252–254, 260–263, 267–268, 277–280
Hewitt, H. Kent
  ancestors, 1
  birth of, 1
  childhood, 1, 2
  high school, 2–4
  church affiliation, 2
  U.S. Naval Academy, 4–11
  in USS *Missouri*, 13–17
  Great White Fleet Cruise, 19–31
  Masons, Order of, member, 30
  in USS *Connecticut*, 33–35
  in USS *Florida*, 39–45
  marriage, 41
  teaching assignment (U.S. Naval Academy), 41–44, 70, 82
  Cuban Revolution, 51–61
  promotion to Lieutenant Commander, 60
  as CO, USS *Dorothea*, 61, 63–64
  World War I, 63–72
  as CO, USS *Cummings*, 66–70, 72
  as CO, USS *Ludlow*, 70, 72
  as Gunnery Officer, USS *Pennsylvania*, 70–71
  as Staff Gunnery Officer, USS *West Virginia* and USS *California*, 76–80
  as Student, Naval War College, 77
  as Commander, Destroyer Division 12, Pacific Fleet, 78–83
  as Staff Operations Officer, Commander-in-Chief, Pacific Fleet, 80
  promoted to Captain , 80
  earthquake, Long Beach, CA, 81–82
  as CO, USS *Indianapolis*, 85–98
  Chief of Staff, Commander, Cruisers, Scouting Force, 101–102
  as Commander, Naval Ammunition Depot, Puget Sound, 102–105
  as Commander, Special Service Squadron, 106–109
  as Commander, Cruiser Division Eight, 110–111, 116, 118
  in Neutrality Patrols, 119–121
  convoy duty, 121–123, 125–127
  Japanese attack on Pearl Harbor, HI, reaction to, 123
  as Commander, Amphibious Force, Atlantic Fleet, 126–128

Operation TORCH 1942 (landings in North Africa), 159–175
Operation HUSKY 1943 (Invasion of Sicily), 177–178
Operation AVALANCHE, 1943, 191–193
Anzio invasion, 195–197
Operation ANVIL-DRAGOON 1944 (Invasion of Southern France), 199–203
as Commander, Twelfth Fleet, 220–231, 233–247, 249–263
as consultant, U.S. Naval War College, 263–264
as member, United Nations Military Staff Committee, 264, 267–275, 277–280
retirement from U.S. Navy, 280–281
Hewitt, Robert Anderson (father), 1, 11, 77
Hillenkoetter, Roscoe H., 235, 247
Hines, John F., 42, 45, 71
Hiroshima, Japan, 227
Hitler, Adolf, 221, 231, 261
Hoboken, NJ, 2
Hoffman, Josiah, 214, 230
Honolulu, HI, 25
Horan, Henry E., 132–133, 147
Hornbeck, Stanley K., 228, 231, 253
Howard, Herbert S., 6, 11
Howe, Alfred G., 65–66, 72
Hughes, Charles F., 69, 71–72, 75
Hughes-Hallett, John, 134, 147
Hutchins, Gordon, 143, 147
Hvalfjördur, Iceland, 125

Ibn Saud Abdul Aziz, King (of Saudi Arabia), 215
Iceland, 118, 123, 125–126, 147, 155
Ingram, Jonas, 121, 123
Inonu, Ismet, 237, 247
Inveraray, Scotland, 134
Ischia, Italy, 241
Ismay, Hastings L., 214, 230
Istanbul, Turkey, 235–238, 240, 247
Ives, Norman S., 142, 147

Jacobs, Randall, 120, 123
James, Jules, 173, 175, 178, 220–221, 229, 235–236, 239–240, 252
Jamestown, RI, 273
Japan, 16, 27–28, 98, 101, 110, 112, 115, 117, 122, 126, 219, 221, 223, 275, 281
Jarman, Sanderford, 107, 109, 112
Jaujard, Robert, 200, 202–204, 206, 217–218
John, William H., 150
Johnson, Bayard S., 130, 146
Johnson, Herschel, 227–228, 231
Johnson, Lee P., 129, 136, 146, 178
Justo, José A. P., 94, 98

Kai-Shek, Chiang, 269
Kelly, Monroe, 141, 144, 147, 149, 151, 155
Kent, Henry Frederick (grandfather), 1, 2
Kent, Mary (mother), 1
Kennedy-Purvis, Charles E., 225, 229, 231
Key West, FL, 59–60, 63–64, 140
Keyes, Geoffrey, 186, 197

Kidd, Isaac C., 105, 112
Kiel, Germany, 34
Kimmel, Husband E., 110–112, 115
King, Ernest J., 102, 112, 118, 120, 123, 126, 176, 178, 182, 187, 209, 214–215, 218, 246
Kingston, Jamaica, 15–16, 49
Kinkaid, Thomas C., 101, 112
Kirk, Alan G., 177–178, 189–191, 196, 207, 217, 220, 252
Kirk, Alexander, 204, 211, 216, 252
Knapp, Harry S., 59, 61
Knollys, Viscount Edward G. W., 173, 175
Knox, Frank, 177, 196

Lahaina Roads, Maui, HI, 25
Lake Maracaibo, Venezuela, 135
Lambert, Roger, 202, 206, 217, 278
Land, Emory, 214, 230
Laning, Harris, 76–77, 83
Lattre de Tassigny, Jean, 221, 231
League Island Navy Yard, 69
League of Nations, 262
Leahy, William, 215, 230
Leathers, Lord Frederick James, 214, 230
Lee, Jerome K., 55–58, 61, 63
Lee, John C. H., 240–241, 247
Le Havre, France, 65, 220, 277
Lemonnier, André, 199–201, 207, 210, 221–222, 278
Lend-Lease Act, 105
Leslie, A. V., 150
Lewis, Spencer S., 178, 180, 196, 220
Lima, Peru, 24, 109
Limerick, Ireland, 136
Lisbon, Portugal, 254, 256–259, 264
Little Creek, VA, 127–128, 138–139, 177
Liverpool, England, 65
Lodge, Henry Cabot, 207, 211
Lodge, John Davis, 207, 211
London, England, 33, 40, 65, 119, 132–134, 136, 155, 177–179, 183, 194, 214–215, 218, 220–221, 223–224, 226, 228–229, 231, 250, 252–253, 259–260, 262, 267, 278, 281
Long Beach, CA, 24, 75, 81–82, 86, 94
Los Angeles, CA, 24, 110
Louis of Battenberg, Prince, 128, 133
Lowry, Frank J., 179, 181, 193–196, 205, 213
Luce, Clare Boothe, 209, 211
Lynnhaven Roads, VA, 127, 149
Lyon, France, 202

Macmillan, Harold, 207, 211
Malta, 29, 143, 189, 192, 194, 214–215
Manila, Philippines, 27–28, 31
Manila Bay, Philippines, 27–28, 31
Mar del Plata, Argentina, 93
Mare Island, CA, 102, 110, 116
Marseilles, France, 199–200, 202, 206–207, 217, 221, 278
Marshall, George, 176, 214–215, 230
Martinique, 129
Masons, Order of, 30
Mayo, Henry T., 61, 64
McBride, Louis, 82–83

McCandlish, Benjamin V., 194, 197, 206, 216, 219
McCluer, Nathan E., 130, 147
McConnell, Riley F., 9, 11, 41
McCreery, Sir Richard L., 269, 275
McMahon, Fred W., 270, 275
McManes, Kenmore M., 220, 231
McNamee, Luke, 80, 82–83
McNarney, Joseph T., 209, 211, 270
McWhorter, Ernest D., 141–142, 147, 151
Mehdiya, Morocco, 139–140, 142, 151, 156, 179, 190
Meknès, Morocco, 216
Melbourne, Australia, 26
Menocal, Mario García, 51, 61
Mers el Kebir, Algeria, 181, 185–186, 205, 216
Messina, Italy, 29, 189
Michelier, Fritz, 163, 165–166, 169, 171, 229
Middlebury College, 83, 224
Middleton, Troy H., 190, 197
Midway Island, 116
Miles, Geoffrey J. A., 205, 211
Mitchell, Edward A., 129, 146
Mitchell, William, 71–72
Mitscher, Marc A., 260, 264
Molotov, Vyacheslav, 244, 247
Monte Carlo, Monaco, 43, 278
Monterey, CA, 24, 40–41
Montevideo, Uruguay, 22, 93, 95–96
Moore, Sir Henry R., 269, 275
Moreau, Jacques, 184, 205, 216, 229, 272, 279–280
Morison, Samuel Eliot, 154, 156, 180
Morocco, 136, 138, 141, 147–148, 156, 178–180, 184, 187, 190, 197, 229, 268
Morris, Edwin L., 269, 275
Morris, Robert, 205, 211, 243
Morse, John. A. V., 208, 211
Mostaganem, Algeria, 182, 185–186
Mountbatten, Edwina Ashley, 134, 147
Mountbatten, Lord Louis, 104, 112, 124, 128, 131, 134, 147, 194
Mumford, Charlotte (grandmother), 1
Munich, Germany, 231
Munroe, William, 117, 123
Muselier, Emile, 200, 211

Naples, Italy, 29, 42, 195, 203–204, 207–208, 210, 214–216, 218, 272
Naval Ammunition Depot, Puget Sound, WA, 102
Nelson, Horatio, 192
Nemours, Algeria, 182, 185, 193
New Brunswick, Canada, 131
New London, CT, 7, 106
New Orleans, LA, 63
New Orleans Navy Yard, 63
New York, NY, 1–2, 105–107, 136, 223, 225, 263–264, 266–268, 272–274, 277, 280–281
New York Navy Yard, 39, 70, 85, 126
Newfoundland, Canada, 121, 123, 131–132, 136, 146–147, 151, 219, 275
Newport, RI, 77, 83, 177, 219–220, 263–264, 267, 273–274

Newport News, VA, 144
Nice, France, 43–44, 200, 211, 278
Nichols, Charles L., 193, 197, 214
Nogues, Charles, 166
Norfolk, VA, 123, 144, 150
Norton, Mary Kent Hewitt (daughter), 75, 83, 103, 106, 224–225, 250, 252–254, 256, 261, 263, 267, 273
Norton, Gerald (son-in-law), 83, 264, 275
Nuremberg trials, 132, 147, 231

O'Daniel, John W., 185, 197
Oahu, Hawaiian Islands, 79, 115
Olga, Queen (of Greece), 29, 31
Operation ANVIL-DRAGOON, 199–211, 222–223 243
Operation HUSKY, 182, 186, 188–189
Operation OVERLORD, 196
Operation TORCH, 137–138, 143, 147, 156, 159–175, 177–183, 186–187, 189–191, 205, 207, 211, 229–230
Oran, Algeria, 178–182, 184–187, 189–191, 193, 203, 205–206, 211, 216, 253
Osborne, Lithgow, 231
Oslo, Norway, 248–249

Paddock, Hubert E., 55, 61
Palermo, Sicily, 188, 193, 203, 205, 213–214, 216
Panama, 71, 76, 85, 106–107
Panama Canal, 19, 76, 107, 116
Panama Canal Zone, 70, 106–107, 109–110, 112
Panama City, Panama, 107
Pan-American Conference, 86, 94, 98
Pará, Brazil, 178
Paris, France, 34, 65, 72, 207, 216–217, 220–222, 229, 260, 262, 272, 277–278
Pasadena, CA, 81–82
Patch, Alexander, 199, 207, 210, 222
Paterson, NJ, 3, 40
Patton, George, 138–140, 143, 145, 147, 149, 151, 154, 156, 182–183, 186–187, 189, 192, 197, 229, 268
Patuxent, MD, 127, 219–220
Pearl Harbor Naval Base, 25, 80, 109–112, 115, 123, 171
Peet, Raymond E., 217, 230
Philadelphia, PA, 6, 11, 42, 68–69, 131
Piraeus, Greece, 29, 238
Pisa, Italy, 208
Pius XII, 211, 241
Pizarro, Francisco, 24, 31
Plymouth, England, 136, 147, 225
Port Angeles, WA, 80
Port au Prince, Haiti, 49, 145
Port Lyautey, Morocco, 139–140, 142, 144, 150–151, 155–156, 178–182, 186–187, 190, 203, 206, 210, 219
Port of Spain, Trinidad, 21, 87, 96
Port Royal, Jamaica, 15
Port Said, Egypt, 29
Portal, Charles F. A., 234, 245, 247
Portland, England, 134
Portland, ME, 122–123, 142
Portsmouth, England, 33, 133
Portsmouth (NH) Navy Yard, 44, 47
Pound, Sir Dudley, 194, 197
Princeton, NJ, 86

Pringle, Joel R. P., 77, 80–81, 83
Provincetown, MA, 11
Puerto Rico, 49, 96
Puget Sound, WA, 25, 76, 78, 80, 102–103
Punta Arenas, Chile, 22, 31
Pupek, Bernard S., 130, 146

Quantico, VA, 71, 75, 126
Queenstown, Ireland, 63, 65, 67–68, 188
Quisling, Vidkun A., 227, 231
Quito, Ecuador, 108–109
Quonset Point, RI, 219

Rabat, Morocco, 206, 216
Raeder, Erich, 234, 247
Ramsay, Sir Bertram, 182, 189, 197, 264
Rankin, John W., 106, 112
Redondo, CA, 24
Reid, Whitelaw, 34–35, 40, 236
Rejkjavík, Iceland, 125, 126
Reuterdahl, Henry, 13–14, 17
Richardson, James O., 110, 112, 115
Ridgway, Matthew, 269, 275
Rio de Janeiro, Brazil, 21, 31, 88–89
Rio de la Plata, 22, 93
Riobamba, Ecuador, 108
Rixey, Presley M., 203, 211, 217
Robinson, Robert E., 220–221, 231
Rockland, ME, 7
Rogers, Edith Nourse, 204, 211
Rome, Italy, 42, 184, 195, 204, 207–208, 216, 275
Rommel, Erwin, 188, 196–197
Rómulo, Carlos, 278, 281
Ronarc'h, Pierre Jean, 164, 175, 216
Roosevelt, Eleanor, 230, 233
Roosevelt, Franklin D., 21, 62, 86, 91, 94–95, 98, 115, 117–118, 121–123, 143, 145, 147, 155, 177, 204, 206, 209, 212–213, 215, 219, 230, 243, 247
Roosevelt, James, 86, 88–89, 98
Roosevelt, Theodore, 10–11, 13–14, 17, 19, 30, 96
Rotterdam, Holland, 252–253
Royal Naval College, 225, 231
Rush, William, 33, 35

Sablé, Louis, 229
Sadler, Frank H., 107, 112
Safi, Morocco, 139–140, 142, 144, 147, 151, 155–156
Salazar, Antonio de Oliveira, 255–259, 264
Salerno, Italy, 104, 147, 193, 195, 197, 205, 215, 260, 269
Salisbury, England, 136, 225
Salonika, Turkey, 30
Salzburg, Austria, 260–261
Samoa, 26, 31
San Diego, CA, 24, 78–81, 106
San Francisco, CA, 19, 24–25, 31, 40–42, 45, 106, 231, 281
San Juan, Puerto Rico, 21, 49
San Pedro, CA, 24, 71–72, 76, 78–79, 98, 101, 110
Santa Barbara, CA, 24
Santa Monica, CA, 24
Santo Domingo, 49, 59–61

Sarajevo, 42
Sawyer, Charles, 220, 231
Schroeder, Seaton, 33, 35
Scotland, 133–135, 263
Scripps College, 106
Seattle, WA, 25
Second World War, 102, 112, 123, 147, 156, 175, 197, 211, 230–231, 247, 264, 269, 275, 281
Selassie, Haile, 215, 230
Sellers, David, 81, 83, 85
Sevastopol, Russia, 213
Shackford, Chauncey, 75, 83
Shelly, Tully, 225, 231
Sherman, Forrest, 260, 264
Ships
    HMS *Ajax*, 199, 210, 221
    USS *Alabama*, 21, 25, 31
    Almirante Brown, 92–93, 98
    USS *Annapolis*, 26
    USS *Antietam*, 5, 11
    USS *Arizona*, 71–72, 105
    USS *Arkansas*, 170, 175
    USS *Augusta*, 118, 123, 142, 149, 151, 155–156, 189
    SS *Baltic*, 65
    USS *Barnegat*, 155–156
    Basque, 200, 211
    USS *Bernadou*, 142, 147
    USS *Birmingham*, 190, 197
    USS *Biscayne*, 187, 197
    Bismarck, 117–118, 123, 269
    USS *Boise*, 190, 197
    USS *Boyle*, 150, 156
    Breslau, 44–45
    USS *Bristol*, 193, 197
    USS *Brooklyn*, 85, 106, 110, 112, 118, 151, 155, 184, 190, 194–195, 205–207
    USS *Buck*, 193, 197
    HMS *Bulolo*, 135, 147
    USS *California*, 76, 80–83
    USS *Calvert*, 149–151, 156
    USS *Carman*, 133
    USS *Catoctin*, 200, 202–203, 210, 213
    Chacabuco, 22–23, 31
    USS *Chandler*, 78, 83
    USS *Charleston*, 112
    USS *Chenango*, 170
    USS *Chesapeake*, 7
    USS *Chester*, 86–87, 90, 92–93, 97–98
    USS *Chicago*, 101, 112
    USS *Cleveland*, 141, 147
    USS *Cole*, 142, 147
    USS *Cone*, 250, 264
    USS *Connecticut*, 21, 29, 31–35, 37, 39
    USS *Conner*, 65–66, 72
    SS *Contessa*, 150–151, 155, 187
    USS *Cummings*, 66–70, 72
    USS *Dallas*, 142, 147, 187
    USS *Delaware*, 33, 35
    HMS *Delhi*, 95, 197
    USS *Delta*, 205, 211

USS *Dolphin*, 30–31
USS *Dorothea*, 61, 63–64
Duguay-Trouin, 200, 206, 211
Dupetit Thouars, 66, 72
USS *Eagle*, 43–51, 53–61, 106, 133, 231, 261
USS *Eberle*, 150, 156
USS *Edward Rutledge*, 169, 175
MS *Elbe*, 119
USS *Electra*, 171, 175
Emile Bertin, 200, 206, 211
USS *Erie*, 107–108, 112
HMS *Ettrick*, 135, 147
SS *Europe*, 221
USS *Florida* (Monitor), 8
USS *Florida*, 8, 11, 39–42, 45, 59, 70
USS *Flusser*, 36, 39, 45
Forbin, 200, 211
USS *Franklin D. Roosevelt*, 254, 258–259, 264
HMS *Frobisher*, 249, 264
General Baquedano, 23, 31
USS *George Washington*, 67–68, 72
Georges Leygues, 200–201, 206, 211, 217
USS *Georgia*, 21
Gloire, 200, 206, 211
Goeben, 44–45, 236
Graf Spee, 96, 98
USS *Gwin*, 120, 123
USS *Hambleton*, 167, 175
USS *Harry Lee*, 149–150, 156
USS *Hartford*, 6–8, 11
HMS *Hecla*, 170, 172, 175
USS *Hogan*, 160, 175
USS *Houston*, 249, 251–255, 258–259, 262
USS *Hovey*, 78, 83
USS *Hugh L. Scott*, 169, 175
USS *Idaho*, 30–31, 42–43, 116–117
USS *Illinois*, 21
USS *Indiana*, 15, 17
USS *Indianapolis*, 84–93, 95, 97–98, 101, 105, 118, 145, 156, 213, 215, 269
Jean Bart, 141, 147, 161, 163–164, 169, 171, 175, 206
Jeanne d'Arc, 206
João de Lisboa, 254, 264
USS *Joseph Hewes*, 167, 175
USS *Kansas*, 21
USS *Kearsarge*, 21
USS *Kentucky*, 21
USS *Lake Champlain*, 229, 231
USS *Lakehurst*, 203
USS *Lamson*, 39, 45
USS *Lang*, 118, 123
Le Fortune, 200, 211
Lemnos, 43
USS *Leonard Wood*, 126, 146
USS *Lexington*, 79, 83
USS *Little Rock*, 249, 252, 254, 264
USS *Long*, 78, 83
USS *Long Island*, 120, 123, 125, 267, 277
Lorraine, 200, 211, 221, 223
USS *Louisiana*, 21

USS *Ludlow*, 70, 72
USS *McLanahan*, 192–193, 197
USS *Maine* (BB-10), 21, 25, 31
USS *Maine* (BB-2/c), 60
Malin, 200, 211
USS *Massachusetts*, 6, 141, 147
USS *Mayflower*, 19, 30
USS *Memphis*, 60–61, 213–218, 221, 223, 230
USS *Meredith*, 120, 123
USS *Miantonomah*, 153–154, 156
USS *Minnesota*, 16–17, 21, 34
USS *Mississippi*, 30–31, 63–64, 71, 116–117
USS *Missouri*, 11–13, 15–17, 21, 26, 29–30, 33, 39, 41, 68, 109, 232, 235–236, 238–240, 242–243
USS *Monrovia*, 192, 197
Montcalm, 200, 203, 206, 211, 217–218
Moreno, 93, 98
USS *Mount Vernon*, 66, 72
USS *Murphy*, 160, 175
USS *Nashville*, 110, 112, 118
HMS *Natal*, 35, 40, 45, 210
USS *Nebraska*, 25, 31
USS *Nevada*, 10–11
USS *New Jersey*, 21
USS *New Mexico*, 116–117, 121, 123
USS *New York*, 163, 165, 175
HMS *Newfoundland*, 172
USS *North Dakota*, 33, 35
USS *Ohio*, 21, 29–31
HMS *Orion*, 215, 230
USS *Parker*, 217, 230
USS *Pennsylvania*, 70–72, 116
USS *Philadelphia*, 100, 110, 112, 116–118, 121–123, 125–126, 140, 155, 190, 201, 211, 242
USS *Plunkett*, 199, 210
USS *Preston*, 39, 45
Primauguet, 184, 197
USS *Providence*, 235, 238, 247,
Queen Elizabeth, 223
USS *Quincy*, 121, 123, 215–216, 230
USS *Ranger*, 141, 147, 153
USS *Reid*, 39, 45,
USS *Rhode Island*, 21
Richelieu, 141, 147, 206, 278
Rivadavia, 93, 98
HMS *Rodney*, 118, 121, 123, 126, 269
HMS *Roxburgh*, 16–17
USS *Samuel Chase*, 178, 180, 184, 193, 196
USS *Sangamon*, 155–156
USS *Santee*, 155–156
USS *Saratoga*, 79, 83
USS *Savannah*, 110, 112, 114, 116–121, 138, 190, 194, 215
HMS *Sirius*, 201, 211
Sister Anne, 133–134
USS *Southard*, 78, 83
Stad Arnhem, 119
USS *Suwannee*, 153, 156
Sverige, 228, 250, 264
USS *Tallahassee*, 8, 11

HMS *Tasajera*, 135, 147
USS *Tasker H. Bliss*, 169, 175
USS *Tattnall*, 108–109, 112
USS *Texas*, 141, 147
USS *Thomas Stone*, 180, 196
USS *Tuscaloosa*, 141, 147
HMS *Venomous*, 170, 175
USS *Vermont*, 21
Victoria, 160, 175
USS *Virginia*, 21, 25, 31
SS *Washington*, 263
USS *Wasp*, 120, 123
HMS *Welshman*, 170, 175
USS *West Virginia*, 76, 80, 83
USS *Wichita*, 141, 147
USS *Wilkes*, 153, 156
USS *Wilson*, 118, 123
USS *Winooski*, 167, 172, 175
USS *Wisconsin*, 25, 31
Yawuz, 236
USS *Yorktown*, 121, 123
Shoup, Aubrey K., 44–45
Sicily, 147, 156, 177, 179, 181–183, 185, 187–193, 195–197, 230, 264, 269, 275
Siena, Italy, 208
Sims, William S., 13, 17, 36, 245
Singapore, 17, 28, 122
Slayter, William R., 269, 275
Smith, Holland M., 120, 123, 126–128
Smith, Robert McLanahan, 167, 175
Smith, Walter Bedell, 180, 196, 207, 214–215
Smith, William W., 110, 112
Snyder, Charles P., 102, 112
Solomons Island, 127
Somerville, James, 214, 230
Soong, Tse-ven, 219, 230
Sorrento, Italy, 240–241
South America, 10, 17, 21, 88, 95, 97–98, 107
Southampton, England, 65, 134, 223, 229, 253–254, 262–263
Spaatz, Carl, 186, 197
Special Service Squadron, 106–107, 110, 112
Spellman, Francis T., 179, 181, 196
Sperry, Charles S., 25, 31
Spruance, Raymond A., 105, 112, 263–264
St. Mandrier, France, 199–200, 278
St. Tropez, France, 199–200, 211, 278
Stark, Harold R., 133, 147, 214–215, 218–220, 223, 225, 230, 263
Steiguer, Louis R. de, 74–77, 83
Stephenville, Newfoundland, 219
Stettinius, Edward R., 208, 211
Stevens Institute of Technology, 2
Stevenson, Adlai, 233, 247
Stimson, Henry, 176–177, 196
Stockholm, Sweden, 227–228, 250–252
Straits of Magellan, 19, 22–23
Strauss, Johann, 233
Subic Bay, Philippines, 28
Suez, Egypt, 25, 29

Swettenham, Sir Alexander, 16–17
Sydney, Australia, 26
Sypher, Jay A., 39–41, 45

Taft, Robert, 280–281
Tangier, Morocco, 29, 44
Taranto, Italy, 195, 197, 209
Tarrant, William T., 101, 112, 118
Tate, Ralph H., 260, 264
Taussig, Joseph K., 101–102, 112, 188
Taylor, Floride Hewitt (daughter), 44–45, 103, 123, 225, 227–228, 263
Taylor, LeRoy (son-in-law), 103, 112, 217
Taylor, Maxwell, 185, 197
Taylor, Myron, 204
Tedder, Arthur W., 186, 197
Ténès, Algeria, 182, 185, 193
Terhume, Warren, 59, 61
Terra, Gabriel, 95, 98
Tobin, Ralph C., 218, 230
Todd, Forde A., 110, 112
Tokyo, Japan, 28
Toulon, France, 199–203, 205–207, 211, 217–218, 278
Trammel, Webb, 233, 247
Trenton, NJ, 1, 5
Trinidad, 21, 87, 96, 121, 178
Tripoli, Lybia, 29
Troubridge, Thomas, 262, 264
Truscott, Lucian K., 132, 140–141, 147, 152, 185, 190
Tunis, Tunisia, 188–189, 197, 216
Turner, Richmond Kelly, 267–268
Tyler, George, 206, 211

Umberto, Prince (of Italy), 232, 240–242, 247
United Fruit Company, 54–56, 106
United Nations, 154, 230, 264, 267, 269–273, 275, 277, 279, 281
U.S. Army War College, 177, 264
U.S. Atlantic Fleet, 14, 17, 19, 21, 24, 32, 35, 37, 45, 48, 50–51, 61, 70, 72, 112, 116, 118, 120, 123, 126, 129, 141, 143, 177, 181, 189, 197, 231, 264
U.S. Eighth Fleet, 19180, 185–186, 189–190, 193–195, 202–207, 210, 213, 216–218
U.S. Naval Academy, 3–4, 7, 9, 11, 17, 31, 34–35, 41, 45, 61–62, 70, 72, 82–83, 85, 96, 98, 110, 112, 123, 126, 129, 138, 146–147, 196–197, 203, 211, 219, 225, 230–231, 264, 275, 281
U.S. Naval War College, 17, 32, 75–77, 83, 112, 130, 177, 196, 263–264, 276
U.S. Pacific Fleet, 24, 70, 72, 75–80, 83, 102, 105–106, 110, 112, 115, 120, 143, 197
U.S. Seventh Army, 182–183, 186, 189–190, 199, 202–203, 207, 210, 222, 279
U.S. Twelfth Fleet, 213, 215, 217, 219–221, 223, 225, 227, 229, 231, 248–249, 251, 253, 255–257, 259–263

Valletta, Malta, 192, 214
Valparaiso, Chile, 23, 31
Van Voorhis, Daniel, 107, 112
Vargas, Getúlio, 90–91, 98
Vermont, 89, 275, 280

Victor Emmanuel, King (of Italy), 240, 247
Victoria, British Columbia, 80
Vienna, Austria, 260
Viggo, Prince (of Denmark), 225–227, 250
Viggo, Princess (of Denmark), 225–227
Villefranche, France, 29, 43, 278
Washington, D.C., 5, 30, 40–42, 47, 49–50, 65, 67–68, 72, 75, 83, 85–86, 119, 128, 131, 137–138, 145, 155, 177, 180, 187, 195, 204, 209, 213, 216, 220, 264, 269, 275, 280
Washington Navy Yard, 42
Watson, Edwin M., 88, 92, 98
Weddell, Alexander W., 235–237, 247
Wellings, Thomas F., 129, 131, 146
Wentworth, Ralph S., 110, 112, 220, 262
West Indies, 14, 44, 48, 144, 231
West Point, NY, 3
Western Naval Task Force, 138–144, 147, 153, 156, 162, 171, 173–175, 182, 189, 191, 203
Wilcox, John W., 106, 112

Wilhelmina, Queen (of the Netherlands), 228, 231, 253
Wilkinson, Theodore, 269, 275
Wilson, Edwin C., 236, 247
Wilson, Henry B., 65, 70, 72
Wilson, Henry Maitland, 209, 211, 214
Wilson, Woodrow, 67–68, 72
Winant, John, 223, 229, 231
Women's Royal Naval Service, 132, 147
Woods, Ralph W. D., 130, 146
Wright, George B., 77, 83
Wright, Jerauld, 180, 196
Wyatt, Ben H., 219, 231

Yalta Conference, 212–215, 217, 230
Yarnell, Harry, 79, 83
Yates, Charles M., 181, 196, 205–206
Yokohama, Japan, 27–28

Zimmerli, Rupert M., 188, 197
Ziroli, Humbert W., 194, 197, 207–208

NAVAL WAR COLLEGE *HISTORICAL MONOGRAPH SERIES*

1. *The Writings of Stephen B. Luce*, edited by John D. Hayes and John B. Hattendorf (1975).
2. *Charleston Blockade: The Journals of John B. Marchand, U.S. Navy, 1861–1862*, edited by Craig L. Symonds (1976).
3. *Professors of War: The Naval War College and the Development of the Naval Profession*, edited by Ronald Spector (1977).
4. *The Blue Sword: The Naval War College and the American Mission, 1919–1941*, Michael Vlahos (1980).
5. *On His Majesty's Service: Observations of the British Home Fleet from the Diary, Reports, and Letters of Joseph H. Wellings, Assistant U.S. Naval Attaché, London, 1940–1941*, edited by John B. Hattendorf (1983).
6. *Angel on the Yardarm: The Beginnings of Fleet Radar Defense and the Kamikaze Threat*, edited by John Monsarrat (1985).
7. *A Bibliography of the Works of Alfred Thayer Mahan*, edited by John B. Hattendorf and Lynn C. Hattendorf (1986).
8. *The Fraternity of the Blue Uniform: Admiral Richard G. Colbert, U.S. Navy, and Allied Naval Cooperation*, Joel J. Sokolsky (1991).
9. *The Influence of History on Mahan: The Proceedings of a Conference Marking the Centenary of Alfred Thayer Mahan's The Influence of Sea Power upon History, 1660–1783*, edited by John B. Hattendorf (1991).
10. *Mahan Is Not Enough: The Proceedings of a Conference on the Works of Sir Julian Corbett and Admiral Sir Herbert Richmond*, edited by James Goldrick and John B. Hattendorf (1993).
11. *UBI SUMUS? The State of Naval and Maritime History*, edited by John B. Hattendorf (1994).
12. *The Queenstown Patrol, 1917: The Diary of Commander Joseph Knefler Taussig, U.S. Navy*, edited by William N. Still, Jr. (1996).
13. *Doing Naval History: Essays Toward Improvement*, edited by John B. Hattendorf (1995).
14. *An Admiral's Yarn*, edited by Mark R. Shulman (1999).